LAW AND MORALITY IN KANT

How do law and morality relate to each other in Kant's philosophy? Is law to be understood merely as an application of general moral principles to legal institutions, or does law have its own normativity that cannot be traced back to that of morality? This volume of new essays is a comprehensive treatment of law and morality in Kant, which also sheds new light on Kant's practical philosophy more broadly. The essays present different approaches to this core issue and address related topics including the justification of legal coercion, the role of freedom and autonomy for law and politics, legal punishment and the question of its ethical presuppositions, moral luck, and the role of permissive laws in Kant's legal and political philosophy. The volume will be of interest to researchers and graduate students working on Kant's moral and legal philosophy. This title is also available as Open Access on Cambridge Core.

MARTIN BRECHER is a faculty member at the Department of Philosophy at the University of Mannheim. He is the author of *Vernunftrecht und Verdinglichung: Eine Rekonstruktion von Kants Eherecht* (2025) and co-editor of *Kant on Sex, Love, and Friendship* (2023).

PHILIPP-ALEXANDER HIRSCH is leader of the Independent Research Group 'Criminal Law Theory' at the Max Planck Institute for the Study of Crime, Security and Law in Freiburg. He is the author of *Kants Einleitung in die Rechtslehre von 1784* (2012) and *Freiheit und Staatlichkeit bei Kant* (2017).

LAW AND MORALITY IN KANT

EDITED BY

MARTIN BRECHER

University of Mannheim

PHILIPP-ALEXANDER HIRSCH

Max Planck Institute for the Study of Crime, Security and Law, Freiburg

CAMBRIDGE
UNIVERSITY PRESS

CAMBRIDGE
UNIVERSITY PRESS

Shaftesbury Road, Cambridge CB2 8EA, United Kingdom

One Liberty Plaza, 20th Floor, New York, NY 10006, USA

477 Williamstown Road, Port Melbourne, VIC 3207, Australia

314–321, 3rd Floor, Plot 3, Splendor Forum, Jasola District Centre, New Delhi – 110025, India

103 Penang Road, #05-06/07, Visioncrest Commercial, Singapore 238467

Cambridge University Press is part of Cambridge University Press & Assessment, a department of the University of Cambridge.

We share the University's mission to contribute to society through the pursuit of education, learning and research at the highest international levels of excellence.

www.cambridge.org
Information on this title: www.cambridge.org/9781009291996

DOI: 10.1017/9781009292030

When citing this work, please include a reference to the DOI 10.1017/9781009292030

We acknowledge financial support by the Max Planck Institute for the Study of Crime, Security and Law and the Max Planck Digital Library.

First published 2026

Cover image: detail from *Jurisprudence,* Gustav Klimt, Österreichische Galerie Belvedere. Image by Google Arts and Culture.

A catalogue record for this publication is available from the British Library

Library of Congress Cataloging-in-Publication Data
NAMES: Brecher, Martin editor | Hirsch, Philipp-Alexander editor
TITLE: Law and morality in Kant / edited by Martin Brecher, Universität Mannheim; Philipp-Alexander Hirsch, Max Planck Institute, Freiburg.
DESCRIPTION: Cambridge, United Kingdom ; New York, NY, USA : Cambridge University Press, 2025. | Includes bibliographical references and index.
IDENTIFIERS: LCCN 2025025096 (print) | LCCN 2025025097 (ebook) | ISBN 9781009291996 hardback | ISBN 9781009292016 paperback | ISBN 9781009292030 epub
SUBJECTS: LCSH: Kant, Immanuel, 1724-1804 | Law–Philosophy | Ethics
CLASSIFICATION: LCC K457.K3 L39 2025 (print) | LCC K457.K3 (ebook)
LC record available at https://lccn.loc.gov/2025025096
LC ebook record available at https://lccn.loc.gov/2025025097

ISBN 978-1-009-29199-6 Hardback

Contents

Contributors

RALF M. BADER is Professor of Philosophy at the Université de Fribourg.

SORIN BAIASU is Professor of Philosophy at the University of Liverpool.

MARTIN BRECHER is a faculty member in the Department of Philosophy at the University of Mannheim.

PAUL GUYER is Emeritus Professor of Philosophy at Brown University and the University of Pennsylvania.

PHILIPP-ALEXANDER HIRSCH is Leader of the Independent Research Group 'Criminal Law Theory' at the Max Planck Institute for the Study of Crime, Security and Law in Freiburg im Breisgau.

CHRISTOPH HORN is Professor of Philosophy at the University of Bonn.

PAULINE KLEINGELD is Professor of Philosophy at the University of Groningen.

BERND LUDWIG is Emeritus Professor of Philosophy at the Georg August University of Göttingen.

J. P. MESSINA is Assistant Professor of Philosophy at Purdue University.

KATE MORAN is Professor of Philosophy at Brandeis University.

JAPA PALLIKKATHAYIL is Associate Professor of Philosophy at the University of Pittsburgh.

GEORGE PAVLAKOS is Professor of Law and Philosophy at the University of Glasgow.

ALICE PINHEIRO WALLA is Associate Professor of Philosophy at McMaster University.

JENS TIMMERMANN is Professor of Moral Philosophy at the University of St Andrews.

MARCUS WILLASCHEK is Professor of Philosophy at Goethe University Frankfurt.

Acknowledgements

In preparation for this volume, we held a three-day conference at the University of Göttingen on 14–16 July 2022. The conference was made possible by support from the German Research Foundation (DFG), the Ministry of Science and Culture, and the Universitätsbund Göttingen. The conference brought together moral and legal philosophers, historians of philosophy, as well as legal and political scientists who draw on or engage with Kant. While it is often the case that the history of (legal) philosophy and contemporary (legal) philosophy take place largely in isolated discourses, this book aims to bring them together in order to establish both the contemporary relevance of exegetical Kant research and the historical awareness of Kantian legal philosophy. We would like to thank the participants of the conference for contributing to insightful discussions. In particular, we would like to thank the people who fostered the discussion by serving as commentators to the papers presented at the conference: Çağlar Çömez, Luke Davies, Luigi Filieri, Micha Gläser, Michael Gregory, Daniel Häuser, Jakob Huber, Marie Newhouse, Daniel Ranweiler, Lara Scaglia, Katja Stoppenbrink, Fiorella Tomassini and Stephan Zimmermann. In addition, special thanks are due to Marlene von Daacke, Oskar Menke, Paul Schreiner, Eila Teizer and Laura Weimer for their help in preparing the manuscript, and in particular to Patrick Joseph Siegle, who coordinated the preparation of the manuscript and provided us with invaluable support at all times. Last but not least, we would like to express our special gratitude to Bernd Ludwig, who supported the project at all stages.

Abbreviations for Works by Kant

GMS	*Grundlegung zur Metaphysik der Sitten* (AA 4, *Groundwork of the Metaphysics of Morals*)
IaG	*Idee zu einer allgemeinen Geschichte in weltbürgerlicher Absicht* (AA 8, *Idea for a Universal History with a Cosmopolitan Aim*)
KdU	*Kritik der Urteilskraft* (AA 5, *Critique of the Power of Judgement*)
KpV	*Kritik der praktischen Vernunft* (AA 5, *Critique of Practical Reason*)
KrV	*Kritik der reinen Vernunft* (*Critique of Pure Reason*)
MS	*Metaphysik der Sitten* (AA 6, *Metaphysics of Morals*)
Refl	Reflexionen (AA 14–19, Reflections/Notes)
RGV	*Religion innerhalb der Grenzen der bloßen Vernunft* (AA 6, *Religion within the Boundaries of Mere Reason*)
RL	*Metaphysische Anfangsgründe der Rechtslehre* (AA 6, *Metaphysical Foundations of the Doctrine of Right*)
SF	*Der Streit der Fakultäten* (AA 7, *The Conflict of the Faculties*)
TL	*Metaphysische Anfangsgründe der Tugendlehre* (AA 6, *Metaphysical Foundations of the Doctrine of Virtue*)
TP	*Über den Gemeinspruch: 'Das mag in der Theorie richtig sein, taugt aber nicht für die Praxis'* (AA 8, *On the Common Saying: 'That May Be Correct in Theory, but Is of No Use in Practice'*)

VARL	Vorarbeiten zur Rechtslehre (AA 23, Preparatory Work for the Doctrine of Right)
VATL	Vorarbeiten zur Tugendlehre (AA 27, Preparatory Work for the Doctrine of Virtue)
VAZeF	Vorarbeiten zu Zum ewigen Frieden (AA 23, Preparatory Work for Towards Perpetual Peace)
V-Met/Dohna	Metaphysik Dohna (AA 28, Lecture notes Metaphysics Dohna)
V-Mo/Collins	Moralphilosophie Collins (AA 27, Lecture notes Moral Philosophy Collins)
V-Mo/Mrongovius II	Moral Mrongovius II (AA 29, Lecture notes Moral Philosophy Mrongovius II)
V-Mo/Powalski	Moralphilosophie Powalski (AA 27, Lecture notes Moral Philosophy Powalski)
V-MS/Vigilantius	Metaphysik der Sitten Vigilantius (AA 27, Lecture notes Metaphysics of Morals Vigilantius)
V-NR/Feyerabend	Naturrecht Feyerabend (AA 27, Lecture notes Natural Law Feyerabend)
VRML	*Über ein vermeintes Recht, aus Menschenliege zu lügen* (AA 8, *On a Supposed Right to Lie from Philanthropy*)
ZeF	*Zum ewigen Frieden* (AA 8, *Towards Perpetual Peace*)

Introduction

Martin Brecher and Philipp-Alexander Hirsch

Aim of the Volume

Research on Kant's legal philosophy has flourished in recent years. This applies both to exegetical research on Kant and to practical philosophy, which pursues normative theorizing in Kant's wake. In view of this enormous interest in Kant's legal philosophy, there is surprisingly still no unified discussion of the fundamental questions of his legal thought. There are two reasons for this: on the one hand, there are contributions to the debate that tend to concentrate on Kant's legal philosophy[1] or his moral philosophy[2] and thus sometimes fail to take the 'other side' sufficiently into account. On the other hand, there is a methodological divergence between more exegetical approaches coming from the history of philosophy[3] and more analytical approaches trying to give a 'Kantian' answer to philosophical problems of law and morality.[4] It is therefore not surprising that there is, first, a need for a philosophical-historical account of the relationship between law and morality in Kant; and secondly, there is a need to clarify the related problem of which path normative theorizing based on Kant can or must take today. This volume takes up these two desiderata in contributions that address these questions from systematic

[1] For instance, Arthur Ripstein, *Force and Freedom: Kant's Legal and Political Philosophy*, Cambridge, MA: Harvard University Press, 2009.

[2] For instance, Allen W. Wood, *Kantian Ethics*, Cambridge: Cambridge University Press, 2008, and *The Free Development of Each: Studies on Freedom, Right, and Ethics in Classical German Philosophy*, Oxford: Oxford University Press, 2014.

[3] For instance, Mary J. Gregor, *The Laws of Freedom: A Study of Kant's Method of Applying the Categorical Imperative in the 'Metaphysik der Sitten'*, Oxford: Basil Blackwell, 1963, and B. Sharon Byrd and Joachim Hruschka, *Kant's* Doctrine of Right*: A Commentary*, Cambridge: Cambridge University Press, 2010.

[4] For example, Christine M. Korsgaard, *Creating the Kingdom of Ends*, Cambridge: Cambridge University Press, 1996, and *The Sources of Normativity*, Cambridge: Cambridge University Press, 1996, and John Rawls, *A Theory of Justice*, Cambridge, MA: Harvard University Press, 1971, and *Political Liberalism*, New York: Columbia University Press, 1993.

and exegetical perspectives. It provides a comprehensive treatment of law and morality in Kant and also sheds new light on Kant's practical philosophy more broadly.

In doing so the volume centres on the fundamental issue that affects almost all debates revolving around Kant's legal and political philosophy: how do law and morality relate to each other? Is legal philosophy to be understood merely as the application of general moral principles to the particular factual circumstances that make law and legal institutions necessary? Or does law have its own normativity that cannot be traced back to that of morality? Scholars generally accept that the *Doctrine of Virtue* (1797), which comprises Kant's ethical doctrine, depends upon the critical foundation of his moral philosophy developed in the *Groundwork for the Metaphysics of Morals* (1785) and the *Critique of Practical Reason* (1788). However, it is very controversial whether Kant's *Doctrine of Right* (1797), too, presents an embodiment or derivation of this critical moral philosophy, or if it rests on an independent foundation. According to the classical reading, Kant's concept of law can be derived from the categorical imperative. Law, like Kant's ethics, is therefore based on the notion of autonomy: legal precepts are categorical imperatives and as such presuppose the transcendental freedom of the subjects of law. According to this view, the doctrine of right and the doctrine of virtue can only be understood as equal parts of a unified, critical practical philosophy. However, some scholars claim that Kant's provisions of right are at odds with central tenets of his moral philosophy: While the categorical imperative prescribes acting upon certain *inner* maxims, rightful conduct depends only on the *outer* form of interaction between persons. While autonomy of pure reason seems to call for the idea of duty itself as the only incentive consistent with it, rightful conduct can be induced by incentives provided by others, such as the political legislator. Such differences are said to preclude any direct appeal to the autonomy of pure reason and the categorical imperative as the grounding principle of the principle of right, so that the latter must have an independent justification.

This 'great divide' in Kantian research is as old as the *Doctrine of Right* itself, in fact, even older, if we take into account Johann Gottlieb Fichte's *Grundlage des Naturrechts* from 1796 which tries to separate radically the normativity of law from the demands of morality. It is not surprising, therefore, that initially there was a lively debate in Germany about the status of Kant's legal philosophy. On the one hand, there was a 'moral-teleological' view of law, particularly held by legal scholars, according to which law has only a serving function vis-à-vis ethics (i.e. that law should merely enable moral development within the framework of ethics).[5] As an opposing position, Julius Ebbinghaus, in particular, developed an 'independentist' reading of Kant's legal philosophy, according to which a derivation of any kind of law from the rest of critical moral philosophy is possible, but not necessary. Kant's legal philosophy could also be explained and justified independently of the rest of moral philosophy.[6] In particular, Ebbinghaus (and other authors such as Georg Geismann and, to a lesser extent, Manfred Baum, who follow him in this[7]) argues that Kant's philosophy of law arises solely from the concept of a general-law compact of external freedom of action. It is therefore independent of the concept of transcendental freedom and thus, in normative terms, also independent of the theory of autonomy. As a reaction to this, a middle position developed – advanced especially by Wolfgang Kersting[8] and Bernd Ludwig[9] – according to which law and ethics represent different areas of morality, but have a common foundation in terms of normative validity, meaning that they necessarily refer to the autonomy and thus the transcendental freedom of the subjects of law.

As we entered the new millennium, this 'great divide' reappeared internationally. Arthur Ripstein, for example, argued in his groundbreaking book *Force and Freedom* that Kant's philosophy of law has a rationale of its own, independent of Kant's moral philosophy. The upshot of his interpretation is that the normativity of law exclusively rests on the conditions of the possibility of external freedom: because people strive for external freedom (i.e. the possibility of making their own decisions independently of restrictions by others), the law and legal institutions (i.e. the

[5] For example, Werner Haensel, *Kants Lehre vom Widerstandsrecht: Ein Beitrag zur Systematik der Kantischen Rechtsphilosophie*, Berlin: Heise, 1926; Karl Larenz, 'Sittlichkeit und Recht: Untersuchungen zur Geschichte des deutschen Rechtsdenkens und zur Sittenlehre', in Karl Larenz (ed.), *Reich und Recht in der deutschen Philosophie*, Stuttgart and Berlin: W. Kohlhammer, 1943, 169–402, and Fiete Kalscheuer, *Autonomie als Grund und Grenze des Rechts: Zum Verhältnis zwischen dem kategorischen Imperativ und dem allgemeinen Rechtsgesetz Kants*, Berlin: De Gruyter, 2014.

[6] See for instance Julius Ebbinghaus, 'Die Strafen für Tötung eines Menschen und Prinzipien einer Rechtsphilosophie der Freiheit', in *Gesammelte Schriften*, vol. 2: *Philosophie der Freiheit: Praktische Philosophie 1955–1972*, ed. by Georg Geismann and Hariolf Oberer, Bonn: Bouvier, 1988, 283–380, and 'Kant und das 20. Jahrhundert', in *Gesammelte Schriften*, vol. 3: *Interpretation und Kritik: Schriften zur theoretischen Philosophie und zur Philosophiegeschichte 1924–1972*, ed. by Georg Geismann and Hariolf Oberer, Bonn: Bouvier Verlag, 1990, 151–74.

[7] See Georg Geismann, 'Recht und Moral in der Philosophie Kants', *Jahrbuch für Recht und Ethik* 14 (2006), 3–124, and Manfred Baum, 'Freiheit und Verbindlichkeit in Kants Moralphilosophie', *Jahrbuch für Recht und Ethik* 13 (2005), 31–43.

[8] Wolfgang Kersting, *Wohlgeordnete Freiheit: Immanuel Kants Rechts- und Staatsphilosophie*, Berlin: De Gruyter, 1984.

[9] Bernd Ludwig, *Kants Rechtslehre*, Hamburg: Meiner, 1988.

state) that make this possible are practically necessary. Kant's philosophy of law is thus independent of his critical *moral* philosophy, especially the categorical imperative and the autonomy of pure practical reason presupposed by it. While this is a controversial interpretation of Kant's works, it is precisely Ripstein's renunciation of these highly metaphysical presupposition of Kant's moral philosophy that makes his interpretation an attractive point of reference for contemporary normative theorizing in the wake of Kant. For instance, Japa Pallikkathayil,[10] Ariel Zylberman,[11] and George Pavlakos[12] build on a non-metaphysical notion of relational and empirically demonstrable freedom, while Louis-Philippe Hodgson[13] and Rafeeq Hasan[14] draw on an innate claim to legal independence as the basis of Kantian approaches to legal and political philosophy. In recent years, Ripstein's and other independentist readings of Kant have increasingly gained traction.[15]

Other scholars, however, reject this idea of a justificatory independence of Kant's legal philosophy from his critical moral philosophy. Instead, Kant's philosophy of law, they claim, can only be understood as a particular application of his moral philosophy: Kant's law of right can and must be derived from the categorical imperative[16] and its normativity can only be justified by recourse to the autonomy of pure practical reason and its underlying doctrine of transcendental freedom.[17] It is not merely external freedom, but rather individual autonomy and moral personality, which

[10] Japa Pallikkathayil, 'Persons and Bodies', in Sari Kisilevsky and Martin Stone (eds.), *Freedom and Force: Essays on Kant's Legal Philosophy*, Oxford: Hart Publishing, 2017, 35–54.

[11] Ariel Zylberman, 'The Public Form of Law: Kant on the Second-Personal Constitution of Freedom', *Kantian Review* 21 (2016), 101–26.

[12] George Pavlakos, 'The Relation between Moral and Legal Obligation: An Alternative Kantian Reading', in George Pavlakos and Veronica Rodriguez-Blanco (eds.), *Reasons and Intentions in Law and Practical Agency*, Cambridge: Cambridge University Press, 2015, 228–43.

[13] Louis-Philippe Hodgson, 'Kant on the Right to Freedom: A Defense', *Ethics* 120 (2010), 791–819.

[14] Rafeeq Hasan, 'Freedom and Poverty in the Kantian State', *European Journal of Philosophy* 26 (2018), 911–31.

[15] For influential contributions cf. Marcus Willaschek, 'Right and Coercion: Can Kant's Conception of Right Be Derived from His Moral Theory?' *International Journal of Philosophical Studies* 17 (2009), 49–70, and Christoph Horn, *Nichtideale Normativität: Ein neuer Blick auf Kants politische Philosophie*, Berlin: Suhrkamp, 2014. For a nuanced account of different possible kinds of (in)dependence of right on (from) morals, cf. Marcus Willaschek's contribution to this volume (Chapter 1).

[16] For instance, Paul Guyer, 'The Twofold Morality of *Recht*: Once More unto the Breach', *Kant-Studien* 107 (2016), 34–63, and Byrd and Hruschka, *Kant's Doctrine of Right*.

[17] For example, Bernd Ludwig, 'Die Einteilungen der "Metaphysik der Sitten" im Allgemeinen und die der "Tugendlehre" im Besonderen', in Andreas Trampota, Oliver Sensen, and Jens Timmermann (eds.), *Kant's 'Tugendlehre': A Comprehensive Commentary*, Berlin: De Gruyter, 2013, 59–84.

constitute the basis of Kant's legal and political philosophy. The binding nature of law arises from the moral requirement not to treat persons as mere means.[18] If according to Kant the '[a]utonomy of the will is the sole principle of all moral laws and of duties in keeping with them' (*Critique of Practical Reason*, 5:33) and if right is 'a universal law [...] that lays an obligation on me' (*Metaphysics of Morals*, 6:231), then the latter must be grounded in Kant's critical moral philosophy.[19] Such a reading, which insists on a dependence of law on morality, has far-reaching implications for present-day Kantian conceptions of law that attempt to eschew such commitments. On this view, a Kantian legal and political philosophy that is decoupled from moral philosophy and its metaphysical presuppositions is incomplete, particularly in terms of the normative bindingness and content of law.[20]

This long-running dispute over the normative basis of Kant's philosophy of law naturally has weighty spillover effects regarding both the interpretation of Kant and current theorizing in the wake of Kant. To the first point, central Kantian theorems, such as the concept of duty and imputation, as well as legal coercion or the criminal law, will be conceptualized differently depending on whether one assumes a derivational link between law and morality or one assumes instead that law has a normativity of its own. To the second point, the question arises as to how philosophically viable current Kantian approaches whose nucleus is the individual claim to external freedom really are. Do they hinge on the normative independence of law from morality? And if so, on what kind of independence? How apt are they for providing conceptual solutions for current challenges in legal and political philosophy?

Overview of the Volume

The contributions in this volume pick up on these and related questions, beginning with a series of essays that examine the issue at the heart of

[18] For instance, Philipp-Alexander Hirsch, *Freiheit und Staatlichkeit bei Kant: Die autonomietheore tische Begründung von Recht und Staat und das Widerstandsproblem*, Berlin: De Gruyter, 2017, and J. P. Messina, 'The Paradox of Outer Necessitation in (and after) Kant's 1784 Course on *Naturrecht*', in Margit Ruffing, Annika Schlitte, and Gianluca Sadun Bordoni (eds.), *Kants Naturrecht Feyerabend: Analysen und Perspektiven*, Berlin: De Gruyter, 2020, 169–83.

[19] For example, Kersting, *Wohlgeordnete Freiheit*; Ludwig, *Kants Rechtslehre*; Gerhard Seel, 'How Does Kant Justify the Universal Objective Validity of the Law of Right?', *International Journal of Philosophical Studies* 17 (2009), 71–94; Byrd and Hruschka, *Kant's Doctrine of Right*; and Hirsch, *Freiheit und Staatlichkeit bei Kant.*

[20] Cf. Katrin Flikschuh, *Kant and Modern Political Philosophy*, Cambridge: Cambridge University Press, 2000.

Kant's understanding of law and morality: does Kant's legal philosophy present an embodiment or derivation of this critical moral philosophy, or does it rest on an independent foundation?

In Chapter 1, **Marcus Willaschek** defends a 'non-derivationist' reading of the relation between morals and right that nevertheless tries to capture the central insight behind 'derivationist' interpretations by arguing that Kantian right instantiates the idea of moral universality, which it shares with ethics. Kantian right and morals both presuppose the idea of universality according to which rights and duties are the same for all. However, this idea – which is captured in the 'supreme principle of morals' of the *Metaphysics of Morals* – must be distinguished from the categorical imperative (CI) as introduced in the *Groundwork for a Metaphysics of Morals*. According to Willaschek the debate so far has failed to do so and thus overlooked the fact that Kantian right (with its supreme principle, the 'Universal Principle of Right', UPR), can be understood as the result of bringing the idea of moral universality to bear on the concept of subjective rights. The supreme principle of morals *alone*, however, is according to Willaschek not sufficient to derive juridical rights and duties. Rather, the normative validity of juridical rights must be presupposed and cannot be derived from anything more fundamental.

In Chapter 2, **Bernd Ludwig** sets out to show that 'non-derivationist' interpretations of Kant have missed the simplicity and brevity of Kant's derivation of right from morals. For Kant, all moral obligation is solely based on the pure legislative will of the free being itself ('autonomy', KpV § 8), and the general formula of obligation is the categorical imperative. Since Kant understands right as a relationship of persons (RL § B), and since personality is the 'freedom of a reasonable being under moral laws' (RL, Intr. IV), the supreme principle of *legal* obligation must be derived directly from the categorical imperative as the origin of *all* obligation. According to Ludwig, it would be wrong to take the externality of right as a proof for its independence from morals. He argues that the provisions of the concept of law from RL §§ A+B taken together with the further insight (which is a commonplace in modern natural law tradition) that there are actions that 'cannot possibly be done in good faith' ('fornication' is the traditional standard example), help us to understand Kant's reference to the externality of right in RL § C ('Every *action* is right that . . .'): It just says that no action is right for which there is no maxim at all that is compatible with the categorical imperative (traditionally: 'for which there is no good intention at all'). But if for any action there is no maxim *at all* compatible with morality, then no moral agent can possibly act according to such a maxim. Consequently, the agent acts (*tertium non datur*) according to a maxim that is contrary to morality, and the action is therefore – as Ludwig argues – simply morally forbidden.

Christoph Horn, in Chapter 3, defends the view that Kant develops a type of legal and political normativity that can neither be satisfactorily characterized on the basis of a 'derivationist reading' (i.e. the interpretation that legitimate legal and political rules must be derived from the moral law) nor on that of a 'separation' or 'independentist' reading (i.e. legitimate political legal rules are *sui generis*, viz. they form a separate kind of normativity). Instead, Horn claims that valid laws and political rules are justified, in Kant, as a significantly non-ideal version of what the categorical imperative (CI) imposes on us. In his essay Horn calls the procedure proposed by Kant the 'General Will Test' (GWT) and highlights the similarities and differences between the CI and GWT. In view of the large debate among scholars on the question of whether or not the CI is present in Kant's description of legitimate juridico-political normativity, Horn tries to highlight a simple, but forceful, observation of a deep ambiguity: on the one hand, Kant says that, ideally, legitimate law (*Recht*) should be based upon a test procedure, while, on the other hand, his concrete procedure – namely GWT – is considerably different from the universalization test (or the humanity-as-end-in-itself test) as we know it from the *Groundwork* or the *Critique of Practical Reason*. Horn goes on to argue that the CI and GWT are related to one another precisely in the sense of ideal and non-ideal normativity. In order to further underpin this claim, Horn refers to and discusses several key passages in Kant's political writings, in particular the 'transcendental formula of Public Right' in *Perpetual Peace*.

In Chapter 4, **Sorin Baiasu** considers and rejects a strategy for defending an independentist interpretation of Kant's legal philosophy. This strategy is based on a particular view of the Universal Principle of Right (UPR) according to which the UPR amounts to two distinct and mutually irreducible normative standards, one concerning formal and the other one identifying material wrongs. Any interpretation which holds that Kant's politico-legal philosophy is dependent on his moral philosophy is thereby faced with the challenge of deriving not just one but two legal principles from the categorical imperative (CI). In fact, as Baiasu goes on to show, the two-standards interpretation makes it impossible to derive the UPR from the purely formal principle of the CI. However, by drawing on Kant's theory of imputation Baiasu argues that this strategy cannot properly track Kant's distinction between formal and material wrongdoing and therefore has to be rejected. This, Baiasu argues, provides indirect support for an alternative, complex dependentist interpretation that can retain the view of Kant's politico-legal philosophy as ethics-sensitive. According to this interpretation, the UPR cannot be derived normatively in an immediate way from the CI, but it can be derived from an intermediary principle.

The volume continues with two contributions that pick up on a topic closely linked to the previous discussion: how can the fact that lawful behaviour can be enforced – and unlawful behaviour punished – be explained against the background of Kant's moral philosophy? In Chapter 5, **Philipp-Alexander Hirsch** tackles the first question. He argues that without grounding right in morality we cannot even understand coercion as a normative problem. The reason is that for Kant coercion becomes problematic only vis-à-vis persons, because they – being ends in themselves – can legitimately claim not to be coerced. Hence, law formulates the necessary conditions for the coexistence of autonomous rational beings and thereby defines equal, relational freedom as a sphere of non-domination, beyond which coercion is morally unproblematic and requires no justification at all. However, proponents of the so-called *independence thesis*, who try to explain coercion as an analytical implication of the idea of equal, relational freedom, fail to provide a *Kantian* justification for the normative bindingness of that very idea and thus for restrictions on the permissibility of coercion. Tracing back coercion to the limits of autonomy, however, does not only explain why coercive force is 'deducible' from moral autonomy (and the categorical imperative as its principle). Even more, this requires us to reconsider whether Kant can consistently argue against the external enforceability of internal perfect duties (e.g. the prohibition of suicide).

In Chapter 6, **Kate Moran** and **Jens Timmermann** take legal punishment as a starting point to address the question whether Kant's legal philosophy is reliant on his mature ethics of autonomy and respect. On the face of it, Kantian law seems to be independent from ethics. Kant holds that law must be externally enforced by coercive measures. The threat that transgressions will be punished acts as a deterrent and thereby ensures compliance with the law. Insofar as law is concerned with external actions only, the state does not concern itself with why citizens break or comply with the law. In this sense, compliance with the law does not depend on the inner motive of duty and respect for the law. However, agents must face a meaningful choice to be responsible for their actions and subject to just punishment. It is at this stage, Moran and Timmermann argue, that the law of land cannot do without the foundations of Kantian ethics: the meaningful choice between right and wrong can only be secured by respect for the law (of ethics), which supports actions required by the law of the land as indirectly ethical. Without the availability of the ethical motive of respect, agents would be exposed to prudential considerations only. But arguably, those who break the law take their criminal act to be prudentially justified – they would not do it otherwise. According to Moran and Timmermann (unsuccessful) criminals might miscalculate in discounting the possibility of being caught and punished. However, it would be absurd to punish them for that. To make what the law prohibits properly illegal thus requires an ethical foundation after all.

The next four chapters deal with particular aspects of the relationship between morality and right in Kant's practical philosophy that are often perceived as puzzling. The first is the issue of moral luck, which is approached by **Ralf M. Bader** in Chapter 7. Kant is often read as being motivated by the idea that morality is something that is within our control, leading him to develop an ethical theory in which there is no room for moral luck. Luck is supposedly excluded by developing an ethical theory that is focused on the maxims of our actions rather than on their consequences. From this perspective a significant chasm opens up between ethics and right. Insofar as right is concerned with external actions, in particular with their effects on the freedom of others, there seems to be plenty of room for luck to come in. If ethics and right were to differ in this way, then it would be hard to see how right could be derived from ethics and how both of them could be integrated into a unified theory based on a single supreme principle. Against this, Bader argues that the role that luck plays in motivating Kant's project needs to be reconceived. His essay develops an account of the morality and legality of actions on which there is no difference in terms of the way in which resultant luck affects ethics and right. In particular Bader sets out to show that Kant is not concerned with resultant luck regarding the consequences of our actions and that the focus on maxims is not motivated by and in fact is not even sufficient for avoiding moral luck. Instead, to the extent that Kant is concerned with moral luck, he is interested in avoiding certain forms of circumstantial and constitutive moral luck. The resulting interpretation, Bader submits, allows for a unified account of morality and legality.

In Chapter 8 **Martin Brecher** discusses Kant's controversial notion of permissive law (*Erlaubnisgesetz*), which comes into play in several key passages of Kant's writings on legal philosophy. Many scholars, such as Reinhard Brandt and Christoph Horn, argue that Kant conceives of permissive laws as suspending moral demands, thus 'permitting' morally wrong actions. In opposition to this view, Brecher proposes another interpretation of Kant's concept of permissive law that takes it to be a kind of moral licence. Brecher lays the foundation of his interpretation through a close reading of Kant's discussion of permissive law in *Towards Perpetual Peace*. As Brecher argues, Kant follows Achenwall and Baumgarten in taking permissive law to be a kind of prohibitive law, developing the concept of a law that specifies under which conditions certain actions are allowed that are otherwise prohibited by it. In this sense, a permissive law *licenses* certain actions with respect to certain conditions. In the sphere of this licence, the actions are not merely tolerated, but genuinely permitted. Brecher then sets out to show that – contrary to Joachim Hruschka's influential interpretation – this concept of permissive law is also at work in the *Doctrine of Right*. He argues that the permissive laws invoked in RL §§ 2, 16, and 22 denote legal capacities to put other agents under enforceable obligations, which capacities are subject to specific conditions that arise from the fundamental prohibition of unilaterally placing obligations on others. These permissive laws, Brecher submits, are thus not invoked to suspend certain legal or moral requirements, but in fact denote how certain actions (in particular, to acquire and possess external objects of one's choice) can be in full conformity with the law of pure practical reason.

Alice Pinheiro Walla, in Chapter 9, addresses the issue of 'provisionality' in Kant's legal writings. She begins by highlighting the problematic status of duties of right in the absence of political institutions, which renders them *inconclusive*, which in turn is what Kant means by *provisional* rights. Against this background, Pinheiro Walla first analyses the need to discharge juridical duties as a matter of personal virtue in the case of lacking or imperfect juridical institutions, which would be the primary duty holders. This introduces – she argues – complications in Kant's account and thus gives rise to additional *ethical* arguments for Kant's *exeundum*: firstly, addressing legal wrongs as a matter of beneficence is incompatible with the dignity of the right holders; secondly, a civil condition is needed in order to avoid overburdening morally responsible agents and thus reconcile moral agency and the human need for happiness. Building on this, Pinheiro Walla criticizes current approaches in Kantian scholarship that take 'provisionality' in Kant as a theory of 'transitionality', able to guide us through messy political developments in the manner of non-ideal theory. In contrast, she argues that the way Kant connects provisional rights and permissive laws has little to do with non-ideal theory, and follows entirely from Kant's apagogical argument for acquired rights in the state of nature.

The next two chapters revolve around the concept of external freedom, which is central to Kant's legal and political philosophy, attempting to reveal the systematic potential of Kantian philosophizing. In Chapter 10, **George Pavlakos** opens this discussion by tackling the long-standing debate between legal non-positivism and legal positivism with a novel Kantian account of radical non-positivism. After highlighting the positivist commitments of contemporary legal non-positivism in giving explanatory priority to institutional rules over legal relations in the account of legal obligation, he uses a Kantian account of legal relations to explore the possibility of a radical non-positivism that gives explanatory priority to legal relations over legal practices. In doing so, he proposes to read Kant's Universal Principle of Right (UPR) as a pre-institutional moral principle that grounds omnilateral demands of rightful action. At the core of this approach is the thesis that freedom as independence does not only generate different normative reasons for individuals but already constitutes a distinct layer of interdependent agency. Hence, Pavlakos argues, we have to take external freedom as requiring the presence of a collective subject. According to Pavlakos, this conception will allow us to better understand the Kantian idea of omnilateral will and it will also demonstrate how relations of justice are not grounded on institutions, for they already constitute an interpersonal structure of normative reasons, to wit a system of 'natural public law'.

In light of the prevalent disagreement of Kantians as to how our external freedom and the corresponding innate right are to be understood, **Japa Pallikkathayil**, in Chapter 11, puts forth a particular concept of external freedom as independence that involves at its core a normative component. According to this conception, one is independent from being constrained by another's choice insofar as one has an effective right against being constrained by them. The innate right to freedom is therefore essentially the right to have a secure place in a system of equal rights. On this basis, Pallikkathayil then demonstrates how this conception of external freedom provides an attractive starting place for present-day thinking about the justification of the state. She argues, first, that the idea of an innate right to external freedom so understood not only provides the basis for an attractive argument for the necessity of the state. It also results, second, in imposing constraints on the state in that the innate right to freedom requires democratic governance and entails certain constitutional requirements which in turn constrain the laws legislators enact. This understanding, she concludes, avoids some powerful objections faced by other approaches proceeding from similar conceptions of external freedom, such as one recently defended by Arthur Ripstein.

The last three chapters bring another perspective to the previous debate, drawing on the foundational elements of Kant's moral philosophy and stressing their importance for his legal and political thinking. In Chapter 12, **J. P. Messina** argues that one cannot have Kant's political theory without his concept of autonomy. He proceeds from the famous puzzle regarding the normative basis of Kant's politics: why did Kant, apparently, not build his politics around the notion of moral autonomy familiar from his moral philosophy, but on the notion of external freedom instead? Messina submits that this question in fact rests on a faulty premise in consequence of conflating two notions of 'external freedom': while the first notion, 'freedom in the external use of choice', refers for Kant to an aspect of the broader capacity for choice, namely that by means of which it is directed towards external objects, the second, 'freedom as independence', describes a normative *status* to which all human agents are entitled, simply insofar as they are free and rational. By drawing attention to this second type of freedom and the place it occupies in Kant's politics, Messina purports to show that, in a real and underappreciated sense, Kant's mature political treatise is grounded in his notion of autonomy.

In Chapter 13, **Pauline Kleingeld**, in turn, considers the positive conception of external freedom in Kant's political philosophy. According to her, scholarly discussion of Kant's republicanism focuses heavily on his 'negative' conception of freedom: independence or not being subject to another master. Much less attention has been paid to Kant's 'positive' conception of freedom: being subject to one's own legislation. Kleingeld argues that Kant's positive conception of external freedom plays a crucial role in his *Doctrine of Right*: external freedom in the negative sense (mutual independence) requires and is realized by freedom in the positive sense (joint self-legislation). After first discussing the 'innate right to freedom', she argues that, on Kant's account, this fundamental right is only fully realized when external freedom is realized in both senses and in all three spheres of public law. Kleingeld concludes that any satisfactory account of Kant's republican theory must complement the focus on independence with an emphasis on citizenship and self-legislation.

In the closing chapter of the volume, **Paul Guyer** completes the circle by picking up the initial debate over the dependence of right on morals and highlighting its implications for the political domain. He argues that any 'independentist' reading of Kant would have to revert to the position that right is founded only on self-love or prudence. But that would be Hobbes, not Kant, and Kant clearly means to dissociate himself from Hobbes at the foundational level of his doctrine of right. Juridical duties are, as Guyer argues, just the subset of moral duties that may be coercively enforced, if the incentive of respect for the moral law is not forthcoming, but they *can* be fulfilled out of respect for the moral law if that is forthcoming. And this is possible just because juridical duties are grounded in the moral law just as much as ethical duties. What is more, only such a foundation of right makes sense of Kant's account of the moral obligations of citizens to enter into and maintain a state and rulers to administer the state in the way that he demands that they must. The existence of a state cannot be compelled, that is, forced on others, out of mere prudence, by people motivated merely by prudence, but must be brought into being by the internally – morally – motivated action of some body of agents. And *rulers* may be seen as having what is essentially an ethical duty, enforceable only by their own respect for the moral law, to rule justly. Politicians must be, as Guyer puts it, moral politicians.

PART I

Law and Morality: Derivation or Separation?

CHAPTER 1

Kant on Moral Universality and the Normative Foundations of Right

Marcus Willaschek

1.1 Introduction

This chapter discusses the relation between Kant's moral philosophy and his legal philosophy in the *Metaphysics of Morals*, where he distinguishes between 'Right' and 'Ethics' and subsumes both under his conception of 'Morals'.[1] There has been some debate about the exact demarcations and relations between the elements of this triad. Specifically, while some argue that Right is *independent* of either Morals or Ethics, others deny this. The debate about the so-called *Independence Thesis* (or *Separation Thesis*), however, is riddled with terminological confusion and ambiguity.[2]

First, it is often unclear what Right is supposed to be independent *of* (or dependent *on*). For instance, Allen Wood suggests that what is at issue is whether Right is independent of *Ethics*.[3] But since Right and Ethics are the two coordinated parts of Morals according to Kant, neither of which is subordinate to the other, there is a sense in which the claim that Kantian Right is independent of Kantian Ethics is *obviously true* and should not be contentious. According to Paul Guyer, by contrast, what is at issue is the

Thanks to Andrews Reath, Pauline Kleingeld, Eric Watkins, Fabian Burt, and audiences in Frankfurt, Bergen, Tromsø, and Providence, as well as the participants of the Göttingen conference, the editors of this volume, and Stephan Zimmermann, who commented on my paper there, for helpful feedback on (various) earlier versions of this chapter. Thanks to Carolyn Benson for correcting my English.

[1] The Kantian term 'Recht' is ambiguous between (i) 'das Recht', which means the legal sphere or 'the law' and (ii) 'ein Recht/Rechte', meaning individual rights (such as my right to free speech). Kant explicitly distinguishes between (i) and (ii) at RL 6:237. In this chapter, I will use 'Right' (with a capital R) for the first meaning. For reasons of uniformity, I will also capitalize 'Morals' and 'Ethics'.

[2] The 'Separation Thesis' (*Trennungsthese*) is often attributed to Ebbinghaus; see Julius Ebbinghaus, 'Kants Rechtslehre und die Rechtsphilosophie des Neukantianismus', in Gerold Prauss (ed.), *Kant: Zur Deutung seiner Theorie von Erkennen und Handeln*, Cologne: Kiepenheuer & Witsch, 1973, 322–36.

[3] See e.g. Allen W. Wood, *The Free Development of Each: Studies on Freedom, Right, and Ethics in Classical German Philosophy*, Oxford: Oxford University Press, 2014, 70.

independence of Right from *Morals* and its fundamental principle.[4] But that Right is independent of Morals is obviously false (as Guyer himself insists), since Right, for Kant, is clearly subordinate to Morals and is in this sense dependent on it. So the independence of Right from Morals *as such* cannot be the issue either. The real question (which I take to be the issue Wood and Guyer are really concerned with) is whether Right depends on what might be called 'Kantian Morality', that is, the conception of morality developed in the *Groundwork* and encapsulated in the Categorical Imperative.

Second, it is unclear what *kind* of dependence is at stake.[5] If we focus on the relation between Kantian Morality and Right, there is the question of whether Kantian Morality is *necessary* for Kantian Right in the sense that the latter presupposes Kant's specific account of morality. Yet there is also the question of whether Kantian Morality is *sufficient* to justify his conception of Right, in the sense that the fundamental principles of Right can be derived from, or normatively justified by appeal to, the Categorical Imperative (or some other general, not yet specifically juridical element of Kantian Morality such as moral autonomy).

Since there are two different directions of logical dependence between Kantian Morality and Right, this leaves us with four options: (i) Kantian Morality is necessary and sufficient to derive/justify Kantian Right; (ii) it is necessary but not sufficient; (iii) it is not necessary but sufficient; or (iv) it is neither necessary nor sufficient.[6] Moreover, among those who think that

[4] See e.g. Paul Guyer, 'Kant's Deductions of the Principles of Right', in Mark Timmons (ed.), *Kant's Metaphysics of Morals: Interpretative Essays*, Oxford: Oxford University Press, 2002, 23–64; Paul Guyer, 'The Twofold Morality of *Recht*: Once More unto the Breach', *Kant-Studien* 107 (2016), 34–63.

[5] See Marcus Willaschek, 'Right and Coercion: Can Kant's Conception of Right Be Derived from His Moral Theory?', *International Journal of Philosophical Studies* 17 (2009), 49–70.

[6] For option (i), see e.g. Guyer, 'Kant's Deductions'; Otfried Höffe, 'Der kategorische Rechtsimperativ: Einleitung in die Rechtslehre', in Otfried Höffe (ed.), *Immanuel Kant: Metaphysische Anfangsgründe der Rechtslehre*, Berlin: Akademie-Verlag, 2010, 41–62, as well as Guyer, this volume (Chapter 14); Stefano Bacin, '"Only one obligation": Kant on the Distinction and the Normative Continuity of Right and Ethics', *Studi Kantiani* 29 (2016), 77–90; Philipp-Alexander Hirsch, *Freiheit und Staatlichkeit bei Kant: Die autonomietheoretische Begründung von Recht und Staat und das Widerstandsproblem*, Berlin: De Gruyter, 2017, as well as Hirsch, this volume (Chapter 5); and Ludwig, this volume (Chapter 2). For option (ii), see e.g. Christoph Horn, *Nichtideale Normativität: Ein neuer Blick auf Kants politische Philosophie*, Berlin: Suhrkamp, 2014, as well as Horn, this volume (Chapter 3); Fiete Kalscheuer, *Autonomie als Grund und Grenze des Rechts: Zum Verhältnis zwischen dem kategorischen Imperativ und dem allgemeinen Rechtsgesetz Kants*, Berlin: De Gruyter, 2014; Arthur Ripstein, *Force and Freedom: Kant's Legal and Political Philosophy*, Cambridge, MA: Harvard University Press, 2009; Fiorella Tomassini, 'Right, Morals, and the Categorical Imperative', *Kant-Studien* 114 (2023), 513–38. For option (iii), see e.g. Ebbinghaus, 'Kants Rechtslehre'; Thomas Pogge, 'Is Kant's *Rechtslehre* a "Comprehensive Liberalism"?', in Mark

Kantian Morality is not sufficient to derive Kantian Right, we can further distinguish between (a) those who hold that what is missing is something *non-normative*, such as embodiment in space or non-ideal political conditions and (b) those who think that what is missing is something *normative*, such as the authorization to use coercion.[7]

In this chapter, I argue for the claim that Kantian Morality is necessary but not normatively sufficient for Kantian Right (that is, for option (ii), variant (b)).[8] In other words, Kant's conception of Right presupposes central elements of his *Groundwork* conception of morality, particularly the idea of moral universality or 'universal law', but requires additional resources (the idea of coercible rights) for its normative justification. I will start by looking at the three supreme principles of Morals, Right, and Ethics that Kant introduces in the *Metaphysics of Morals* (Section 1.2). I will then consider the Formula of Universal Law (FUL) from the *Groundwork* (Section 1.3) and argue that it cannot be straightforwardly identified with the supreme principle of Morals (SPM) to which Kant refers in the *Metaphysics of Morals*. Next, I will show, primarily against recent suggestions by Paul Guyer, that the supreme principle of Right cannot be derived from FUL or any other version of the Categorical Imperative alone. In effect, I will argue that although Kantian Right is a special instantiation of Morals, this does not mean that its supreme principle can be derived (without additional resources) from any principle that is more fundamental (Section 1.4). Thus, the relation of Right to Morals is one of *subsumption without derivation*. I will then indicate how Kantian Right can be derived, in some sense, by combining the ideas of individual rights and of moral universality (Section 1.5). I will close by

Timmons (ed.), *Kant's Metaphysics of Morals: Interpretative Essays*, Oxford: Oxford University Press (2002), 133–58. Finally, for option (iv), see e.g. Marcus Willaschek, 'Why the Doctrine of Right Does Not Belong in the Metaphysics of Morals: On Some Basic Distinctions in Kant's Moral Philosophy', *Jahrbuch für Recht und Ethik/Annual Review of Law and Ethics* 5 (1997), 205–27; Allen W. Wood, 'The Final Form of Kant's Practical Philosophy', *The Southern Journal of Philosophy* 36 (1998), 1–20. There are also intermediate positions that do not easily fit into this schema, such as that found in Sorin Baiasu, 'Right's Complex Relations to Ethics in Kant: The Limits of Independentism', *Kant-Studien* 107 (2016), 2–33. For a helpful overview of the debate, see Kalscheuer, *Autonomie als Grund und Grenze des Rechts*, ch. 3.

[7] On the two possibilities mentioned under (a), see Ripstein, *Force and Freedom*, and Horn, *Nichtideale Normativität*, respectively. On option (b), see Willaschek, 'Right and Coercion'.

[8] I have thus revised some of my earlier formulations, according to which Kantian Morality is not even necessary for Kantian Right (see Willaschek, 'Why the Doctrine of Right Does Not Belong in the Metaphysics of Morals'; Willaschek, 'Right and Coercion'). However, the revision is less substantial than it may seem, since the necessity of Kantian Morality for Kantian Right that I now acknowledge does not go beyond the dependence of Right on pure practical reason outlined, for instance, in the final pages of Willaschek, 'Right and Coercion'.

sketching the resulting overall picture of the relation between Morals, Right, and Ethics in Kant and by indicating how the resulting conception of Right can be rationally justified (Section 1.6).[9]

1.2 Three Supreme Principles

According to the *Metaphysics of Morals*, Morals, Right, and Ethics each has its own *supreme principle*. In what follows, we will approach the question of how Right relates to Morals and Ethics by looking at the relation between their supreme principles.

In the Introduction to the *Metaphysics of Morals*, Kant writes: 'The supreme principle of the doctrine of morals (*Sittenlehre*) thus is: act on a maxim that at the same time can hold as universal law' (MS 6:226) – a principle that, one page prior, he calls the 'categorical imperative, which as such only affirms what obligation is' (MS 6:225). While a *maxim* is a principle followed by an individual agent (for some purpose, and given the right circumstances), a *universal law* consists in *everyone's* acting on a particular maxim (see e.g. GMS 4:400n; GMS 4:420n; KpV 5:19). Thus, a maxim can hold as universal law if it is possible (in some suitable sense of 'possibility') for everyone to act on it. Let us call maxims that can hold as universal laws 'universalizable'. Thus, the SPM requires us to act on universalizable maxims.

In the Introduction to the Doctrine of Virtue, which presents his account of Ethics, Kant claims that the 'supreme principle of the Doctrine of Virtue is: act on a maxim of ends the having of which can be a universal law for everyone' (TL 6:395). Kant does not explain what he means by a 'maxim of ends', but the ends in question are presumably the two 'ends that at the same time are duties', namely one's own moral perfection and the happiness of others (TL 6:385; cf. TL 6:391–94). So the supreme principle of Ethics (SPE) can be understood as requiring us to act on universalizable maxims that are suitably related to these two

[9] Note that my reading of the relation between Morals, Right, and Ethics is based on the *Metaphysics of Morals*. As I have argued in earlier work, Kant's views in the *Metaphysics of Morals* differ from what he had anticipated twelve years earlier in the *Groundwork*. Things are complicated further by the fact that even in the *Metaphysics of Morals* we find remnants of Kant's earlier view, according to which juridical rights and obligations can be derived directly from the Categorical Imperative (Willaschek, 'Why the Doctrine of Right Does Not Belong in the Metaphysics of Morals'). What I reconstruct in this chapter is what I take to be the best version of Kant's mature view of the relation between Morals, Right, and Ethics in the *Metaphysics of Morals*.

ends (e.g. to act on a maxim of beneficence to promote the happiness of others).

While Kant does not explicitly state a 'supreme principle of the Doctrine of Right', it seems that the 'universal principle of Right' (UPR) has exactly that function. It reads: 'Any action is rightful that is such that, or in accordance with its maxim, the freedom of choice of each can coexist with everyone's freedom in accordance with a universal law' (RL 6:230).[10] One page later, Kant formulates a 'universal law of Right' (ULR), which I take to be substantially the same principle as UPR but that brings out the parallel with the other two 'supreme principles' even more clearly: 'act externally such that the free use of your choice can coexist with everyone's freedom in accordance with a universal law' (RL 6:231). Since UPR (in the German original) is not grammatically well formed[11] and is thus more difficult to interpret, while ULR is formulated in a way that is parallel to SPM and SPE, I will concentrate mainly on ULR. ULR requires us to act 'externally' (that is, irrespective of one's motivation) in such a way that one's own free acts ('free use of your choice') 'can coexist' with those of others 'in accordance with a universal law'. If we read 'coexist' as 'being jointly realized' and 'in accordance with a universal law' as 'affecting everyone in the same way', we can paraphrase ULR as follows: restrict your exercise of free agency in such a way that your acts do not prevent others from exercising their free agency in the same way.

In sum, Kant formulates three 'supreme principles', one for Morals (SPM), one for Ethics (SPE), and one for Right (UPR/ULR). Each of these three principles invokes the idea of universal law: in fact, this idea seems to be the only element common to all three principles. (SPM, SPE, and ULR are also all formulated as imperatives, while UPR is not.) Only SPM and SPE require that one's maxim *be able to be* (or to hold as) a universal law; by contrast, ULR does not even mention one's maxim and only requires that one's freedom *be able to coexist* with the freedom of others in accordance with a universal law. (UPR does mention a maxim

[10] Translation altered.

[11] The German reads: 'Eine jede Handlung ist Recht, die oder nach deren Maxime die Freiheit der Willkür eines jeden mit jedermanns Freiheit nach einem allgemeinen Gesetze zusammen bestehen kann', where the first disjunct 'die' of the subordinate clause 'die oder nach deren Maxime . . .' does not fit grammatically with the rest of the construction. While the remainder of the clause is governed by 'nach', which in turn requires a word like 'maxim', the first disjunct 'die' refers back to 'Handlung', which does not admit a construction with 'nach'. The infelicity becomes obvious once we remove the second disjunct: 'Eine jede Handlung ist Recht, die . . . die Freiheit der Willkür eines jeden mit jedermanns Freiheit nach einem allgemeinen Gesetze zusammen bestehen kann' is not a well-formed German sentence.

but does *not* require that it be able to hold as a universal law.) Before we look at the difference between SPM and ULR more closely, let us first turn to the relation between SPM and a fourth principle, namely the Categorical Imperative we know from the *Groundwork*.[12]

1.3 Is SPM Identical with the Categorical Imperative Introduced in the *Groundwork*?

In the *Groundwork*, Kant offers (at least) four different formulations of the Categorical Imperative (cf. GMS 4:436), all of which are meant to be expressions of the same 'supreme principle of morality' (GMS 4:440; cf. GMS 4:392). The most general and fundamental of these formulations, and the one closest in wording to SPM, is FUL. It reads:

> FUL: 'act only on that maxim through which you can at the same time will that it become a universal law' (GMS 4:421).

For a maxim to *become* a universal law, I take it, is for it to *hold* as a universal law on which everyone acts. To will *through one's maxim* that one's maxim become a universal law is to want the *conjunction* of two things, namely that one acts on that maxim and that everyone else does the same. FUL thus prescribes a two-step procedure: (i) imagine that everyone acts on one's maxim and (ii) ask whether one can rationally want *both* that one acts on that maxim oneself *and* that everyone else acts on that maxim. If the result of step (i) is that this is logically impossible, or if the result of step (ii) is that you cannot rationally want this (GMS 4:424), then the action is prohibited, and otherwise it is permitted.

Now compare FUL with SPM, which says: 'act on a maxim that at the same time can hold as universal law' (MS 6:226). SPM and FUL are similar in various respects; most importantly, both require us to act on universalizable maxims. But there is at least one important difference: while FUL requires that one be able to 'will' that one's maxim become a universal law, SPM only requires that the maxim be able to 'hold' as a universal law. Apparently, the second step required by FUL has fallen away in SPM. In order to determine what is required by SPM, all one needs to do is ask whether it is *possible* for everyone to act on one's maxim.

[12] For the place of SPM, ULR, and SPE in Kant's wider system of rational principles, see Marcus Willaschek, 'The Structure of Normative Space: Kant's System of Rational Principles', in Beatrix Himmelmann and Camilla Serck-Hanssen (eds.), *The Court of Reason: Proceedings of the 13th International Kant Congress*, Berlin: De Gruyter, 2021, 245–66.

What is the significance of this difference? In the *Groundwork*, Kant identifies the duties that emerge from the first step of FUL (based on a 'contradiction in conception') with narrow or strict duties and those that emerge from the second step (based on a 'contradiction in willing') with wide or meritorious duties (GMS 4:424). Does this mean that SPM is only a principle of narrow and not of wide duties? This is unlikely, since SPM is supposed to be the fundamental principle of the *Metaphysics of Morals*, which includes both narrow duties (which Kant now tends to identify with juridical duties) and wide duties (which are ethical duties).[13]

Could it be that the difference between FUL and SPM does not have any significance at all because Kant is simply expressing the same thing in the different formulations? This also seems unlikely. First, the idea of '*willing* one's maxim (at the same time) to be a universal law' is so prominent in the *Groundwork* that it can hardly be a coincidence that Kant deleted it from the formulation of the SPM.[14] Second, in the *Metaphysics of Morals*, the idea that the Categorical Imperative provides a test procedure for determining our duties recedes into the background and is replaced by a catalogue of juridical rights and ethical virtues.[15] It seems plausible that this change (whether substantial or merely expository) is reflected in the formulation of SPM.

In any case, we cannot straightforwardly identify SPM with FUL. Whatever the reason for Kant's dropping of the reference to 'willing through one's maxim', the two principles differ in subtle ways that presumably reflect the different roles they play in the *Groundwork* and in the *Metaphysics of Morals*.[16] And this means that we cannot simply identify the principle that covers both Right and Ethics as parts of Kant's conception of Morals with the fundamental principle of Kantian Morality as defined in the *Groundwork*.

I think that the difference between SPM and FUL goes even further than indicated thus far, however. As the architecture of the *Metaphysics of Morals* demands, SPM is supposed to hold for both Right and Ethics. But how can that be? As we saw, ULR in effect requires us not to act in ways

[13] Hirsch claims that SPM is a principle only of perfect duties, that is, of juridical duties, and thus must be 'extended' to include imperfect, that is, ethical, duties (see Hirsch, *Freiheit und Staatlichkeit bei Kant*, 94 and 99). But then SPM would not be a principle that holds in the same way for both parts of the *Metaphysics of Morals*.

[14] Reference to willing had already disappeared from the formulation in the second *Critique* (KpV 5:30), which is substantially the same as SPM.

[15] See Wood, 'The Final Form of Kant's Practical Philosophy'.

[16] That SPM is not the same as FUL has also been noted by Tomassini, 'Right, Morals, and the Categorical Imperative'.

that prevent others from doing what they have a right to do, where our rights and theirs are allocated 'in accordance with universal law', that is, in the same way for all. But on Kant's own account, not infringing on other people's rights is something one can do while acting on a maxim that is not universalizable. For instance, Kant claims that lying as such (unless under oath, in a contract, etc.) does not infringe on other people's juridical rights, since it is up to them to believe us or not (RL 6:238). But clearly, the maxim of lying whenever it is convenient is not universalizable, according to Kant (GMS 4:403). Similarly, Kantian Right permits us not to cultivate our talents and abilities, while Kantian Ethics requires this (TL 6:392; cf. GMS 4:422–23). The list of acts and maxims that are juridically permitted according to ULR but not universalizable could easily be extended.[17] So the problem is this: if SPM requires us to act on universalizable maxims but the supreme principle of Right, ULR, does not require this, how can SPM also hold for Right – or conversely, how can ULR fall under SPM as a special case?

We will return to this question soon. For now I want to suggest that we can see how SPM can cover both Right and Ethics if it is understood, despite its imperatival form, as giving expression to (nothing more than) the following twofold claim: (i) there are moral rights and obligations (ii) that are the same for all rational beings. While the imperatival form of SPM can be taken to give indirect expression to (i), the idea of moral universality (ii) is contained in the expression 'universal law'. As Kant himself points out, SPM 'only affirms what obligation is' (MS 6:225). SPM requires us to act on maxims that can be universal laws. But if a maxim *can* be a universal law, then it *is* a universal law in the sense that *everyone* is at least permitted to act on it. Conversely, if my maxim cannot be a universal law, then everyone else is prohibited from acting on it too. Thus, according to SPM, acting on some maxim is morally permitted (prohibited) for one person if and only if it is morally permitted (prohibited) for everyone else. This means that SPM in effect 'affirms what obligation is' on a formal level by saying that *rights and obligations, whether*

[17] Hirsch seems to deny this: 'Was rechtlich erlaubt bzw. verboten ist, das ist auch moralisch (d.h. nach dem kategorischen Imperativ) erlaubt bzw. verboten' (Hirsch, *Freiheit und Staatlichkeit*, 108). He argues for this by criticizing my claim that moral permissions can conflict while rights cannot (Willaschek, 'Right and Coercion'; cf. § 5). While I think that his critique relies on a different understanding of 'conflict' between actions/permissions and thus does not disprove my point, more importantly for our present concerns he does not address the examples just given, which to my mind clearly show that Kant allows for actions that are prohibited by FUL but permitted by UPR.

juridical or ethical, must be the same for all. It thus gives expression to the idea of moral universality.

Only if read in this minimal way can SPM serve as the supreme principle of both Ethics *and* Right. Put differently, what is common to Right and Ethics is not the command to act only on universalizable maxims (because that command, according to Kant, does not hold for Right), but rather the idea that there are moral rights and duties and that they take the form of 'universal law', which means that what is permitted (prohibited) for one must be permitted (prohibited) for all. Note that implicit in SPM and the idea of moral universality is the idea of moral autonomy. If moral rights and obligations must be the same for all rational beings, this is because they are based only on what all rational beings as such share, namely the capacity of (pure practical) reason. But this means that we can understand these rights and obligations not as external requirements but as an expression of our own will insofar as it is rational.

There are two things I would like to take away from our discussion of the relation between SPM and FUL. First, SPM and FUL are distinct principles in that only FUL, but not SPM, requires us to act only on maxims we can *will* to be universal laws. Thus, the supreme principle of the *Metaphysics of Morals* is not identical with (the basic formulation of) the supreme principle of morality Kant introduces in the *Groundwork*. Second, despite its imperatival form, SPM should be read as claiming that there are moral rights and obligations that, because they are based on pure practical reason, are the same for all rational beings. Only if read in this minimal way can SPM serve as the fundamental principle of both Right and Ethics.

1.4 Why ULR Cannot Be Derived from the Categorical Imperative Alone

According to a widespread reading of the Introduction to the Doctrine of Right, ULR can be derived from FUL (or at least falls under FUL as a special case). On this reading, the three features of Right that Kant mentions in RL §B (externality, efficaciousness, and formality) and that take him to his definition of Right and to UPL/ULR (RL 6:230–31) restrict FUL to the 'formal' compatibility of 'external' actions insofar as they can affect others. Since ULR requires me to restrict my sphere of external agency to the conditions under which it is formally compatible with the same sphere's being granted to everyone else ('in accordance with a universal law'), ULR may thus seem to be a restricted version of FUL.

But this picture cannot be correct. First, note that Kant himself never explicitly claims that ULR, UPR, or his conception of Right can be *derived* from FUL (or from any other version of the Categorical Imperative or from Kantian Morality more generally). He only says that Right is one of two branches of Morals, under which it falls or can be subsumed. Second, FUL commands us to act only on maxims we can will as universal laws. But as we have just seen, ULR in no way requires us to act on maxims that qualify as universal laws. All it says is that our actions (UPR: and their maxims) should be compatible (in a specific respect) with everyone else's actions in accordance with a universal law. Thus, the appeal to universal law serves to qualify the way in which one's actions and maxims are to be made compatible with everyone else's, *not* to characterize the quality of one's maxim. But if FUL requires us to act on universalizable maxims while ULR does not, ULR cannot be a special case of FUL (in the sense in which, say, 'Do not lie under oath' is a special case of 'Do not lie'). And if it is not a special case of FUL, then it cannot be derived merely by *restricting* FUL to a specific set of actions or conditions.

Against this, one might respond that for ULR to be a restricted case of FUL it is not necessary for all acts permitted by ULR to be permitted by FUL. Since ULR only concerns external acts, irrespective of whether their motive is duty, lying, for instance, might well be permitted by ULR and prohibited by FUL, even if ULR is derived from FUL by restriction to external acts. Lying as such, except under oath, etc., is simply not an action type that falls under ULR.[18]

While this is correct as far as it goes, it does not show how ULR can be derived as a special case of FUL. The problem is not simply that there are acts that are permitted by ULR but prohibited by SPM. Rather, the *reason* why something is permitted or prohibited according to ULR differs from the reason it is permitted or prohibited according to FUL. In the case of FUL, an act is permitted because its maxim is universalizable. In the case of ULR, an act is permitted not because its maxim is universalizable (since there are permissible acts whose maxim is not) but because it can coexist with everyone's external freedom in accordance with universal laws. If ULR were just a special, restricted case of FUL, one would expect the reason why something is permitted (or prohibited) to be the same for both principles (or at least that the reason in the more general case forms part of the reason in the more specific case). But that is not so. Rather, FUL and ULR impose substantially different normative requirements on us

[18] Thanks to Ralph Bader for raising this objection.

(act on universalizable maxims; respect the equal freedom of others). Given the substantial differences between FUL and ULR, it seems unlikely that there is any other way to derive ULR directly from FUL or any other version of the Categorical Imperative.

Against this conclusion, Paul Guyer has proposed not one but three ways in which ULR (or rather UPR, which is the principle on which Guyer focuses) can be derived from the Categorical Imperative without additional normative input.[19] First, according to Guyer, the most fundamental value that grounds Kant's ethics is the value of freedom, and its most fundamental principle is thus to act in such a way that the 'greatest use of freedom is possible'.[20] UPR is then supposed to follow 'from application of the idea of the "greatest use of freedom" to the interpersonal case'.[21] Second, Guyer asks whether the 'maxim of arrogating as much freedom for themselves as they like regardless of the effect on the freedom of others' is universalizable (according to him, it is not).[22] Third, UPR 'can also be derived from the Formula of Humanity' (FH), which on Guyer's reading requires that I 'exercise my own capacity to set ends only in ways consistent with the capacity of all others to set ends', from which it presumably follows that 'the formula of humanity tells me always to exercise my freedom of choice only in ways that leave others equal freedom of choice – precisely what is required by the Universal Principle of Right'.[23]

I think that the first derivation fails because it does not distinguish between two notions of external freedom at issue in Kant's conception of Right: one's 'pre-juridical' freedom of choice and one's juridical freedom (the latter being both limited and protected by universal laws of Right).[24] Clearly, it cannot be a fundamental moral principle to secure the 'greatest use of freedom' if by that we mean the unrestricted use of one's freedom of choice, since this would include unrightful and immoral uses of freedom. But if the principle is restricted to *juridical* freedom, it just becomes a version of UPR: secure the greatest possible freedom for yourself that is compatible with the same freedom for everyone else. UPR would then be

[19] Guyer, 'The Twofold Morality of *Recht*'.

[20] Guyer, 'The Twofold Morality of *Recht*', 43, quoting a lecture Kant probably held in 1777, V-Mo/Collins 27:346.

[21] Guyer, 'The Twofold Morality of *Recht*', 44.

[22] Guyer, 'The Twofold Morality of *Recht*', 44.

[23] Guyer, 'The Twofold Morality of *Recht*', 45.

[24] Note that this distinction is fundamental to Kant's entire conception of Right, which limits one's pre-juridical freedom of choice to the conditions under which it is compatible with the same freedom for everyone. The freedom resulting from this limitation is what Right guarantees.

derived not from FUL but from a principle that is just another version of UPR and that, therefore, cannot be the supreme principle of both Right and Ethics. Perhaps there is some third notion of external freedom (let us call it *moral* freedom) that is fitting for a moral (not specifically juridical) principle of greatest freedom – perhaps 'freedom as constrained by FUL'. But if so, Guyer does not provide it here.[25]

The second derivation rests on the claim that the maxim of arrogating more freedom for oneself than one grants to others is not universalizable. Bringing this idea even closer to a possible derivation of ULR or UPR, we can ask whether the maxim of *not* (always) acting in accordance with ULR (that is, not always 'act[ing] externally such that the free use of your choice can coexist with everyone's freedom in accordance with a universal law') passes the FUL test. Obviously, it is *logically* possible for this maxim to be a universal law, since such a situation is just what Kant, with the tradition, calls 'the state of nature' (*natürlicher Zustand*, RL 6:306). Now according to FUL, we must next ask whether one can rationally *will* such a situation, and Kant is ultimately committed to the claim that one cannot (cf. RL 6:307).

But note that his argument for this claim is that only in a civil state (*bürgerlicher Zustand*, a state in which Right is realized) can people's juridical *rights* be secured and conflicts about such rights resolved in a non-arbitrary way (namely in court) (RL 6:306). Thus, Kant's argument against the state of nature already presupposes what he calls 'private Right' (with its presumptive subjective rights, e.g. to freedom of speech and to property) and thus presupposes UPR. Moreover, Kant claims that in the state of nature 'no one is bound to refrain from encroaching on what another possesses if the other gives him no equal assurance that he will observe the same restraint toward him'. He concludes:

> Given the intention to be and to remain in this state of externally lawless freedom, men do *one another* no wrong at all when they feud among themselves; for what holds for one holds also in turn for the other, as if by mutual consent . . . But in general they do wrong in the highest degree. (RL 6:307)

Thus, Kant himself argues that, at least from the perspective of the individual agent, willing to live in the state of nature is rationally possible ('as if by mutual consent') as long as we ignore each other's juridical rights.

[25] Moreover, if the moral notion of freedom is freedom as constrained by FUL, then the reasons that tell against deriving ULR from FUL outlined at the beginning of this section also tell against deriving ULR from a principle of greatest freedom using that notion.

It is only once we take into account the *additional* requirement to leave the state of nature, which already presupposes private Right and ULR, that this maxim can no longer be willed as universal law. But this means that the maxim in question (of not always acting in accordance with ULR) fails to be universalizable only if we already presuppose that there are juridical rights according to ULR, which is just what was meant to be derived.

Finally, we can see that something is amiss with Guyer's third derivation from the fact that its conclusion ('to exercise my freedom of choice only in ways that leave others equal freedom of choice') contains an idea not contained in FH as interpreted by Guyer ('exercise my own capacity to set ends only in ways consistent with the capacity of all others to set ends'), namely that of '*equal* freedom'. FH requires me always to treat others in ways to which they can rationally consent. But in not respecting their juridical rights (not granting them equal freedom), I do not necessarily violate this requirement. The reason, again, is that in the state of nature, as long as others do not grant equal freedom to me, I am not morally required to grant *equal* freedom to them. Thus, it is not the case that in the state of nature, where there is no 'equal freedom' because, 'as if by mutual consent', the strongest prevails, I automatically violate FH (treat others as mere means), since our relation may still be entirely reciprocal and consensual.

I conclude that Guyer's three proposed derivations of UPR/ULR from FUL and FH are unsuccessful. Ultimately, I think that no such derivation is possible because Kantian Right is not a state in which everyone voluntarily acts in accordance with ULR (that is, respects equal spheres of freedom for all), but rather a state in which everyone is *guaranteed* to act that way, willingly or unwillingly, where this guarantee involves the use of coercion where necessary. As I have argued elsewhere, this 'authorization to use coercion', which according to Kant is analytically linked to the concept of Right (RL 6:231), cannot be justified merely by appeal to FUL, FH, or SPM.[26] Let me close this section by briefly commenting on Guyer's discussion of one of my arguments for this claim.[27]

The argument in question is that if FUL were to include the authority to use coercion in the juridical case, it would also include that authority for some ethical cases, which would clearly be inappropriate. Guyer thinks

[26] Willaschek, 'Right and Coercion'; Willaschek, 'The Non-Derivability of Kantian Right'.

[27] Guyer, 'The Twofold Morality of *Recht*', Appendix. I am not convinced by his rejection of the other two arguments, but this is not the place to pursue this point further. Also cf. Hirsch, this volume (Chapter 5), for a different critique of my claim that the authorization to use coercion cannot be derived from the Categorical Imperative.

that 'this is the most promising' of the arguments I offer and rightly points out that the 'difficult cases' for someone who wants to resist this argument 'will be perfect duties to others, such as simply keeping promises, that do not seem to be desirable candidates for coercive enforcement'.[28] Guyer's main line of response is that failure to keep non-contractual promises is 'not really a hindrance to freedom' and that therefore the keeping of such promises cannot be coercively enforced. So the idea is that while we are morally obligated to keep our non-juridical promises, this obligation cannot be coercively enforced because breaking such a promise does not hinder the promisee's freedom. Guyer admits that this 'may seem implausible', but he then argues that 'rational agents do not place too much weight on promises that do not take the form of legally enforceable contracts'.[29] Therefore, according to Guyer, their freedom is not hindered by someone's breaking such a promise. But that still seems implausible. We often rely on promises that are not legally enforceable, such as a friend's promise to stand by my side even in difficult times or a wedding vow of mutual faithfulness. In many ways, non-juridical promises can be more important to us than legally binding contracts, and important parts of our lives depend on them. Moreover, breaking a non-juridical promise can very well limit our freedom in that it can hinder us from doing something we could, and would, otherwise have done. Thus, we still lack a principled way to distinguish between duties that are coercively enforceable and those that are not without already presupposing a Kantian conception of Right (with its analytic link to coercion).[30]

In sum, there is reason to doubt that ULR can be derived from FUL alone (or from any other version of the Categorical Imperative) without introducing additional normative resources, and recent attempts to provide such a derivation remain unconvincing.

1.5 How ULR *Can* Be Derived from SPM (in Conjunction with the Idea of Subjective Rights)

In this section, I will argue that ULR (and thus Kant's conception of Right) can be understood as combining SPM with the claim that there are

[28] Guyer, 'The Twofold Morality of *Recht*', 62. [29] Guyer, 'The Twofold Morality of *Recht*', 63.

[30] Guyer also claims that by requiring normative resources in addition to FUL/SPM for the derivation of legitimate coercion, I 'give up the game of a purely analytic argument for the authorization to use coercion' (Guyer, 'The Twofold Morality of *Recht*', 61). But this misrepresents my view. The purely analytic argument is the one Kant offers in § D, which starts *from* the concept of Right and leads to the authorization to use coercion. The additional normative resources are needed to *derive* the concept of Right (the one *from* which the analytic argument in § D starts) from FUL/SPM.

coercible juridical rights. If there are such rights, then, according to Kant, it follows analytically that they must form a system, which Kant calls Right. (Note that the following 'derivation' of ULR does not in itself constitute a justification of juridical coercion but presupposes that there are coercible juridical rights. I will return to the question of how to justify coercion at the end of this chapter.)

Let us start from the claim that juridical rights must form a system. This follows from a principle I have elsewhere called the Impossibility of Conflicting Juridical Rights (ICJR).[31] It says that if you have the right to do *F*, then no one else can have a right to do something that makes it impossible for you to do *F*:

> ICJR: Necessarily, if *A* has a juridical right to do F_1 and if *B*'s doing F_2 makes it impossible for *A* to do F_1, then *B* does not have a juridical right to do F_2.

Thus, ICJR implies that all juridical rights must be compossible, that is, that it must be possible for all juridical rights to be jointly exercised. In recent legal and political theory, this claim has been the subject of much debate.[32] Nevertheless, I take ICJR to be a *conceptual truth* about juridical rights in Kant's sense. To be sure, there can be 'rights' in a wider sense that do conflict – such as my 'right' to privacy and your 'right' to security. But these are not all-things-considered juridical rights in the Kantian sense, which are coercively enforceable, but rather *pro tanto* rights (or perhaps, in analogy with Kant's resolution of conflicting duties, *grounds* of rights; cf. MS 6:224). Only when it has been determined (typically by a court of law) whether in a particular case your 'right' to security or my 'right' to privacy prevails do we have a juridical right in Kant's sense that can be coercively enforced (e.g. my right to keep my email messages private or your right to have them searched). Even though Kant does not explicitly articulate ICJR, he is clearly committed to it by the way he argues for the analytic link between right and coercion (RL 6:231).[33]

Now, ICJR implies that different people's spheres of legally protected freedom (subjective juridical rights) must be *limited* in a way that avoids the possibility of conflicting rights. If *A* has an unrestricted right freely to

[31] I appealed to ICJR in previous work in order to explain Kant's claim that Right is coercible (Willaschek, 'Right and Coercion'; Willaschek, 'The Non-Derivability of Kantian Right'), but I now think that its significance is even wider.

[32] See e.g. Adina Preda, 'Are There Any Conflicts of Rights?', *Ethical Theory and Moral Practice* 18 (2015), 677–90, and the works cited there. Thanks to Jesse Tomalty for alerting me to this body of literature and for suggesting the example that follows.

[33] See Willaschek, 'Right and Coercion'.

speak her mind and *B* has an unrestricted right not to be spoken ill of in public, these rights can conflict if *A* thinks ill of *B* and makes use of her right to say so publicly. Thus, because of ICJR, either *A*'s or *B*'s right must be limited in order to form a system of compossible rights. In principle, this can be done in many possible ways, for example by giving all rights to one person and none to all others, or many rights to women and few to men. Any distribution of juridical rights that avoids conflicts between rights would satisfy ICJR. But clearly, unequal distributions of rights violate the idea of moral universality expressed in SPM, which requires that juridical rights (spheres of legal freedom) must be the same for all.

But if ICJR is combined with SPM, what results is the idea of Kantian Right and ULR. While ICJR implies that spheres of freedom must be limited (or 'united') so as not to conflict, SPM means that this limitation must be the same for all ('in accordance with universal law'). Taken together, they require us to limit people's spheres of freedom in a way that grants everyone a sphere of juridically protected freedom that is compatible with granting the same sphere of freedom to everyone else. Thus, given the idea of moral universality, if there are any juridical rights at all, they must conform to ULR. Assuming that there can be no justification of Kantian Right (with its emphasis on 'universal law') that does *not* appeal to the idea of moral universality, this means that SPM is *necessary*, and in conjunction with ICJR also *sufficient*, for justifying ULR.[34]

I hope that the reading developed here can capture what I take to be the correct insight in interpretations of Kantian Right that aim to derive ULR or UPR from FUL or SPM, namely that Kantian Right is one instantiation of a more general idea that is also instantiated, although in a different way, in Ethics. What is common to Right and Ethics is the assumption that there are moral rights and obligations which, because they arise from rational principles, are the same for all rational beings, a universality which is expressed in SPM (as well as in ULR and SPE) by appeal to 'universal law'. Where the reading proposed here differs from those other readings, however, is in its denial that either FUL or SPM alone is sufficient to

[34] In itself, the combination of SPM and ICJR does not imply that each person's sphere of freedom must be limited *only* as far as is made necessary by the idea of moral universality. And in fact, it does not seem that a requirement of *maximal* freedom is included in Kant's conception of Right. After all, Kant allows for the possibility of taxation that goes beyond the bare minimum required to keep the state functioning in that it also includes provisions for 'public security, convenience and decency' (RL 6:325). Since taxation of course restricts the freedom to use one's financial resources, such taxation would be compatible with Kantian Right but would result in spheres of freedom that are more limited than is strictly necessary to satisfy both ICJR and SPM.

justify Kantian Right. On the reading suggested here, what is needed in addition to SPM (i.e. in addition to the idea of moral universality) in order to justify Kantian Right is the assumption that there are coercively enforceable rights. While Right applies the idea of moral universality to subjective juridical rights (requiring that the coexistence of individuals' rights results in equal rights for everyone), Ethics applies it to people's maxims and ends (requiring us to act only on universalizable maxims).

1.6 The Resulting Picture

In this chapter, I have tried to elucidate the relation between Kantian Morals, Right, and Ethics by discussing the relation between their 'supreme principles' (and the Categorical Imperative from the *Groundwork*). The basic principle of Kantian Morals is SPM, which Kant formulates as the imperative to act on maxims that can hold as universal laws. As I have argued, however, SPM is best understood as an expression of the claim that there are moral rights and obligations which, because they arise from pure practical reason, are the same for all rational beings.

This general claim has two basic applications: Right and Ethics. In Right, the idea of moral universality is applied to juridical rights. Since the juridical rights of different people cannot conflict, they must be (coercively) 'united' in a system of rights. SPM requires that these rights be distributed equally, 'in accordance with a universal law'. In this sense, Right is a special case of Morals, and its supreme principle (UPR/ULR) is a special case of SPM. But this does not mean that ULR can be derived from SPM alone. What can be derived from SPM in conjunction with the idea of juridical rights is the conditional claim that *if* there are juridical (coercible) rights, they must take the form of a system of equal rights for all. In order to derive UPR/ULR itself, the existence of juridical rights must already be presupposed. But note that this does not mean that juridical rights are normatively prior to, or more basic in the order of justification than, UPR/ULR. It only means that we can understand UPR/ULR as a combination of central elements of Kantian Morality (rights and obligations based on pure practical reason, moral universality) and the idea of enforceable rights (which necessarily form a system). When it comes to *justifying* UPR/ULR or to explaining its normative validity, there is nothing more basic on which UPR/ULR could be grounded, because the fundamental juridical rights that are normatively valid for us, according to Kant, are those that hold equally for all rational beings, that is, those defined by UPR/ULR.

In Ethics, the idea of moral universality is applied to the two ends reason prescribes to each of us: moral self-perfection and the happiness of others. As Kant maintains, these ends must be pursued only in ways that respect the equal moral standing of all, which means that they must be pursued in maxims that can hold as universal laws (SPE). Even though this has not been the topic of this chapter, there is little reason to assume that SPE, so understood, can be derived from SPM alone. For instance, that the happiness of others is ethically important is something that does not follow from the idea of moral universality (SPM). Rather, the two ethical ends must be presupposed, and combined with the idea of moral universality, in order to arrive at SPE. Again, this does not mean that self-perfection and the happiness of others are normatively more fundamental than SPE, but only that SPE can be understood as a combination of these two ends with other elements of Kantian Morality. When it comes to justifying SPE, there is nothing more basic to which one could appeal and that would explain the validity of SPE without already presupposing SPE in one way or another.

Thus, Kant's conception of Morals is united by the ideas (i) of rights and obligations based on reason and (ii) of 'universal law' or moral universality. It is these ideas that are shared by both Right and Ethics. As I have argued, however, this does not mean that the supreme principles of Right and Ethics can be derived from something more fundamental (such as SPM or FUL). On the reading defended here, Right and Ethics are both equally fundamental and underivable expressions of Kantian Morals, with its idea of moral universality.

Now it may seem that, unlike Ethics, Right stands in need of further rational justification because it involves the authorization to use coercion. Since coercion consists in making people do something they would not have done freely (cf. RL 6:231; TL 6:379), we need to explain what gives us the right to coerce someone and thus to restrict their freedom. But note that if Right cannot be derived from anything more fundamental, this does not mean that it cannot be rationally justified from *within* the perspective of Right. The inherent rationality of Right (including the authorization to use coercion) is evident in the fact that someone who violates other people's rights cannot *reasonably* complain if she is coerced into respecting those rights (as long as the coercive measures are proportionate, of course).[35] In particular, she cannot rationally insist on her *right* to do as she pleases, or her *right* not to be coerced, since juridical rights, as we have

[35] See Ludwig, this volume (Chapter 2), for a similar argument.

seen, necessarily form a *system* in the sense that one person's right is mutually dependent on any other person's right. (This is implied by ICJR.) It is therefore rationally impossible to insist on one's own rights without granting equal rights to everyone else. (This is implied by ICJR in conjunction with SPM.) Thus, while it may be rationally possible to reject the whole idea of Kantian Right, it is impossible to rationally object to the fact that other people protect their own rights and the rights of others coercively, since doing so would amount to insisting on one's own right not to be coerced, which in turn implies granting equal rights to all others. This, it seems to me, is entirely sufficient as a normative justification of Kantian Right.

CHAPTER 2

Kant's Direct Route from the Categorical Imperative to the Universal Law of Right

Bernd Ludwig

2.1 Obligation in Classical Theories of Natural Law

In the Natural Law tradition since Francisco Suarez and Hugo Grotius there is a broad consensus that all kinds of obligation derive in the final instance from a *single* source: from the divine will, from the reason-guided *voluntas Dei*: 'Thy *WILL* be done in earth, as it is in heaven'. Accordingly, all obligations arising from *human* legislation must also be traceable to this single source: Fundamental natural law is ultimately *divine law*. Gottfried Achenwall, the author of the textbook Kant used for his lectures on Natural Law, can hardly be surpassed in clarity on this point:

> The law of nature is the moral law or the divine one, as far as it [1] can be recognized from philosophical principles; it is a rule according to which we [2] are obliged to direct our actions because of God's will – so far as we can recognize it by reason alone. (§ 50)[1]

Of course different legal scholars in that period attributed the law-giving authority of God to different qualities in God, whether it is that he does not allow contradiction because of his *omnipotence* (as in Hobbes – in reference specifically to legislation for the Commonwealth Ecclasiasticall), or that no reasonable doubt about his prescriptions is possible because of his *omniscience* and *omnibenevolence* (as in Leibniz), or that this authority simply derives from his privilege as *creator* of the world (as in Locke and Achenwall) – or (as for instance in Pufendorf) from some combination of these elements. But these are differences that have a common ground.

1 'Lex naturalis est lex moralis sive divina, ex principiis philosophicis cognoscibilis; est propositio, secundum quam, ob voluntatem divinam – quatenus sola ratione cognoscere possumus – actiones nostras dirigere obligamur' (Achenwall, *Prolegomena iuris naturalis*, 2nd ed., Göttingen: Bossiegel, 1763; the English translation: *Prolegomena to Natural Law* (1763), ed. by Pauline Kleingeld, trans. by Corinna Vermeulen, Groningen: University of Groningen Press, 2020).

The *unity of all kinds of obligation* cannot arise from contingent properties of (human) nature or community, but requires a peculiar source. This is also indisputable for Immanuel Kant:

> Everyone must grant that a law, if it is to hold morally, that is, as a ground of an obligation, must carry with it absolute necessity [. . .], that [. . .] the ground of obligation here must not be sought in the nature of the human being or in the circumstances of the world in which he is placed, but a priori simply in concepts of pure reason; and that any other precept [. . .] can indeed be called a practical rule but never a moral law.[2]

2.2 The Concept of Law

The Law (*Jus*), the natural law *sensu stricto* or *simpliciter* (see Achenwall, *Prolegomena* § 99), is essentially distinguished within general morality (i.e. natural law in the broader sense, *late dictum/latius dicta*) by the fact that it refers solely to those actions that (1) can be perceived through the *external* sense ('*sensu externo aliorum percipi possunt*'), that is, also *by other people* and (2) on the other hand, constitute an injury *to other people* (a '*violatio alteri homini*'; see Achenwall §1 and § 112). Kant, of course, is familiar with the relevant discussion since Hugo Grotius' time from Gottlieb Hufeland's *Versuch über den Grundsatz des Naturrechts* of 1785 (which he reviewed immediately after its publication, see Rez Hufeland 8:127 ff.): only 'external' actions of this kind are both (1) *capable* of external (i.e. human) legislation (because only they are epistemically as well as practically *accessible to other* human beings) and (2) also *in special need* of it (because only they also *affect other* human beings). And these two aspects are also directly connected, as we already find in Grotius, who refers to the Christian tradition here. Briefly:

> The very nature of injustice consists in nothing else but in the violation of another's rights; but it does not signify, whether it proceeds from avarice, or lust, or anger, or imprudent pity, or ambition, which are usually the Sources of the greatest injuries.[3]

[2] 'Jedermann muß eingestehen, daß ein Gesetz, wenn es moralisch, d.i. als Grund einer Verbindlichkeit, gelten soll, absolute Nothwendigkeit bei sich führen müsse [. . .], daß mithin der Grund der Verbindlichkeit hier nicht in der Natur des Menschen, oder den Umständen in der Welt, darin er gesetzt ist, gesucht werden müsse, sondern a priori lediglich in Begriffen der reinen Vernunft, und daß jede andere Vorschrift, [. . .], zwar eine praktische Regel, niemals aber ein moralisches Gesetz heißen kann' (GMS 4:389).

[3] 'Iniustitia non aliam natura habeat quam alieni usurpationem; nec referat, ex avaritia illa, an ex libidine, an ex ira, an ex imprudente misericordia proveniat, an ex cupuditate excellendi, unde

And within the framework of this tradition, the law of justice or of right, to emphasize this once again, is in the final instance also *divine* law.

2.3 Obligation in Kant

At the latest since his *Grundlegung zur Metaphysik der Sitten* of 1785, any kind of obligation for Kant is quite explicitly no longer dependent on the *voluntas Dei* endowed with punitive authority.[4] Any obligation is ultimately based solely on the pure legislative will ('reiner Wille', GMS 4:390) of the free being itself: Morality and *autonomy* are inseparable.

> The dependence upon the principle of autonomy of a will that is not absolutely good (moral necessitation) is obligation.[5]
>
> Accordingly the moral law is for them an imperative that commands categorically because the law is unconditional; the relation of such a will to this law is dependence under the name of obligation.[6]

The formula for all varieties of *obligation* is thus the Categorical Imperative – or the one and only moral law, which in Kant has systematically taken the place of the *one divine* law:

> An obligation determined by law is a duty. There are various duties, but only *one* duty at all with regard to all of them. The latter has no plural. [. . .] Obligation is moral necessitation of action, i.e. the dependence of a will that is good in itself on the principle of autonomy or objectively necessary practical laws. Duty is the objective necessity of an action out of obligation.[7]

maximae iniuriae nasci solent' (Hugo Grotius, *De jure belli ac pacis libri tres*, Paris: Nicolaus Buon, 1625, Prolegomena, § 45).

[4] As was still the case in Kant's proof of God's existence in the 'Canon' of the First Critique from 1781 (see A 811). This proof was disposed of and replaced by another one in the Second Critique (KpV 5:124 ff.).

[5] 'Die Abhängigkeit eines nicht schlechterdings guten Willens vom Princip der Autonomie (die moralische Nöthigung) ist [!] Verbindlichkeit' (GMS 4:439).

[6] 'Das moralische Gesetz ist daher bei jenen ein Imperativ, der kategorisch gebietet, weil das Gesetz unbedingt ist; das Verhältniß eines solchen Willens zu diesem [!] Gesetze ist Abhängigkeit, unter dem Namen der Verbindlichkeit' (KpV 5:32).

[7] 'Eine durchs Gesetz bestimmte Verbindlichkeit ist Pflicht. Es giebt verschiedene Pflichten aber nur *eine* Verbindlichkeit überhaupt in Ansehung ihrer aller. Letztere hat keine [P]lurale' (VARL 23:250). See also: 'Verbindlichkeit ist moralische Neceßitation der Handlung, d.i. die Abhängigkeit eines an sich guten Willen vom Princip der Autonomie, oder objectiv nothwendigen praktischen Gesetzen. Pflicht ist die objective Nothwendigkeit der Handlung aus Verbindlichkeit' (V-NR/Feyerabend 27:1326). On 'autonomy' vs 'heteronomy' see *Groundwork*, sect. III.4 and KpV § 8, in contrast with KrV A 633, 811, 813 and 818f.

There are no *obligations*, no *duties* without the moral law (period!). Since Kant also explicitly understands law or right as a relationship of *persons* (RL 6:230), and since *personality* for him is the 'freedom of a rational being under moral laws' (RL 6:223), the highest principle in respect of legal obligation must for him in the final instance be derived from the Categorical Imperative as the origin of *any* obligation, of *all* duties: *alterum non datur*;[8] and this is precisely what Kant succeeds in doing quite directly, as will be shown below.

2.4 The Principle of Right and the Principle of Morality

This derivation draws the formula of the *General Law of Right* directly from the formula of the *Categorical Imperative*, the supreme 'principle of morality'. Here are the two formulas:

> The supreme principle of the doctrine of morals is, therefore, *act on a maxim which can also hold as a universal law.*[9]
>
> Thus the universal law of right, so *act externally that the free use of your choice can coexist with the freedom of everyone in accordance with a universal law.*[10]

The derivation in question is of almost stenographic brevity and presumably therefore increasingly difficult to understand with greater distance from the natural law tradition. This has led to various elaborate strategies of reconstruction, up to the assumption that legal obligation is for Kant – contrary to the natural law tradition as well as contrary to Kant's own explicit statements – not a *special case* of obligation (i.e. *moral* necessitation) through the Categorical Imperative at all, but a *sui generis* complex of 'obligations'. The *Doctrine of Right* would thus – even against Kant's architectural decision to include it in that very book – *not* be part of a *Metaphysics of Morals* at all,[11] which nevertheless explicitly presupposes the doctrine of freedom from the *Critique of Practical Reason*:

[8] As far as I can see, there is not a single instance in Kant's critical writings where he leaves room for any kind of obligation that might be independent from the moral law. All relevant text passages considered, a 'non-moral-obligation' seems to be a kind of *contradictio in adiecto* to Kant.

[9] 'Der oberste Grundsatz der Sittenlehre ist also: *handle nach einer Maxime, die zugleich als allgemeines Gesetz gelten kann*' (RL 6:226, emphasis B.L.).

[10] 'Also ist das allgemeine Rechtsgesetz: *handle äußerlich so, dass der freie Gebrauch Deiner Willkür mit der Freiheit von jedermann nach einem allgemeinen Gesetze zusammenbestehen kann*' (RL 6:231, emphasis B.L.).

[11] This was prominently proclaimed by Marcus Willaschek in 1997 in his paper titled: 'Why the Doctrine of Right Does Not Belong in the Metaphysics of Morals'; see for the further discussion: Willaschek, 'The Non-Derivability of Kantian Right from the Categorical Imperative: A Response

> The *critique of practical reason* was to be followed by a system, the *metaphysics of morals*, which falls into metaphysical first principles of the *doctrine of right* and metaphysical first principles of the *doctrine of virtue* (this is a counterpart of the metaphysical first principles of natural science, already published).[12]

The so-called independence thesis, which breaks up the systematic unity of the *Doctrines of Right* and *of Virtue*, must then consequently give its *own* answer to the question of what the binding nature of juridical laws, the *obligation*, is supposed to be based on (if *not* on the *moral* law), since no explicit answer to *that* question can be found in Kant's texts. An additional hurdle here is that for Kant, obligation, as shown, is already a *moral concept* by definition, and this also refers, as we saw, directly to the theory of autonomy from the *Groundwork* and the second *Critique*.

If one starts with the above-mentioned, traditional definition of *Jus* (*Recht*) as a concept of *external* legislation (RL 6:229f.) and then adds the familiar[13] insight that there are *actions* or ways of acting that 'cannot possibly be done with good intentions' (fornication, adultery, drunkenness, blasphemy, and theft are the traditional standard examples), then one immediately will arrive at Kant's formula in § C:

> Any action is right if it can coexist with everyone's freedom in accordance with a universal law, – or if on *its maxim* the freedom of choice of each can coexist with everyone's freedom in accordance with a universal law.[14]

The part of the quotation after the dash (and starting with an 'or') might be irritating especially for readers who are *too* familiar with Kant's moral

to Nance', *International Journal of Philosophical Studies* 20 (2012), 557–64 and Hirsch, *Freiheit und Staatlichkeit bei Kant: Die autonomietheoretische Begründung von Recht und Staat und das Widerstandsproblem*, Berlin: De Gruyter, 2017 (ch. 3). In the present volume the debate between 'derivationist' (Baiasu, Chapter 4; Messina, Chapter 12) vs 'non-derivationist' interpretations (Willaschek, Chapter 1; Horn, Chapter 3) continues.

[12] 'Auf die *Kritik der praktischen Vernunft* sollte das System, die *Metaphysik der Sitten*, folgen, welches in metaphysische Anfangsgründe der *Rechtslehre* und in eben solche für die *Tugendlehre* zerfällt (als ein Gegenstück der schon gelieferten metaphysischen Anfangsgründe der Naturwissenschaft)' (RL 6:205).

[13] See as the locus classicus: Augustinus, *De sermone domini in monte*, 2, 18(59): 'For when it is written, "By their fruits ye shall know them" [Matthew 7.1] the statement has reference to *things which manifestly cannot be done with a good intention*; such as debaucheries, or blasphemies, or thefts, or drunkenness, and all such things, of which we are permitted to judge, according to the apostle's statement: "For what have I to do to judge them also that are without? do not ye judge them that are within?" (Cor. 1,5)' (Aurelius Augustinus, *De sermone domini in monte libri II*, ed. by Almut Mutzenbecher, Turnhout: Brepols 1967; emphasis mine, B.L.).

[14] 'Eine jede Handlung ist recht, die – oder nach deren [!] Maxime die Freiheit der Willkür eines jeden – mit jedermanns Freiheit nach einem allgemeinen Gesetze zusammen bestehen kann' (RL 6:230, emphasis and hyphens B.L.).

philosophy as it is presented in the *Groundwork* and the *Second Critique*. There seems to be a problem in joining the concept of a *maxim* from his earlier writings to the formula in § C. In these earlier writings, there are no maxims of *actions* at all, but only maxims of the *agents*, these maxims being the *subjective* principles of their actions. And the moral *worth* of these *actions* depends on these subjective *principles* being in conformity with the Categorical Imperative.

But for Kant the individual *subjective* maxim or the intention of the *agent* cannot be recognized by other persons (and at least in some cases not even by the agent himself: GMS 4:407) and is thus, *e suppositione*, inaccessible to any external legislation (see § B, RL 6:230) – and thus *this* maxim cannot be the one that is meant here in § C. Why then does Kant add the phrase with the 'maxim of the *action*' and why does he add it with help of an 'or'? The answer is straightforward: because Kant has to make sense of the expression that an *action* 'can coexist with everyone's freedom in accordance with a universal *law*' in the framework of his own theory of action. How can an *action* be in conformity or in conflict with any *law*, if not by a *maxim*?

If an agent *acts willingly* at all (and does not merely *behave* unconsciously like a brute or even a plant), he acts according to *some* maxim (*propositio maxima*), that is, 'according to the idea of laws, i.e. according to principles' (GMS 4:412). And these principles are either compatible with the Categorical Imperative or they are not: Even the *criminal* is supposed to act on a *maxim* (RL 6:320n.) when he commits a *crime*. In short: Where there is no (subjective) *principle*, there is no (voluntary) *action* at all:

> as a freely acting being, man cannot actually do anything without will – he always [!] acts according to maxims, even if not universally.[15]

Only where there is a *maxim*, can there be a conflict with a *rule* or with a *law*. In the absence of any plausible alternative, the phrase 'maxim of an *action*' in fact *has* to be (and naturally *can* be) read as meaning that an action is right precisely if at least *one* (subjective) maxim can be conceived for this action that would be compatible with the Categorical Imperative (traditionally speaking: 'for which there is some *good intention*').

It is important to note that the *externality* of right (as defined in § A and then spelled out in § B) is the guiding idea here to transform (or to mitigate) Kant's *general moral* commandment (his 'Sittengesetz') into his

[15] 'als freihandelndes Wesen kann der Mensch eigentlich nichts nicht mit Willen thuen – immer [!] handelt er nach Maximen wenn auch nicht universaliter' (V-Met/Dohna 28:678).

(mere) *legal* commandment (his 'Rechtsgesetz'). In this step, Kant follows his point of reference Achenwall (see Section 2.2) seamlessly and without any attempt to distinguish his position from that of Achenwall. The maxim (or intention) according to which the agent actually acts cannot be judged *in Jus*, namely externally, '*sensu externo aliorum*', *e suppositione* – and this is even mirrored in Kant's definition:

> The sum of those laws for which an *external* lawgiving is *possible* is called the Doctrine of Right (*Jus*).[16]

And hence we read in a preliminary note to the *Metaphysics of Morals*:

1. Doctrine of law. The concept of duties that take place independently of all incentives for their observation.
2. The Doctrine of virtue is the epitome of duties that make themselves the incentive of movement.[17]

Kant had already emphasized in the *Groundwork* (GMS 4:397) that in the case of the prudent merchant, for example, his clients cannot know what his maxim or his motive is, that is, whether he is acting only out of self-interest, merely 'pflichtgemäß', or whether he is acting out of duty (and whether his subjective *maxim* therefore has 'moral content', i.e. 'value'). But – and this is the underlying thought, at least implicitly, and not only for Kant – if and *only if* no morally compatible maxim, that is, no maxim compatible with duty, can be conceived for an action in the given context, is it then definitely certain – even for an *external* legislation – that the agent *is not* acting according to such a maxim: simply because there is none. And if there is in fact *no possible maxim* at all compatible with the Categorical Imperative, the *action itself* (more precisely: the type of action as such) is therefore *necessarily* 'pflichtwidrig', morally forbidden: there is a *duty* to refrain.

On the other hand, if, for example, for any alleged act of 'fornication or theft', even *one single* subjective maxim could actually be conceived that is in accordance with the Categorical Imperative (i.e. if, traditionally speaking, 'fornication or theft' were also possible 'with good intention'), then it would not be possible for any (external) *human* legislation to conceive of that particular act of fornication or theft itself as forbidden. For in order to

[16] 'Der Inbegriff der Gesetze, für welche eine *äußere* Gesetzgebung *möglich* ist, heißt die Rechtslehre (*Ius*)' (RL 6:229, emphasis B.L.).

[17] '1. Rechtslehre. Der Inbegrif der Pflichten die unabhängig von allen Bewegursachen zu ihrer Beobachtung statt finden 2. Tugendlehre. Der Inbegriff der Pflichten die sich selbst zur Bewegursache machen' (VATL 27:377).

recognize the unlawfulness of one's action, one would have to know, besides the external action (or behaviour), that the particular subjective maxim of the person acting *is not the one* compatible with the Categorical Imperative. For this, however, one would need a 'Herzenskündiger' ['heart's discerner'] who 'see[s] through the innermost part of everyone's mind' (KU 6:22 ff.) and in the given case actually recognizes the particular underlying *subjective* maxim of the agent and not only its 'appearance' in actions (*ibid.* 72; or RGV 6:99). Only then could we apply to it the standard of virtue (*moralitas*) over and above the standard of legal obligations (*legalitas*). Such an examination, at least according to the canonical view, only happens through God and, moreover, not 'in time':

> Therefore judge nothing before the time, until the Lord come, who both will bring to light the hidden things of darkness, and will make manifest the thoughts of the hearts: and then shall every man have praise of God. (Cor. 1.4.5)

Thus, by definition, law is only concerned with permitted (or prohibited) *actions* (*legalitas*), types of action for which a 'pflichtgemäße' maxim is *possible* (or *not*):

> And on this rests the distinction between consciousness of having acted in conformity with duty and from duty, that is, respect for the law, the first of which (*legality*) is possible even if the inclinations alone have been the determining grounds of the will whereas the second (*morality*), moral worth, must be placed solely in this: that the action takes place from duty, that is, for the sake of the law alone.[18]

The *value* of a particular *action* – more precisely: the 'moral content' of the respective subjective maxim (GMS 4:398) of the agent – is the sole concern of *ethics*, because the subjective maxim of the agent, if there is any, is only accessible to the agent himself:

> If we want to explain them [sc. the actions] according to their morality [!] (which we have in mind in regard to them), we cannot explain them from the nature of the *actions* in relation to the law but only from the attitudes and maxims which *we ourselves* have made the basis of those actions [. . .].[19]

[18] 'Und darauf beruht der Unterschied zwischen dem Bewußtsein, pflichtmäßig und aus Pflicht, d.i. aus Achtung fürs Gesetz, gehandelt zu haben, davon das *erstere* (die *Legalität*) auch möglich ist, wenn Neigungen blos die Bestimmungsgründe des Willens gewesen wären, das *zweite* aber (die *Moralität*), der moralische Werth, lediglich darin gesetzt werden muß, daß die Handlung aus Pflicht, d.i. blos um des Gesetzes willen, geschehe' (KpV 5:81, emphasis B.L.).

[19] 'Wollen wir sie [sc. die Handlungen] nach ihrer Moralität [!] erklären (die wir an ihnen denken) so können wir sie nicht aus der Beschaffenheit der *Handlungen* in Beziehung aufs Gesetz sondern nur

As far as I know, Kant never speaks of *external* actions that are in *accordance with duty* and that would themselves be possible *exclusively from duty*. And one should not even expect this, since in fact there is no 'right'/ 'just' (external) *action* that one could not do for the 'wrong'/'evil' *reasons* (while there are no 'morally good' *pro tanto* reasons for 'unjust' actions). In a given context, for every external action whose maxim *has* moral content one can easily *imagine* maxims that in fact do not have any such content. Think, for instance, of the prudent merchant with the subjective maxim, contrary to duty, of keeping contracts (if and) only if it benefits him. As long as he assumes that no breach of contract goes unpunished in the state, he will keep his contracts no less than the most virtuous merchant who always keeps them 'from duty'. The '*sensus externus aliorum*' will not be able to make out any relevant difference between the particular acts of the two – and will accordingly have to treat them the same in *Ius*. Kant expresses this with all the clarity one could expect:

> Now through experience we can indeed notice unlawful *actions*, and also notice (at least within ourselves) that they are consciously *contrary to law*. But *we cannot observe maxims*, we cannot do so unproblematically even within ourselves; hence the judgment that an agent is an evil *human being* cannot reliably be based on experience.[20]

And it is precisely for this reason that Kant can claim in the *Friedensschrift* (ZeF 8:366) that a republican state would also be possible for ('für', not 'by') a 'people of devils' (if they only had sense, reason, and demanded their preservation). Clever sanctioning institutions could turn even such *Kantian* 'devils' (like the strictly rational and selfish merchant just mentioned) into law-abiding 'good citizens' without having first transformed them into morally 'good people' – and, one can add: even without having to presuppose in them any 'consciousness of obligation for the law', namely *pure* practical reason, at all. This is what Kant pointedly wrote in 1795 for those German princes who wanted to justify their unwillingness to reform by saying that republicanism was suitable only for a nation of gods or angels (as Rousseau implicitly admitted).

Even more fundamentally (as we learn from the last quote), the *positive* value of an individual action (that it really 'happened solely out of duty'),

aus den Gesinnungen und Maximen erklären die den Handlungen *von uns selbst* zum Grunde gelegt werden [. . .]' (VARL 23:142).

20 'Nun kann man zwar gesetzwidrige *Handlungen* durch Erfahrung bemerken, auch (wenigstens an sich selbst) daß sie mit Bewußtsein *gesetzwidrig* sind; aber die *Maximen kann man nicht beobachten*, sogar nicht allemal in sich selbst, mithin das Urtheil, daß der Thäter ein böser *Mensch* sei, nicht mit Sicherheit auf Erfahrung gründen' (RGV 6:20, emphasis B.L.).

namely the moral content of its subjective maxim, not only remains hidden from legal-political authorities and fellow citizens, but, as Kant emphasizes here again, in the end it is not even reliably revealed to the agent himself (see RGV 6:20, TL 6:393, 441, 447). Therefore, *a fortiori*, all attempts to access the subjective maxims of the agent in the assessment of *legalitas* are at best a stopgap:

> All principles of law should not be such that they appear to be derived from ethical sources. The *provocatio ad forum conscientiae* or to an oath *coram foro externo* is to be regarded as something that is an emergency aid, and which does not belong to it at all.[21]

2.5 Persons and Things

But why then do we still need the status of a *person*, namely an *awareness* of the binding nature of moral laws in the *Doctrine of Right*, at all? The answer is evident if we take a broader point of view and recognize that the *Doctrine of Right* not only deals with the *right to coerce* but at the same time with *limits of legitimate coercion* vis-à-vis *persons*, vis-à-vis beings who can have duties and thus rights in the first place (see RL 6:239 note). § E of the *Doctrine of Right* leaves no question open here:

> Only a completely external right can therefore be called strict right (in the narrow sense). This is indeed [1] based on everyone's consciousness of obligation in accordance with a law;[22] but if it is to remain pure, [2] this consciousness need[23] not and cannot be appealed to as an incentive to determine his choice in accordance with this law.[24] Strict right rests instead [*tertium non datur*; B.L.] on the principle of its being possible to use

[21] 'Alle principia des Rechts müßen nicht [read: 'sollen nicht'] so beschaffen seyn, daß sie aus ethischen Quellen abgeleitet zu seyn scheinen. Die *provocatio ad forum conscientiae* oder zum Eide *coram foro externo* ist anzusehen als etwas was eine Nothhülfe ist, und was demselben gar nicht competirt' (V-Mo/Powalski 27:162).

[22] Because legal subjects are persons but not mere things without duties and rights, see § B and RL 6:239: 'Wir kennen unsere eigene Freiheit (von der alle moralische Gesetze, mithin auch alle Rechte sowohl als Pflichten ausgehen) nur durch den *moralischen Imperativ*, welcher ein pflichtgebietender Satz ist, aus welchem nachher das Vermögen, andere zu verpflichten, d.i. der Begriff des Rechts, entwickelt werden kann' ('The reason is that we know our own freedom (from which all moral laws, and so all rights as well as duties proceed) only through the *moral imperative*, which is a proposition commanding duty, from which the capacity for putting others under obligation, that is, the concept of a right, can afterwards be explicated').

[23] Up to Kant's time 'darf . . . nicht' primarily had the same meaning as 'bedarf . . . nicht', 'braucht . . . nicht' or 'muss . . . nicht' has in modern German. Thus 'need not' is the proper English translation here. With 'may not' Mary Gregor gives an incorrect one.

[24] Because *Jus* by definition is about mere *external* legislation, which the maxims of the agents epistemically and practically elude.

> external constraint that can coexist with the freedom of everyone in accordance with universal laws.[25]

It is of course beyond question for Kant's contemporaries and needs no further emphasis that one is *allowed* to treat any being (rational or not) *at will* as long as it does *not* have the status of a *person*, in Kant's terms, as long as it lacks any awareness of obligation by the Categorical Imperative. In the Kantian sense these beings are mere things ('Sachen', RL 6:223) without duties and thus without rights. To treat such a 'thing' nonetheless like a person is not unjust at all.[26] Hence the *legal* status of 'personhood' is mainly the *privilege* of being 'right-bearers'. And often we can grant such a privilege even to beings who do not deserve it (or at least: to those of whom we do not know[27] whether they deserve it or not). This might be *imprudent* in a given case (to open the tiger's cage), but it is no *injustice to* these beings. In sum, no *rational* being can complain if it is coerced by others to act according to the Kantian *imperative of right*:

> [A]ct externally that the *free use of your choice* can coexist with the freedom of everyone in accordance with a universal law.[28]

This means: act in such a way that your subjective maxim *could* be one that would pass the test of the Categorical Imperative, even if the action in fact proceeds from fear of punishment (or even 'from Avarice, or Lust, or Anger, or imprudent Pity, or Ambition, which are usually the Sources of the greatest Injuries', see the quote from Grotius above). *Persons* as autonomous beings have no right to act against *the Principle of Right* in particular and thus have no moral reason to complain if they are coerced suitably – and *non*-persons have no rights at all and therefore no 'moral' reason to grumble if they are coerced.[29]

[25] 'Ein strictes (enges) Recht kann man also nur das völlig äußere nennen. [1] Dieses gründet sich nun zwar auf dem Bewußtsein der Verbindlichkeit eines jeden nach dem Gesetze, aber [2] die Willkür darnach zu bestimmen, darf und kann es, wenn es rein sein soll, sich auf dieses Bewußtsein als Triebfeder nicht berufen, sondern fußt sich deshalb [*tertium non datur*; B.L.] auf dem Princip der Möglichkeit eines äußeren Zwanges, der mit der Freiheit von jedermann nach allgemeinen Gesetzen zusammen bestehen kann' (RL 6:232).

[26] See Hirsch's chapter in this volume (Chapter 5).

[27] In fact, nobody can know whether other humans are in fact conscious of the moral law or not. But often we have strong reasons to assume that they are (e.g. if they give and keep promises). In any case: I cannot demand any greater evidence for the personality of other humans than these can have for mine: Hence treating other human beings as persons is the *default position* for those human beings who themselves demand to be treated as persons.

[28] 'Handle äußerlich so, dass der freie *Gebrauch Deiner Willkür* mit der Freiheit von jedermann nach einem allgemeinen Gesetze zusammenbestehen kann!' (RL 6:231, emphasis B.L.).

[29] For Kant persons have duties *concerning* animals, but these are not 'grounded' in a personality of the animal but are duties vis-à-vis oneself (TL 6:443).

2.6 Right and Morals

If we reconstruct[30] Kant's path from his 'Principle of Morality' to the 'General Principle of Right' in RL §§ A–E as proposed above it is short and completely transparent in substance – at least if we read it against the background of both the natural law tradition and Kant's own doctrine of obligation. However, it is not necessarily easy for us later readers to follow. When we turn to the *Doctrine of Right*, after all, we usually have fewer preconceptions based on the teachings of the natural law tradition than on Kant's writings in moral philosophy (such as the *Groundwork* and the *Second Critique*) with their dominant interest in the *value* of the actions and maxims. It can therefore easily appear to us as a shortcoming of Kant's presentation that he (as it were entirely without preparation) speaks of an 'action' and '*its* maxim', that is, of a 'maxim of action' *sensu stricto* (and not – as in the aforementioned writings – in the sense of a particular 'maxim of the *agent*' as an expression of his 'Gesinnung').

But then we overlook that two things seem to be self-evident *for Kant* – and should also be so for his readers: (1) Every action *sensu stricto* is performed under some maxim, for only in this way is it an expression of a *will* (or *choice*) which, as *liberum arbitrium*, determines itself not only according to *stimuli* (as the *arbitrium brutum*) but always also according to *principles* (A 802; GMS 4:412.26f.), be these conformable to morality or not. And (2): in *Jus*, the actual maxim of the agent (his or her *subjective* principle of action) must, by default, remain unknown and thus *cannot* play any role at all (thus it *must* not). Hence, the only thing that matters for the doctrine of right is (3) that an external behaviour in question (a) *can be conceived* as an action according to some maxim at all (and not merely as unreflective, as it were 'brute', *behaviour*). And if so, that this maxim *can then also be thought of* (b) as one which and under which the action 'can coexist with everyone's freedom according to a general law'. Then and only then is the external *behaviour* to be regarded as an external *action* (per 'a') and as *morally permitted* (per 'b'), that is, as *e definitione* right. Thus others have a *duty* to refrain. All other behaviour may – this now almost goes without saying – be prevented by others with coercion anyway. They have no duty to refrain, since a person's freedom is always already 'restricted in

[30] Of course, this is merely a reconstruction since we have no explicit statement by Kant about the difference between the 'maxim of the agent' and the 'maxim of an action'. But, at least, this reconstruction is in conformity with Kant's statements concerning his theory of action and obligation – and with his claim, that his *Metaphysische Anfangsgründe der Rechtslehre* are an integral part of his *Metaphysik der Sitten.*

the idea of it [*sc.* to lawful action]' (§ C, RL 6:231). The obstruction of an obstacle to freedom, whatever else it may be, is at least not a restriction *of freedom* (§ D, RL 6:231) – and thus, for its part, cannot constitute a moral and thus, *a fortiori*, legal breach of *duty*:

> If another does violence to me, we are acting rightly if we force him. But if he does not do us wrong, it is wrong if we force him. [...] If someone violates my rights, does not fulfil his obligation [or] does not compensate me for damage done, I can force him by force.[31]

By bringing into play his *new* concept of (moral) obligation, which he had precisely spelled out since the 1770s in terms of the Categorical Imperative – that is, by speaking *not* of the appropriate *intention* (*intentio recta, animus bonus*, etc.) of the *agents* but, more precisely, of their *maxims* and thus also about the *possible maxims* for the respective *actions* – Kant sharpens the distinction between *Jus naturae* and *Theologia moralis* already pointed out by Pufendorf in the Introduction of his *De officio hominis et civis* (1673).

We can also recognize that Kant already had precisely this separation of *Jus* and *Ethica* in mind for a long time, even if he first specified it definitively in his *Introduction* to the *Doctrine of Right* in 1797 with his *new* concept of 'legislation' ('Gesetzgebung', RL 6:218). He was able to be so brief in demarcating *Ius* from *Ethica* at that time because he could assume that everything that might be unfamiliar to his contemporary readers, namely his decisive *philosophical* innovations, had already been sufficiently dealt with in the *Second Critique* and in the Introduction to the *Metaphysics of Morals*, which explicitly (RL 6:222) precedes *both* parts, the *Doctrine of Right* and the *Doctrine of Virtue*. This was his new theory of the *entia moralia*, namely of personhood as autonomy, and thus of all laws of morality as categorical imperatives for maxims (RL 6:213f., 221ff.). And what was then still missing he summarized in the final definition of strict law (§ E), which I have already quoted (see Section 2.5).

2.7 Coercion in Natural Law

This also brought to an end the debate about the appropriate definition of *Ius*, which was widely documented in Hufeland's book from 1785. For

[31] 'Wenn ein andrer mir Gewalt thut, so handeln wir recht, wenn wir ihn zwingen, thut er uns aber nicht unrecht, so ists unrecht, wenn wir ihn zwingen. [...] Wenn jemand meinen Rechten Abbruch thut, seine Obligatio nicht erfüllt, mir einen zugefügten Schaden nicht erstattet, kann ich ihn mit Gewalt zwingen' (V-NR/Feyerabend 27:1342).

Kant the power of coercion is indeed *analytically* contained in the concept of Ius (thus RL 6:231 TL 6:396), but coercion need not therefore be a component of the *definition* of the concept of *Ius*/Right. The legal possibility of coercion is rather an immediate *consequence* of the externality of *Ius* – if we add the important insight that every *external* legislation for rational beings with sensibility requires some *motive force* in addition to the binding law in order to be able actually to determine actions (RL 6:222). Only in this way does a *law* become a component of a *legislation* ('Gesetzgebung'). In the (merely external) *Ius*, only the threat of coercion in conformity with the law can serve as a motive force, since *respect* ('Achtung') for the law, which can fulfil this task in the (internal) *Ethics*, is reserved for the latter alone – and *tertium non datur*.

It was precisely the obvious requirement of a *motive* for bringing about humans' compliance with the laws in *Jus* and *Ethics* that had led Wolff and the Wolffians to the wilfully exaggerated doctrine that obligation itself consisted *essentially* in a nexus of action and motivation, *actio* and *motivum*.[32] This doctrine was still followed by the young Gottfried Achenwall when, freshly appointed from Marburg to Göttingen, he published his first textbook on *Natural Law* in 1750 together with J. S. Pütter.[33] In Göttingen, Achenwall was the successor of Samuel Treuer, who had already led a sharp polemic against Wolff's doctrine of obligation in the 1730s and defended Pufendorf's classical *theistic* doctrine against Wolff's (and Leibniz's) objections. In the year of Wolff's death, Achenwall published a rehabilitation of Pufendorf's theory of obligation fuelled by the writings of his predecessor.[34] When he wrote the third edition of his textbook (and the *Prolegomena*) one year later he was no longer the Wolffian in the theory of obligation he had started out as in Halle and Marburg, but had turned into a Pufendorfian (see his *Prolegomena* § 50,

[32] See for example C. Wolff, *Vernünftige Gedancken von der Menschen Thun und Lassen &c.*, 4th ed., Frankfurt am Main and Leipzig: Johann Benjamin Andreä & Heinrich Hort, 1733, § 8. For the following see: Bernd Ludwig, 'Von der coactio hypothetica zum kategorischen Imperativ: Was Kants Autonomie-Lehre Achenwalls Naturrecht von 1755 verdankt', in *Rechtphilosophie – Zeitschrift für Grundlagen des Rechts* 6 (2020), 352–67, and Bernd Ludwig, *Aufklärung über die Sittlichkeit: Zu Kants Grundlegung einer Metaphysik der Sitten*, Frankfurt am Main: Klostermann, 2020, ch. 4.

[33] Gottfried Achenwall and Johann S. Pütter, *Anfangsgründe des Naturrechts (Elementa Iuris Naturae)* (1750), ed. and trans. by Jan Schröder, Frankfurt am Main: Insel, 1995, here §§ 82ff. It is remarkable that in this book on Natural Law there is no reference to God at all (see especially the definition of the 'obligatio naturalis' in §§ 96–103 in contrast to Achenwall's later *Prolegomena* §§ 49–97).

[34] Gottfried Achenwall, *Observationes iuris naturalis, Specimen II [secundum], De obligatione et imputatione*, Göttingen: Bossiegel, 1754.

quoted in Section 2.1) – and this is exactly how Kant then came to know him as the author of his textbook. Here legal *obligation* does not coincide with the effectiveness of the motive (provided, for example, by the threat of punishment), but stems from the *authority* of the *will* that links such a motive to the action. This is either the will of God as lawgiver, or of a human lawgiver authorized by divine natural law. Obligation is thus essentially a relationship of *will* and does *not depend* on the motive *alone* as in Wolff and in the early Achenwall but mainly on the authority of the law itself.

But even the later Achenwall still took for granted, that obligation presupposes that God's lawgiving will makes the rules of reason obligatory *by adding a motive* (e.g. like the threat of punishment) to it:

> the natural laws are armed with divine rewards and punishments, [. . .] because without a proposed good or bad consequence there is no obligation at all, nor, as a consequence, does there exist any law.[35]

In his lecture on natural law from 1784 Kant rebutted sharply even this 'Achenwallian blend' of Wolffianism and Pufendorfianism for the first time:

> Our author [Achenwall] and others speak of *obligatio per poenas*, as does Baumgarten. But to connect one by *poenas* and *praemia* is *contradictio in adjecto*; for there I move him to acts which he does not out of obligation but out of fear and inclination.[36]

2.8 Kant's New Concept of 'Lawgiving' (*Gesetzgebung*)

It took more than ten years until Kant could wrap this fundamental insight from 1784 into his new definition of a 'Gesetzgebung' (lawgiving), which puts together the 'Gesetz' (i.e. the source of *obligation* on one side) and the 'Triebfeder' (i.e. the source of *motives* on the other) into *one* new concept:

> In all lawgiving [. . .] there are two elements: first, a law, which represents an action that is to be done as objectively necessary, that is, which makes the action a duty; and second, an incentive, which connects a ground for

35 Prolegomena § 55: 'leges naturales praemiis atque poenis divini armatae [sunt] [. . .] quum sine bono vel malo consectario proposito nulla omnino detur obligatio, nec consequenter ulla lex existat'. This was even Kant's position in 1781 (see note 4)!

36 'Unser Autor [sc. Achenwall] und andre reden von der *obligatio per poenas*, so auch Baumgarten. Aber durch *Poenas* und *Praemia* einen verbinden ist *contradictio in adjecto*; denn da bewege ich ihn zu Handlungen, die er nicht aus Verbindlichkeit sondern aus Furcht und Neigung thut' (V-NR/ Feyerabend 27:1326).

> determining choice to this action subjectively with the representation of the law.[37]

We *know* that we are *obliged* from the moral law *alone* whose binding force is a fact of reason (and the only '*ratio cognoscendi*' of our freedom and personality, KpV 5:4, RL 6:239). And our *motives* to *act* in accordance with that moral law are twofold: the very idea of being obliged by one's *own* reason itself (in *ethical* lawgiving by *respect* for the law) or something different (in *juridical* lawgiving by '*praemia et poenas*'). In the case of external actions, the latter may be even the threat of legal punishment by other *human* beings.

The *unity* of *Jus* and *Ethica* is guaranteed by the unity of the source of *obligation* alone: the one and only *moral law*. Their (only) *difference* lies in the source of *motives* for our *acting* in accordance with that law. These motives are thus *not* the *grounds* (or sources) of our *obligation* (*pace* Wolff) nor even necessary *parts* of it (pace Achenwall, Baumgarten – and the *Canon* of Kant's *First Critique*). Since his *Groundwork* (1785) Kant thinks the other way round: motives are only *morally* possible, as long as they are in conformity with our *duties* from the moral law.

Therefore Kant's terms '*juridical* duty' and '*ethical* duty' *both* refer to *moral* duties.[38] The former refers to those kinds of moral duties that *can* be part of *juridical lawgiving* (see § A), the latter to those that *cannot* (RL 6:219). And since we can fulfil *any* duty *from* duty alone (since we are *autonomous*), all *juridical* duties are *indirect-ethical* duties when considered as part of ethical lawgiving (RL 6:221). 'Pacta sunt servanda!' is a *juridical* duty, but it does not cease to *oblige* us if the threat of enforcement or punishment is actually missing (RL 6:219).

Indeed, we find the core of the classical natural law doctrine in Kant's Introduction to the *Metaphysics of Morals* – but, of course, without the heteronomistic reference to the Will of God, and without any reference to *motives*:

> We can think of an external lawgiving that contains only positive laws; but then a *natural law* would still have to precede it, which would

[37] 'Zu aller Gesetzgebung [. . .] gehören zwei Stücke: erstlich ein Gesetz, welches die Handlung, die geschehen soll, objectiv als nothwendig vorstellt, d.i. welches die Handlung zur Pflicht macht, zweitens eine Triebfeder, welche den Bestimmungsgrund der Willkür zu dieser Handlung subjectiv mit der Vorstellung des Gesetzes verknüpft' (RL 6:218).

[38] For Kant the term 'moral duties' is, of course, a pleonasm: 'Duty' is the 'matter of obligation' (RL 6:222), and obligation is the necessity of an action under the Categorical Imperative, which is the principle of *morals* (see Section 2.4).

establish the authority of the lawgiver (i.e., his *authorization* to bind others by his mere choice).[39]

Accordingly, a central task of the main text of the *Doctrine of Right* will be to demonstrate our obligation (as *persons*) to submit to an external legislation that represents the idea of a general legislative will of the people (Rousseau's *volonté générale*): Thus we will impose new juridical duties on ourselves *as persons*. The first step of that demonstration essentially takes place in §§ 1–9 of Private Right, where Kant shows that any juridical reference of persons to external objects ('Äußeres Mein und Dein'), in particular to the finite land supply of the earth, the 'globus terraquaeus' (RL 6:352), can only coexist with the freedom (see § C, RL 6:230) of those persons through an omnilateral contract, namely through establishing a *common will* of all those concerned as an *artificial*[40] source of their obligations (§§ 8f., RL 6:255ff.). Hence the *moral* imperative to establish public right, according to Kant its *categorical* imperative, is: *exeundum est e statu naturali* (RL 6:307). And since this (*moral*) duty 'allows for an incentive other than the idea of duty' it is a *juridical duty* – and thus, of course, an *indirect-ethical* duty too (RL 6:219).

2.9 Epilogue

Returning to the core idea of our reconstruction of the argument in §§ A–E of the Doctrine of Right, I would like to point out that (to paraphrase a formulation of the *Groundwork*, GMS 4:454) 'the practical use of common legal reasoning confirms the correctness of Kant's deduction of the general principle of Right'. Those who convince the court, for example, that their conduct can be interpreted as an expression of acting according to a permissible maxim are usually acquitted – albeit often grudgingly: think, for example, of major economic offences, when it is said, *mutatis mutandis*, 'An intention to defraud could not be *proved*'.

Some external conduct, on the other hand, can *only* be declared an *attributable act* by assuming such an 'intention to defraud' – and as such would then definitely be unjust. Of course, it is always a question of the

[39] 'Es kann also eine äußere Gesetzgebung gedacht werden, die lauter positive Gesetze enthielte; alsdann aber müßte doch ein *natürliches Gesetz* vorausgehen, welches die Autorität des Gesetzgebers (d.i. die *Befugniß*, durch seine bloße Willkür andere zu verbinden) begründete' (RL 6:224, emphasis B.L.).

[40] This raises the familiar political challenge for any natural law theory of the state: the possibility of conflict between positive laws of the state (*lex humana*) and the natural law that establishes the legislative authority of the state in the first place.

extent to which the external conduct (including the previous history and the expected course of action) can and must be taken into account in this consideration. But let us take as an example someone who in a department store carefully stows a tiny umbrella in his bag and immediately rushes out into the sun-drenched pedestrian zone without paying and disappears into the crowd. He will not be able to explain convincingly to the store detective who has rushed over (and later to a judge) that he only wanted to try out the umbrella once in order to bring about the decision to buy it.[41] But if he somehow managed to explain his behaviour convincingly as being compatible with another 'legal' maxim formerly undisclosed, for the court his *behaviour* would count only as the misleading expression of an essentially lawful *action*, according to whose maxim his freedom may well coexist with that of others (perhaps a 'mere *fault*', not a serious crime; RL 6:224). And because not only the judge, but also any possible lawyer, is not a 'heart's discerner' and therefore can at best *assume* the maxim, it is in principle morally possible for the lawyer to plead before the judge for the acceptance of *that* possible maxim, according to which the conduct of his client does deserve the least drastic punishment or no punishment at all: *In dubio pro reo.*

41 The same applies for example in the case of someone who slits someone's throat before taking his wallet. He will not be able to defend the slitting convincingly by saying that he is doing the same thing a surgeon does before removing a thyroid tumour: obviously, the set of possible maxims for a particular action is strongly situational. For this well-known 'accordion-effect' see e.g.: Joel Feinberg, 'Action and Responsibility', in M. Black (ed.), *Philosophy in America*, London: Cornell University Press, 1965, 134–60, at 146.

CHAPTER 3

Kant on the General Will Test and the Categorical Imperative Procedure

Christoph Horn

According to Kant, it is possible to differentiate between legitimate and illegitimate laws by means of a certain formal procedure. His criterion for the legitimacy of a draft law is whether or not it corresponds to the 'General Will' of a people. The test question Kant has in mind is this: could a people give its consent to a proposed particular law? Let us call this the 'General Will Test' (GWT). The GWT is presented by Kant on several occasions in slightly different formulations (e.g. in RGV 6:98; RL 6:263, 6:314 and TP 8:304). It is sometimes even described as a formal procedure which can be used like a thought-experiment which should be enacted by the legislator who is, for Kant, in principle the people itself, but in fact it is the monarch.[1] Maybe the most prominent passage appears in his treatise *What Is Enlightenment?* (8:39; trans. H. B. Nisbet):

> The touchstone of whatever can be decided upon as law for a people lies in the question: whether a people could impose such a law upon itself.

As the word 'touchstone' (*Prüfstein*) begins to bring into view he is thinking of a formal procedure. In this chapter, I want to explore the question of whether and, if so, to what extent, this test outlined by Kant resembles the universalization procedure of the Categorical Imperative, the CI procedure (henceforth CIP), understood according to the 'Formula of Universal Law' and the 'Formula of a Law of Nature'. I will arrive at the conclusion that the two test processes, the GWT and the CIP, are indeed somewhat similar. They actually have certain properties in common. And these commonalities amount to more than a mere 'family resemblance' in the Wittgensteinian sense. It will turn out that the GWT and the CIT are interrelated in a quite characteristic manner, namely according to a relation

[1] This is clear from *Theory and Practice* 8:305 and especially from the *Conflict of the Faculties* 7:91. In *Idee* 8:23 Kant explains that men need a master who has to impose the General Will on them. Kant sees the 'greatest problem' in the morality or immorality of this master.

of ideal and non-ideal normativity. The GWT is a specifically attenuated form of the CIP.

By highlighting this, I hope to strengthen my interpretation, developed in my book on Kant's non-ideal normativity.[2] My fundamental idea in this book was, and still is, that the type of normativity presented by Kant in the *Doctrine of Right* and elsewhere in his political and legal writings can be satisfactorily characterized neither by following (what I call) a 'derivation reading', which attributes to Kant the claim that legitimate juridical and political rules must be immediately derived from the moral law, nor by what could be referred to as a 'separation reading', which argues that legitimate political and legal rules are, on Kant's view, *sui generis*, that is, they form an independent kind of normativity. Instead, I claim that normatively valid laws are justified, in Kant's view, by the fact that their content is established in a significantly non-ideal way, by a quasi-CI, namely the GWT. Thus, I maintain an intermediary position between the two well-known camps of the derivation reading and the separation reading.

There has been a large debate among scholars on the question of if and in what sense the CI is present in Kant's description of legitimate juridico-political normativity. The elementary but, as I believe, forceful point I wish to make in this article rests upon the observation of a deep ambiguity: on the one hand, Kant says that, ideally, legitimate right (*Recht*) should be based upon a formal test procedure, while, on the other hand, his concrete procedure – namely the GWT – is considerably weaker than the universalization test of the Categorical Imperative, the CIP, as we know it both from the *Groundwork* and from the second *Critique*.

In what follows, I will first outline some of the main characteristics of Kant's notion of a General Will and then turn to the profound differences that exist between the GWT and the CIP. Starting from § 46 of the *Doctrine of Right*, my main point of reference will be the Universal Principle of Right in § C (Section 3.1). My reading finds confirmation through a close examination of key passages from *Religion within the Boundaries of Mere Reason* and *Conflict of the Faculties* (Section 3.2). Following this, I will develop my interpretation with reference to selections from the second appendix of *Towards Perpetual Peace* in which Kant characterizes his GWT more precisely than anywhere else (Section 3.3). In a final remark, I will add some considerations on a problematic consequence to Kant's idea of right: namely the fact that GWT only ensures that the external liberties of citizens

[2] Christoph Horn, *Nichtideale Normativität: Ein neuer Blick auf Kants Philosophie*, Berlin: Suhrkamp, 2014.

must be ordered by some rules does not guarantee specific contents as, for example, human rights do (Section 3.4).

3.1 Affinities and Differences between the GWT and the CIP

Kant repeatedly uses the test operation which I called the GWT based on his account of the Rousseauian notion of a General Will (*volonté générale*). Both philosophers see the General Will or popular sovereignty as the foundation of legitimate lawgiving. In contrast to Rousseau's use of the term, however, Kant understands his notion of an *allgemeiner Wille* in the sense of an a priori unified multilateral will.[3] The apriority plays a crucial role in Kant's version of contractarianism, which relies neither on a Hobbesian prudential thought-experiment nor on a Lockean historical scenario. Instead, Kant interprets the General Will as a 'command of practical reason'. The General Will is thus designed to resolve the exeundum issue of establishing a state, that is, the problem of how there can be a legitimate transition from a first acquisition of property, in the context of private right, to a mutually accepted possession, that is, to public right.[4] For Kant, the General Will is what constitutes and legitimizes public right.

The following passage contains some further crucial aspects of his view (RL § 46, 6:313–14; trans. M. J. Gregor):

> The legislative authority can belong only to the united will of the people. For since all right is to proceed from it, it *cannot* do any wrong by its law. Now when someone makes arrangements about another, it is always possible for him to do the other wrong; but he can never do wrong in what he decides upon with regard to himself (for *volenti non fit iniuria*). Therefore, only the concurring and united will of all, insofar as each decides the same thing for all and all for each, and so only the general united will of the people, can be legislative.

[3] But already for Rousseau, the General Will can never be mistaken; see Patrick Riley, 'Rousseau's General Will', in Patrick Riley (ed.), *The Cambridge Companion to Rousseau*, Cambridge: Cambridge University Press, 2001, 124–53. On Rousseau's influence on Kant regarding the General Will and the differences between their usage of it see Patrick Riley, 'Kant on the General Will', in James Farr and David L. Williams (eds.), *The General Will: The Evolution of a Concept*, New York: Cambridge University Press, 2015, 333–49, and Christoph Horn, 'Rousseau und Kant über Gemeinwille und Gesellschaftsvertrag', in Paul Geyer, Volker Ladenthin, and Anke Redecker (eds.), *Rousseau über Rousseau: Beiträge zum 300. Geburtstag*, Würzburg: Ergon, 2016, 31–46.

[4] See RL 6:256 (trans. M. Gregor; slightly amended): 'A unilateral will cannot serve as a coercive law for everyone with regard to possession that is external and therefore contingent, since that would infringe upon freedom in accordance with general laws. So it is only a will putting everyone under obligation, hence only a collective, general (common) and powerful will, that can provide everyone this assurance.'

According to Kant, all legitimate right must proceed from the United or General Will of the people. So far, this is the Rousseauian principle of popular sovereignty. Each and every citizen must be involved in the process of lawgiving in which the same rules are established for all of them. Justified law must not do wrong to anybody; and the General Will guarantees this since it includes everyone's confirmation. Kant further adds to this the Hobbesian principle that someone is not damaged as long as he has given his consent (*volenti non fit iniuria*).

Now, how close is this to the Categorical Imperative? Note that the General Will as it is described here is that of a concrete people, that is, of a spatiotemporally limited group – and not the omnitemporal united will of humanity at large. This does not contradict the fact that it is described as a priori: the General Will rests on the purely formal (i.e. a priori) idea of the united volitions of a concrete people. Furthermore, it rests upon collective voluntarism and thus points in the direction of a Hobbesian notion of authority conception of law: it takes a concrete authority to establish a law. I understand this aspect likewise in the sense of a historically situated community which chooses laws according to their concretely given situation while the same law could be rejected by another people, living under different conditions. This implies, additionally, that the GWT is a formal procedure by which one can establish highly diverging legal constitutions. Kant explicitly claims, in the Introduction to the *Metaphysics of Morals* (MS 6:224), that a legal order could completely consist of positive laws which go back to the arbitrary choice of the legislator. The lawgiver has an 'authority to obligate others by mere arbitrary choice' (*Befugniß, durch seine bloße Willkür andere zu verbinden*), provided that a preceding natural law authorizes him (MS 6:224, trans. M. J. Gregor):

> So it is possible to think of an external legislation, which would contain only positive laws; but then a natural law would have to precede, which would establish the authority of the legislator (i.e. the power to bind others by his mere arbitrariness).

On my reading, the natural law, which has to precede acts of external legislation in order to fully authorize a lawgiver's arbitrary external legislation, is the innate right to freedom (RL 6:237–8). In accordance with the innate right understood as an a priori rule for appropriate lawgiving, the monarch is obliged to respect the principles of full individual freedom, equality, and self-determination (being *sui juris*) for all citizens.

With the idea that a certain people voluntarily imposes a law onto itself Kant *a limine* excludes the possibility of a self-violation. As I pointed out, he quotes the *volenti* formula and thereby, under the condition of the innate right, subscribes to the Hobbesian principle *auctoritas, non veritas, facit legem.*[5] This does not of course mean that he is a legal positivist. On the contrary, Kant remains strongly committed to the classical idea of natural law, which he takes in the sense of an a priori law and identifies with the innate right to freedom. Seen in this way, the procedural and formal character of the GWT, as described by Kant, does not merely result from the principle of non-contradiction applied within a generalization procedure. Rather, the idea is that each citizen must be seen, simultaneously, as the lawgiving author and the obligated subject of a piece of legislation, which might take this or that concrete form – as long as it conforms to the principles of freedom and equality.

When we look at these details, one can see how closely the GWT is connected to Kant's 'Universal Principle of Right' (UPR) in B of the *Doctrine of Right* (RL 6:230; trans. M. J. Gregor):

> Right is therefore the sum of the conditions under which the choice of one can be united with the choice of another in accordance with a universal law of freedom.[6]

In section C, the UPR is taken up as follows (RL 6:230; trans. M. J. Gregor):

> Any action is *right* if it can coexist with everyone's freedom in accordance with a universal law, or if on its maxim the freedom of choice of each can coexist with everyone's freedom in accordance with a universal law.

As both the GWT and the UPR express, right must restrict and enable each citizen to make use of his freedom of choice according to a formal principle that unites all individual ranges of freedom. This thought closely resembles the universalization test of the CIP. Legitimate right, for Kant, has to pass an examination: namely that it must be capable of coordinating everybody's free choice with that of everyone else, according to a general rule. Almost the same holds true for the CIP: it is a formal procedure to select those maxims as morally possible which can be adopted simultaneously by all rational agents.

There is a formulation used by Kant some lines below the UPR, where he provides an articulation of the maxim in a second-person imperative

[5] For Kant's reception of Hobbes see Karlfriedrich Herb and Bernd Ludwig 'Kants kritisches Staatsrecht', *Jahrbuch für Recht und Ethik/Annual Review of Law and Ethics* 2 (1994), 431–78.

[6] RL 6:230: 'Das Recht ist also der Inbegriff der Bedingungen, unter denen die Willkür des einen mit der Willkür des andern nach einem allgemeinen Gesetz der Freiheit zusammen vereinigt werden kann.'

mood. He calls it the 'Universal Law of Right' (ULR) (RL 6:231, trans. M. J. Gregor):

> Thus the universal law of Right, so act externally that the free use of your choice can coexist with the freedom of everyone in accordance with a universal law [. . .].[7]

This imperative formulation of the UPR, namely ULR, is clearly close to the CIP. Let us compare the UPR with the Universal Law Formula of the CIP (GMS 4:421; trans. M. J. Gregor/J. Timmermann):

> Act only according to that maxim through which you can at the same time will that it become a universal law.

The version put forward in the second *Critique* is as follows (KprR, 5:30; trans. M. J. Gregor):

> So act that the maxim of your will could always hold at the same time as a principle in a giving of universal law.[8]

An initial difference is immediately visible. The term 'maxim' (or 'maxim of your will') in the CIP is replaced by 'arbitrary choice' (*Willkür*) in the ULR. The notion of a maxim (and the 'maxim of your will') refers to the inner freedom of autonomy connected by Kant with the term *Wille*, whereas the concept of arbitrary choice (*Willkür*) is restricted to external freedom. The limitation to external freedom is explicitly discussed in the passage RL 6:231. This can be seen as the second difference: Kant explicitly tells us that the ULR does not commit the agent to an inner motivation. It is, according to Kant, completely sufficient to abide by the law in one's external actions.[9]

A third point is closely related to this. Kant characterizes the ULR in §C of the *Doctrine of Right* as:

> indeed a law, which lays an obligation on me, but it does not at all expect, far less demand, that I myself should limit my freedom to those conditions just for the sake of this obligation; instead, reason says only that freedom is

[7] RL 6:231: 'Also ist das allgemeine Rechtsgesetz: handle äußerlich so, daß der freie Gebrauch deiner Willkür mit der Freiheit von jedermann nach einem allgemeinen Gesetze zusammen bestehen könne [. . .].'

[8] KpV 5:30: 'Handle so, daß die Maxime deines Willens jederzeit zugleich als Princip einer allgemeinen Gesetzgebung gelten könne.'

[9] The relevant quote is this: 'It also follows from this that it cannot be required that this principle of all maxims be itself in turn my maxim, that is, it cannot be required that make it the maxim of my action.'

> limited to those conditions in conformity with the Idea of it and that it may also be actively limited by others [. . .].[10]

As we learn from this quote, Kant believes that reason does not require from us that we ourselves should limit our freedom due to the normativity of right. Rather, reason presents it merely as an 'idea' that our freedom should be limited according to the ULR and that this limitation should be actively limited by others. We see that, in the case of legal normativity, his point of reference are the citizens of a state, not the *homo noumenon* within us. Hence, the third difference between the Law of Right and the Categorical Imperative is that right always has to be imposed on us by others; it is not our duty to follow the mere idea of right, but only its concrete realization in this or that legal order. Therefore, the right that is meant in the UPR and the ULR must be that of a concrete state, not an abstract right of omnitemporal and universal validity.[11]

And in fact, Kant claims, as we already saw, that the laws legitimately established in a state are always in force in a spatiotemporally limited form; they are the laws of a historical individual state and thus do not require full universality concerning their authors and addressees. Instead, they go back to a concrete voluntaristic will of a people (*de facto* normally by its legislator, i.e. the monarch) and consequently do not apply objectively and unconditionally. This is the fourth difference: the CIP verifies or falsifies certain maxims independently of time and place while the GWT leaves room for contextual circumstances. Positive laws are valid, even if they are strongly suboptimal, by the legitimate authority of the lawgiver, as Kant says, and they must be obeyed as long as they do not directly violate morality (RGV 6:99 fn.; trans. A. W. Wood/G. di Giovanni):

> As soon as something is recognized as a duty, even if it should be a duty imposed through the purely arbitrary will of a human lawgiver, obeying it is equally a divine command. Of course we cannot call statutory civil laws divine commands; but if they are legitimate, their observance is equally a divine command. The proposition 'We ought to obey God rather than men' means only that when human beings command something that is bad

[10] 'ein Gesetz, welches mir eine Verbindlichkeit auferlegt, aber ganz und gar nicht erwartet, noch weniger fordert, daß ich ganz um dieser Verbindlichkeit willen meine Freiheit auf jene Bedingungen selbst einschränken solle, sondern die Vernunft sagt nur, daß sie in ihrer Idee darauf eingeschränkt sei und von andern auch thätlich eingeschränkt werden dürfe [. . .].'

[11] As Flikschuh ('Elusive Unity: The General Will in Hobbes and Kant', *Hobbes Studies* 25 (2012), 21–42, at 34) correctly remarks: 'In contrast to both Rousseau and Hobbes, Kant holds that whereas ethical obligation binds only internally, juridical obligation binds only externally. Importantly, not just enforcement of juridical obligation is external in the juridical domain – the very source of juridical obligation is external to (the will of) the individual agent.'

> in itself (directly opposed to the ethical law) we may not, and ought not, obey them.

As Kant claims in this quote, the citizens should, on the one hand, regard even the statutory laws of a legislator as quasi-divine ones; on the other hand, they need not and even must not obey those statutory laws that are 'directly opposed to the law of morality'. Obedience to suboptimal laws is seen here as the standard case, disobedience is described as an exception. Note that Kant even admits that the monarch does not have to improve suboptimal laws immediately as long as he accepts that their improvement must be realized in the future.[12]

An important consequence follows from this for the translation of the UPR and the ULR. I quoted Mary J. Gregor's translation in which the original 'allgemein' gets the English equivalent 'universal'. But on my reading, this translation is mistaken; I think that Kant's wording 'nach einem *allgemeinen* Gesetz' should be rendered as 'according to a *general* law'. A universal law would be an omnitemporal one for humanity at large; this is clearly not meant here. Generalization is, for Kant, a legitimate procedure, but of reduced value compared to full universalization.[13] However, even if the correct translation of the UPR and the ULR is then 'in accordance with a *general* law', I still believe that it remains appropriate to speak of a *Universal* Principle of Right and a *Universal* Law of Right – since these formulations are given from a second-order perspective. The UPR and the ULR in themselves are in fact invariant and omnitemporal. We can identify here a fifth difference: whereas the CIP leads to invariant results in the sense of strict universality, the GWT only arrives at a certain generality of rules.

What does all of this mean for the comparison between the GWT and the CIP? The main parallel between the two is their character as formal procedures. We saw that legitimate right, like each appropriate maxim, must successfully pass an examination: juridical laws are correct if and only if the range of everybody's free choice is guaranteed by them according to a general rule. Likewise, maxims are morally permissible if and only if they are universalizable as laws for any rational agent. Juridical laws must be capable of mutually coordinating the individual freedom margins of the citizens of a certain state in an equal, neutral, and unbiased way. Moral

[12] Important passages for Kant's permission that legal improvements might be delayed by the monarchs are *Towards Perpetual Peace* 8:372 and RL 6:321–2.

[13] In the *Groundwork* 4:424, Kant explicitly distinguishes between a strict *universalitas* and a mere *generalitas*. The latter is characterized as a decrease of the full validity of the CI.

laws must enable an order of action where all rational beings can follow the same rules. At the same time, Kant's description of how the process of establishing normatively correct legislation actually should go is far from what is specified under the CIP. Let me highlight the differences which exist between the two formal procedures in the following contrasting juxtaposition (Table 3.1):

Table 3.1 *Comparison of CIP and GWT*

Moral normativity according to the CIP	Legal normativity according to the GWT
(a) Moral duties are based on individual freedom as autonomy (*Wille*). Every individual subject to the moral law is at the same time the author of morality (following the idea of self-legislation).	(a*) Legal duties are based on freedom as arbitrary choice (*Willkür*), the negative concept of freedom). Lawmaking is usually done by the monarch; the legal subjects are not directly involved.
(b) For moral duties, compliance based on intrinsic motivation is indispensable; they are internally enforced by practical reason.	(b*) For legal duties, compliance out of external obedience to the law is sufficient; they are externally enforced by the authority of a state.
(c) Moral duties are objectively given by practical reason (or by the *homo noumenon*) and addressed to all human beings, even to all rational beings.	(c*) Legal normativity is a mere idea which need not be followed by an individual agent unless he lives in a legal order.
(d) The normativity of moral laws is strict and inescapable. Maxims are always either morally permissible or impermissible.	(d*) Juridical laws can be invalid if they directly contradict the innermost of morality. And they can be suboptimal so that they need improvement over time.
(e) Moral laws are universally mandatory. Their validity is invariant and omnitemporal.	(e*) Juridical laws are generally valid. In legislation, there is room for voluntarism and contextualism.

Thus reconstructed, an important implication of Kant's concept of law is that legal relations do not establish a true omnilateralism since this would imply that all human beings enter into a legal relationship with all others. There is only a constellation of regionally and temporally limited multilateralism.[14] Kant's idea is that a legal order can be justified even if it is no more than a historically situated and contextualized phenomenon.

[14] From this point of view, it is not correct to characterize law, as Arthur Ripstein does, as 'normative omnilateralism'; it is a mere multilateralism, since law is always group-related and spatiotemporally limited and does not exclude associated persons (Arthur Ripstein, *Force and Freedom: Kant's Legal and Political Philosophy*, Cambridge, MA: Harvard University Press, 2009, 24; cf. 183): 'Each of the defects of the state of nature requires an omnilateral authorization to solve it [. . .].' At least, it must be clarified who exactly the 'all' meant by the term omnilateralism are: all members of the legal order? Certainly, they are not all human beings in every place and at every time.

In addition to this, he also recognizes the necessity of universalizing the juridical relations between all men. This is why, in *Towards Perpetual Peace* and elsewhere in Kant's writings, international law remains to be established even when legal orders in individual states are already existing.

But how is it possible that Kant, the theorist of universality, objectivity, intrinsic motivation, inner coercion, and autonomy, confines the level of juridical and political normativity to a contextual, situated phenomenon? A plausible answer to this question arises from the historical dimension of his idea of non-ideal normativity. If the external conditions allow only a lesser form of realization of what might ideally be mandatory, one has to consider preliminary ways in which one can reduce the full normativity while, at the same time, preserving as much as possible of its core. This is exactly what happens in Kant's conception of right. He is convinced that on the historical path towards a full inner moralization of humanity, external juridification is needed since, once people live under stable legal relations, they can more easily take steps towards morality. And if robust republican legal structures exist on a national level, it is to be expected that a 'League of Nations' (*Völkerbund*) will emerge, an alliance of freedom-oriented states which is seen by Kant as the basis for a moral cosmopolitanism.

This is why I think that the relationship between morality and law, represented by the contrast between the CIP and the GWT, is neither that of an equivocity of the normative concepts employed in both formulas, nor is it based on a mere 'family resemblance', namely, showing some overlapping affinity between otherwise deeply different usages of a term. On the contrary, the CIP and the GWT substantially refer to each other insofar as the latter preserves an important residue of the kind of normativity of the former, whereas full normativity, realized (as we will see in a moment) in an 'ethical commonwealth', would be characterized by the fact that it is directly based on moral law. The relation between the CIP and the GWT is that of normative ideality and normative non-ideality respectively.

3.2 The Ethical Commonwealth as Kant's Ideal of a Moral Community

The topic of Kant's legal and political philosophy is the concrete juridical order, established in a historical state, not the idea of a perfectly moral right. And this is absolutely appropriate. He would be an idealistic dreamer, a *Gesinnungsethiker* in the problematic sense of the word, had he taken full moral normativity, according to the left side of Table 3.1, as the basis of his view on what is required for the legal sphere. Given that

Kant does not make such a commitment, as we have seen so far, there is good reason for abandoning the derivation reading, which wants to defend the thesis that, for Kant, there is a direct moral basis for legal normativity. As he writes, for example, in one of the posthumously edited notes on the constitution of a legal order (Refl 7961 19:565): 'Whether the constitution requires unanimity. In the idea of good people, yes. But as they are, so much, that others can be forced. According to the principle *exeundum e statu naturali*.'[15] Kant here gestures towards the fact that grounding the normative foundation of a state in the unanimity (*unanimia*) shared among a morally good people would leave us with an entirely utopian outlook. In reality, one must proceed differently: bad as men are, establishing a state of order does only require that the majority force those others who are unwilling into this state, such that all will live in the future under the General Will. Following these considerations, it is clear that the idea of a General Will is not immediately a moral one, a view which is also expressed in *Idea for a Universal History with Cosmopolitan Purpose* as follows (8:23; trans. H. B. Nisbet): 'He [i.e. man] thus requires a master to break his self-will and force him to obey a generally valid will (*einem allgemeingültigen Willen*) under which everyone can be free.'[16] According to the 'Sixth Sentence' of the *Idea*, human beings are so bad that they are in need of a master. This master has to break their individual will and force them under a General Will which then turns out to be the rule according to which the citizens can be free.

What would an authoritative will look like in the case of a genuinely moral community? We are in the fortunate situation that Kant addresses this question explicitly in the 'Third Part' of his *Religion within the Limits of Reason Alone* through differentiating between a juridical and an ethical commonwealth. Note that Kant's ethical community consists of all men without exception; 'the whole human race' should belong to it (6:94). To this universality he adds the moment of intrinsic moral motivation; in the ethical community each individual is genuinely motivated by morality and not merely subject to the pressure of legal sanction. An important further point about Kant's ethical commonwealth is that it is an idealized, but at the same time still concrete, historical community, namely the true church.[17] Kant is not thinking here of an otherworldly moral ideal

[15] Refl 7961 19:565: 'Ob die constitution *unanimia* erfordere. In der Idee guter Menschen, Ja. Aber so wie sie sind so viel, daß andere können gezwungen werden. Nach dem *principio exeundum e statu naturali*.'

[16] I changed Nisbet's translation 'universally valid will' into 'generally valid will'.

[17] RGV 6:101.

community. Rather, it is introduced as a concrete precondition for preserving the morality of a community (RGV 6:98–9; trans. J. Bennett):

> If a commonwealth is to come into existence, all individuals must be subject to a public legislation, and it must be possible to regard all the laws that bind them as commands of a common lawgiver. For a juridical commonwealth, the mass of people uniting into a whole would itself have to be the lawgiver (of constitutional laws), because the legislation comes from the principle: Limit the freedom of each individual to the conditions under which it can be consistent with the freedom of everyone else according to a common law, and thus the general will sets up an external legal control.

In this passage, Kant formulates a clear contrast between the ethical commonwealth he is concerned with and a juridical one. The former, as the notion of the 'people of God' indicates, lives under the rule of a common (divine) legislator. In the latter, however, the 'mass of people' serves as the lawgiver; such a community is oriented to the principle of the General Will, that is, to the principle that the freedom of each must be restricted in accordance with the freedom of every other. The juridical commonwealth establishes its laws by means of external coercion. But this is precisely not the case in an ethical community. Kant continues (RGV 6:98–9):

> But if the commonwealth is to be ethical, the people as such can't itself be regarded as the lawgiver. In such a commonwealth the laws are all expressly designed to promote the morality of actions, which is something inner, and so can't be subject to public human laws. (In a juridical commonwealth, in contrast, the public laws concern the legality of actions, which is out in the open, visible.) So someone other than the people must be specifiable as the public lawgiver for an ethical commonwealth. But ethical laws can't be thought of as coming originally, basically, from the will of this superior being (as statutes that might not have been binding if he hadn't commanded them), because then they wouldn't be ethical laws, and conforming to them would only be a matter of coerced obedience to the law, not the free exercise of virtue.

Here, Kant emphasizes the differences which exist between a juridical and a purely ethical community: whereas the former is based on the unified will of all people and expresses its laws by means of the authoritarian element of collective voluntarism, the latter is based on inner morality. Morality cannot be regulated by external laws; hence, morality is not the object of a General Will. In the first case, the community of individuals has to follow the principle of legality of actions, in the second, the distinct principle of morality. Kant explicitly claims that, in the second case, the people are not the lawgiver. As he adds, the source of moral normativity (moral normative authority) can originate neither from the people, nor from the divine will, even though God plays the role of a 'moral ruler of the world' (*als einem moralischen Weltherrscher*). What Kant means is that the normativity of an ethical commonwealth must be based on a good (moral) will, namely, that which follows the Categorical Imperative instead of that which obeys a General Will.

Shortly after this passage, Kant raises the question of whether one could combine the concept of an ethical commonwealth with that of the legality of statutory laws (RGV 6:99–100). In this case God would still be the legislator, but his laws would be taken as rules for an external order. Kant rejects this theocratic proposal, since it would amount, as he writes, to an aristocracy of priests; such a state would bring in God only externally. He then characterizes his own ethical commonwealth explicitly as 'an institution whose laws are purely inward – a republic under laws of virtue, i.e., a people of God "zealous of good works"' (RGV 6:100).

As Stephen Palmquist rightly points out, Kant describes the ethical commonwealth or invisible church according to the pattern of the four categories which he introduced in the first *Critique*: quantity, quality, relation, and modality. Palmquist gives the following convincing reconstruction:[18]

> *Universality*. The *quantity* of the true church is one.
>
> *Integrity*. The church's *quality* aims at its members' moral edification.
>
> *Freedom*. The *relation* of church members must be free of coercion both (a) inwardly (i.e., members will not exercise control over each other) and (b) outwardly (i.e., the church and political state will operate independently).
>
> *Unchangeability*. The *modality* of the church's constitution is (a) *necessary*, in the sense that these four basic precepts will *never* change, while also being (b) *possible*, in the sense that all *other* aspects of church governance are *always* open to change.

As one can see from these features of the invisible church, Kant interprets it as an ideal universal and invariant community based on morality. Therefore, this passage from the *Religion* provides welcome support of my non-ideality interpretation. If the derivation reading were correct, we would expect that Kant might describe the normativity of a juridical commonwealth precisely in terms of the Categorical Imperative – which he apparently does not. Instead, as we can see, the community directly

[18] Stephen R. Palmquist, 'How Political is the Kantian Church?', *Diametros* 17 (2020), 95–113, at 100.

based on the CI would be the ethical commonwealth. Kant sees such a community as important, yet it should be restricted to the tasks of an invisible church. If it were institutionally realized as a state, it would adopt the form of a theocracy, that is, a mistaken attempt to implement a divine, morally perfect legislation under historical conditions. The legislation resulting from a General Will, by contrast, involves everyone as author and addressee of the right and is therefore the normatively appropriate way of organizing a state.

But the separation reading, on the other hand, is misguided, too, since it falsely assumes that law and morality are without connection. The link that connects the General Will and the Categorical Imperative lies in the person of the legislator. This can be concluded from those passages in which Kant deals with the GWT as a concrete test procedure to be conducted by the monarch. In the *Idea for a Universal History with Cosmopolitan Purpose*, he claims that 'the supreme leader should be just for himself and yet a man' (IaG 8:22: '*Das höchste Oberhaupt soll aber gerecht für sich selbst und doch ein Mensch sein*'). Kant requires him to possess a 'good will' (ibid.). As this implies, the GWT cannot appropriately be done without inner morality, but it is the monarch who transforms his inner reflections into a concrete set of laws. This again shows how the notion of a General Will encompasses the idea of a non-ideal normativity.

Likewise, in *The Conflict of the Faculties* Kant demands that the monarch follows the obligation to treat his people according to republican principles. In this text, he describes a state organized with regard to the idea of General Will – the citizens being at the same time obedient to the law and legislators – as the Platonic ideal of a *respublica noumenon* (SF 7:90–1):

> The Idea of a constitution in harmony with the natural right of man, one namely in which the citizens obedient to the law, besides being united, ought also to be legislative, lies at the basis of all political forms; and the body politic which, conceived in conformity to it by virtue of pure concepts of reason, signifies a Platonic Ideal (*respublica noumenon*), is not an empty chimera, but rather the eternal norm for all civil organization in general, and averts all war.

As this passage confirms, the normative foundation of any appropriate constitution lies in the natural rights of man, namely, the a priori (innate) right to freedom, and its realization is done by the idea of a General Will. Then Kant continues (SF 7:91):

> A civil society organized conformably to this ideal is the representation of it in agreement with the laws of freedom by means of an example in our experience (*respublica phaenomenon*) and can only be painfully acquired after multifarious hostilities and wars; but its constitution, once won on a large scale, is qualified as the best among all others to banish war, the destroyer of everything good. Consequently, it is a duty to enter into such a system of government, but it is provisionally the duty of the monarchs, if they rule as autocrats, to govern in a republican (not democratic) way, that is, to treat the people according to principles which are commensurate with the spirit of libertarian laws (as a nation with mature understanding would prescribe them for itself), although they would not be literally canvassed for their consent.

The monarch should not reign, we are told, as an autocrat; instead, he has the 'provisional' duty to rule according to a republican idea of government. This confirms that Kant should not be interpreted on the basis of a separation reading, since the procedure that is prescribed here is clearly an internal one. The concrete legislator, namely, the monarch, has to practice some sort of private thought-experiment in which he should imagine 'how a people with mature understanding would prescribe it for itself' (*wie ein Volk mit reifer Vernunft sie sich selbst vorschreiben würde*). The monarch is only bound to the correct execution of the GWT internally and morally, not externally or legally. We can thus extend our list by a point (f–f*), namely through the opposition of two types of contradiction-in-will procedure (Table 3.2).

The above-quoted passage from the *Conflict of the Faculties* contains important elements of a philosophy of history. The Platonic ideal of a perfect constitution, we learn, is not outside our world, for we can in fact

Table 3.2 *Extended Comparison of CIP and GWT*

Moral normativity	Legal normativity
(f) The CIP is successfully applied if an agent, following their strictly formal process, identifies a maxim as passing the universalist contradiction-in-will test.[19]	(f*) The *GWT* is successfully applied if a monarch, in an imaginative thought-experiment in which he envisions his people as being mature, finds no contradiction in his generalist contradiction-in-will test.

[19] Kant clearly says that the contradiction-in-will test is the fundament of the Categorical Imperative while the contradiction-in-conception test only helps to identify perfect duties (GMS 4:422).

attain it, namely, through an order based on a General Will. Before we arrive at a concrete example of such a well-organized state (a *respublica phaenomenon*), we have to face 'multifarious hostilities and wars'. I take Kant here to be claiming that the GWT cannot be fully and appropriately applied under contemporary, heavily non-ideal circumstances; for the time being, history has to proceed according to the teleological scheme (as formulated in the *Idea for a Universal History with Cosmopolitan Purpose* (1784) and elsewhere). In the future, however, there will be a historical moment when such a constitution (a *respublica phaenomenon* which is the closest approximation to a *respublica noumenon*) can be established. This, then, will banish all war. We have the duty to enter into such a condition of government, which means that we must follow the *exeundum est e statu naturali*, although such an ideal constitution is still far away. In the meantime ('provisionally'), while the monarchs are often reigning as autocrats, they should, following Kant, rather rule 'in a republican (not a democratic) way'. They have to do this even if, as he admits, the citizens cannot be asked for their consent. Note here that the GWT should be practised by the monarchs as a mere thought-experiment, and there is no right to resistance or civil disobedience against this procedure, since nobody except the king is entitled to practise the thought-experiment or to determine its adequate execution.

The distinction between a *respublica noumenon* and a *respublica phaenomenon* in this passage sheds some light on Kant's view of a non-ideal political normativity, which includes two different aspects. First, concerning the two formal procedures which are testing universalizability and generalizability respectively, it denotes the difference between moral and political normativity. The norms derived from the Categorical Imperative are the ideal version, while the norms taken from the General Will are the non-ideal ones. Second, regarding the implementation, Kant describes degrees of realization of political norms as mediated by a historical process: while we are living nowadays under conditions of a defective *respublica phaenomenon*, future generations may arrive at full version of it (which is then still not a *respublica noumenon*).[20]

3.3 The Transcendental Conception of Public Right as a Form of GWT

I now turn to a text in which Kant presents a very detailed version of the GWT. Notably the GWT is presented here not as a procedure to be done

[20] I am grateful to Rainer Forst for having drawn my attention to this point.

by the legislator, but instead by a general public. I mean the passage entitled 'Of the Accordance of Politics with Morals according to the Transcendental Conception of Public Right' from *Towards Perpetual Peace* (ZeF 8:381–2). Kant there explicitly speaks of a formal test criterion for public law, namely that of publicity. Let us call it the Publicity Test (PT). He introduces the PT by differentiating between a material and a formal view of public right:

> We may think of Public Right in a formal way after abstracting from all the matters to which it is applied in detail, such as the different relations of men in the State, or of the States to each other, as presented in experience; and this is the way in which jurists usually think of it. But apart from the *matter* of public right, there remains only the *form of publicity*, the possibility of which is implied in every pretension of right; for without such publicity there would be no justice, this being thinkable only as what is publicly declarable, and hence without this publicity there would be no right, as right is only administered or distributed by it.

Kant's idea is that each future element of public right must have a content and a form. Now, we might expect him to say something about the formal aspect of each future element of public right in the sense of the inner coherence of a law or its outer applicability, which itself must be free from contradiction. Instead, he maintains that every claim or pretension to the legitimacy of right must be publicly declared. At first, this seems to be a rather procedural and strictly formal aspect of lawgiving. But what Kant has in mind is a procedure by which the general approbation is tested:

> This character of publicity must belong to every pretension of right; and, as it can easily be judged whether it accompanies any particular case, and whether it can therefore be combined with the principles of an agent, it furnishes a criterion, which is at once presented *a priori* in reason and which it is easy to use in experience. Where it cannot be combined with the principles of an agent, the falsity and wrongness of a pretended right can thus be immediately recognized, as if by an experiment of the pure reason.

In this part of the passage, Kant even explicitly speaks of the PT as a 'criterion' and an 'experiment of pure reason'. He claims that it is an a priori criterion: it helps to figure out whether or not 'a pretended right can be combined with the principles of an agent' (*ob sie sich mit den Grundsätzen des Handelnden vereinigen lasse oder nicht*). This implies that he is not thinking of a concrete political procedure like a public announcement; again, it sounds instead like a thought-experiment. This is confirmed by the observation that Kant characterizes the PT in the following lines as an 'abstraction from everything empirical' (*Abstraction von allem Empirischen*):

> Abstraction being thus made from everything empirical that is contained in the conceptions of national and international right, (such as the evil disposition of human nature which makes coercion necessary) the following proposition arises, and it may be called the *transcendental formula* of Public Right. 'All actions relating to the rights of other men are wrong, if their maxim is not compatible with publicity.'

Kant speaks of a 'Transcendental Formula of Public Right'. This makes it clear that the PT is a version of the GWT: what he means is that all human beings affected by a pretended law must be able to give their consent. The fact that he does not use the expression 'General Will' may have to do with the extension of the Transcendental Formula which applies both for national and for international law. We can find further evidence for the strong overlap between the PT and the GWT: the idea of a general consent is indirectly present when Kant in the next lines says that by a publicly presented illegitimate law would 'inevitably aroused [. . .] the resistance of all men against my purpose' (*dadurch unausbleiblich der Widerstand Aller gegen meinen Vorsatz gereizt werde*):

> This principle is not to be regarded merely as *ethical*, and as belonging only to the doctrine of virtue, but it is also to be regarded as *juridical* and as pertaining to the rights of men. For a maxim cannot be a right maxim which is such that I cannot allow it to be *published* without thereby at the same time frustrating my own intention, which would necessarily have to be kept entirely secret in order that it might succeed, and which I could not *publicly confess* to be mine without inevitably arousing thereby the resistance of all men against my purpose. It is clear that this necessary and universal opposition of all against me on self-evident grounds, can arise from nothing else than the injustice which such a maxim threatens to everyone. Further, it is a merely *negative* maxim, in so far as it only serves as a means of making known what is *not* right and just towards others. It is like an axiom which is certain without demonstration. And, besides all this, it is easily applicable; as may be seen from the following examples and illustrations of Public Right.

On my reading, under the title of a Transcendental Formula of Public Right, Kant discusses the General Will. The PT is a slightly different version of the GWT.

For my interpretation, it is an interesting detail that Kant explicitly claims that the Formula connects morals and politics. The heading of the passage is formulated as *Of the Accordance of Politics with Morals* (*Von der Einhelligkeit der Politik mit der Moral*). Furthermore, in the last portion of the text, it is said that the Formula is valid both in the ethical and in the legal sphere.

The PT as a test criterion works in the following way: whenever a maxim, namely the pretended law, can only be successfully established if the legislator keeps it secret, it is illegitimate; whenever the lawgiver can publicly confess his intention without provoking the resistance of all men against his purpose, it is legitimate. This means that the PT, very much like the GWT, is applied to a multitude of concrete people (not to humanity at large) and is intended to ascertain either their protest or their acceptance. The wording by which the PT is formulated also suggests that it is a procedure analogous to the CIP: 'All actions related to the right of other people, whose maxim is not compatible with publicity, are unjust.' It excludes, like a litmus test, all unreasonable legal actions. Kant notes, however, that a people can use the test criterion only *negatively* – a point that is repeated in the treatise *Theory and Practice* (TP 8:304).[21]

In which way should a ruler publicly announce his or her legal maxim? And how is the possible resistance of the citizens to be understood? Given the fact that Kant leaves no room for legitimate civil disobedience or political resistance, one wonders what reactions on the part of the citizens Kant might be thinking of here. He could certainly admit nothing more than a weak form of a written expression of concerns (according to the 'freedom of the pen' as described in TP 8:304). So the only protest against a proposed law would be on the basis of a quite narrow form of freedom of expression. Or should the legislator simply imagine that his announcement causes uncontrolled public anger? In the first case, it seems somewhat far-fetched to speak of a 'resistance of all against my intention'; written concerns are certainly not a kind of general resistance. Moreover, Kant does not explicitly tell us whether he wants to impose on the lawgiver the obligation to announce his intentions publicly in advance, as a matter of principle, in order to then wait for the reaction of the citizens as the test procedure. The PT and GWT as outlined would only make full sense if they were established as formal, constitutionally based, and legally regulated procedures. But even then, one could not be sure; in a regime of terror, even the public announcement of unjust laws might not trigger protest, because no one would dare to object. The problem of the Transcendental Formula seems to be that it presupposes what it is

[21] 'The universal principle, however, according to which a people is to judge its rights negatively, i.e. only to judge what the highest legislature would like to be regarded as not having decreed with its best will, is contained in the sentence: What a people cannot decide about itself, the legislator cannot decide about the people.' On this negative principle see Jens Kulenkampff, 'Über die Rolle des ursprünglichen Vertrages in Über den Gemeinspruch: Das mag in der Theorie richtig sein, taugt aber nicht für die Praxis', *Jahrbuch für Recht und Ethik* 16 (2008), 165–81.

supposed to achieve: a legally oriented state with a defensively acting legislator and a critical civil society.

However, it is not only the lack of clarity of the GWT procedure (as described here) that must be viewed with scepticism, but also the fact that a non-institutional and uncontrolled test procedure is unlikely to lead to normatively appropriate results.

3.4 Some Critical Remarks on Kant's GWT

The GWT is not directly based on morality, and it is not based on prudential rationality either. We saw that, by taking the General Will as the legitimizing basis of any legal order, Kant does not simply defend the idea of an aggregation of individual self-interested wills as the fundament of a legitimate state. A legitimate state has, as its grounding principles of justification, criteria that share characteristic similarities in common with CIP. The GWT is a reduced or attenuated form of the CIP, formulated to deal with political reality.

Kant's General Will is meant to coordinate the individual freedom ranges of agents in an objective, neutral, and unbiased way, as opposed to coordinating them with respect to each person's interests. It starts from the idea of the innate right to freedom attributed to all citizens. But nevertheless, this does not imply that a state has a directly moral foundation. Instead, the essential characteristic of right is, according to Kant, that each individual's leeway in exercising their arbitrary freedom must be made compatible with all other such exercises, in a formal manner as well as in a generalizable way, by means of law that is justified as legitimate. Let me close with two critical remarks on Kant's notion of a General Will.

(1) *The procedure of the GWT is vague and unclear.* Most of Kant's formulations of the GWT leave it open to which precise test he is referring. Under which conditions can a legislator assume that the hypothetical consent of a people has or has not been given, and under which not? At least four aspects seem to be clear: first, the law to be established must allow for the free arbitrary action of the individual; second, it must coordinate this use of freedom on the basis of a general rule; third, this rule must be something enforceable, that is, it must limit external actions; fourth and finally, it must have the form of a juridical law (i.e. be connected with such moments as promulgation, permanent validity, judicial enforceability, and factual enforcement). However, these four criteria are certainly too underdetermined to be normatively satisfactory. To apply them would not sufficiently limit the range of permissible rules, for rules of

the type 'Men should have substantive privileges compared to women in political, social, and economic life' and 'Not all citizens of a state should count as active ones, but only those who are economically independent' do also fulfil all the requirements mentioned: they leave room for the free arbitrary action of all, they coordinate it on the basis of a general rule, they are externally enforceable, and they can be established as laws. We can see evidence of this normative underdetermination at work in Kant's own analysis; in RL §46, for example, he does not envisage a full equality of rights for men and women – just as he does not give the full status of active citizenship to those living in economic dependence.

(2) *The GWT is not based on a theory of political and legal goods.* The General Will Test could be constructed in much more plausible form if Kant had integrated into it the idea of political or legal goods. For any citizen who wants to see his or her freedom of arbitrary choice protected, it is relevant that the necessary means to free actions are available. These are one's bodily integrity, physical and mental health, sufficient material wealth, political participation, the access to information and education – among many others. These and many other goods could serve as success criteria for ensuring that the General Will is actually respected. In his purely formal procedure, Kant ignores these goods and, in fact, is even eager to do so, in order to carefully avoid the presence of any empirical and material components in his theory. But the flip side of this formalism, which ends up exposing a weak point in the Kantian theory, is that it remains unable to guarantee the kinds of concrete political and legal goods that, for example, find articulation and justification in and through human rights discourses. Nothing in Kant's theory impedes the monarch from restricting what we see as human rights, as long as he does so in a formally correct way. Additionally, the fact that the Kantian monarch has the right to remain behind and is not forced to guarantee a complete set of freedoms accessible to everyone cannot be clearly formulated in this account either since the notion of a 'full set of freedoms' has strong material implications. Moreover, there are strongly diverging degrees of importance in a list of such freedoms. It makes a difference if a ruler restricts, for example, public opinion by censorship or limits shopping opportunities on Sundays. The Kantian model seems unable to account for such differences.

CHAPTER 4

Kant's Right as Normatively Independent

One Strategy Considered and Rejected

Sorin Baiasu

4.1 Introduction

Recent debates on the relation in Kant between the Categorical Imperative, as the fundamental principle of ethics,[1] and the Universal Principle of Right, as the fundamental principle of politico-legal norms,[2] are underpinned by the significant question of how politics and ethics are supposed to connect (if at all) – not only in Kant's work, but also more generally in our societies.[3] The range of plausible answers with regard to Kant is surprisingly varied: from the claim that politico-legal principles

I am very grateful to Bernd Ludwig, Martin Brecher, and Philipp-Alexander Hirsch for the invitation to present an earlier version of this chapter as a paper at their excellent international conference on the topic of 'Law and Morality in Kant'. The discussions after the paper, both during the question-and-answer session and, following that, during the social events have been very useful in revising the chapter. I am in particular grateful to Lara Scaglia (who acted as commentator for my paper), Marie Newhouse, Pauline Kleingeld, Paul Guyer, Martin Brecher, George Pavlakos, and Luke Davies for perceptive suggestions, comments and criticisms. Special thanks are also due to the editors of this volume, Philipp-Alexander Hirsch and Martin Brecher, for detailed written comments on earlier versions of this chapter. All remaining errors are mine.

[1] Henceforth CI. I have here in mind the fundamental principle of the doctrine of virtue (TL 6:395). It is true that Kant also talks about a CI as the fundamental principle of the 'doctrine of morals [*Sittenlehre*]' (e.g. MS 6:226), but he specifies that this 'as such only affirms what obligation is' (MS 6:225). I take, with Kant, the various formulations of the CI to be 'so many formulae of the very same law', with the difference between them being 'subjectively, rather than objectively practical' (GMS 4:435). I understand this as follows: the CI, as the fundamental principle of the doctrine of morals, affirms what obligation in general is and without concern for the motivation with which the obligation is to be fulfilled. This contrasts with the CI, as the fundamental principle of ethics or the doctrine of virtue, where the way the obligation is to be fulfilled is important. A proper discussion of the relation, in Kant, between the various formulations of the CI must be left for another occasion. A discussion of the fundamental principles of morals, doctrine of right, and doctrine of virtue is provided in this volume by Marcus Willaschek (Chapter 1).

[2] Henceforth UPR.

[3] As Willaschek notes in his contribution to this volume (Chapter 1), it is not always clear what the debate on the connection between politics and ethics refers to. What I am interested in, in this chapter, is the connection between ethical and juridical lawgiving [*Gesetzgebung*]. (MS 6:218–19) I assume that the UPR is the fundamental principle of juridical lawgiving, whereas the CI is the fundamental principle of ethical lawgiving. I clarify further in n. 11.

should depend normatively on ethical ones, to the view that the former are independent of the latter and even to a conception of a complex relation of dependence of legal duties on ethical principles.[4]

One interesting implication of readings which dismiss a relation of simple dependence of politico-legal principles on ethical ones is that they contest one of the stereotypical views of Kant's practical philosophy as impractical and idealistic, as what texts such as 'Perpetual Peace' and 'On a Supposed Right to Lie from Philanthropy', seem to suggest (ZeF; VRML).[5] While interpretations according to which the UPR is independent from the CI run

[4] In a previous text (Baiasu, 'Right's Complex Relation to Ethics in Kant: The Limits of Independentism', *Kant-Studien* 107 (2016), 2–33), I called these positions Simple Dependentist (for instance, Jürgen Habermas, *Between Facts and Norms: Contributions to a Discourse Theory of Law and Democracy*. Cambridge, MA: MIT Press, 1996, esp. 105–6), Simple Independentist (among others, Allen Wood, 'The Final Form of Kant's Practical Philosophy', *The Southern Journal of Philosophy* 36 (1997), 1–20 and Willaschek, esp. 'Why the *Doctrine of Right* Does Not Belong in the *Metaphysics of Morals*: On Some Basic Distinctions in Kant's Moral Philosophy', *Jahrbuch für Recht und Ethik/Annual Review of Law and Ethics* 5 (1997), 205–27, but also 'Recht ohne Ethik? Kant über die Gründe, das Recht nicht zu brechen', in Volker Gerhardt (ed.) *Kant im Streit der Fakultäten*, Berlin: De Gruyter, 2005, 188–204; 'Right and Coercion: Can Kant's Conception of Right be Derived from His Moral Theory?', *International Journal of Philosophical Studies* 17 (2009), 49–70; 'The Non-Derivability of Kantian Right from the Categorical Imperative: A Response to Nance', *International Journal of Philosophical Studies* 20 (2012), 557–64) and Complex or Relative Dependentist (e.g. Paul Guyer, 'Kant's Deductions of the Principles of Right', in Mark Timmons (ed.), *Kant's Metaphysics of Morals: Interpretative Essays*, Oxford: Oxford University Press, 2002, 23–64; Arthur Ripstein, *Force and Freedom: Kant's Legal and Political Philosophy*, Cambridge, MA: Harvard University Press, 2009; and Bernd Ludwig, 'Whence Public Right? The Role of Theoretical and Practical Reason in Kant's Doctrine of Right', in Mark Timmons (ed.), *Kant's Metaphysics of Morals: Interpretative Essays*, Oxford: Oxford University Press, 2002, 159–84), respectively. One aim of that text was to account for this relation of complex dependence, since although a few Kant interpreters did suggest the UPR cannot simply be derived from the CI and a more complex relation of dependence between them should be considered, there was no account of this more complex relation. In another text (Baiasu, 'Ethical and Politico-Juridical Norms in the *Tugendlehre*', *Studi Kantiani* 29 (2016), 59–76), I argued that the relation is in fact even more complex, when we take into account some of Kant's claims in the 'Doctrine of Virtue' (TL).

[5] To give just a few examples, talking about Kant's political writings in general, including *Zum ewigen Frieden*, Graciela Fernández observes that, in reading them, 'one has the impression of having put foot on the soil of Utopia' ('Utopia and Perpetual Peace', in Valerio Rohden, R. R. Terra, G. A. de Almeida and Margit Ruffing (eds.), *Recht und Frieden in der Philosophie Kants: Akten des X. Internationalen Kant-Congresses*. Berlin: De Gruyter, 2008, 311–21, at 311). Christine Korsgaard, in a text about Kant's 'Über ein vermeintes Recht, aus Menschenliege zu lügen', claims in general about his moral philosophy that it 'sets a high ideal of conduct and tells us to live up to that ideal regardless of what other persons are doing' (Korsgaard, 'The Right to Lie: Kant on Dealing with Evil', *Philosophy and Public Affairs* 15 (1986), 325–49, at 325). Concerning *Zum ewigen Frieden*, see also Kleingeld, 'Kant's Theory of Peace', in Paul Guyer (ed.), *The Cambridge Companion to Kant and Modern Philosophy*, Cambridge: Cambridge University Press, 2006, 477–504, at 477). With regard to 'Über ein vermeintes Recht, aus Menschenliege zu lügen', see also Paul Formosa, '"All Politics Must Bend Its Knee Before Right": Kant on the Relation of Morals to Politics', *Social Theory and Practice* 34 (2008), 157–81, at 157.

the risk of depriving Kant's moral philosophy of a feature attractive to many (namely, the ethics-sensitivity of his legal and political philosophy), they also seem to align his thought with that of contemporary influential political theorists, such as Rawls, who respond to the pluralism of our societies by separating politics from ethics, metaphysics, and even philosophy in general.[6]

I have two aims in this chapter. First, I develop, examine, and reject one interesting strategy for defending the independentist position.[7] This starts from a particular view of the UPR, according to which, contrary to the dominant reading, which regards it as representing a single standard, the UPR includes, in fact, two distinct principles – one for formal, and the second for material, wrongs.[8] This two-standard interpretation of the UPR (TSI) makes more difficult the task of the dependentists, who claim to be able to show that the UPR can be derived from the CI: with the TSI in place, they need to show that not only one, but two, principles can be derived from the CI. In addition, however, at least on a standard reading of the CI, TSI can make the dependentist's task impossible, if the distinct parts of the UPR are viewed as normatively irreducible.[9]

Before moving on to the second aim, I mention that my focus on this strategy is motivated by its philosophical significance: it challenges the dominant readings of Kant's politico-legal philosophy as ethics-sensitive by pointing to features internal to Kant's practical philosophy. Thus, if the TSI were correct (a claim which I will challenge in what follows), then the

6 'Thus, justice as fairness deliberately stays on the surface, philosophically speaking' (Rawls, 'Justice as Fairness: Political not Metaphysical', *Philosophy and Public Affairs* 14 (1985), 223–51, at 230). See also Rawls, *Political Liberalism*, rev. ed., New York: Columbia University Press, 2005 [1993].

7 The chapters by Willaschek (Chapter 1), Ludwig, Christoph Horn (Chapter 3) and Guyer (Chapter 14) in this volume all reject an independentist position, but they do so by defending specific aspects or forms of dependentist views. For instance, Ludwig thinks that 'the formula of the *General Law of Right* [can be derived] directly from the formula of the *Categorical Imperative*' (p. 39). Horn also rejects an independentist position and argues that 'the GWT [the 'General Will Test' for the legitimacy of a draft law] and the CIP [the Categorical Imperative procedure] are interrelated in a quite characteristic manner, namely according to a relation of ideal and non-ideal normativity' (p. 54–5). Finally, Guyer also rejects independentism, but his focus is on what he thinks is 'the more interesting and timely issue of the need for individual morality – virtue – in the actual practice of justice' (p. 289). My aim here is to reconstruct an independentist position starting from a particular interpretation of the UPR and then to reject it, while at the same time providing support for a complex dependentist view on the relation in Kant between ethics and right.

8 Call this the Two-standard Interpretation – henceforth TSI.

9 This would, of course, not hold true, if the CI itself were viewed as including two or more normatively irreducible parts; yet, the CI is standardly viewed as normatively unitary and I am not aware of any dissenting readings.

UPR could not depend normatively in a straightforward way on a normatively unitary CI. That conclusion would vindicate an independentist position in the debate on the relationship between the CI and the UPR.

By developing the argument against the TSI, my second aim in this chapter is to defend indirectly a complex dependentist position in the debate on the relationship between the UPR and the CI. According to this view, the UPR cannot be derived normatively in an immediate way from the CI, but can be derived from an intermediary principle,[10] from which the CI can also be derived.[11] This is a view I presented and argued for directly elsewhere, but the argument in this chapter provides additional support for it.[12]

4.2 The Independentism-Justifying Strategy

4.2.1 *The TSI*

Consider the UPR: 'Any action is *right* if it can coexist with everyone's freedom in accordance with a universal law, or if on its maxim the freedom of choice of each can coexist with everyone's freedom in accordance with a universal law' (MS 6:230).

[10] The principle is intermediary, although it will turn out to have priority over both the CI and the UPR, from the perspective of the problem discussed in this chapter, as well as in other chapters of this volume (such as those by Guyer (Chapter 14), Willaschek (Chapter 1), Ludwig (Chapter 2) and Horn (Chapter 3)), of the relation in Kant between ethics and right. My claim is that the UPR is not directly derivable from the CI, but we can link the two through this principle, which, in *this* specific sense, is intermediary – it is a link *between* two other principles.

[11] We can roughly regard the UPR as derivable from the CI, when we restrict the CI to the domain of external action. Yet, the CI so restricted still does not yield the UPR, since the motivation to act out of duty remains a requirement, which does not apply to the UPR. The intermediary principle from which we can normatively derive the UPR is a principle similar in its generality to the CI, but which, like the UPR, allows for action merely in accordance with duty and action for the sake of duty. Please note: this does not commit me to a reading of the CI, according to which the CI would impose action out of duty as a duty. I agree that such a reading would lead to various issues (for discussion, see, for instance, Michael Walschots, 'Kant and the Duty to Act from Duty', *History of Philosophy Quarterly* 39 (2022), 59–75; I also agree that readings of the CI, such as Ludwig's (Chapter 2 in this volume), or Hirsch's (*Freiheit und Staatlichkeit bei Kant: Die autonomietheoretische Begründung von Recht und Staat und das Widerstandsproblem*, Berlin: De Gruyter, 2017, 108ff.), avoid these problems, by regarding the CI as merely stating that a certain duty is to be fulfilled, but not how this is to be done. On my reading, the CI would need to require ethical motivation (although, as already mentioned, not as a duty), if it is to represent the fundamental principle of ethics. Hence, if the question is the relation, in Kant, between the CI, as the fundamental principle of ethics, and the UPR, as the fundamental principle of right, then the CI would need to be connected with a requirement of ethical motivation. It can do so, however, in a weak sense – for instance, as the CI applies to ethical maxims, ethical motivation can be seen as required by what ethical maxims mean by definition. Of course, a proper discussion of these claims would need serious consideration of alternative interpretations of the CI, which needs to be left for another occasion.

[12] See n. 4.

The first part of the UPR, call it P1, can be read as formulating, in inverse form, Kant's standard for material wrongs. According to P1, action A is right, if it can coexist with everyone's freedom in accordance with a universal law. We can understand a material wrong as an action *physically* incompatible with the rights of one or more individuals. On this construal, that action A cannot coexist with everyone's freedom in accordance with a universal law means that A is physically incompatible with the rights of one or more individuals. For instance, A may interfere with an individual's use of what is theirs or may actually use what is theirs.

The second part of the UPR, call it P2, can be seen as expressing, in inverse form, Kant's standard for formal wrongs. On this reading, A is right, if, on A's maxim, the freedom of choice of each can coexist with everyone's freedom in accordance with a universal law. We can understand a formal wrong as a wrong against the right of human beings as such, rather than as a wrong against particular individuals (e.g. MS 6:307n). Hence, the specific wrong for this type of action is not given by physical incompatibility with the rights of specific individuals. For instance, the maxim of being willing to be and remain in the state of nature is formally wrong, even when we are in a rightful condition and even when acting in accordance with that maxim happens not to have any effect on the rightful condition. Similarly, attempted murder is formally wrong, even when it is unsuccessful.

Many Kantians read the UPR as formulating one standard of right conduct.[13] Yet, given Kant's distinction between material and formal wrongdoing (e.g. MS 6:307–8 and 307n) and the specific formulation of the UPR, the TSI argues that the UPR is better read according to the previous interpretation: P1 is the inverse form of a standard of what is materially wrong, whereas P2, of what is formally wrong.[14]

4.2.2 *Formal and Material Wrongs*

On the TSI, a *merely* material wrong may occur by accident, if a person fails to realize that she is using something that belongs to someone else.

[13] This, for instance, has been my default understanding of Kant's UPR. See also Allen Wood, *Kantian Ethics: A Hermeneutic of Freedom*, Cambridge: Cambridge University Press, 2008, 243, and Arthur Ripstein, 'Means and Ends', *Jurisprudence* 6 (2015), 1–23, at 8.

[14] Marie Newhouse, 'Two Types of Legal Wrongdoing', *Legal Theory* 22 (2016), 59–75; I am not aware of other commentators who defend an interpretation of the UPR as formulating two normatively distinct and irreducible standards, so, in this chapter, I engage with this text. The example of Richard and Edward in the next section, for instance, is in Newhouse's text. I should add that Newhouse's article does not link the TSI she proposes to the debate on the relation of dependence between the CI and the UPR. I am also not aware of any other commentator who would develop this independentism-justifying strategy from the TSI in the way in which I do in this chapter.

Consider Arthur Ripstein's example of a tort of innocent trespass: if I build a treehouse on your property, because I misread the map, then my innocent intention (and maxim) to build the treehouse on my property leads nevertheless to a material wrong – I use your property without your authorization.[15]

Merely formal wrongs, by contrast, occur when someone tries to wrong another person, yet fails to do so. Say, Richard and Edward want the same job.[16] To prevent Edward from attending the interview, Richard tries to steal the spark plugs from Edward's car, so that Edward cannot drive to the interview; yet, by mistake, Richard removes the spark plugs from his own car. Richard has not wronged Edward, but this does not mean that he has not acted wrongly at all – this is a merely formal wrong.

According to the TSI, a confirmation of the accuracy of this reading is provided by Kant's definition of 'transgression' ('a deed contrary to duty', MS 6:224), which includes both material and formal wrongs:

> An *unintentional* transgression which can still be imputed to the agent is called a mere *fault* (*culpa*). An *intentional* transgression (i.e. one accompanied by consciousness of its being a transgression) is called a *crime* (*dolus*). (MS 6:224)

For the TSI, an intentional transgression generates a formal wrong; by contrast, an unintentional transgression, which can still be imputed to the agent, leads to a material wrong. For instance, misreading the map and mistakenly building my tree house on your property would be considered a mere fault, a merely material wrong. Such mistakes, on this reading, although innocently committed, can still be imputed to the agent in a civil lawsuit, but they are not crimes. Crimes have objectionable maxims, such as that of interfering with another person's property, in order to deprive them of a chance to compete for a job.

Again, for the TSI, Kant seems to confirm this, because he says that material wrongs do 'not always presuppose in the subject a principle of doing so [namely, committing an injustice]' (VRML 8:429). In other words, on TSI's reading of Kant, merely material wrongs are not performed on wrongful maxims (but on innocent maxims). Moreover, Kant suggests that a formal wrong which 'escapes being punishable merely by accident can be condemned as wrong even in accordance with external laws' (VRML 8:427). In the example of Edward and Richard above, if Richard mistakenly removes his own spark plugs, then Edward will be able

[15] Ripstein, *Force and Freedom*, 380–1. [16] Concerning this example, see n. 14.

to drive to the interview on the next day. To the TSI, this seems to suggest that, although by accident Richard does not commit a material wrong, his action might still be condemned as wrong even according to external laws; given its maxim of intending to wrong another person, the action is (merely) formally wrong.

On this interpretation of the distinction between material and formal wrongs, certain wrongs are both formal and material – the performed actions represent intentional transgressions, but also violate the rights of individuals (for instance, in the case of a thief, the right to property). Other wrongs are merely formal, when the perpetrators are unsuccessful in their attempt to violate a particular person's or specific individuals' rights. Still other wrongs are merely material, as in the case of an unintentional, but still imputable, transgression.[17] Moreover, on this interpretation, P1 and P2 are normatively irreducible, since a merely material wrong, which does not pass P1, will nevertheless pass the test offered by P2 (given that the action which does not pass P1 as a merely material wrong is performed on an innocent maxim); similarly, a merely formal wrong, which does not pass P2, will nevertheless satisfy P1 (given that the respective action is performed on a maxim rejected by P2, but produces no material wrong, so will not be rejected by P1).

4.2.3 *Merely Material Wrongs and Unintentional Transgressions*

Now, the notion of a merely formal wrong and its connection with the notion of an intentional transgression seem quite clear. By contrast, the notions of a merely material wrong and of an unintentional transgression seem more obscure. To be sure, Kant is quite clear about the notion of something's being unintentional; in his definition of intentional transgression, he specifies that by an intentional transgression he means one accompanied by consciousness of its being a transgression. (MS 6:224) Hence, an unintentional transgression is one which is not accompanied by consciousness of its being a transgression. It follows that, for the TSI, a merely

[17] P1 and P2 are stated in Kant's UPR, but separated as disjuncts. Given that P1 and P2 are supposed to be normatively distinct and possibly irreducible, an action is right if it meets *both* P1 and P1; either of them would not be sufficient. Yet, Kant does formulate the UPR as a *disjunction* with P1 and P2 as disjuncts. A possible reply is that this is an editorial mistake. Another reply is that the UPR is not meant to set the conditions for an action's rightness, but to describe the ways in which an action may be right: satisfying P1 just shows one way in which an action may be right (materially) and satisfying P2 just shows another way in which an action may be right (formally). Why did Kant not specify the UPR in this way? The answer related to poor editorial work could be invoked again here.

material wrong is supposed to be such an unintentional transgression, which is still imputable; however, when is such a transgression imputable?

4.2.3.1 Conceptual Framework of Imputation

Kant's account of imputation is complex, particularly if we consider the context in which he was writing.[18] Nevertheless, for my argument here, it is sufficient to mention the general framework of his account and one particular aspect; first, concerning the general framework, Kant says:

> *Imputation* (*imputatio*) in the moral sense is the *judgement* by which someone is regarded as the author (*causa libera*) of an action, which is then called a *deed* (*factum*) and stands under laws. If the judgement also carries with it the rightful consequences of the deed, it is an imputation having rightful force (*imputatio iudiciara s. valida*); otherwise it is merely an imputation *appraising* the deed (*imputatio diiudicatoria*). (MS 6:227)

One preliminary clarification concerns the notions of author of an action and of a deed. A deed is a specific type of action, more exactly, an action 'insofar as it comes under obligatory laws and hence insofar as the subject, in doing it, is considered in terms of the freedom of his choice' (MS 6:223). Some actions may not have moral import and, hence, may not fall under the jurisdiction of obligatory laws. For instance, whether I choose orange or papaya juice as a drink when offered is an action without moral relevance, unless some relevant conditions are in place (such as, that the orange juice producer is unethical). In this case, my choice will not be constrained by any moral obligatory laws. By contrast, for those actions, which do have moral import, we can further consider whether the agent will observe the respective moral obligation(s) or not.

Now, for Kant, '*freedom* of choice is this independence from being *determined* by sensible impulses' (MS 6:213). Because a deed is that action which comes under obligatory laws, the agent who performs a morally relevant action would need to act on the obligatory laws, even when her sensible impulses motivate her to act differently. So it is for this reason that Kant regards a deed as an action for which the subject, in performing the action, is considered in terms of the freedom of their choice. By contrast, a morally irrelevant action is not considered in relation to morally obligatory laws and, hence, the question whether the person performing it could have

[18] For instance, for a discussion of Kant's engagement with what is called today the '*versari*' rule, as well as Wolff's and Pufendorf's accounts, see Sharon B. Byrd and Joachim Hruschka, *Kant's* Doctrine of Right*: A Commentary*, Cambridge: Cambridge University Press, 2010, esp. ch. 14 §4 and Appendix II.

observed the laws even when this required acting independently from the sensible impulses (and, hence, whether the person had freedom of choice) does not apply.

Now, for the notion of the author of an action, we have the necessary conceptual background. Kant notes that, by performing such an action (i.e. a deed), the agent 'is regarded as the *author* of its effect, and this, together with the action itself, can be *imputed* to him' (MS 6:223). In other words, a person is the author of an action when the person has freedom of choice, that is, when the person could act independently of her sensible impulses. This does not mean that a person who satisfies some subjective impulses by acting could not count as being the author of the action, since what is important is that the person *could have acted* independently from sensible impulses.

4.2.3.2 Moral Imputation

With the notions of author of an action and deed clarified, we can return to Kant's general account of imputation. In the previous quotation, we had a threefold distinction between moral, appraising or judging, and rightfully forceful imputation ['Zurechnung (*imputatio*) in moralischer Bedeutung'/ 'beurteilende Zurechnung (*imputatio diiudicatoria*)'/'rechtkräftige Zurechnung (*imputatio iudiciaria s. valida*)']. Moral imputation judges whether the agent can be considered the author of the respective action. Appraising imputation evaluates the attributed action as right or wrong, and, as a result, as we will see, whether the action and its consequences require that the agent be rewarded, punished, or simply not considered for the purpose of punishment or reward. Finally, the rightfully forceful imputation determines the reward or punishment appropriate in the case of an action or its consequences, for which a reward or punishment is appropriate.

According to Kant,

> [i]f someone does *more* in the way of duty than he can be constrained by law to do, what he does is *meritorious* (*meritum*); if what he does is just exactly what the law *requires*, he does *what is owed* (*debitum*); finally, if what he does is *less* than the law requires, it is morally *culpable* (*demeritum*). (MS 6:227)

Doing what is meritorious, owed, and culpable is defined by Kant in relation to what the law requires and, in particular, as doing more than, exactly what, and less than, the law requires. Kant specifies, however, that: 'The good or bad results of an action that is owed, like the results of omitting a meritorious action, cannot be imputed to the subject [. . .]. The good results of a meritorious action, like the bad results of a wrongful action, can be imputed to the subject [. . .]' (MS 6:228).

Doing exactly what the law requires is doing what is owed, so the agent does not qualify either for a reward or for punishment. Omitting an action which would do more than the law requires and simply doing what the law requires, again, do not qualify the agent either for reward or for punishment. Moreover, the good or bad consequences of such actions are not imputable to the agent. By contrast, doing less than the law requires or doing more than the law requires makes the agent culpable or meritorious, respectively, and, hence entitles the agent to punishment or reward. The bad or good results of these actions can also be imputed to the agent.

This point can be illustrated with Kant's famous examples from 'A Supposed Right to Lie from Philanthropy'. The would-be murderer is pursuing my friend, who tries to escape by taking refuge in my house; the murderer knocks on the door and asks me whether I know my friend's whereabouts; according to Kant:

> If you have *by a lie* prevented someone just now bent on murder from committing the deed, then you are legally accountable for all the consequences that might arise from it. But if you have kept strictly to the truth, then public justice can hold nothing against you, whatever the unforeseen consequences might be. It is still possible that, after you have honestly answered 'yes' to the murderer's question as to whether his enemy is at home, the latter has nevertheless gone out unnoticed, so that he would not meet the murderer and the deed would not be done; but if you had lied and said that he is not at home, and he has actually gone out (though you are not aware of it), so that the murderer encounters him while going away and perpetrates his deed on him, then you can by right be prosecuted as the author of his death. For if you had told the truth to the best of your knowledge, then neighbours might have come and apprehended the murderer while he was searching the house for his enemy and the deed would have been prevented. (VRML 8:427)

Hence, a wrong action makes the agent culpable not only for the action itself, but also for all of the action's consequences, no matter how unforeseeable. By contrast, the right action leaves the agent irreproachable, from the perspective of justice, both with regard to the action and to its consequences. While Kant has been criticized for his answer to the problem of the murderer at the door, his account of imputation has been defended as plausible.[19] However, one question about this account

[19] See, for instance, Andrews Reath, 'Agency and the Imputation of Consequences in Kant's Ethics', in *Agency and Autonomy in Kant's Moral Theory: Selected Essays*, Oxford: Oxford University Press, 2006, 250–69.

concerns the notions of right and wrong actions, which lead differently to imputation. According to TSI, we have two types of notion of right/wrong, which are normatively irreducible. Hence, the question is whether both material and formal right/wrong actions have the same implications for imputation.

I think the answer here is that only formally wrong/right actions should be considered. This is because a material wrong is defined as an action physically incompatible with the rights of other individuals. Yet, an action's physical incompatibility is not a matter of the agent's will; it is, however, a matter of the agent's will to be aware of existing legislation, to draw conclusions about legal restrictions in specific circumstances, and to formulate a maxim and rules of actions that are in accordance with what the law requires. An action's physical incompatibility with other individuals' rights might be the result of various contingent factors beyond the agent's control. An agent may be blown by strong winds onto another person's property or may be misguided by the directions of a distracted police officer or may damage another person's property due to a device's manufacturing fault.[20] Hence, there can be no conclusions drawn about imputation from a material wrong.

This is one reason why the distinction between material and formal wrongs, as presented by the TSI, cannot track Kant's distinction between intentional and unintentional transgressions. Unintentional transgressions are always transgressions, that is, deeds contrary to duty, but material wrongs need not always be contrary to duty, although they are physically incompatible with the rights of some individuals. Material wrongs can be starting points for a consideration of whether the agent can be regarded as the author of the action under consideration, whether another agent is the author, or whether there is no moral agent authoring the action, but only a natural factor causing a particular effect.[21]

4.2.3.3 Complex Moral Imputation and Judging Imputation

This is, in fact, the particular aspect of Kant's account of imputation, which I said would be useful for my purpose in this chapter. Consider a

[20] For instance, '[y]ou are not a trespasser if the wind blows you onto your neighbor's land, but you are if you are mistaken about where the boundary is, because you are still using another person's land' (Ripstein, *Force and Freedom*, 381).

[21] To be sure, the implication is that, contrary to the TSI, according to Kant, if it turns out that a physical incompatibility with the rights of some individuals is the effect of some natural factor, then the source of this incompatibility is not a wrong. The TSI would regard it as a 'merely material wrong', but, in fact, 'wrong' here would not be the appropriate term, since the source of this incompatibility is not morally imputable. I am grateful to Philipp-Alexander Hirsch and Martin Brecher for suggesting I clarify the expression 'material wrong' here.

situation in which more than one action contributes to a particularly bad outcome. If some of these contributing actions are performed in accordance with their respective obligatory laws, whereas others are performed against these laws, then the bad outcome will be imputed to the author(s) of the wrongful actions. It might well be that this bad outcome would not have been possible without the actions which observe obligatory laws; yet, according to the rules of imputation which represent Kant's account, the moral author of the bad outcome will be the author(s) of the wrongful actions.

For instance, say I need to pay my mortgage rate by a certain day of the month. Throughout the month I am being very careful about how I spend my monthly salary, in order to have sufficient funds to pay to the bank. On the day my mortgage rate is due, on my way to the bank, I go to a shop to buy some food, pay for the food, and the shopkeeper gives me the right change, part of which is needed for my mortgage payment. Without being aware of this, the shopkeeper includes in the change counterfeit money, with which another customer had just paid. When I go to the bank to pay, I end up being arrested. In order for the bad outcome of circulating counterfeit money to occur, a series of actions have had to take place, which represent exactly what the law requires (such as, the fact that I spend my money carefully in order to be able to pay the amount I owe or the fact that the shopkeeper gives me the right change, which includes money for the mortgage rate); yet, culpable for this outcome is only the person who produced the fake money and used it.[22]

Let us assume, however, that I am the author of the action which takes me on my neighbour's property (which, as we have seen, only requires my freedom of choice) – I get onto my neighbour's property, as a result of a set of decisions I make. We have seen that, for Kant, the process of moral imputation involves also a process of assessing the moral status of the action I authored – together, these two forms of judgement are called by Kant appraising imputation. Again, the fact that the action under consideration is physically incompatible with, say, the rights of another person is just a starting point for the process of appraising imputation. Since there are rights of other individuals, which need to be considered, and since, in this case, I can be expected to be aware of these rights (and the fact that I follow a map is an indication that I am), the question is how my action did lead to a physical incompatibility with those rights.

[22] The shopkeeper might also be culpable if there is an expectation that she verifies the authenticity of the banknotes before accepting them.

Various things may concur to produce this result: I may have taken the wrong edition of the map or I may be an incompetent map-reader or I may be negligent or any combinations of these and other similar factors. All these are situations in which what I do is wrong, since I fail to take reasonable steps to make sure I am not trespassing and, hence, not infringing on the legitimate rights of other individuals. It follows that I am liable for my action and for the consequences of this action. For instance, as my action leads me to being on my neighbour's property, the fact that the treehouse I built is on the neighbour's property, rather than on mine, is a result of my initial wrongful action and I need to compensate the neighbour for this appropriately.

But imagine now that I am being careful to take with me the latest edition of the map, I have just refreshed my knowledge of map-reading the day before, and I am concentrating to read the map and follow its guidance. There is nothing more that I can reasonably be expected to do, in order to make sure that the existing legitimate norms (for instance, those constituting the relevant rights of other persons) are respected. Yet there is a mistake in the map, and I end up building a treehouse for my children on the neighbour's property. Hence, the fact that I am mistaken about the boundary of my property does not necessarily imply that the action which takes me on my neighbour's property is wrongful.

The case of the mistake in the map, which leads (precisely because I am careful to follow the map accurately) to being on my neighbour's property is, I take it, the outcome of a series of actions; some of these are my actions, but, in performing them, I do the right thing and am irreproachable; as Kant puts it, 'public justice can hold nothing against [me]' (VRML 8:427); yet, various factors beyond my control affect the performance of my action. My actions satisfy what is owed in accordance with the relevant obligatory laws and, hence, these actions are right, and the bad results are not imputable (in any sense) to me (but perhaps to the cartographer, editor, or publisher of the map).[23]

[23] Let me mention, for the sake of completeness, that, when it turns out that my action is less than it is owed by obligatory laws, there is still the question of judiciary imputation, namely, the judgement of the punishment that is the appropriate response to my wrongful action and its bad results. This, too, is a complex process, because, according to Kant, 'the state of mind of the subject, whether he committed the deed in a state of agitation or with cool deliberation, makes a difference in imputation, which has results' (MS 6:228). The issue of judiciary imputation, however, goes beyond the scope of this chapter and will not be discussed further here. I make one note of clarification: I might end up compensating the neighbour for the damage, although I am irreproachable – this is, of course, not because the treehouse would be the result of some wrongful action I performed (since otherwise I would not be irreproachable); it might be a

4.3 The Argument against the Independentist Strategy

To sum up, one of the issues of the TSI is the construal of Kant's distinction between formal and material wrongs. For instance, Kant talks about this distinction at MS 6:307–8; in the footnote to 6:307, he says: 'This distinction between what is merely formally wrong and what is also materially wrong has many applications in the doctrine of right.' This, however, suggests a different distinction from that offered by the TSI: Kant does not mention anything about a merely material wrong; he only talks about formal wrongs, which may or may not be at the same time material. The intention to be and remain in the state of nature may be incompatible with no particular person's rights, but, Kant adds, in general it does 'wrong to the highest degree by willing to be and to remain in a condition that is not rightful, that is, in which no one is assured of what is his against violence' (MS 6:307–8).

Wrongs are, therefore, always formal; when they also go against particular individuals' rights, they are also material; otherwise, they are merely formal. It follows that the distinction between intentional and unintentional transgressions is also misconstrued by the TSI: both these transgressions are formal wrongs and both may be merely formal or, if not merely formal, then formal and material. The case of negligence seems to be one case Kant has in mind, when he talks about the second type of transgression, the unintentional transgression he calls fault. This is unintentional, since, for instance, I do not intend to misread the map (in the case where the map is accurate and I am distracted), although I can be said to intend to be negligent or at least I can be said to accept the risk, given that I do not do anything to address this; instead, misreading the map is an unintended, although perhaps expected, result of being negligent when I try to get a treehouse built on my property.[24] There are contemporary

pragmatic decision on my part not to waste time by trying to get the publisher of the map to pay or a decision not to upset my neighbour by delaying the compensation and reparation of the damage or it might be a mistake (assuming the account presented here is correct) in the judgement of the person who has the authority to make the decision and who happens to have a different account of imputation than the Kantian account I presented here; other similar practical or pragmatic reasons are possible.

[24] A similar example considered in the literature is that of a philosopher, who acts on the maxim 'I will drive to the store to get some milk.' On the way, she is distracted by thoughts about metaethics, fails to notice a red light, and hits another vehicle. This is also a case of negligence, and the maxim of action should reflect this. Consider now those cases, in which we fail to pay particular attention and also fail to realize that we have not paid sufficient attention (I am grateful to Luke Davies for raising this example). I think that, for the purposes of imputation, the situation is the same as that in which I realize I am being negligent. Say I am distracted by the conversation in the car; I do not realize that

accounts of negligence along Kantian lines, which attempt to account precisely for this 'paradox' of imputability without intention.[25]

We have seen that the interpretation of the distinction between material and formal wrongs as part of the TSI seems to be confirmed by two of Kant's claims concerning these wrongs. First, Kant says that material wrongs do 'not always presuppose in the subject a principle of doing so [namely, committing an injustice]' (VRML 8:429). Yet, as we have seen, this applies to cases of negligence and also cases of wrongful acts which have unexpected bad consequences. Secondly, Kant suggests that a formal wrong, which 'escapes being punishable merely by accident can be condemned as wrong even in accordance with external laws' (VRML 8:427). The context for this claim is Kant's example of the murderer at the door, from 'On a Supposed Right to Lie from Philanthropy', in particular, the situation in which a lie told to the murderer may not be punishable, given the context (which is accidental), but, through its consequences, can become punishable, as in the case of Kant's imagined situation, where the potential victim leaves the house without the owner's knowledge, the owner tells a lie to the would-be murderer, and the murderer encounters the potential victim and kills her. Again, here we have a case of accidental consequences of wrongful actions, rather than a case of a merely formal wrong.

I started with a brief presentation of an approach, which can use the TSI, that is, the view that the UPR has in fact two normatively irreducible parts – one concerning formal, and the other one identifying material, wrongs. If correct, this would mean that Kant's view could not be classed

the conversation distracts me, and I end up scratching my car. The situation in which I do not realize I am being distracted might actually be more serious than that in which I am aware I am distracted. Unless some pathological elements are involved, not being aware that I was not paying attention might mean that I will be required to undertake some exercises of concentration and reflection.

[25] For instance, for Erasmus Mayr, 'Unwitting Omissions, Mistakes and Responsibility', in George Pavlakos and Veronica Rodriguez-Blanco (eds.), *Agency, Negligence and Responsibility*, Cambridge: Cambridge University Press, 2021, 37–56: '[i]n everyday life, we hold one another responsible not only for what we do, or fail to do, intentionally or knowingly, but also for many things we do or fail to do unintentionally or inadvertently. [. . .] That these reactions are so commonplace suggests one can be morally responsible for one's actions and omissions even when one has neither decided on them nor been aware, at the time, that one was acting in a morally problematic way' (Mayr, 'Unwitting Omissions', 37). The account proposed by Mayr is that 'we are only blameworthy for an unwitting omission or similar failure, [. . .] if it manifests a failure to care sufficiently about morality and its general principles and values' (Mayr, 'Unwitting Omissions', 38). See also Joseph Raz, 'Responsibility and the Negligence Standard', *Oxford Journal of Legal Studies* 30 (2010), 1–18, for an analysis of negligence and a new conception of responsibility. I am grateful to George Pavlakos for suggesting these texts as useful for my argument.

as dependentist (whether simple or complex[26]); on the contrary, this may even suggest that the UPR can be a ground (perhaps in a complex way) for the CI (say, P1 or P2 could ground the CI). In this section, I have, however, claimed that the two normative components identified by TSI as part of the UPR (P1 and P2) are not irreducibly distinct in their normative functions. They both formulate what it means for an action to be formally wrong with a difference of emphasis – P1, on actions, and P2, on maxims. There are no actions without maxims and no maxims without actions in Kant's philosophy of action, and the focus on the action or its maxim places emphasis on distinct important aspects – the physical, external character of the action and its intention.[27] There is, therefore, nothing surprising in the fact that Kant formulates the UPR in the way in which he does in the *Metaphysik der Sitten*.

4.4 Conclusion

In this chapter, I have developed, considered, and rejected a significant strategy that an independentist about the relation in Kant between ethics (in particular, the CI) and right (specifically, the UPR) can mobilize to motivate their reading. In my response, I identified some problems with this strategy and with the reading of Kant it relies on (more exactly, the TSI) and indirectly provided some further support for a complex dependentist position, which I find more convincing.

Systematically, what I find particularly significant about the complex dependentist reading is that it enables an account of political-juridical standards, which preserves a significant connection with ethical normativity, while at the same time it gives serious consideration to those aspects of political-juridical standards which distinguish them from ethical principles.

Even if we accept that the UPR represents a single standard – as I have argued in this chapter – a number of other strategies for supporting independentism can be formulated, including an argument from the innate right of humanity[28] and two paradoxes – one concerning juridical

[26] As these positions have been presented in Section 4.1.

[27] In this volume, Ludwig (Chapter 2) and Hirsch (Chapter 5) are in agreement with this interpretation of Kant.

[28] This is suggested by certain readings of Ripstein (for instance, *Force and Freedom*, 381) as defending an independentist, rather than a dependentist, account of the relation between the UPR and the CI, e.g. Ruhi M. Demiray, 'The Intrinsic Normativity of Law in Light of Kant's *Doctrine of Right*', *Contextos Kantianos* 3 (2016), 161–87; for a more detailed presentation of the context of his

imperatives[29] and a second one concerning their performance's motivation.[30]

I have argued elsewhere how the paradox of juridical imperatives can be answered and why the best account of the relation between the CI and the UPR is a complex dependentist one.[31] Although I think the other independentism-justifying strategies can be rejected, these arguments are not needed for the purpose of this chapter and they will have to be presented elsewhere; in rejecting the argument of the first strategy, this chapter has also offered indirect support for the complex dependentist position, which I view as both the most philosophically convincing and the most accurate reading of Kant.

argument, see Demiray, 'Natural Law Theory, Legal Positivism and the Normativity of Law', *The European Legacy* 20 (2015), 807–26. A related argument is also offered by Christian Rostbøll, 'Kant and the Critique of the Ethics-First Approach to Politics', *Critical Review of International Social and Political Philosophy* 22 (2019), 55–70. For a related discussion of the role the innate right of humanity plays in Kant, see Katrin Flikschuh, 'Innate Right and Acquired Right in Arthur Ripstein's *Force and Freedom*', *Jurisprudence* 1 (2010), 295–304.

29 See, for instance, Marcus Willaschek, 'Which Imperatives for Right? On the Non-prescriptive Character of Juridical Laws in Kant's Metaphysics of Morals', in Mark Timmons (ed.), *Kant's Metaphysics of Morals: Interpretative Essays*, Oxford: Oxford University Press, 2002, 65–88.

30 See Andre S. Campos, 'Kant on Acting from Juridical Duty', *International Journal of Philosophical Studies* 27 (2019), 498–514.

31 Baiasu, 'Right's Complex Relation'.

PART II

Sanctions and Coercion: A Problem for a Derivational Reading?

CHAPTER 5

Legal Coercion as a Moral Problem?

Kant on the Enforcement of Rights and the Limits of Moral Personality

Philipp-Alexander Hirsch

The question of whether or not Kant's Philosophy of Right[1] can be understood as part of his critical moral[2] philosophy has always been disputed. One of the main arguments in favour of the independence of Right from morality relates to the coercive power that is, according to Kant, conceptually associated with Right: 'Right and authorization to use coercion [. . .] mean one and the same thing.'[3] Accordingly, proponents of the *independence thesis* hold that if Right and the power to coerce were analytically linked, then Right as the epitome of heteronomy (i.e. external lawgiving) could not possibly appeal to moral autonomy (or the categorical imperative) as its grounding principle.[4] However, does the authority to

Ancestors of this chapter were presented at the 'Law and Morality in Kant' conference held at the University of Göttingen and a workshop of the MAEN-Network. I am indebted to the respective audiences for valuable feedback, in particular to Luke Davies and Fiorella Tomassini, who acted as my brilliant commentator at the Göttingen conference.

1 I have opted to use the term 'Right', since the German 'Recht' and its cognates (such as 'rechtlich') have no exact English equivalent. Using 'Right' holds the merit of preserving some of this ambiguity in a way that 'law' does not.

2 I use the term 'moral' as an attribute of laws in the Kantian sense, i.e. 'moral(s)' is the common generic term for 'Right'/'doctrine of right' (*Recht, Rechtslehre*) on the one hand and 'ethics'/'doctrine of virtue' (*Tugend, Ethik, Tugendlehre*) on the other. Where 'morality' does not refer to laws, but instead (as the opposite of 'legality') describes the specifically ethical relationship of actions to moral laws, I will indicate this.

3 RL 6:232.

4 This objection has been raised in particular by Markus Willaschek, 'Right and Coercion: Can Kant's Conception of Right be Derived from His Moral Theory?', *International Journal of Philosophical Studies*, 17/1 (2009), 49–70, at 59f.; Markus Willaschek, 'The Non-Derivability of Kantian Right from the Categorical Imperative: A Response to Nance', *International Journal of Philosophical Studies*, 20/4 (2012), 557–64, at 557. Also cf. Willaschek in this volume (Chapter 1). According to him, coercive power can neither be derived from the autonomy theorem nor from the categorical imperative (neither as per the Formula of Humanity nor as per the Formula of Universal Law). Arthur Ripstein, *Force and Freedom: Kant's Legal and Political Philosophy*, Cambridge, MA: Harvard University Press, 2009, 355, 359, 388 voices similar doubts. In addition, this objection is at a minimum implicit in most independentist readings, cf. Allen W. Wood, 'The Final Form of Kant's Practical Philosophy', in Mark Timmons (ed.), *Kant's Metaphysics of Morals: Interpretative Essays*, Oxford: Oxford University Press, 2002, 1–21, at 5ff. or Thomas Pogge, 'Is Kant's *Rechtslehre* a

coerce really call into question the dependence of Right on Kant's moral philosophy? In this chapter, I will propose the alternative, opposite view that – on Kantian grounds – coercion as a normative problem only becomes explicable *against* Kant's critical moral philosophy. For it is the moral personality of the coerced that calls for a normative justification of coercion in the first place (1). That said, coercion that does not violate one's moral personality becomes morally irrelevant since moral personality is conceptionally restricted. Thus, the very embedding of Right in Kant's critical moral philosophy provides a two-way solution: an explanation for why coercion is a normative problem in the first place; and a justification as to what extent coercion is legitimate. However, proponents of the *independence thesis* aim to explain coercion as an analytical implication of the notion of equal, relational freedom and thus miss this crucial dual dependence on Kant's critical moral philosophy. Consequently, they are neither able to offer a *Kantian* justification for the normative bindingness nor for the enforceability of Right. (2). Conversely, tracing coercion back to the limits of moral personality does not only explain why coercive force is grounded in moral personality (and autonomy as its constitutive principle). Even more importantly, it requires us to reconsider whether Kant is able to argue consistently against the external enforceability of internal perfect duties (e.g. the prohibition of suicide) (3).

5.1 Coercion as a Moral Problem and Unlawful Treatment as a Mere Means

Why is somebody legally entitled to coerce someone else? – Before explaining why this is fundamentally the wrong question, I would first like to clarify what I mean when I use the term *coercion* with reference to Kant. From Kant's perspective – echoed by contemporary legal theory – coercion can mean two things: first, physical coercion in the sense of *vis absoluta* (i.e. the factual restriction of action); and, second, psychological coercion in the sense of *vis compulsiva* (i.e. the pathological motivation by conflicting sensual inclinations, e.g. fear of punishment). When Kant analytically

"Comprehensive Liberalism"?', in Mark Timmons (ed.), *Kant's Metaphysics of Morals: Interpretative Essays*, Oxford: Oxford University Press, 2002, 133–58, at 141f. However, some proponents of a derivationist reading of Kant's legal philosophy also see a problem here, e.g. Wolfgang Kersting, *Wohlgeordnete Freiheit: Immanuel Kants Rechts- und Staatsphilosophie*, Berlin: De Gruyter, 1984, 29f. For a view questioning or at least problematizing the derivation of Right from the categorical imperative in view of legal coercion, cf. Paul Guyer, 'Kant's Deductions of the Principles of Right', in Mark Timmons (ed.), *Kant's Metaphysics of Morals: Interpretative Essays*, Oxford: Oxford University Press, 2002, 23–64, at 46ff. and Christoph Horn, *Nichtideale Normativität: Ein neuer Blick auf Kants politische Philosophie*, Berlin: Suhrkamp, 2014, 46ff.

derives the authority to coerce from the concepts of *right* and *wrong* in § D of the Introduction into the Doctrine of Right, he speaks of coercion in the former sense:

> [C]oercion is a hindrance or resistance to freedom. Therefore, if a certain use of freedom is itself a hindrance to freedom in accordance with universal laws (i.e., wrong), coercion that is opposed to this (as a *hindering of a hindrance to freedom*) is consistent with freedom in accordance with universal laws, that is, it is right.[5]

Since Kant is concerned with factual resistance to a wrongful act here, coercion under § D can be taken to mean only physical coercion in the sense of *vis absoluta*. This is to be distinguished from psychological coercion in the sense of *vis compulsiva*, which consists in the prospect of physical coercion in response to potential wrongdoing. In connection with a universal law, such psychological coercion can even be considered the epitome of external, juridical lawgiving as referred to by Kant in the Introduction into the Metaphysics of Morals.[6] To compel someone to do something in this latter sense means nothing other than to act as an external, juridical legislator – that is, as someone who declares the duty to the obligor and links it to a pathological incentive.[7] This chapter will focus on coercion in the sense of *vis absoluta* and disregard *vis compulsiva*.

My main argument is that the coercive power of Right is less a problem than evidence for a derivational reading of Kant's legal philosophy. This is due to the fact that the authority to coerce does not need to be derived from the categorical imperative at all if one understands Right as an integral part of Kant's critical moral philosophy. While on the surface this might sound surprising, it becomes clear when we realize that Kant's actual issue is to demonstrate the inadmissibility of coercion. The central question for Kant is therefore not *Why and when may I coerce someone?*, but rather *Why and when may I* ***not*** *coerce someone?*.

[5] RL 6:231. [6] Cf. RL 6:218f.

[7] That coercion is part of every lawgiving (be it ethical or juridical) follows directly from Kant's concept of duty, to which every form of lawgiving refers: 'The very *concept of duty* is already the concept of a necessitation (constraint) of free choice through the law. This constraint may be an *external constraint* or a *self-constraint*' (TL 6:379). What makes this coercion entailed in the concept of duty an external constraint (i.e. *external lawgiving*), however, is that it is someone other than the obligor who 'is the *lawgiver* (*legislator*)' and 'commands (*imperans*) through a law. He is the author (*autor*) of the obligation in accordance with the law' (RL 6:227). What is more, if this external lawgiving does not make the 'duty the incentive' but draws the incentive 'from pathological determining grounds of choice' (RL 6:219), then it constitutes *juridical lawgiving*, which is nothing other than *vis compulsiva*. For more details on Kant's concept of *lawgiving* in this context, cf. Philipp-Alexander Hirsch, *Freiheit und Staatlichkeit bei Kant: Die autonomietheoretische Begründung von Recht und Staat und das Widerstandsproblem*, Berlin: De Gruyter, 2017, 123ff.

Coercion (in the sense of using physical force) only becomes a normative problem when someone can legitimately claim not to be coerced. Therefore, use of force or coercion in any form towards stones, plants, or animals[8] is always normatively permissible. This is the case because, according to Kant, stones, plants, and animals lack moral personality, that is, they are not suitable subjects of moral (i.e. legal and ethical) entitlements and duties.[9] Coercion does not become a normative problem until a person is involved.[10] This is already implied in Kant's definition of the 'concept of right, insofar as it is related to an obligation corresponding to it (i.e., *the moral concept of right*)' in § B of the 'Introduction to the Doctrine of Right',[11] according to which Right concerns the intersubjective relationship of persons. Consequently, the question of the permissibility of legal coercion, which is raised in §§ C–E, arises only for them. Kant mapped this out clearly as early as 1784 in the Feyerabend lecture on natural law:

> *Res* is that in regard to which another's freedom can in no way be limited if it is used. The thing has no freedom, thus it can certainly not be wronged, thus it does not limit my freedom. But *persona*, a free being, limits my freedom. [. . .] A freedom is limited through itself. Things that have no freedom can thus not be limited in their freedom. In relation to beings who do have freedom the freedom of everyone else is limited. The latter is a person, the former a thing.[12]

Unlike things, persons enjoy the status of being subjects of rights and duties and as such cannot be coerced to do something or used by others

[8] While this might be a somewhat odd way of framing coercion and force, it enables me to illustrate the core of my argument.

[9] Animate and inanimate matter without pure practical reason is at most the object of rights and duties, but never the subject of them. Thus, in RL 6:241, Kant states that there is no 'relation in terms of rights of human beings toward beings that have neither rights nor duties [. . .] [f]or these are beings lacking reason, which can neither bind us nor by which we can be bound'. Animals also fall under this category. They are only being protected reflexively, insofar as cruelty to animals violates a duty of man against himself. Cf. TL 6:443.

[10] This is also pointed out by Bernd Ludwig, 'Sympathy for the Devil(s)? Personality and Legal Coercion in Kant's Doctrine of Law', *Jurisprudence* 6 (2015), 25–44, at 42: 'If the other rational being is a non-person, that is, a mere *thing* without any rights, then any kind of coercion is morally permissible under all possible circumstances.'

[11] Cf. RL 6:230.

[12] V-NR/Feyerabend 27:1335 (my translation; the translation by Rauscher and Westphal is not reliable here, nor in the other passages I have quoted from V-NR/Feyerabend as well as VARL and VATP). The restriction of freedom that Kant speaks of here is subsequently identified in the lecture as self-legislated, with which he refers to the autonomy theorem and the doctrine of transcendental freedom. For a more detailed account, cf. Philipp-Alexander Hirsch, *Kants Einleitung in die Rechtslehre von 1784: Immanuel Kants Rechtsbegriff in der Moralvorlesung 'Mrongovius II' und der Naturrechtsvorlesung 'Feyerabend' von 1784 sowie in der 'Metaphysik der Sitten' von 1797*, Göttingen: Universitätsverlag Göttingen, 2012, 90ff. and with the same reasoning, also cf. Kant's remarks in GMS 4:428ff.

without further justification.[13] It follows that the plurality of persons generates the problem of legitimate coercion in the first place. Yet why should it be that a person has this special standing not to be coerced? As I will outline in this chapter, Kant sees the reason for this in the fact that a person is an autonomous being and as such an end in herself or himself. Or to put it differently: without presupposing Kant's critical moral philosophy and the autonomy theorem on which it is based, coercion – at least for Kant[14] – ceases to be a normative problem.[15] This raises two questions: what is the justificatory relationship between the doctrine of Right and Kant's critical moral philosophy? And how can legal coercion be explained with reference to this?

Let me start with the first question:[16] If we interpret Kant's legal philosophy against his critical moral philosophy, then someone only has rights because and to the extent that she is an end in herself. A violation of rights is nothing more than a treatment of that person as a mere means; and, although often incorrectly denied, any treatment of another person as a mere means constitutes a breach of a legal duty.[17] A legally valid contract, for example, requires that the other party not be treated merely as a means, that is, that his contractual interests are met. Likewise, to infringe upon

[13] This is most clearly stated by Kant in TL 6:462, where he says that the human being 'must always be used at the same time as an end. It is just in this that his dignity (personality) consists, by which he raises himself above all other beings in the world that are not human beings and yet can be used, and so over all things.'

[14] My aim here is to explain Kant's concept of things. However, whether we can substitute a different account of the value/moral worth of a person for Kant's account is another story. I do not think that it is impossible to build a Kantian philosophy of law and politics on a different foundation. However, this would require a more detailed elaboration, which lies outside the scope of this chapter.

[15] Here and in the following, I refer to a 'normative' problem or a 'normative' justification; for now, this leaves the question unanswered whether or not Kant endorses a separate, genuinely independent normativity of Right in addition to the normativity of morality. However, subsequent sections (cf. pp. 106ff.) will clarify that Kant does not acknowledge such normativity – making all normativity moral.

[16] For a detailed account of the relationship between law and morality according to Kant, cf. Hirsch, *Freiheit und Staatlichkeit bei Kant*, 67ff.

[17] As the focus of this chapter is legal coercion, I can only touch on this point: contrary to what some authors (e.g. Willaschek, 'Right and Coercion', 61) claim, Kant even considers promissory courtesies (e.g. the promise to help a friend move house) to represent enforceable legal obligations. Such a promissory courtesy also involves an agreement to transfer one's choice to another and, on Kantian principles (cf. RL 6:271ff.), in this respect establishes a personal right that is contractually binding and, if necessary, enforceable (also cf. Gerhard Seel, 'How Does Kant Justify the Universal Objective Validity of the Law of Right?', *International Journal of Philosophical Studies* 17 (2009), 71–94, at 78ff.). If this is to be avoided and the legal obligation is to lapse under certain circumstances (e.g. in the case of a family emergency or even if one suddenly regrets the promise made), this should – as Kant himself emphasizes (cf. ZeF 8:348, n. *; RL 6:298, 300) – be included in the contractual agreement as a reservation or resolving condition. For a detailed account, cf. Hirsch, *Freiheit und Staatlichkeit bei Kant*, 106ff.

another's property for one's own enrichment without consent means to treat this person as a mere means. This justificatory nexus can be identified for the first time in Kant's *Feyerabend* lecture on natural law.[18] It also finds its way into the *Grundlegung* with Kant's analysis of perfect duties against others. In the case of fraud ('a false promise') and 'assaults on the freedom and property of others [. . .] he who transgresses the rights of human beings intends to make use of the person of others merely as means'.[19] Kant's examples show that legal duties – for here, without exception, we are dealing with perfect external duties – essentially consist in not using others merely as a means. He made this explicit in the *Vorarbeiten* on the *Doctrine of Right*:

> Outer *freedom* is the independence of a human being from the choice of others, so that he need not act solely in accordance with their ends but may, in doing so, also act in accordance with his own ends; that is, so that he *need* not serve *merely* as a means to any end of another (i.e. so that he cannot be compelled to do so).[20]

External freedom as Kant describes it here is obviously nothing other than the innate right to freedom presented in the *Doctrine of Right*: '*freedom*' as the 'independence from being constrained by another's choice'.[21] This is made even clearer in the *Vorarbeiten* for *Theory and Practice*, according to which '*freedom* as a *human being* according to the innate right [consists in] not being subject to the choice of others merely as a means'.[22]

This justificatory nexus of violating one's right by treating a person merely as a means highlights an important clarification of the concept of

[18] Cf. V-NR/Feyerabend 27:1319f. (my translation): 'The human being can, however, be used as a means by another rational being, but it is never a mere means, instead it is always an end at the same time, e.g.: if the mason serves me as a means of building a house, I serve him back as a means of obtaining money. [. . .] If I make a contract with my servant then he must also be an end just as I am, and not a mere means. [. . .] I cannot take something from another's field in order that it serves my own, for then the other would be a mere means.' These remarks in the *Feyerabend* lecture on natural law reflect a justificatory nexus between morality and law to which Kant subsequently essentially adhered and which thus ultimately also found its way into the *Doctrine of Right* of 1797. For more details, cf. Philipp-Alexander Hirsch, 'Kant über Recht, Autonomie und Selbstzweckhaftigkeit: Naturrecht Feyerabend als Geburtsstunde Kants kritischer Rechtsbegründung?', in Dieter Hüning, Stefan Klingner, and Gianluca Sadun Bordoni (eds.), *Auf dem Weg zur kritischen Rechtslehre?*, Leiden: Brill, 2021, 197–228 and, for a critical assessment in this respect, Markus Willaschek, 'How Can Freedom Be a Law to Itself? The Concept of Autonomy in the "Introduction" to the Naturrecht Feyerabend Lecture Notes (1784)', in Stefano Bacin and Oliver Sensen (eds.), *The Emergence of Autonomy in Kant's Moral Philosophy*, Cambridge: Cambridge University Press, 2020, 141–57 and Günther Zöller, '"[O]hne Hoffnung und Furcht": Kants Naturrecht Feyerabend über den Grund der Verbindlichkeit zu einer Handlung', in Bernd Dörflinger *et al.* (eds.), *Kant's Lectures*, Berlin: De Gruyter, 2015, 197–210.

[19] Cf. GMS 4:429ff. [20] VARL 23:341 (my translation). [21] RL 6:237.

[22] VATP 23:136 (my translation).

freedom in Kant's *Doctrine of Right*. External freedom is the 'object' protected by Right. It represents what the innate right consists in and what the legal duties corresponding to that innate right refer to. However, the legal validity, that is, the bindingness of legal obligations protecting this very freedom, depends on the obligee and the obligor both being ends in themselves and thus follows from their shared moral autonomy. It follows that external freedom is not a specifically human capacity (e.g. physical freedom of movement, or psychological freedom as in the ability to determine oneself according to one's purposes). Instead, external freedom is nothing other than 'freedom in the *external* use of choice [...] insofar as it [*sc.* choice] is determined by laws of reason'.[23] External freedom refers to human choice in external actions (i.e. the faculty to perform external actions as one pleases) insofar as one's choice is subject to autonomous laws of reason. In other words, the choice or the exercise of one's choice is morally indifferent if the choice is not subject to a moral law and is *therefore* not regulated in a certain way (e.g. restricted to a specific scope of action). Consequently, human choice is only free choice in that it can be determined by laws of reason, and it is precisely this determinability by the laws of reason in which moral autonomy finds its expression.

In consequence, external freedom as the 'object' protected by law (i.e. independence from another's necessitating choice) is the normative demand that the laws of Right specify for the external use of choice *because* human beings are morally autonomous and thus necessarily ends in themselves.[24] A person exists '*as an end in itself* (which is the supreme limiting condition of the freedom of action of every human being)',[25] and 'hence so far limits all choice'[26]. This is why, for Kant, coercion by others is *prima facie* normatively problematic, as by coercing someone the coerced would 'serve *merely* as a means to any end of another'.[27] Thus, legal subjects being morally autonomous and therefore ends in themselves is not only crucial for the validity of Right, but also gives rise to legal coercion as a normative problem in the first place.[28]

[23] RL 6:214.
[24] Cf. J. P. Messina's essay in this volume (Chapter 12); Messina's reading also goes in this direction.
[25] GMS 4:430f. [26] GMS 4:428. [27] VARL 23:341 (my translation).
[28] It seems a bit premature when Willaschek, 'Right and Coercion', 60 objects: 'It [*sc.* the value of autonomy] resides entirely in its self-legislation and thus in its not being conditioned by anything empirical and contingent. [...] [T]he value of autonomy alone cannot be a reason for or against the legitimacy of coercion: it cannot be a reason against its legitimacy, because it is not affected by coercion; and it cannot be a reason for its legitimacy, because it cannot be promoted by coercive measures.' For Kant, however, physical body and moral personality form a unit, so that respect for personality and the preservation of one's physical integrity are closely connected: '[A]cquiring a

Before turning to legal coercion in more detail, let me address – albeit briefly – three possible objections to this reading of Kant: first, one might object that Kant had abandoned this justificatory nexus in the *Doctrine of Right* since he does not explicitly refer to moral autonomy or the end-in-itself-formula of the categorical imperative in the Introduction to the Doctrine of Right. However, this objection overlooks the fact that stipulating legal subjects to be ends in themselves is implicit in Kant's notion of moral personality, which is – as shown above – central to the *Doctrine of Right.* This is most evident in Kant's treatment of criminal law when he states that 'a human being can never be treated merely as a means to the purposes of another or be put among the objects of rights to things: his innate personality protects him from this'.[29] A person is not a thing and therefore cannot be treated arbitrarily. This would disregard his or her moral 'personality, by which alone they are ends in themselves'.[30] Consequently, as Right refers to the 'practical relation of one person to another',[31] Kant implicitly traces legal freedom back to the legal subjects being ends in themselves and being morally autonomous.[32] This is the case as it follows from '*[m]oral* personality' 'that a person is subject to no other laws than those he gives to himself (either alone or at least along with others)'.[33]

A second objection might be rooted in the view that the moral value of being an end in itself is in fact normatively too ambitious and thus an ill-suited foundation for Right. This would be the case if one assumes the end-in-itself-formula of the categorical imperative ultimately to require us to treat everyone else as an end. However, Right is obviously not about promoting ends in themselves in this positive way. Instead, Right can be deduced analytically from the concept of freedom of choice in its external use. Therefore, rightful behaviour is possible without taking into account

member of a human being is at the same time acquiring the whole person, since a person is an absolute unity' (RL 6:278). In a similar vein, cf. V-Mo/Collins, 27:369 and Immanuel Kant, *Vorlesung zur Moralphilosophie*, ed. by Werner Stark, Berlin: De Gruyter, 2004, 216. According to Kant's (admittedly strong) claim, moral personality (at least of human beings) is thus always embodied. Consequently, coercion only poses a moral problem for autonomous beings and therefore beings that are ends in themselves. In this respect, personality or its moral value is – as I have tried to show – the only reason why coercion is *prima facie* illegitimate vis-à-vis autonomous rational beings and thus requires justification in the first place. For a similar take, cf. Bernd Ludwig, '"Positive und negative Freiheit" bei Kant? Wie begriffliche Konfusion auf philosophi(ehistori)sche Abwege führt', *Jahrbuch für Recht und Ethik* 21 (2013), 271–305, at 300ff.

29 RL 6:331.

30 KpV 5:87. likewise cf. KpV 5:131; GMS 4:428 and RL 6:359 and RL 6:423, 434ff.

31 Cf. RL 6:230.

32 On Kant's line of reasoning, also cf. Ludwig, 'Sympathy for the Devil(s)?', 34ff.

33 RL 6:223.

the special interests and wishes of others (as external duties of virtue-demand),[34] which is a prerequisite for treating them as an end. 'If I do not contribute to another's happiness, I do not infringe upon his freedom, but let him do what he wants.'[35] Thus, Right is only about the moral value of being an end in itself in the *negative* sense of not treating others as a mere means.

A third objection to the justificatory nexus outlined above could be that Right according to Kant abstracts from the ends the legal subjects are pursuing and thus cannot be derived from the categorical imperative (in whatever formula). While it would go beyond the scope of this article to discuss the complex question of the derivability of the general law of Right from the categorical imperative,[36] we can nevertheless point out that Right restricts legally legitimate actions to the extent that at least one permissible maxim can be found for them. This is the case despite the fact that Right does not specifically prescribe any maxims, this being the function of the doctrine of virtue. Thus, if at least one permissible maxim can be found for a rightful action, then that action does not amount to treating other legal subjects merely as means.[37] Irrespective of the disputed derivability of Right from the categorical imperative, Right hence reflects the fact that legal subjects are ends in themselves.

5.2 Coercing without Treating merely as a Means

How does all this help us to understand the legitimacy of legal coercion? As I have tried to show, Right protects our independence from someone else's necessitating choice, precisely because as persons we are ends in ourselves and may not be used merely as a means. And since applying coercive force is the paradigmatic case of using someone merely as a means,

[34] Cf. TL 6:385ff., 395, 448ff.

[35] V-NR/Feyerabend 27:1329. In a way, Right precedes virtue: the doctrine of virtue requires our use of choice to conform with the wishes and ends of others. However, the *conditio sine qua non* for this is always that our use of choice is compatible with the choice of others in the first place. Cf. V-NR/Feyerabend 27:1336 and V-MS/Vigilantius 27:669.

[36] For a detailed account, cf. Hirsch, *Freiheit und Staatlichkeit bei Kant*, 90–138 and the contribution by Bernd Ludwig in this volume (Chapter 2).

[37] Ludwig, 'Sympathy for the Devil(s)?', 39 nicely puts it in a nutshell: 'Since by definition juridical lawgiving is indifferent to the motives for conformity with its laws, it cannot be concerned with the particular maxim of the *actor*. But if for a given *act* there is *no* morally possible maxim at all (e.g. arbitrarily killing innocent people), the maxim of the *actor*, whatever it may be, cannot be in conformity with the categorical imperative. And since freedom of *persons as persons* is *a priori* limited by the categorical imperative [. . .], their *external freedom* is thus *a priori* limited by the principle of right.'

any form of coercion is *prima facie* impermissible. Right therefore generally prohibits any form of coercion, since it contradicts the claim of autonomous rational beings to be respected in their moral personality and not to be treated as a mere means.[38] Moral personality, however, does not amount to inviolability and does not render any coercion illegitimate. This is the case because the moral laws which govern personality, and which are an expression of persons being ends in themselves, also restrict moral personality. When it comes to the use of choice in external relations, these restrictions necessarily follow from the plurality of autonomous rational beings. Precisely because human beings form a community with other persons, their own use of choice is subject to the normative stipulation that it must be reconciled with the others being ends in themselves. The minimum conditions for this – that is, the necessary conditions under which beings that are ends in themselves can coexist according to a universal law – are formulated by Right. It guarantees each legal subject a use of choice according to a universal law. At the same time, Right restricts each legal subject's external freedom to this very use. Therefore, any use of choice beyond this restriction can no longer be understood as an expression of the moral personality of the legal subject. The legitimacy of legal coercion is just the flipside of this, as Kant nicely put it in the *Vorarbeiten* to the Metaphysics of Morals:

> Duties of right [. . .] are based solely on the necessary conformity with the law of freedom in relation to one's own person or to others [and are] hence proper laws, that is, strictly determining principles, and here these laws which restrict a human's own freedom due to his personality are a prerequisite of restricting the freedom of others.[39]

To the extent that Right restricts the use of choice according to a universal law, it only reflects that moral personality – and thus the scope or sphere in which persons are in fact ends in themselves that must not be treated merely as a means – is conceptually restricted. In § C of the Introduction of the Doctrine of Right, Kant puts this in a nutshell by saying that 'freedom *is* limited to those conditions [*sc.* the conditions according to the universal law of right] in conformity with the idea of it [*sc.* freedom] and that it may also be [in fact] actively limited by others'.[40] In other words, anyone who commits a violation of rights is *in this respect* (i.e.

[38] Both psychological coercion (*vis compulsiva*) and physical coercion (*vis absoluta*) prevent people from freely pursuing their self-chosen ends. The coerced person functions only as the means for another person and can no longer determine himself as he sees fit.

[39] VARL 23:392 (my translation). Also cf. VARL 23:383.

[40] RL 6:232.

insofar as he violates the rights of others) no longer a moral person worthy of protection from interference. Consequently, his or her moral personality, which is to be legally protected, is not affected by opposing coercive acts. As a corollary, the need to normatively justify the legitimacy of coercion never does arise in the first place.[41] Insofar as the concept of Right can be analytically derived from the concept of free external choice of moral persons according to universal laws, the permissibility of external coercion corresponds directly to this:

> The conformity of the action with the universal laws of freedom is thus the measure by which to determine whether anyone possesses a coercive right, and another one can be subject to him; and I can thus have authority to coerce the will of another person against his freedom only insofar as my freedom is at the same time in conformity with the general freedom according to universal laws. [. . .]. *From this it follows that I have a right to all actions that are not contrary to the other's right, i.e. contrary to his moral freedom; for to that extent I do not derogate his freedom, and he has no right to coerce me.* From this, it also follows that the right to coerce the other consists in resisting his use of freedom, insofar as it cannot coexist with universal freedom according to universal law; and this is the right of coercion.[42]

Just to reiterate: coercion or coercive force against non-persons (stones, plants, animals) is morally indifferent in relation to them;[43] this is the case because moral personality calls for a normative justification of coercion in the first place. However, moral personality is not unlimited but conceptually restricted due to the plurality of persons interacting with each other. It follows that this restriction marks the limit of morally permissible or impermissible coercion. For Kant, Right and coercive power both follow from the fact that moral personality – and thus the sphere within which interference with others amounts to treating them merely as a means – is

[41] Those who act wrongfully are in this respect no longer worthy of moral protection. Coercion against the wrongful act does not affect the moral personality of the coerced person. Contrary to Willaschek's assumption in 'Right and Coercion', 60ff. and 'The Non-Derivability of Kantian Right from the Categorical Imperative', 558ff. this is not a question of whether the coercion may be wanted as an end by the coerced person. The end-in-itself formula says nothing about this, since I do not have to include the coerced person – insofar as he acts unlawfully – in my moral deliberation. It follows that it cannot be deduced whom I have the authority to coerce from the end-in-itself formula. Rather, it can only be shown whom I may *not* coerce, i.e. treat merely as a means. For a similar criticism of Willaschek, cf. Ludwig, '"Positive und negative Freiheit" bei Kant?', 301 with n. 47.

[42] V-MS/Vigilantius 27:525f. (my translation and emphasis).

[43] This means that mistreating non-human animals (or other non-persons) does not violate any duty owed to them. For Kant, of course, mistreating them is not morally indifferent *tout court*, but still violates a duty that the agent owes to himself. Cf. TL 6:443.

conceptually restricted. This could be called a scalable 'sphere of protection' that comes with being a moral person and that gives rise to legal duties which protect one's moral personality. Beyond this sphere of protection, coercion does not violate the 'moral freedom [of the other], for to that extent I do not derogate his freedom'.[44] This is how Kant can analytically equate Right and coercion in § E of the Introduction to the Doctrine of Right.[45] Thus, there is no need for a positive derivation of 'a legal entitlement to coerce' from the categorical imperative. On the contrary, the permissibility of coercion or use of coercive force is the default case since coercion is morally irrelevant if it does not violate one's moral personality. According to this view, coercion is always permissible as long as the legally protected freedom of the other – namely his or her moral personality in legal terms – is not impaired.

However, one might think that the proponents of the independence thesis would come to similar conclusions, since they too hold the view that coercive power is nothing other than the flip side of relational freedom: '[T]he entitlement to coerce is simply the entitlement that others exercise their freedom consistent with your own.'[46] This reading of Kant, however, presupposes a concept of freedom as independence from being constrained by the choice of another person, without being able to explain the categorically binding nature of this idea. By invoking the independence of law from morality, proponents of the *independence thesis* cannot refer to the aforementioned notion of autonomy and persons being ends in themselves. They are left with having to resort to prudential reasons. It would go beyond the scope of this chapter to go into detail on this and outline the (in my view) shortcomings of the various independentist readings of Kant's legal philosophy and the justifications of legal coercion that go hand in hand with them.[47] However, the most common line of reasoning seems to be as follows: independentists understand freedom of choice pursuant to Kant as the ability to set and pursue one's own ends.

[44] V-MS/Vigilantius 27:526. It is therefore wrong to ask, as Willaschek does in 'The Non-Derivability of Kantian Right from the Categorical Imperative', 562, whether one is authorized 'to limit the freedom of *others*' or '[*sc.* to infringe] upon some other person's external freedom'. For unlawful acts are not subject to one's external freedom (understood as the 'object' protected by Right) in the first place. Consequently, coercion opposing the wrong does not pose a moral problem in the first place.

[45] RL 6:232. [46] Ripstein, *Force and Freedom*, 56.

[47] For a detailed account, cf. Hirsch, *Freiheit und Staatlichkeit bei Kant*, 147ff. A good, albeit a little outdated overview of the various positions represented in the debate is also provided by Willaschek, 'Right and Coercion', 49–54 and Seel, 'How Does Kant Justify the Universal Objective Validity of the Law of Right?'.

This ability presupposes only practical freedom,[48] but not transcendental freedom. This is why Kant's doctrine of Right, which reconciles and guarantees freedom of choice according to a universal law, is said to be independent of Kant's critical moral philosophy.[49] Since every person naturally wants to realize his or her own ends, no person can 'reasonably' reject legal restrictions of freedom because Right defines the conditions that enable us to realize our own ends in accordance with everyone else.[50] As a corollary, legal coercive power just means exercising the freedom to which everyone is entitled who wants to freely realize his or her purposes.

However, on Kantian grounds this independentist argument is flawed in two ways: first conceptually, since it conceives of external freedom as some capacity, whereas it is actually – as shown above – the 'object' protected by Right.[51] Second, it is normatively flawed since the *categorical* bindingness of legal standards and restrictions on the legitimate use of coercive force cannot be explained in this way. This is the case because according to the independentist reading, compliance with legal standards is (if authors do not resort to postulating quasi-moral principles governing Right)[52] only

[48] Meaning 'praktische Freiheit' as Kant defines it in KrV, A798/B826. However, Kant abandoned the idea that this concept of freedom is sufficient for the justification of law and morality with the *Groundwork* and the *Second Critique*. In the latter work, he belittles this practical freedom (to which he adhered in the *First Critique*) as 'the freedom of a turnspit, which, when once it is wound up, also accomplishes its movements of itself' (KpV 5:97). In parts, Kant also refers to such a use of reason in contrast to a moral-practical use of reason (which freedom is about) as *technical-practical*, cf. e.g. KpV 5:26, n. *; KdU 6:172–5; VAZeF 23:163; V-MS/Vigilantius 27:577 and RL 6:217ff. On this also cf. the insightful remarks by Ludwig, '"Positive und negative Freiheit" bei Kant?' and Ludwig, 'Sympathy for the Devil(s)?', 27ff.

[49] Cf. Julius Ebbinghaus, 'Die Strafen für Tötung eines Menschen und Prinzipien einer Rechtsphilosophie der Freiheit', in *Gesammelte Schriften*, vol. 2: *Philosophie der Freiheit: Praktische Philosophie 1955–1972*, ed. by Georg Geismann and Hariolf Oberer, Bonn: Bouvier, 1988, 283–380, at 296ff. and following him Manfred Baum, 'Freiheit und Verbindlichkeit in Kants Moralphilosophie', *Jahrbuch für Recht und Ethik* 13 (2005), 31–43, at 37ff. and Georg Geismann, 'Recht und Moral in der Philosophie Kants', *Jahrbuch für Recht und Ethik* 14 (2006), 3–124, at 10ff., 66ff. In a similar vein, cf. also Wood, 'The Final Form of Kant's Practical Philosophy', 5ff.; Pogge, 'Is Kant's *Rechtslehre* a "Comprehensive Liberalism"?', 149; Arthur Ripstein, 'Authority and Coercion', *Philosophy and Public Affairs*, 32 (2004),), 2–35, at 8ff., as well as Ripstein, *Force and Freedom*, 355ff. and Horn, *Nichtideale Normativität*, 50ff., 171.

[50] Cf. Julius Ebbinghaus, 'Kant und das 20. Jahrhundert', in *Gesammelte Schriften*, vol. 3: *Interpretation und Kritik: Schriften zur Theoretischen Philosophie und zur P hilosophiegeschichte 1924–1972*, ed. by Georg Geismann and Hariolf Oberer, Bonn: Bouvier, 1990, 151–74, at 167; Pogge, 'Is Kant's Rechtslehre a "Comprehensive Liberalism"?', 146ff.; Geismann, 'Recht und Moral', 72ff. or Ripstein, *Force and Freedom*, 31ff.

[51] Cf. above, p. 100f. But also cf. J. P. Messina's contribution to this volume (Chapter 12), which identifies two different ways of speaking of 'external freedom' under Kant.

[52] Cf., for example, Flikschuh, 'Justice without Virtue', 51 ff., who defends a concept of Right as public morality and, as such, as systematically distinct from the personal morality of Kant's ethics. In a similar vein, cf. also Christoph Horn's contribution to this volume (Chapter 3). From my point

hypothetically required, namely insofar as it is conducive to one's own interest in self-preservation. This is best illustrated by the example of the nation of devils which Kant refers to in *Towards Perpetual Peace* and which is, ironically, often cited by independence theorists in an attempt to defend their position.[53] The devils[54] are exactly the kind of beings that possess the qualities that are said to be necessary to be a suitable subject of rights and legal obligations: they are rational in the sense that they can set and pursue their own ends. However, they lack moral personality because they are not transcendentally free and thus not autonomous.[55] Such beings would certainly be able to act in accordance with the prescripts of Right. However, even if *legality* is achievable for a nation of devils, devils would never have a concept of legal *validity* or legal *obligation*:

> The problem of establishing a state, no matter how hard it may sound, is *soluble* even for a nation of devils (if only they have understanding) and goes like this: 'Given a multitude of rational beings all of whom need universal laws for their preservation but each of whom is inclined covertly to exempt himself from them, so to order this multitude and establish their constitution that, although in their private dispositions they strive against one another, these yet so check one another that in their public conduct the result is the same as if they had no such evil dispositions.'[56]

Devils can indeed be subjected to an external coercive mechanism that – despite egoistic self-interests – guarantees prudentially lawful behaviour. However, this is at best a legal order in the *technical* sense. It does not suffice for the *moral* concept of Right that Kant has in mind, in which Right corresponds to a moral *obligation*. This is what Kant himself says when he talks about the natural guarantee safeguarding perpetual peace. For, according to Kant, the natural guarantee merely answers the following question:

of view, Flikschuh and Horn are going in the right direction, but only halfway. This is the case because the *a priori* notion of the general united will (governing public morality) does not – as Flikschuh and Horn claim – replace the principle of autonomy as the basis of moral obligation, but only transfers it to external relations. For more details, cf. Hirsch, *Freiheit und Staatlichkeit bei Kant*, 201 ff.

53 Cf., for example, Pogge, 'Is Kant's *Rechtslehre* a "Comprehensive Liberalism"?', 150.

54 This refers to the devils that Kant has in mind in *Towards Perpetual Peace*, who only have technical-practical reason, but not to the evil devil of the *Religion*, who elevates 'resistance to the law [...] to [the] incentive' of his actions (RGV 6:35).

55 Ludwig, 'Sympathy for the Devil(s)?', 41 also rightly points out that 'Kantian devils, in this passage at least, are mere *rational* and thoroughly *selfish* beings. As devils, they cannot be assumed to have a consciousness of the moral law. Kant explicitly attributes to them *only* "understanding", not "reason", and not at all "*pure* practical reason".'

56 ZeF 8:366.

> [w]hat nature does for this purpose with reference to the end that the human being's own reason makes a duty for him, hence to the favouring of his *moral purpose*, and how it affords the guarantee that what man *ought* to do in accordance with laws of freedom but does not do, it is assured he *will* do, without prejudice to this freedom, even by a constraint of nature [. . .]. When I say of nature, it *wills* that this or that happen, *this does not mean, it lays upon us a duty to do it (for only practical reason, without coercion, can do that) but rather that nature itself does it, whether we will it or not* (fata volentem ducunt, nolentem trahunt).[57]

Legality within a nation of devils merely proves that the prudent devils will opt for a legal order out of cleverly calculated self-interest. This is how 'nature comes to the aid of the general will grounded in reason [. . .] precisely through those self-seeking inclinations'.[58] Devils, however, have no concept of moral obligation because they are not persons. This lack of moral personality not only puts an end to any form of categorical moral obligation (be it ethical or legal), but also to the normative problem of justifying coercion.[59] A devil is not a person and therefore needs to be considered as a thing in moral terms. To force him to do something, to injure him, or even to kill him are simply normatively irrelevant acts. Or to put it differently: any independentist reading of Kant that seeks to justify the binding nature of Right independently of Kant's critical moral philosophy fails even to explain why coercion is a normative problem in the first place.[60] It may be unwise for a devil to coerce others unilaterally and without limits. However, this is neither categorically forbidden nor in need of normative justification.

5.3 With Kant beyond Kant, or: Are Internal Perfect Duties Externally Enforceable?

As we have seen, the permissibility of legal coercion is just the flipside of the moral personality being conceptually restricted: if you try to hit me and

[57] ZeF 8:365 (my emphasis). [58] TP 8:366.

[59] This is also the conclusion by Ludwig, 'Sympathy for the Devil(s)?', 42: 'For *non-persons, rational or not*, as beings incapable of imputation, there are no moral restrictions at all on their behaviour against others, *persons* and *non-persons* alike. As *rational* non-persons, they only have rules of *prudence*, and any talk about rights and duties is pointless.'

[60] With that in mind, the validity of Right remains entirely stipulative if, for example, Ripstein, *Force and Freedom*, 21 claims that Right is grounded in the 'simple but compelling normative idea that, as a matter of right, each person is entitled to be his or her own master'. As Ripstein aims to justify Right independently of Kant's critical moral philosophy, he fails to answer why persons have this special status and why it should – consequently – be normatively problematic to interfere with a person's 'purposiveness – [her] capacity to choose the ends [she] will use [her] means to pursue' (Ripstein, *Force and Freedom*, 34). For Kant, however, purposiveness has no moral value if it is not the purposiveness of a transcendentally free and autonomous subject.

I violently push your arm away, I am not treating you merely as a means since your wrongful action is not an expression of your moral personality that I must respect. According to Kant, however, Right is restricted to intersubjective relations among persons, 'insofar as [. . .] actions [. . .] can have (direct or indirect) influence on each other'.[61] Consequently, coercive power also finds a corresponding limitation and depends on the injury of another person in this intersubjective relationship. Thus, Kant claims that only *external* legal obligations (i.e. legal obligations *towards* others) are coercively enforceable. But is this claim actually warranted?

If coercion is legitimate if and only if it does not amount to treating others merely as a means, then this seems to endorse more coercive action than Kant claims. For if coercive power ultimately results from the fact that moral personality is conceptually limited in a way that renders all coercive acts permissible that do not affect the moral personality of the coerced, then this also seems to hold true for the realm of perfect duties against oneself: the legal internal duty of *honeste vive* and the internal perfect duties presented in the *Doctrine of Virtue*.[62] These duties do not only reflect a conceptual restriction of our moral personality in a specifically legal sense, namely the 'right of humanity in our own person'.[63] They, too, are in principle externally enforceable insofar as they prohibit external actions.[64] This holds for internal legal duties (not to prostitute oneself, not to sell oneself into slavery, etc.) and the perfect duties against oneself in the *Doctrine of Virtue* (prohibition of suicide, prohibition of harming oneself, etc.).[65] If legitimate coercion represents the flipside of our moral personality being conceptually restricted, and if internal perfect duties reflect such a conceptual restriction, then these duties should also be enforceable.

Kant himself opposes a conceptual equation of perfect duties and enforceable duties, as it has been implemented in contemporary natural law philosophy. Rather, he sees a requirement to substantiate the authority

[61] Cf. RL 6:230.

[62] Cf. RL 6:236 and TL 6:421ff. In the lecture on Metaphysics of Morals *Vigilantius*, however, all these duties belong to a unified category (cf. V-MS/Vigilantius, 27:581ff.). Only in the *Metaphysics of Morals* did Kant divide the perfect duties against oneself into inner duties of right (*honeste vive*) and inner perfect duties of virtue. On this and on the question whether this division is consistent, cf. Philipp-Alexander Hirsch, 'Von Rechtspflichten zu vollkommenen Tugendpflichten? Kants ungelöstes Problem der Pflichtensystematik', in Beatrix Himmelmann, Camilla Serck-Hanssen (eds.), *The Court of Reason*, Berlin: De Gruyter, 2021, 1457–66, at 1457ff.

[63] Cf. RL 6:240.

[64] External actions are in principle enforceable because they take place in space *and* time. Inner actions (like setting an end), in contrast, take only place in time and thus cannot be externally enforced, cf. RL 6:239.

[65] On this, also cf. Hirsch, *Freiheit und Staatlichkeit bei Kant*, 194ff.

to coerce based on the concept of law. In the lecture on Metaphysics of Morals *Vigilantius*, Kant complains that until his time it had been

> [. . .] an unproved assumption of right, to consider the authority to coerce as a legal axiom. [. . .] But since nobody can exercise a right to coerce, who has not obtained a right thereto from a higher ground, which consists, however, in one's own freedom and its conformity with the freedom of everyone according to universal law, it is clear that the authority to coerce can only be derived from the idea of right itself.[66]

If we take Kant at his word, any restriction of the authority to coerce would depend on whether such a restriction can be derived from the idea of Right that 'the choice of one can be united with the choice of another in accordance with a universal law of freedom'.[67] In the case of perfect duties towards oneself, however, such a restriction seems questionable for two reasons.

First, as shown above, Right and coercive power according to Kant both follow from the fact that by virtue of being persons, our choice in external actions is subject to moral laws. By designating certain acts as impermissible, Right also describes morally permissible coercive acts, for those who commit a legal wrong are not affected in their moral personality by opposing coercive acts. However, this line of reasoning applies quite generally to perfect duties, be they external or internal: self-harming actions that violate perfect duties against oneself are just as little an expression of one's own moral freedom in the external use of choice as actions that harm others and violate external legal duties. In either case, the moral personality is unaffected by the opposing coercive actions. The 'right of humanity in one's own person', which is the basis of all perfect duties against oneself,[68] sets the morally permissible external use of choice apart from the morally impermissible external use of choice. By recognizing perfect duties against oneself, Kant thus identifies certain forms of behaviour or actions as not morally worthy of protection and thus as potentially subject to coercion – regardless of whether someone else is harmed by them or not.

Second, restricting legitimate coercion to the fulfilment of external duties (and exempting perfect internal duties) would be self-contradictory.

[66] V-MS/Vigilantius 27:526. Also cf. V-NR/Feyerabend 27:1335. Kant thus opposes a conceptual equation of perfect duties and coercive duties, as it has been implemented in the contemporary natural law philosophy, cf. for instance Georg Achenwall and Johann S. Pütter, *Anfangsgründe des Naturrechts (Elementa Iuris Naturae)* (1750), Frankfurt am Main: Insel, 1995, § 185.

[67] Cf. RL 6:230. [68] As Kant states in RL 6:240.

For if the right of humanity in our own person prohibits certain behaviour, it cannot at the same time designate it as legally worthy of protection vis-à-vis other persons. If it did, then this would mean that I would be allowed to commit an act that is at the same time forbidden. This can be illustrated by the example of the prohibition of suicide: if I prevent a suicidal person from killing himself by coercion (e.g. by grabbing his arm), then he would not have the right to resist my intervention. He would only have this right if he could claim that he had been wronged by my intervention. However, the suicidal person neither has a right nor any other moral entitlement to kill himself; otherwise we could not say that he has a perfect duty not to commit suicide. It follows that my use of coercive force in this scenario is not wrong. This follows trivially from the principle of contradiction to which Kant refers in § C of the Introduction into the Doctrine of Right: a legal wrong is committed by me only where the other person has a legal right. *Tertium non datur.*

One can go even further in this respect: according to Kant's concept of Right, I even have a right to prevent the other person from committing suicide, since my choice is compatible with the choice of the suicidal person according to a universal law of freedom. This is the case because this very law of freedom prohibits suicide. However, it would be wrong to justify my coercive power by saying that the suicidal person legally has an obligation *towards me to preserve* his moral personality. He certainly does not. Yet the suicidal person does have an obligation *towards me to tolerate* the intervention. For my conduct is in complete harmony with the Universal Principle of Right[69] and is in this respect an expression of my innate right to freedom.[70] This seemingly odd conclusion becomes clear by focusing on the *debitum* and distinguishing *what* is owed to whom: in the case of perfect duties against oneself, there is no external legislation because the obligor owes the fulfilment of the duty only to himself. Thus, in the example previously outlined, the suicidal person owes the preservation of his life to himself, but not to me. Consequently, I have no moral authority to oblige him to stay alive under the threat of coercion, that is, to bind him by means of external legislation. Or to put it differently: with regard to the *debitum* 'preservation of his life', I have no moral standing and therefore no entitlement to enforce this duty. However, since the prohibition of suicide is a perfect duty, it simultaneously defines the scope of my innate right and thus also of the corresponding duty of *neminem laede*. With regard to the latter *debitum* 'respect for my innate right', the

[69] RL 6:231. [70] RL 6:237ff.

suicidal person does indeed owe it to me to tolerate my physical intervention. The reason for this obligation does not lie in the perfect duty against oneself (prohibition of suicide), but in the fact that resistance to my intervention would violate my innate right.

Seen in this way, the morally owed behaviour (*debitum*) and the normative reason for morally legitimate coercive actions (physical coercion) diverge when viewed against perfect duties to oneself. Kant certainly did not aim to argue for a prohibition of suicide that could be enforced by others. But if for Kant the power to coerce begins where moral personality ends, then it cannot be limited to external legal obligations. Instead, use of coercive force in accordance with internal perfect duties is also legitimate, even though – strictly speaking – it is not the internal duty that is being enforced, but the innate right of the coercer.

CHAPTER 6

Should Criminals Be Punished for Their Folly? On the Ethical Foundations of Kant's Legal Philosophy

Kate Moran and Jens Timmermann

6.1 Introduction

It is commonly thought that the legislation germane to the first part of the *Metaphysics of Morals*, the Doctrine of Right, is purely external. The state secures the rights of its citizens by coercive means, namely by reliable mechanisms of restraint, deterrence, and restitution. These measures prevent some crimes directly and provide strong disincentives to commit others. Wrongdoing that still occurs must be adequately dealt with. Any wrong must be righted. This is what distinguishes the juridical condition from the state of nature. As the law of the land is coercive and external, the state does not expect it to be obeyed out of respect for its normative authority. It does not police an agent's inner dispositions. It is content with *legality*, since juridical duty need not be done from duty. The requirement of *morality* is the hallmark of ethical obligation, which is the subject of the second part of the book, the Doctrine of Virtue.

In what follows, we shall argue that this common account of juridical obligation is incomplete. The state cannot, it is true, expect citizens to be motivated by respect for either its own laws or the law that is the supreme principle of morality in general (if only because it is impossible to ascertain moral worth in individual cases). But the coercive measures of the penal system require that agents have the motive of duty at their disposal.[1] Without the support of internal or ethical legislation, those who transgress the law could not be held to account for their behaviour. Put slightly paradoxically, without the support of ethical obligation no crime would ever be committed. But not in a good way.

[1] Our focus will lie on the role of the duty motive in Kant's theory of punishment. Another consideration that connects the two spheres of moral legislation, the duty to exit the state of nature or *exeundum*, will briefly be mentioned at the end of the chapter.

6.2 What Is Kantian Legislation?

In the general introduction to the *Metaphysics of Morals*, Kant tells us that legislation, whether ethical or juridical, consists of both an objective and a subjective element. It requires, first, a law that objectively 'represents an action that is to be done as necessary' and, secondly, an incentive that subjectively 'connects a determining ground for the faculty of choice [...] with the representation of the law' (RL 6:218.13–17). Contemporary moral philosophy tends to neglect the second, subjective part. But it is important to realize that legislation would be incomplete without a motivational element. An objectively valid law would not be a law *for us* – it would lack authority – if there were no connection to our faculty of choice or *Willkür*. That law would remain 'merely theoretical' (RL 6:218.20), that is, the state would not be able to hold us to it because we would be unable to act on it. So, how do juridical and ethical legislation differ?

As to the first element, this is a highly contentious question. The minutiae of the debate lie beyond the scope of this chapter, but it is worth noting that at least some juridical laws will be positive laws not grounded in a priori reasoning. Trivially, the categorical imperative does not decide the question whether we should drive on the left side of the road or the right. That is a matter of convention. However, once a state has settled the question one way or the other, the law is binding for anyone driving a vehicle on its territory. The Highway Code can be coercively enforced. Other legal obligations can, perhaps, directly or indirectly be derived from the principle of morals. But, again, the details need not concern us.

As to the second element, it is uncontroversial that there the perspectives of law and ethics diverge sharply. This is how the issue is introduced in the general introduction to the *Metaphysics of Morals*:

> Legislation that makes an action a duty and also makes this duty the incentive is *ethical*. But legislation that does not include the incentive of duty in the law, and hence also [!] admits of an incentive other than the idea of duty itself, is *juridical*. (RL 6:219.2–6)

There is a designated ethical incentive (*Triebfeder*), variously called 'respect' (or 'reverence') for the moral law (*Achtung*), 'moral interest', or 'moral feeling'. That much is clear from the *Groundwork* and the *Critique of Practical Reason*. An action that coincides with what the moral law says (an action that is, in that thin sense, *right*) has moral worth (it is morally valuable or good) only if it proceeds from the appropriate inner attitude, from the right maxim. From the viewpoint of ethics, motives other than respect are illegitimate. When the moral law speaks, we must obey it; we must do what it says because we appreciate its unconditional authority. Juridical legislation, however, is independent of any *particular* incentive as long as there is an incentive that enables agents to do their duty.[2] The details of this will become clearer as we proceed. For now, let us note that while the juridical sphere does not privilege the duty motive, it does not exclude that motive either.[3] In fact, there is a sense in which it is our ethical duty to obey the laws of the state.[4] Kant says that, though there are many '*directly ethical* duties', internal legislation makes 'the remaining duties' – that is to say, juridical duties – 'one and all indirectly ethical' (RL 6:221.1–3).[5] Note that the conception of ethics now in play is not restricted to duties of virtue but rather encompasses all categorical imperatives. It coincides with the discipline Kant normally calls 'moral philosophy'.

6.3 Why is External or Coercive Legislation Needed?

In a juridical state, external legislation relies on coercive institutions. It arises as human beings exit the state of nature. The state of nature, Kant tells us, is a 'a state devoid of justice' (RL 6:312.24–5), if not entirely devoid of rights. It is possible to acquire property in that state, but any such acquisition can only be '*provisional* as long as it does not yet have the sanction of public law, since it is not determined by public (distributive) justice and secured by an authority exercising this right' (RL 6:312.30–3).

Kant emphasizes the importance of provisional rights. They generate the *exeundum*, that is, it is by virtue of these rights that we are forced to enter the juridical state, which turns provisional right into actual or 'conclusive' right. Accordingly, the juridical state – commonly equated with the 'state' *simpliciter* – is characterized as 'that relation of human beings among one another that contains the conditions under which alone everyone is able to enjoy [*theilhaftig werden*] his right [. . .]' (RL 6:305.34–306.1).

2 The notion of legislation does not as such include any particular incentive; this much is obvious, since the two can come apart.

3 This is evident from the little word 'also' (*auch*) at RL 6:219.5 (see Bernd Ludwig, 'Die Einteilungen der "Metaphysik der Sitten" im Allgemeinen und die der "Tugendlehre" im Besonderen', in Andreas Trampota, Oliver Sensen, and Jens Timmermann (eds.), *Kant's 'Tugendlehre': A Comprehensive Commentary*, Berlin: De Gruyter, 2013, 59–84, at 60).

4 Assuming that the state deserves its name and law's demands are legitimate (that they do not, for instance, violate human rights).

5 Kant uses his theory of space and time as pure intuitions to illustrate this point, 6:214.19–30: just as we can regard the objects of outer sense as spatial, we can regard the laws of juridical legislation as external. But these are both abstractions. Overall, the objects of outer sense are temporal as well as spatial; and the laws of juridical legislation are ethical as well as juridical.

Note, however, that the notion of a 'provisional right' is problematic. On the one hand, Kant wants to break away from the Hobbesian paradigm. There are, he tells us, actual, practically relevant rights in the state of nature. On the other hand, these rights are not conclusive because they are not secured by coercive means and thus, in a sense, not really rights at all. Only rights that can be claimed are rights in the proper sense of the word. As such, only conclusive rights are rights; and conclusive rights exist only in the juridical state.[6]

6.4 How Does the State Secure the Rights of Its Citizens?

Let us turn to the coercive measures put in place by state institutions to secure the rights of individuals. Once again, the right to property can serve as an example. The state must, among other measures, promulgate and enforce laws to the effect that those who steal other people's property will not only not be allowed to keep their spoils.[7] Stolen goods must be returned to the original owner. If restitution turns out to be impossible, the owner deserves compensation.[8] In addition, they will be punished, that is, they will suffer an ill that is proportional to the crime. These measures are intended as a clear signal that it is in no one's interest to break the law. Crime will be severely discouraged.

To make external legislation work, Kant has to assume that human beings take a natural and unavoidable interest in their own well-being.[9] As this interest is general – it aims at whatever gives us pleasure – it needs to be made determinate. Initially, we do not have a very good sense of what is in our interest. Prudential deliberation helps us discover what promises satisfaction long-term. Though this is often difficult to achieve, the threat of punishment makes this task a little easier by impressing upon us, as citizens of the state, that breaking the law will not be to our advantage.[10]

[6] The only promising way out of this dilemma would seem to be this. Provisional rights are not wholly ineffectual. For even though we cannot directly claim provisional right, they can be claimed indirectly in that they necessitate our entering into a juridical state, which allows us to claim these rights. That is why, in a roundabout way, they should count as actual rights after all. But some problems remain even if this approach can be made to work. For instance, as law cannot be applied retrospectively, any violations of (provisional) right that occurred in the state of nature will not be corrected or punished.

[7] This is often difficult to achieve, see RL 6:332–4.

[8] As, for example, in the famous case of the stolen horse, see RL 6:301.28–302.2.

[9] And indeed he does, see e.g. GMS 4:415.28–33.

[10] It is still very rare that any prudential consideration can lay claim to conviction that approximates certainty. The second 'gallows case' comes close, see KpV 5:30.27–35.

6.5 Elements of Kant's Theory of Punishment

It is apparent from what has been said so far that Kant's theory of punishment is not purely 'retributive'. As Sharon Byrd has argued, three elements need to be distinguished with care.[11] There is, first of all, the general threat contained in the law as promulgated by the state. The purpose of this threat is deterrence. The second element is the execution of this threat, namely the act of punishing an individual, which is legitimate only if the law was in force (promulgated, publicized) at the time it was broken. Retrospective legislation would fall foul of the rule of law. Thirdly, every law has to specify a sentence, which for Kant must be informed by the principle of retribution (*ius talionis*). Everyone who has broken the law is thus meant to receive the same fixed and fair punishment.[12]

From the perspective of juridical legislation, the particular motivation of citizens is not only irrelevant when they comply with the law; it is also irrelevant when they – consciously, wilfully[13] – break it. The state does not punish criminals because they acted on this or that morally objectionable motive, for example out of hatred, jealousy, or greed. Criminals are punished because they have broken the law, that is, because they have committed a crime. And there was no good reason, no justification, to do so. As long as certain conditions of rational agency (such as conscious deliberation or premeditation) are met, what matters is that unconditional law was violated. From the point of view of the law, motivation – which can never be ascertained with certainty – cannot make an action worse or better, let alone excuse it.

6.6 Why Do Criminals Break the Law?

Still, punishment must be proportionate to the crime. The state is not allowed to impose draconian sentences even if threatening such measures would prevent transgressions more effectively.[14] Moreover, even the best of states cannot ensure that all crimes are duly punished. Anyone inclined

[11] Cf. B. Sharon Byrd, 'Kant's Theory of Punishment: Deterrence in Its Threat, Retribution in Its Execution', *Law and Philosophy* 8 (1989), 151–200.

[12] The condition that sanctions be, in various ways, legitimate is a first indication that there is some reliance on ethics.

[13] These qualifications are introduced to exclude the complications raised by negligent action.

[14] There are, moreover, cases in which *ius talionis* is inapplicable; strict retribution would have a greater deterrent effect than the legitimate measure, but it would violate – as we might put it – human rights. It is thus illegitimate to threaten torturers with torture to deter them from torturing others. See RL 6:362–3.

to break the law will be acutely aware of this. As a consequence, there is only so much a state can legitimately do to discourage crime.[15] Deterrence can never be perfect – or else, no law would ever be broken, no right would ever be infringed and, a fortiori, no citizen would ever be punished.[16] The crucial question, then, is this: what goes on in the mind of citizens when they decide to commit a crime?

On Kant's view, human beings do not break the law because they want to defy it; such a desire would be diabolical (see RGV 6:37.21). Immoral action in general, and illegal action in particular, are governed by the principle of happiness (see KpV 5:22). Human beings break the law because they expect to profit from the illicit deed, the state's best efforts notwithstanding. And this is possible only if the prohibited course of action appears to be in their interest. This impression may well be wrong. But prudential calculation is notoriously complicated, in part because we cannot predict the future with certainty. We can misjudge the situation, for example because we do not expect to be found out or convicted, or because punishment cannot be sufficiently severe to make it the case that crime is not worth our while. Also, some people may be more risk averse than others, and so more likely to take chances with compliance.[17]

6.7 What Makes Self-Interested Behaviour Punishable?

So, if crimes are committed out of self-interest, if the crime is taken to be prudentially adequate at the time it is done, the state cannot, it would

15 In the light of this, Kant's 'sales pitch' (so to say) that the state will make provisional rights conclusive may well be an exaggeration. Are they really 'secured by an authority' that exercises public justice (RL 6:312.32–3, quoted above). Is it really the case that 'everyone is able to *enjoy* his rights' (RL 6:305.36–306.1, quoted above)?

16 This is actually implicit in Willaschek's analysis of the realm of right as a descriptive system of norms. It would not be descriptive if agents could fail to act on hypothetical imperatives whose incentives are provided by the state. As he puts it, 'the idea of a juridical "ought" would not be applicable to a people under a perfect legal system, since they are forced to obey its laws anyway' (Marcus Willaschek, 'Which Imperatives for Right? On the Non-prescriptive Character of Juridical Laws in Kant's Metaphysics of Morals', in Mark Timmons (ed.), *Kant's Metaphysics of Morals: Interpretative Essays*, Oxford: Oxford University Press, 2002, 65–88, at 85). But we do not live in such a system. And that is why juridical law is imperatival after all. A little later, Willaschek concedes that juridical laws 'are indeed prescriptive, but only when considered from an ethical perspective' (Willaschek, 'Which Imperatives for Right?', 86). We contend that this perspective is inevitable even from the point of view of the Doctrine of Right.

17 We cannot have a different set of sanctions for those willing to take risks, because (a) it is impossible to know whether a person is willing to take such risks and (b) otherwise we would have different laws for different agents. (NB: this is different from the suggestion that the punishment itself be tailored to the person's circumstances, for example that a wealthier person should pay a heavier fine than a poor person or that the threat should be two-pronged; see RL 6:332–3.)

seem, punish the criminal for *that* – even though the *threat* of punishment appeals to the human desire to be happy.[18] Consider the following quotation from the *Critique of Judgement.* Kant is engaging in a thought experiment. What would be the result if the human will could only be determined by the expected agreeableness or disagreeableness of prospective options, which are commensurable and can be ranked on a single scale?

> [T]his would be the agreeableness in the sensation of one's condition, and since in the end all the workings of our faculties are directed to what is practical and must be united in it as their goal, one could not seek to impose upon them any other estimation of things and their value than that which consists in the gratification that they promise. The manner in which they achieve this does not, in the end, matter at all; and since the choice of means alone can make a difference in this, human beings could very well accuse each other of folly or lack of understanding [*Unverstand*], but never of baseness [*Niederträchtigkeit*] or malice [*Bosheit*]: because all of them, each seeing things his own way, hurry towards one goal, which for everyone is gratification. (KdU 5:206.7–18)

We cannot punish criminals for their folly. In fact, in the second *Critique* Kant himself indicates that imprudence and punishability are different in kind – so different, in fact, that they are quite distinct even in the judgement of the agent who is justly punished (KpV 5:37–8). There must therefore be something (broadly) immoral about crime for judicial punishment to be appropriate.

Roughly, criminals are punished because they have wilfully broken a law promulgated and valid at the time it was broken.[19] The Kantian state does not punish criminals because of any particular kind of moral deprivation, a task that is left to the Deity (see TL 6:460.33). And as with complying with the law, the state does not pay attention to the particular motive of the criminal *as long as* it is clear that he was responsible for the act, namely that the decision to break the law was based on a free choice. But even though the law does not concern itself with the specific motive of the agent, there is an assumption that (i) the agent had no legitimate motive at his disposal and (ii) that there was a legitimate motive to which he did have access, a motive that would have been sufficient to produce an action in conformity with external legislation. The law thus takes account of the agent's mindset without paying attention to specific motivations, which were one and all illicit. This idea is reflected in the following definition:

[18] See Jens Timmermann, *Kant's Will at the Crossroads: An Essay on the Failings of Practical Rationality*, Oxford: Oxford University Press, 2022, 10–29.

[19] Again, malice in the above quotation from KdU, 5:206 means action on inclination in the face of the voice of the moral law, not wilful defiance of the law *because* it is the law.

> An intentional transgression (i.e. one that is coupled with the consciousness of its being a transgression) is called a crime (*dolus*). (RL 6:224.5–7)

But this raises further questions about the conditions that need to be given for an agent to be conscious of a prospective transgression in a way that renders it punishable by right.

6.8 How Can an Act That Is Judged Prudentially Adequate Be Punishable?

Consciousness of a transgression as such cannot merely consist in being conscious of what one is doing, such as appropriating someone else's property. One must also be conscious of its wrongfulness. One must be conscious that one ought – and therefore can – do otherwise.[20] This qualification is vital. Without this consciousness, it would be manifestly inappropriate to hold criminals to the legal standards set by the state. To abide by the law, it needs to be a live option. And for that we need conscience, whose task it is to watch the legality of action in particular.[21] As a result, internal legislation is needed to back up external legislation. After all, all juridical duties are indirectly ethical.

Only external compliance is required in the sphere of right; but at times the motive of duty is the only motive that can secure external compliance. The motive of duty is not required from a juridical point of view, which is motivationally neutral – and thus does not preclude our acting on the duty motive as such. So, it is contingently demanded that we act for the sake of the law – not as such, but because it is the only way we can secure conformity with law (or 'legality').[22] That is why it is so important that all duties are indirectly ethical.[23]

[20] In technical terms: a *formal* wrong is required (Marie Newhouse, 'Two Types of Legal Wrongdoing', *Legal Theory* 22 (2016), 59–75), though the material wrong done may well determine the severity of the crime in terms of its punishability.

[21] See Jens Timmermann, '*Quod dubitas, ne feceris*: Kant on using Conscience as a guide', *Studi Kantiani* 29 (2016), 163–7.

[22] There is, perhaps, a trace of our view in Martin Annen's discussion of the duty to honour contracts: 'Die Ethik geht insofern über die Rechtspflicht hinaus, als sie die Einhaltung von Verträgen auch dann fordert, wenn der äußere Zwang wegfällt. [...] Erst die Kombination von Rechts- und Tugendpflicht kann gewährleisten, daß die mit dem Vertrag eingegangene Verpflichtung, das Versprechen einzuhalten, nicht vom Wohlwollen des Handelnden abhängig ist' (Martin Annen, *Das Problem der Wahrhaftigkeit in der Philosophie der deutschen Aufklärung: Ein Beitrag zur Ethik und zum Naturrecht des 18. Jahrhunderts*, Würzburg: Königshausen & Neumann, 1997, 184).

[23] RL 6:220.19–21. If so, juridical legislation cannot simply be equated with external legislation. Rather, legislation that can *also* be external is juridical legislation (cf. Bernd Ludwig, 'Einteilungen', 65 and 66, where he argues that any duty of right is tied to an ethical duty and does, in fact, include

> [T]he system of the general doctrine of duties is now divided into that of the doctrine of right (*ius*), which is capable of external laws, and that of the doctrine of virtue (*Ethica*), which is not capable of it [. . .]. (TL 6:379.8–11)[24]

Note that this does not mean that the state can demand that we act in accordance with duty out of duty on any particular occasion;[25] rather, it must assume that we face a meaningful choice, that we can refrain from breaking the law even if we judge it to be in our interest. Agents do not think they are justified overall[26] as they violate the law (though they do think they are prudentially justified, or at least likely to give it a good shot).[27] In some cases (in cases in which the criminal act is, despite the state's best efforts, judged to be in the interest of the agent) the motive of duty is needed to make sure that obeying the law is more than just a theoretical option for the agent – a theoretical option already dismissed on

it). The imposition of an ill as a legitimate sanction presupposes that an action that is to be sanctioned is not just epistemically but also motivationally accessible.

[24] Compare Allen Wood's much starker attempt to separate law and ethics. Wood insists that juridical legislation as such is exclusively external. He is right that 'juridical duties are precisely those where the incentive need not be duty – it may, for example be the threat of coercion connected to the law by the legislative authority that promulgates it'; but this does not entail that ethical motivation relates only to the moral worth of the action, or that 'it would be superfluous, and even contradictory, to the very concept of the juridical, to include the rational incentive of duty as part of its principle' (Allen W. Wood, 'The Final Form of Kant's Practical Philosophy', in Mark Timmons (ed.), *Kant's Metaphysics of Morals: Interpretative Essays*, Oxford: Oxford University Press, 2002, 1–21, at 8). It may have to be *included* as one incentive among many, though it is not, as in the ethical sphere, the *privileged* moral motive. Or, to argue against another prominent advocate of 'justice without virtue', Katrin Flikschuh, it is indeed Kant's view that – sometimes – '[w]hether or not our rights claims are met [. . .] depends on others' good will' (Katrin Flikschuh, 'Justice without Virtue', in Lara Denis (ed.), *Kant's Metaphysics of Morals: A Critical Study*, Cambridge: Cambridge University Press, 2010, 51–70, at 63–4). These are cases in which external legislation fails; and if it does, a well-functioning juridical state will mete out punishment. On Kant's behalf, Flikschuh rejects the distinction between acting justly and being just, since the former would call for a role of autonomy and its motive, respect for the law, in the juridical sphere (Flikschuh, 'Justice without Virtue', 51, 64). But these are precisely the terms in which Kant distinguishes material and formal wrong in the Feyerabend lecture notes: *unrecht handeln* is different from *ungerecht sein*, V-NR Feyerabend 27:1344.40–1345.1. In much the same vein, Kant distinguishes 'being served honestly' from 'being served by an honest shopkeeper' in Section I of the *Groundwork* (GMS 4:397.25–7). We are assuming Marie Newhouse's distinction between formal and material (see Newhouse, 'Two Types of Legal Wrongdoing').

[25] Cf. RL 6:219.17–20: there is *no requirement* that the idea of juridical duty, which is internal, be by itself the determining ground of the action.

[26] As evidenced by the fact that we can all recognize a distinction between civil disobedience and folly. The person who practises civil disobedience thinks his action is justified, but is willing to be punished (i.e. he is not prudentially irrational).

[27] In the Doctrine of Virtue, Kant even argues that all duties – including external duties and thus presumably duties of right? – are impossible without (ethical) duties to self. Cf. TL 6:417.25.

prudential grounds. There is no free choice without the duty motive. The duty motive is thus a background condition of moral responsibility.[28]

6.9 Hegel's Dog

Without the availability of the duty motive, Hegel's criticism of Feuerbach's deterrence theory of punishment would pose a problem for Kant's view as well:

> Feuerbach bases his theory of punishment on threat and thinks that if anyone commits a crime despite the threat, punishment must follow because the criminal was aware of it beforehand. But what about the justification of the threat? A threat presupposes that a man is not free, and its aim is to coerce him by the idea of an evil. But right and justice must have their seat in freedom and the will, not in the lack of freedom on which a threat turns. To base a justification of punishment on threat is to liken it to the act of a man who lifts his stick to a dog. It is to treat a man like a dog instead of with the freedom and respect due to him as a man. But a threat, which after all may rouse a man to demonstrate his freedom in spite of it, discards justice altogether. – Coercion by psychological factors can concern only differences of quantity and quality in crime, not the nature of crime itself, and therefore any legal codes that may be products of the doctrine that crime is due to such coercion lack their proper foundation. (G. W. F. Hegel, *Elements of the Philosophy of Right*, § 99, first published in 1820)

This is a common concern. Readers and commentators are worried that Kant cannot espouse a deterrence theory of punishment – not even if, to use Sharon Byrd's memorable phrase, deterrence in threat of punishment is coupled with retribution in its execution – because this kind of external manipulation would amount to treating human beings as mere means rather than persons. But on the reading given above, Kant's theory of punishment

[28] The widely held view that hypothetical imperatives are expressions of practical rationality that agents can violate, or that there is a prescriptive principle called *the* Hypothetical Imperative, would have disastrous consequences for Kant's theory of punishment. According to this view, it is reason that can motivate us – and at times fails to motivate us – to do instrumentally rational acts. It would then be possible for us to fail to do what is instrumentally adequate even if we are fully committed to an end, we know the means necessary to bring it about, and the means is at our disposal. Note that we do not punish people for being instrumentally irrational, that is, for the kind of irrationality that consists in the failure to realize an end to which one is fully committed. Indeed, as has been argued elsewhere, there is reason to believe that Kant did not allow for such cases of 'true irrationality'. Note that an additional threat would not help – on the contrary, it would threaten to undermine Kant's entire system of deterrence. Providing a further incentive to do something to which one is already fully committed does not guarantee that one will do it if such slips are possible. Kant's theory of punishment thus relies on the impossibility of 'true' irrationality in the prudential – and generally in the instrumental – sphere.

is dependent on the personality of those who think that breaking the law might be in their interest. It is their autonomy – and the availability of the duty motive that is tied up with it – that makes them a fit object of a legal punishment that is neither 'natural' nor unduly moralized.[29]

6.10 Backups in Law and in Ethics

Our account of the conditions of juridical punishment has an interesting implication for Kant's moral philosophy as a whole. So far, we have argued that, appearances notwithstanding, Kant needs to rely on the duty motive in his legal theory. Respect needs to be available to motivate action in accordance with the law when – on, one would hope, rare occasions in a well-ordered state – agents judge that such action is not in their interest and are therefore inclined to break the law. Without the availability of moral interest, juridical punishment would be illegitimate.

Now, the idea that the motive of duty should serve as a backup has been ascribed to Kant's moral philosophy before – if to his ethics, rather than his philosophy of law. Scholars like Richard Henson and Allen Wood maintain that we need to act from duty or respect for the moral law only when inclination-based motivation fails to point in the right direction. For the most part, action can thus be determined by benign inclination. They reject motivational rigorism on Kant's behalf.[30] On these views, which can be seen as a response to broadly virtue ethical concerns, Kant's ethics does not include a requirement that obligatory action always be done for the sake of duty. Rather, the moral motive – or an action that has moral worth – is required only in cases of conflict. Even from the point of view of ethics, there would then be nothing objectionable about acting on inclination as long as what one wants to do coincides with what one morally ought to do.[31] But doing away with Kant's motivational rigorism in this manner means *legalizing* the sphere of ethics, which, in Wood's case, goes

[29] The natural consequences of breaking the law are irrelevant from a legal point of view (cf. RL 6:331.22) – presumably because natural punishment is unpredictable and a bad deterrent and, relatedly, because it boils down to prudence from the agent's point of view. Desert plays no role in the apportionment of natural punishment.

[30] See Richard G. Henson, 'What Kant Might Have Said: Moral Worth and the Overdetermination of Dutiful Action', *The Philosophical Review* 88 (1979), 39–54 and Wood, *Kant's Ethical Thought*, Cambridge: Cambridge University Press, 1999, 26–40.

[31] See Jens Timmermann, 'Acting from Duty: Inclination, Reason and Moral Worth', in Jens Timmermann (ed.), *Kant's 'Groundwork of the Metaphysics of Morals': A Critical Guide*, Cambridge: Cambridge University Press, 2009, 45–62.

hand in hand with *de-ethicizing* the sphere of right. We would argue that both tendencies should be resisted.

In the end, however, external legislation is an abstraction. The ethical perspective is more fundamental and it is, importantly, inevitably the perspective of the agent. From a first-person point of view, all moral decision-making is ethical, that is, the legal perspective exists only from a third-person point of view. As an agent, it would be weird for me to say: I care only about conforming with the law of the land; in one area of practical normativity, there is no need for me to do my duty from duty. I cannot say: I *ought* to do it, juridically, because the state forces me to do it – if only the state's forcing me to do it makes me *want* to do it, and what I want cannot be regulated by oughts. I ought to obey the law whether I want to do it – whether I judge it to be in my interest – or not. We are experiencing juridical obligations as categorical imperatives, not as the hypothetical imperatives the legislator employs to enforce them.[32] And that is possible only because they fall within the sphere of ethics. In fact, our view can even accommodate Willaschek's 'paradox of juridical imperatives'.[33] His worry is that 'juridical laws cannot find expression in categorical imperatives, after all, because juridical laws do *not* require obedience for their own sake'.[34] The answer is that even if from the point of view of the state they do not, from the point of view of the agent they do – which is why they are proper categorical imperatives after all.[35] The paradox can be resolved in true Kantian fashion by distinguishing two standpoints from which we can view juridical obligation.[36]

6.11 Objection: What about Kant's 'State of Devils'?

Our view faces one obvious objection. What, we may wonder, about Kant's dictum that establishing a state is a problem that can be solved even for a people or nation of devils (ZeF 8:366.15–17)? Surely, the state must sustain the threat and execution of punishment? And devils, for the lack of respect for the law, cannot do their duty from duty? So, how can it be right to punish them?

[32] Cf. Oliver Sensen, 'Tugendlehre als Lehre von Zwecken (Einleitung zur Tugendlehre, I–VI)', in Otfried Höffe (ed.), *Immanuel Kant: Metaphysische Anfangsgründe der Tugendlehre*, Berlin: De Gruyter, 2019, 29–43, at 40–1.

[33] See Willaschek, 'Which Imperatives for Right?', 69–73.

[34] Willaschek, 'Which Imperatives for Right?', 70.

[35] This way, we can save Jürgen Habermas' distinction of perspectives (cf. Willaschek, 'Which Imperatives for Right?', 73–5).

[36] Respect for the law is tied to autonomy, so there can be no juridical duties without autonomy.

It is clear from the historical context of this passage that Kant is exaggerating. First of all, Kant is reacting – maybe overreacting – against August Wilhelm Rehberg's allegation of utopianism.[37] The state does not rely on the divine nature of its citizens; on the contrary, even devils can live together in a well-ordered state. Secondly, the devils he has in mind are not endowed with a diabolical will in the sense defined in the *Religion* (see, again, RGV 6:37.21). They do not violate the law for the sake of violating the law. For a nation of truly diabolical devils, the task of establishing the state *would* be insoluble. Rather, the devils envisaged in *On Perpetual Peace* are a race of egotistical maximizers of self-interest.

So, rational, less than diabolical devils can make use of a state in a Hobbesian fashion, because it is in their interest. However, they do not have a state with the same kind of practical normativity as ours. There would be no *exeundum* either. This is Kant's advice:

> Given a multitude of rational beings all of whom need universal laws for their preservation, whilst each of whom is inclined covertly to exempt himself from them, so to order this multitude and establish their constitution that, even though in their private dispositions they strive against one another, these yet so check one another that in their public conduct the result is the same as if they had no such evil dispositions. (ZeF 8:366.17–23)

Would those devils that violate the laws of the land be punishable? Yes and no. They would not be punishable if by that expression we mean the infliction of *just* punishment. Making good on the threat of punishment would not be deserved. But any pain inflicted on such creatures does not count as undeserved either. It might thus still be in the interest of devil citizens to live in a state that is, by and large, to everyone's advantage.

Human beings are importantly different from this breed of devils in that in their case acts of punishment are morally, not just instrumentally, justified.

6.12 Conclusion

So, the sphere of right and the sphere of ethics are less distinct than one might think. The former relies on the latter via the notion of legal obligation as *indirectly* ethical. The state cannot tell us: You have to do your (juridical) duty *from duty*. But the state can tell us: You have to do

[37] August Wilhelm Rehberg, 'Über das Verhältniß der Theorie zur Praxis', *Berlinische Monatsschrift* 23 (1794), 114–43, at 136.

your (juridical) duty, period. It just happens to be the case that when committing a crime seems means–ends rational, the motive of duty – moral interest or respect for the law – is the only incentive available. And we cannot act without an incentive. If we then refrain from breaking the law, we do so from duty; if we do not, we should and could have decided not to break the law from duty. That is why, when we commit a crime, we deserve to be punished.

Let us note in conclusion that there are other ways in which the sphere of right rests on internal legislation. Most prominently, the *exeundum* does not depend on external legislation since it is only by virtue of our leaving the state of nature that external legislation arises in the first place. As Onora O'Neill puts it, 'this duty to leave the state of nature and to enter a civil society is necessarily *unenforceable,* since it is a duty to establish the possibility of enforcement'.[38] So, our conclusion should not come as a surprise.[39]

[38] Onora O'Neill, Enactable and Enforceable: Kant's Criteria for Right and Virtue. *Kant-Studien* 107 (2016), 111–24, at 123. What about the principle of *honeste vive,* namely the command not to let oneself be treated as a thing by other people, which made its way into the Doctrine of Right quite late in the day, cf. Ludwig, 'Einteilungen', 68? Is this merely a matter of external behaviour (qua duty of right), or is there a remnant of reliance on ethical motivation? Also TL 6:390.30.

[39] What are we to make of equity and necessity in the light of this theory? Should the plank be punishable? If not, how is the plank different from the standard case (in which deterrence equally fails)?

PART III

Issues across the Boundaries of Law and Morality

CHAPTER 7

Morality, Legality, and Luck

Ralf M. Bader

7.1 Introduction

Kant is often read as being committed to the idea that morality is within our control, which leads him to develop an ethical theory in which there is no room for moral luck.[1] Luck is supposedly excluded by focusing on the maxims of our actions rather than on their consequences. Whereas consequences are subject to luck and depend on factors that are beyond our control, our maxims are considered to be entirely up to us. Kant's political and legal philosophy, by contrast, is taken to be concerned with external actions, in particular with their effects on the freedom of others, and thus seems to be far from immune to luck.

From this perspective a significant chasm opens up between ethics and right. The former seems to be an internal domain that is immune to luck due to focusing on the agent's maxims. The latter seems to be an external domain that is susceptible to luck due to focusing on consequences.[2] If ethics and right were to differ in this way, then it would be hard to

Thanks to Christopher Benzenberg, Luke Davies and audiences at Göttingen, Fribourg and Bern as well as the editors of this volume. Special thanks to Marie Newhouse for her helpful comments at the 'Law and Morality in Kant' conference. Translations of Kant's works are my own.

1 For the locus classicus cf. Bernard Williams, 'Moral Luck', *Proceedings of the Aristotelian Society*, supplementary volume 50 (1976), 115–35 and Thomas Nagel, 'Moral Luck', *Proceedings of the Aristotelian Society*, supplementary volume 50 (1976), 137–52. Nagel helpfully distinguishes moral luck into different types, three of which are relevant to our discussion: (1) resultant luck concerns the consequences of one's actions, (2) circumstantial luck concerns the circumstances in which one acts, and (3) constitutive luck concerns the agent's constitution, such as his desires, abilities, and dispositions.

2 A striking statement of this view has been put forward by David Heyd: 'While the agreement of the action with the law is always contingent upon external circumstances, the agreement of the incentive to obey the law with the action is independent of any such contingent factors, since the action is "internal". Kant's strategy for securing the necessity and hence the absolute supremacy of the moral is by restricting "the ground determining the will of the agent" to a pure inner sphere of the person, hermetically isolated from any contaminating occurrences in the world. This leaves the moral realm completely immune to chance or luck.' David Heyd, 'Moral and Legal Luck: Kant's Reconciliation with Practical Contingency', *Jahrbuch für Recht und Ethik* 5 (1997), 27–42, at 27.

see how right could be derived from ethics and how both of them could be integrated into a unified theory based on a single supreme principle. Moreover, it would be difficult to motivate such an asymmetric treatment of luck in these two domains, since the considerations that make susceptibility to luck problematic at the level of morality would seem to carry over to the level of legality. After all, it is rather strange to claim that moral luck needs to be rejected on the grounds that it is objectionable if an agent can be blamed for things that are outside his control, yet at the same time claim that legal luck is unobjectionable even though it implies that an agent can be coerced or punished for things that are not up to him.

This chapter argues that the role of luck in Kant's practical philosophy needs to be reconceived and that considerations of luck do not stand in the way of a unification of ethics and right. Section 7.2 argues that morality and legality do not differ in terms of resultant luck. Legality, like morality, is based on maxims, so that neither is susceptible to resultant luck. Otherwise, it would neither be possible to account for the way in which the good will ensures non-accidental rightness (Section 7.2.1), nor for the way in which legality can be ensured by means of legal sanctions (Section 7.2.2). Though imputation is subject to resultant luck, this applies equally to juridical and ethical imputation (Section 7.2.3). Section 7.3 argues that the moral worth of our actions is susceptible to constitutive and circumstantial luck (Section 7.3.1) and that a state that effectively enforces justice excludes morally worthy behaviour (Section 7.3.2). By demonstrating that there is no duty to act out of duty, it shows that this does not generate a conflict between ethics and right (Section 7.3.3). Finally, by establishing that a bad will can act out of duty, it shows that the moral worth of actions, unlike the moral worth of the agent, is merely derivative and does not add anything to the value of the world, so that this type of moral luck is innocuous (Section 7.3.4).

7.2 Maxims, Consequences, and Luck

The contrast between morality and legality is not a distinction between internal maxims and external actions. What is at issue in both cases is actions, where these are individuated and evaluated in terms of their maxims. The universal principle of right, like the categorical imperative, is concerned with maxims. It states that actions are right only if their maxims are such that 'the freedom of choice of each can coexist with everyone's freedom according to a universal law' (RL 6:230).[3] The legality of an action is entirely a function of its maxim, not of its consequences. Accordingly, no gap opens up between the maxim and the legality of the action. Legality, like morality, is thus immune to resultant luck.

The difference between an action that is moral and a corresponding action that is merely legal lies, not in the form of their maxims (since they are both universalizable), but in the incentive that is motivating the agent to perform the action in question. Legality, in particular, is less demanding than morality since it abstracts from incentives and only requires universalizability of the maxim. The morality of an action, by contrast, requires the action to have respect for the law as its incentive.

7.2.1 *Non-accidental Rightness*

The fact that legality is based on maxims rather than consequences and thus not susceptible to resultant luck makes it possible for a good will to ensure non-accidental rightness. Having a good will, which consists in adopting a fundamental maxim that subordinates self-love to duty, ensures that only universalizable maxims will be adopted and that impermissible maxims put forward by instrumental reasoning will be rejected, since the adoption of the maxims on which one acts proceeds on the basis of one's fundamental maxim (cf. RGV 6:36). The actions of an agent who has a good will are thereby guaranteed to be right, namely to accord with duty.[4]

[3] Newhouse has objected that this claim ignores the first part of the universal principle of right, which is not concerned with maxims. On her two-standard interpretation, only formal wrongs are understood in terms of maxims, whereas material wrongs are understood in terms of physical incompatibilities. Cf. Marie Newhouse, 'Two Types of Legal Wrongdoing', *Legal Theory* 22 (2016), 59–75. If her interpretation were correct, then the account given here would be restricted to formal wrongs. Luck could then come in at the level of material wrongs, most notably in the case of mere faults (cf. RL 6:224), thereby threatening the unification of right and ethics. Fully addressing this challenge would require an account of the normative importance of imperfect epistemic access to the facts, which includes both false information and limited information. The arguments of Sections 7.2.1 and 7.2.2 will show that if a two-standard interpretation were correct, then (i) a good will would not be able to ensure non-accidental rightness, since it cannot rule out physical incompatibilities, and (ii) compliance with the requirements of right could not be coerced via sanctions, since epistemic problems, unlike compliance problems, cannot be resolved by providing incentives, which renders the state unable to provide assurance by guaranteeing that rights are respected. Moreover, conceiving of material wrongs as transgressions of duties is in tension with restricting the universal law of right to formal wrongs (cf. ibid. 72–3).

[4] Non-accidental rightness is explained at the level of the *Gesinnung* (= fundamental maxim), that is, in terms of a good will, not at the level of the maxim, nor the incentive. What is at issue is whether the agent would still have done the right thing, that is, whether he would still have acted according to duty, even if his inclinations or the circumstances had been different (not whether he would have performed the very same action, nor whether that action would still have been right, but whether he

The legality of the actions of a person with a bad will, by contrast, is a matter of constitutive and circumstantial luck.[5] Conformity with duty is then accidental. This is not to be understood in terms of one and the same action being legal or illegal depending on luck, but rather in terms of a bad person performing a legal action or an illegal action depending on luck.

Whether a person with a bad will acts in conformity with duty or not depends on circumstances beyond his control. This is because free choice applies in the first place to the agent's *Gesinnung*. One freely chooses one's fundamental maxim. Non-fundamental maxims are then adopted on the basis of this *Gesinnung*. Non-fundamental maxims cannot be arbitrarily made up and are not selected at will but are a function of the agent's fundamental maxim and the context in which the agent finds himself.[6] This allows luck to come in at the level of the adoption of non-fundamental maxims.

When holding the bad will fixed but varying the context, one can end up with permissible as well as impermissible actions. Two people who do not differ in terms of having a bad will can nevertheless differ insofar as the actions of the one are permissible while those of the other are impermissible. This difference is not due to those agents having made different choices at the level of their fundamental maxims, given that both of them have a bad will, but due to factors that can be a matter of luck, such as the circumstances in which the agents find themselves, which can in part determine the non-fundamental maxims that instrumental reasoning will put forward and that will be adopted in accordance with their fundamental maxim independently of their permissibility.[7]

would have performed an action that was right). Acting according to duty has to be non-accidental, which is guaranteed by the good will. The fact that someone acts out of duty, by contrast, does not guarantee rightness, since someone who has a bad will can act out of duty, yet does so only accidentally (cf. Section 7.3.4). While moral worth excludes luck, since moral worth presupposes a good *Gesinnung*, it is the moral worth of the agent and not the moral worth of the action that is responsible for excluding luck. In short, neither motivation nor maxim but *Gesinnung* ensures non-accidentality.

5 Kant cautioned against having a self-congratulatory assessment of oneself on the basis of one's compliance with the requirements of morality, pointing out that such behaviour may well be the result of circumstantial and constitutive luck, most notably luck relating to temperament, abilities, and circumstances of time and place, rather than the result of a good will, cf. 8:329–30 and RGV 6:38.

6 Cf. Ralf M. Bader, 'Kant on Freedom and Practical Irrationality', in Dai Heide and Evan Tiffany (eds.), *The Idea of Freedom: New Essays on the Kantian Theory of Freedom*, Oxford: Oxford University Press, 2023, 198–216.

7 Though it is a matter of luck whether an agent with a bad will acts permissibly, it is up to the agent whether to adopt a bad will and thereby open himself up to this type of moral luck. Indeed, one has to adopt a good will precisely in order to avoid opening oneself up to luck. One is not allowed to leave it up to luck whether one complies with duty but has to exercise one's freedom in a way that

The non-accidental rightness that results from a good will goes hand in hand with the accidental rightness that results from a bad will. Moral luck in the form of accidental rightness in the case of a bad will is a corollary of the absence of moral luck due to the non-accidental rightness in the case of a good will. This means that a form of moral luck is at the centre of Kant's ethical theory.

7.2.2 *Coercing Legality*

The fact that legality is based on maxims is required to make it possible to enforce legality coercively. Legality can be ensured by external coercion. This is particularly clear in the case of juridical duties, where it is not only possible but also permissible to use coercion to ensure compliance with the law. When the state reliably threatens sufficiently severe punishment, the incentive for complying with juridical laws will be sufficiently strong to outweigh other incentives of self-love. Morality, by contrast, cannot be coerced. This difference arises because legality is compatible with acting on a heteronomous principle and allows for sensible incentives that can be provided by coercion, whereas morality presupposes acting on an autonomous principle and has to be based on the incentive of respect.

Coercion can affect the agent's choice of maxim. By suitably changing the incentive structure that the agent is facing, one can determine which action will be prudentially optimal and will be supported by instrumental reasoning.[8] This enables legal sanctions to ensure legality. The threat of sufficient punishment makes it the case that duty and self-interest align. In particular, it ensures that the omission of illegal actions will be prudentially rational. An agent who acts on the basis of self-love will perform the very same action that a person motivated by duty would choose. Such agents perform the same action but are motivated by different incentives. In this way coercion can ensure compliance with the law: no matter whether one has a good will or a bad will, one will act in conformity with

renders one immune to luck and ensures that one's actions are non-accidentally right. This type of moral luck, accordingly, is avoidable and hence does not contradict the idea that what ultimately matters, namely having a good will, is within everyone's reach.

8 Coercion is here understood in terms of the threat of sanctions, not in terms of the actual use of force, and hence does not circumvent choice/agency but affects the prudential evaluation of options. Put differently, it is to be understood in terms of *vis compulsiva* rather than *vis absoluta*. (For a discussion of the latter, cf. Philipp-Alexander Hirsch's contribution to this volume (Chapter 5).)

the law. One is thus guaranteed to act according to duty even if one might not do so out of duty.[9]

One can only coerce actions but not consequences. One can coerce someone to act one way rather than another way, in particular to act in a way that conforms to the laws rather than in a way that contravenes them.[10] However, coercion cannot ensure consequences, since there is a gap between actions and consequences where luck can intervene. Which consequences follow from coerced actions is a matter of luck just as much as which consequences follow from non-coerced actions. Since legality can be coerced and since coercion can only ensure that someone acts in a certain way, not that they bring about certain effects (given that there is a luck-susceptible gap between action and effect), legality only consists in the agent acting in conformity with the law, not in terms of the agent bringing about certain effects. Legality is thus a matter not of consequences but of actions and is hence immune to resultant luck. Accordingly, there is no difference between morality and legality with regard to resultant luck.

7.2.3 Imputation

Though consequences do not affect the legality of an action, they are nevertheless important for juridical imputation. Since actual, as opposed to intended or expected, consequences are imputed there is room for resultant luck.[11] Luck can affect which consequences result from an action and can accordingly affect which effects can be imputed to an agent. While the details of Kant's theory of imputation are intricate and interesting, two points are important for the topic at hand.[12]

[9] The claim that coercion ensures that someone lacking a good will performs the same action as someone with a good will concerns the performance of obligatory actions as well as the omission of impermissible actions. It does not extend to the choice of permissible actions, which depend on the agent's desires, abilities, and circumstances and in terms of which there can be variation amongst agents having a good will.

[10] Only legality but not illegality can be coerced. By means of coercion one can effect an alignment of prudence and duty, thereby ensuring legality. Since one cannot exclude the possibility of respect for the law overriding prudence, one cannot coerce illegality.

[11] Since one can impute not only consequences but also actions, juridical imputation can also encompass the intended or expected consequences of actions even when these did not in fact eventuate.

[12] For a helpful discussion of imputation see Joachim Hruschka, *Kant und der Rechtsstaat und andere Essays zu Kants Rechtslehre und Ethik*, Freiburg: Karl Alber, 2015, ch. 6. For recent discussions of the way in which Kant's account of imputation makes room for moral luck see Samuel Kahn, 'Kant's Philosophy of Moral Luck', *Sophia* 60 (2021), 365–87 and Robert J. Hartman, 'Kant Does Not Deny Resultant Moral Luck', *Midwest Studies in Philosophy* 43 (2019), 136–50.

First, imputation is not restricted to juridical imputation but also encompasses ethical imputation (cf. V-Mo/Collins, 27:290). Both domains allow for imputation of consequences that is susceptible to resultant luck. In the same way that there can be resultant luck in the case of juridical imputation, there can likewise be resultant luck in the case of ethical imputation. This implies that there are no differences between ethics and right as regards the possibility of resultant luck at the level of imputation.

Second, although there is room for resultant luck, it is possible for the agent to avoid the imputation of bad consequences. Since it is only in the case of impermissible actions that bad consequences can be imputed to the agent (cf. RL 6:228), it is possible for the agent to render himself immune to bad luck, given that it is always possible for the agent to act permissibly. The agent can avoid being in a situation in which something that is not under his control can have a negative effect on what can be imputed to him. More generally, if luck comes in, then it is because the agent has acted in such a way as to make himself susceptible to luck. Since no imputation takes place either in the case of obligatory actions or in the case of merely permissible actions, it is completely within the agent's control whether to make room for luck or not.

7.3 Moral Worth and Luck

There is no room for moral luck at the level of the good will. Since the good will is unconditionally good, it is good independently of which effects it brings about. This implies that its goodness is immune to resultant luck. Moreover, the choice whether to have a good will by giving priority to duty over self-love, or a bad will by adopting the inverted priority ordering, is a transcendentally free choice that is not in any way determined or influenced by empirical factors.[13] This choice is, accordingly, immune to constitutive and circumstantial luck. The agent's *Gesinnung*, which makes up his worth, is entirely up to that agent.

7.3.1 Accidental Moral Worth

Whereas the moral worth of the agent is immune to luck, the moral worth of actions is susceptible to luck, even when one has a good will. Someone

[13] Free choice is independent of the empirical not only in terms of not being determined by empirical facts. It is also independent of empirical content. A transcendentally free choice is not about the empirical circumstances, insofar as the choice between a good and a bad *Gesinnung* is not a choice between empirically characterized options.

who has a good will is guaranteed to act according to duty. Such a person, however, is not guaranteed to act out of duty. Whether someone with a good will acts out of duty is a matter of luck. Having a good will, though necessary, is not sufficient for our actions to have moral worth. Non-accidental legality goes together with accidental morality. The moral worth of our actions is susceptible to circumstantial and constitutive luck. Instead of morality being immune to luck and legality being susceptible to luck, the opposite is true.

A good will guarantees legality by only adopting universalizable maxims. Morality, however, cannot be guaranteed in this way, since morality, unlike legality, is not determined solely by maxims. Maxims by themselves do not suffice for morality. Something more is needed in order for the action to have moral worth, namely an ethical incentive in the form of respect for the law that is incorporated into the maxim.[14] One needs to act on a universalizable maxim out of respect for the law in order for the action to have moral worth.

Whether this ethical incentive is available for incorporation in a given situation, however, is a matter of luck. This is because one can act out of respect for the law only when the maxim put forward by instrumental reasoning is impermissible. Moral rules are practical rules of exception.[15] Morality only comes in when rejecting or limiting impermissible maxims put forward by instrumental reasoning. As long as instrumental reasoning puts forward permissible maxims, morality does not even come in. Accordingly, one can act out of duty only in case of a conflict between morality and prudence, given that only then is there a practical rule of exception that can incorporate respect for the law as an ethical incentive.

When acting permissibly and even when acting in a way that is obligatory, it is not the case that there is one practical rule into which one can either incorporate the incentive of duty or the incentive of self-love. Although duty and self-love can enjoin the same action, practical rules of exception have a different logical form from their corresponding practical rules of commission and omission. For instance, whereas prudence would

[14] The incentive is not part of the maxim but is that which makes a practical rule the maxim of the agent. One adopts a practical rule and makes it one's maxim, namely the principle of one's action, by joining it with an incentive. The incentive is what motivates one to act on that maxim and thus cannot itself be part of the maxim. Since the motivating reason for the action is not contained in the maxim, the maxim by itself does not tell us whether the agent does the right thing for the right reason but only whether he does the right thing.

[15] Cf. Ralf M. Bader, 'Kant and the Categories of Freedom', *British Journal for the History of Philosophy* 17 (2009), 799–820, at 809–11.

tell one to do *phi*, morality would require one to omit non-*phi*. Respect for the law can only be incorporated into practical rules of exception and such rules are available for adoption only when the practical rules proposed by prudence are impermissible such that exceptions need to be made. This means that in the absence of a conflict between morality and prudence it is not only the case that the moral incentive is not available, since respect requires morality to strike down self-conceit, but also that the relevant practical rule of exception that is generated by limiting or rejecting an impermissible practical rule will not be available.

Whether there is a conflict between morality and prudence in a given situation depends on factors that are beyond the agent's control, thus rendering it a matter of luck whether the agent can act in a way that has moral worth. Which maxims are put forward by instrumental reasoning is not entirely up to the agent. Whereas the agent's fundamental maxim is freely chosen and immune to luck, the adoption of non-fundamental maxims is susceptible to circumstantial and constitutive luck. Which maxims are put forward depends on the inclinations and abilities of the agent and the circumstances in which he is acting. These factors together determine which maxims will be proposed by instrumental reasoning and will then be adopted or rejected in light of the agent's fundamental maxim. Since the agent's inclinations and abilities are partly a function of luck and since the circumstances in which the agent finds himself are likewise partly a function of luck, the moral worth of actions is susceptible to both constitutive and circumstantial luck.

The required conflict between morality and prudence does not imply that there cannot be concurrent inclinations when acting out of duty. An agent can do something from duty while at the same time having a desire to perform that action. There is no need to have an aversion to the action in question. What is required instead is that the practical rule put forward by instrumental reasoning is not universalizable, since only then does pure practical reason kick in and become operative. For that to be the case, the concurrent inclinations need to be outweighed by other inclinations that suggest a different course of action. Instead of an aversion to the action that is performed out of duty, one needs a prudential preference for an impermissible alternative. The action needs to be rejected comparatively rather than absolutely. One can enjoy doing the action that one performs out of duty as long as one would have enjoyed even more an impermissible alternative that one is setting aside due to one's commitment to morality. The conflict between prudence and morality is to be found at the level of maxims: one can have concurrent inclinations but not concurrent maxims.[16]

7.3.2 *Justice Excludes Virtue*

Performing an action that has moral worth is only possible when instrumental reasoning puts forward a non-universalizable maxim that can then be rejected by pure practical reason. Whether instrumental reasoning does put forward such a maxim depends on the context in which the agent finds himself. This means that external circumstances can render virtuous behaviour impossible, that is, they can render it impossible to act out of duty. Interestingly, the mechanism by means of which the state can coerce legality is such as to exclude virtuous behaviour. The state precludes morality when it successfully coerces legality by using coercion to ensure that self-interest and duty align.

If the threatened punishment in case of violations of the law is both sufficiently strong and sufficiently assured, then instrumental reasoning will only put forward permissible maxims. Violating the laws will then never be in the agent's own interest. No conflict will arise between the maxims suggested by self-love and the demands of pure practical reason. A conflict, however, is necessary for acting in a way that has moral worth, since this requires rejecting or limiting impermissible maxims. When all maxims that are put forward by instrumental reasoning are permissible, then no exceptions need to be made, such that the possibility of acting out of duty does not even arise. When acting contrary to duty is not an option for prudence, then it is not possible to act against prudence and choose something over it. The agent's actions, accordingly, will always be in conformity with duty but will lack moral worth due to being motivated by self-love rather than by the motive of duty.

A state guaranteeing complete assurance through sufficiently severe and likely punishment will, accordingly, preclude morality with respect to all

[16] Accordingly, Schiller's famous objection is misguided (cf. Friedrich Schiller, *Sämtliche Werke*, vol. 1, Munich: Carl Hanser Verlag, 1962, at 299–300). It mistakenly assumes that moral worth requires opposed inclinations, when all that is required for moral worth is a conflict at the level of maxims. (Additionally, it assumes that moral worth is something that we are supposed to bring about, whereas it is nothing but a form of signatory value, cf. Sections 7.3.3 and 7.3.4.) The required conflict is to be understood in a weak sense such that the prudential maxim can permit an action contrary to duty without requiring such an action. This means that one can act out of duty in cases involving disjunctive maxims where prudence is indifferent between two actions, one of which is impermissible – in particular, one can refrain from performing the impermissible action, despite the fact that the prudential maxim does not require the performance of an impermissible action.

juridical duties. There is thus an important sense in which justice excludes virtuous behaviour. The effective enforcement of rights that is constitutive of justice excludes the manifestation of virtue by ruling out actions that have moral worth. Since juridical duties are a subset of duties, there is still room for the manifestation of virtue in a just state, namely with respect to non-enforceable duties (most notably imperfect duties, such as the duty of beneficence, but also perfect duties to oneself), yet compliance with juridical laws will in all cases lack moral worth.

The claim that justice excludes virtuous behaviour holds not only for worldly justice but also for divine justice, which establishes a necessary connection between virtue and happiness. If one were to know that God exists, then one would never be able to act out of duty (cf. KpV 5:146–8).[17] Since actions contrary to the law would be punished, all maxims proposed by instrumental reasoning would then accord with duty. The problem here is not that the inclination to avoid divine punishment is too strong for morality to outweigh it, but rather that morality never comes in when prudence is guaranteed to result in legality. Divine punishment (and reward) would make conformity with duty the only instrumentally rational course of action. Morality would then not have to limit instrumental reasoning. All limitations would already be internalized at the level of prudence. Pure practical reason would play no role in shaping the agent's maxims, given that no proposals put forward by prudence would have to be rejected or limited. This would preclude pure practical reason from ever striking down self-conceit and requiring one to make exceptions to prudential reasoning. Respect for the law would never be operative as an incentive.

Though virtue would not manifest itself and actions would not have moral worth, this does not imply that one cannot have a good will in such a situation. The fact that a person's actions lack moral worth does not mean that the person does not have a good will and that the person's will lacks moral worth. The good will can be latent and need not manifest itself in action in order to have its worth.[18] The unconditional goodness of the

[17] More generally, acting out of duty is impossible whenever one has a doxastic attitude that enters into instrumental reasoning and that asserts the existence of God. Accordingly, the postulate of pure practical reason not only has to fall short of theoretical knowledge but must not enter into instrumental reasoning, if it is not to exclude the possibility of morally worthy actions.

[18] At KpV 5:147 Kant suggests from the perspective of a developmental account that involves strengthening the will in conflict cases that there may be problems in acquiring a good will in this case. This suggestion, however, would seem to be an empirical story that is difficult to accommodate at the level of transcendental choice.

good will is not only independent of the consequences that one brings about but also independent of whether it manifests itself.

An agent in such a situation could either have a good or a bad *Gesinnung*. This, however, would not lead to any differences at the level of the choice of non-fundamental maxims. The agent would act in the same way independently of whether he had a good will or a bad will, given that instrumental reasoning only puts forward permissible maxims.[19] The distinctive effects of a good will, namely that such an agent would omit impermissible actions and perform obligatory actions out of duty, would then not be found in the actual world but would be entirely counterfactual. Since one would be guaranteed to do one's duty independently of whether one had a good will or not, the good will would become dispensable as far as doing one's duty is concerned.

Correspondingly, excepting the choice of the fundamental maxim, such an agent would not be able to rise to the level of positive freedom. Indeed, in a sense even negative freedom would drop out, which is why Kant says that actions would become mechanical (cf. KpV 5:147). This is because the issue of acting contrary to inclinations would never arise, such that the agent would never have alternatives amongst which *Willkür* could choose.

7.3.3 *Duty and Moral Worth*

The enforcement of rights by a just state precludes prudence from coming into conflict with morality. It thereby makes it impossible for someone to act out of duty and perform morally worthy actions when fulfilling juridical duties. In a state that effectively enforces justice, no one will perform a juridical duty out of duty. Justice in this way excludes virtuous behaviour.

This might seem to generate a deep-seated conflict between ethics and right. Ethics seems to require virtuous behaviour, yet justice rules out such behaviour. If we are required, from the point of view of ethics, to engage in virtuous behaviour and perform actions having moral worth (as opposed to merely acting in accordance with duty), then ethics and right are in conflict. In that case, ethics requires that we act out of duty, yet right requires the establishment of a rightful condition in which fulfilling our juridical duties out of duty is not possible, given that the state makes it

[19] If this were not possible, then prudence would be self-undermining since acting on the basis of inclinations would then undermine the condition, namely having a good will, that has to be satisfied in order to avoid divine punishment and receive divine rewards.

prudentially irrational to act contrary to these duties. Ethics then requires something that cannot be realized in a rightful condition.

This apparent conflict between ethics and right can be avoided, since there is no duty to act out of duty. It cannot be the case that acting out of duty is what one's duty consists in, that is, that one fails to do one's duty unless one acts out of duty. First, respect for the law motivates one to do what duty requires, so that what one's duty consists in has to be specified independently of the incentive that motivates one to act in this way. Second, if one's duty were to consist in acting out of duty, then this would imply that one would act contrary to duty if one were to act merely according to duty, which would be incompatible with the existence of both imperfect duties and actions that accord with duty without being performed out of duty.

Nor can there be a separate duty to act out of duty. First, if it were a perfect duty to act out of duty, then merely acting according to duty would be impossible, so that there would again be no permissible behaviour not motivated by duty, since one would be violating the second-order duty whenever one would be acting according to but not out of the first-order duty. Second, the very idea of it being a duty to act out of duty would seem to be confused, since it presupposes that the incorporation of incentives is itself an action that is based on maxims that are subject to the categorical imperative. This is misguided since incentives are incorporated on the basis of the *Gesinnung*, which has a different status from ordinary maxims.[20]

There is no need to act out of duty, except when doing so is necessary for acting according to duty.[21] Only when morality and prudence conflict, such that one has to set prudence aside and act on the basis of respect for

[20] The idea of a duty to act out of duty might also seem objectionable due to generating an infinite regress of actions, so that agency would never get off the ground. Or, as is sometimes suggested, that there would be an infinite regress of duties (cf. Michael Walschots, 'Kant and the Duty to Act from Duty', *History of Philosophy Quarterly* 39 (2022), 59–75, especially section 1). This is mistaken. If one complies with the second-order duty, that is, if one acts out of duty, then it follows that one does so out of duty. This is because one cannot act out of duty out of self-interest (i.e. one cannot genuinely act out of duty and do something on the basis of respect for the law when one is motivated by self-interest to do so), so that there is no room for a third-order duty to act out of the second-order duty when acting out of the first-order duty. Put differently, in the case of the first-order duty there is not only the question whether one complies with duty, but also the subsidiary question in case of compliance whether one complies out of duty or not. The second-order duty concerns precisely this issue, since it amounts to a duty to comply out of duty. Here the question is whether one complies with this second-order duty by acting out of duty. Since it is not possible for the agent to act out of duty out of self-interest, there is no corresponding subsidiary question that could be the object of a third-order duty.

[21] Also cf. Philipp-Alexander Hirsch, *Freiheit und Staatlichkeit bei Kant: Die autonomietheoretische Begründung von Recht und Staat und das Widerstandsproblem*, Berlin: De Gruyter, 2017, 119.

the law if one is to act permissibly, does one have to act out of duty. In that case merely acting according to duty is not an option. The only situations in which acting out of duty is possible, namely when there is a conflict between morality and prudence, are also the only situations in which acting out of duty is required. Yet even then one ought to act out of duty not because doing so has moral worth but because doing so is necessary for acting according to duty.[22]

The categorical imperative requires us to act on universalizable maxims, but it does not require that we do so out of duty. Our maxims have to be universalizable but they do not have to be motivated by respect for the law. We need to see to it that we do our duty, but there is no need to do our duty out of duty. A rightful condition in which compliance with laws is guaranteed by the threat of punishment and in which the fulfilment of juridical duties lacks moral worth is thus unproblematic from the perspective of morality.

7.3.4 Signatory Value

The moral worth of our actions is susceptible to luck. The possibility of performing an action that has moral worth is contingent on instrumental reason putting forward a non-universalizable maxim, which is in part a function of constitutive and circumstantial luck. This type of moral luck is relatively benign because the moral worth of our actions is a derivative kind of worth that results from the manifestation of a good will. Non-derivative moral worth is had by the good will and is immune to luck.

The fact that the worth of our actions derives from manifesting the worth of a good will can be brought out by considering someone who has a bad will yet nevertheless acts out of duty and is motivated by respect for the law. Having a bad will yet acting out of duty is possible since an agent

[22] If ensuring that our actions had moral worth were required of us, then this would have the troublesome consequence that we should create contexts in which instrumental reasoning puts forward impermissible maxims such that it becomes possible for the agent to act out of duty. This would imply not only that one should avoid a rightful condition, but also that one should engage in morally risky behaviour, such as making promises that are difficult to keep, cultivating troublesome inclinations (cf. Schiller: 'Decisum: Da ist kein anderer Rat, du mußt suchen, sie zu verachten, | Und mit Abscheu alsdann tun, wie die Pflicht dir gebeut'), or seeking out circumstances in which one's ends can only be achieved impermissibly. Relatedly, if one thinks that moral worth comes in degrees and is a function of the difficulty of resisting inclination and siding with duty (as seems to be suggested by some of Kant's remarks about merit), then one would have to bring about contexts in which acting out of duty is particularly praiseworthy, for example by cultivating recalcitrant inclinations that are difficult to overcome. If anything, the opposite is true due to the indirect duty to pursue one's happiness in order to avoid potential conflicts between prudence and morality.

who has a bad will subordinates duty to self-interest. This means that he always pursues self-interest, except that he pursues duty when doing so is not detrimental to self-interest.[23] He will, consequently, act out of duty when doing so does not require him to make any sacrifices.[24]

When two alternatives are equally good from the perspective of self-interest, that is, when they are all things considered prudentially equivalent, instrumental reasoning puts forward a disjunctive practical rule requiring us to perform either of them. Whenever one disjunct is impermissible, pure practical reason will reject this disjunctive maxim and restrict the maxim to the permissible disjunct. An agent who has a bad will is going to be motivated by respect for the law to reject the disjunctive maxim that contains the impermissible disjunct and instead perform the permissible action. Neither self-interest nor duty could motivate him to act otherwise, since considerations of self-interest do not decide amongst the two alternatives and since considerations of duty favour the permissible action. The subordinated principle of duty, accordingly, determines how someone who has a bad will acts when two (undominated) options are tied in terms of self-interest but differ in terms of permissibility, since the fact that self-love does not care which of them is performed allows the subordinated principle of duty to come in.[25]

The possibility of acting out of duty while having a bad will is the analogue of the possibility of acting out of self-interest while having a good will. A good will and a bad will differ in terms of the ordering of duty and self-love. If various actions are morally permissible, that is, they are 'indifferent' from the point of view of morality, then someone who has a good will chooses amongst them on the basis of self-love, selecting the one that makes them most happy. By contrast, if various actions are prudentially

[23] A bad will, which prioritizes self-love over duty, is to be distinguished from a diabolical will that is actively opposed to morality and from a will that is completely indifferent to morality. A bad will treats duty as a tie-breaker, such that one chooses the right action conditional on it being prudentially permissible. A diabolical will, by contrast, acts wrongly even when the right action is prudentially permissible. A will that is indifferent to morality randomizes amongst prudentially permissible actions. Human beings are only capable of having either a good will or a bad will and cannot be opposed or indifferent to morality (cf. RGV 6:35).

[24] Accordingly, the three types of actions: (1) out of duty, (2) according to duty, (3) contrary to duty, and the two types of will: (1) good will, (2) bad will, combine to yield five possibilities. One can act out of duty both when having a good will and when having a bad will. Likewise, for acting according to duty. Yet one can act contrary to duty only when having a bad will.

[25] Put differently, any agent who is exclusively motivated by self-love when two alternatives are prudentially but not morally equivalent will be indifferent to morality. Since we are not indifferent to morality, but can at most subordinate morality, and since the only alternative for us to acting on the basis of self-love is acting on the basis of duty, it follows that we have no option but to act out of duty in such situations, even when we have a bad will.

'permissible', so that they are indifferent from the point of view of prudence, then someone who has a bad will chooses amongst them on the basis of duty, selecting the one that is universalizable. The two cases are symmetrical (though the former scenario is much more likely to arise than the latter, since it can easily happen that multiple actions are permissible, yet not so easily happen that multiple undominated actions are prudentially indifferent).

Since respect for the law is playing an entirely subordinated role in the case of an action that is performed out of duty by someone who has a bad will, insofar as it merely functions as a tie-breaker that tips the scale in favour of the permissible action, it seems inappropriate to consider such an action to have moral worth. Though the correct incentive is operative, the agent has the incorrect *Gesinnung*, which means that the incentive is not assigned its proper role. The action, accordingly, fails to manifest the subordination of self-interest to morality that is to be found in the case of a good will and that gives morality its dignity.

The crucial issue is thus not acting out of duty but manifesting a good will. The latter involves the former. The former, however, does not imply the latter, since acting out of duty is not sufficient for moral worth. Moral worth pertains to the manifestation of a good will, which consists in the combination of having a good will and acting out of duty. An action has moral worth iff it is performed out of duty on the basis of a good will.[26] Both elements need to be combined. Having a good will is not by itself sufficient for an action to have moral worth, since someone who has a good will can out of self-interest perform actions that accord with duty and that lack moral worth.[27] And acting out of duty is not by itself sufficient, since an action performed out of duty by someone who has a bad will lacks moral worth.[28]

[26] Both commissions and omissions can have moral worth. Cf. Refl 7115: 'Doing good and omitting evil (the former without motives of self-love, the latter under motives of self-love) are both morally good, that is, equivalent in terms of morality; we can therefore regard omissions of the opposite as actions' (19:252).

[27] The good will is not sufficient in general for acting out of duty, but is only sufficient for acting out of duty when doing so is necessary for doing one's duty. If acting out of duty and having a good will were to go together, then not acting out of duty would imply not having a good will, from which it would follow, given rigorism (cf. RGV 6:22 fn.), that acting according to duty would imply having a bad will. Yet, since acting according to duty is permissible, there is no reason to think that it implies having a bad will.

[28] These cases also constitute exceptions to the claim that only those actions have moral worth that one would not have performed if one would have had a bad will. Since duty can be operative and motivate the same action even when subordinated, it follows that the good will need not make a difference in terms of whether an action is performed.

The moral worth of an action is then to be understood as a form of signatory value that does not add anything to the value of the world. It is a derivative value that is due to manifesting the goodness of the good will. What is of ultimate significance is the moral worth of the good will and not the moral worth of our actions. What matters is virtue, not its manifestation in the form of virtuous behaviour. Put differently, the moral worth of an action does not add anything to but merely manifests the moral worth of the good will. Having a good will and acting out of duty is not better than having a good will and merely acting according to duty. To think otherwise would be to engage in double counting. Correspondingly, the unconditioned component of the highest good, namely the supreme good, is to be understood in terms of the having of a good will and not in terms of the manifestation of a good will. The unconditional goodness of the good will extends to the point where its goodness is independent even of its own manifestation. For the highest good to be realized, individuals need to have a good will, but they do not need to manifest their good will through virtuous behaviour.[29]

7.4 Conclusion

From the perspective of luck, no significant differences open up between morality and legality. In particular, the legality of an action is just as much immune to resultant luck as the morality of an action. This is because legality is a function, not of the consequences of our actions, but of the maxims on which we act. And while juridical imputation allows for resultant luck, ethical imputation does the same. Morality and legality are thus closer to each other than might initially seem to be the case, which raises the hopes for a unification of ethics and right.[30]

[29] Otherwise, it would be a matter of luck whether the highest good could be realized. Moreover, moral luck would have an effect on the extent to which different agents would be worthy of happiness.

[30] The legality vs morality contrast applies to all duties. All duties admit of the possibility of either acting out of duty or merely according to duty. A suitable restriction of the relevant actions focuses on juridical duties, most notably enforceable duties that concern the way in which actions affect the freedom of choice of others. (Difficulties arise in specifying the relevant restriction due to the duty of *honeste vive*, which is a non-enforceable duty to self yet nevertheless is classified as a duty of right. For a discussion of some of these complexities cf. Luke Davies, 'Whence "Honeste Vive"?', *European Journal of Philosophy* 29 (2021), 323–38.)

CHAPTER 8

Kant on Permissive Law

Martin Brecher

8.1 Introduction

The concept of permissive law (*Erlaubnisgesetz*) figures prominently in both *Towards Perpetual Peace* and the *Doctrine of Right.* In both writings permissive laws come into play to establish special privileges for juridical agents – states in the former, individuals in the latter. In the literature on Kant's legal and political philosophy, there is considerable debate about how to understand Kant's notion of permissive law. In particular, there are two prominent but opposing views.[1] The first, which has long been the common view, is that permissive laws are meant to permit certain actions that are legally or morally forbidden. Thus, Reinhard Brandt in his landmark contribution to the discussion has suggested that permissive law has the function of provisionally permitting something that is prohibited as such. Thus, according to Brandt, permissive laws provisionally enable the use of force in lieu of right, and in some sense even contrary to it, and prevent other agents from enacting their rightful claims against the agent who acts on the basis of the permissive law. In this way, Brandt

The interpretation of permissive law that I present here has been originally developed in the context of my work on Kant's marriage right, in order to account for the 'natural permissive law' of marital acquisition (6:276) (see Martin Brecher: *Vernunftrecht und Verdinglichung: Eine Rekonstruktion von Kants Eherecht*, Berlin: De Gruyter, 2025, ch. 8). For valuable feedback on previous versions of the present chapter I thank audiences at XXIV. Deutscher Kongress für Philosophie, Berlin 2017, at GAP.11, Berlin 2022, and at the conference, 'Law and Morality in Kant', Göttingen 2022. I especially thank my commentator Jakob Huber for his nuanced criticism and helpful remarks.

[1] Joel T. Klein adds as a third main kind of approach Brian Tierney's reading that 'stress[es] the systematic-conceptual unfitness of permissive laws' (Joel T. Klein, 'Permissive Laws and Teleology in Kant's Juridical and Political Philosophy', *Kantian Review* 27 (2022), 215–36, at 215). See Tierney's 'Kant on Property: The Problem of Permissive Law', *Journal of the History of Ideas* 62 (2001), 301–12, and 'Permissive Natural Law and Property: Gratian to Kant', *Journal of the History of Ideas* 62 (2001), 381–99. In what follows, I will not discuss Tierney's interpretation.

argues, the permissive law is required in order to actually bring about juridical and legal institutions, that is, to enable the realization of right.[2]

The second prominent account has more recently been put forward by Joachim Hruschka. Hruschka opposes the common assumption that Kant would employ the same notion of permissive law in both *Perpetual Peace* and the *Metaphysics of Morals*, and he argues that we find a revised understanding of permissive law in the *Metaphysics of Morals*: the permissive law in the *Doctrine of Right*, Hruschka submits, should not be taken as a norm establishing exceptions to prohibitions (as in *Perpetual Peace*), but as a norm regulating previously *indifferent* actions. Specifically, the permissive law, Hruschka argues, changes the legal character of certain actions by conferring particular legal powers on the agents who act in these ways, specifically the power to acquire external objects of choice.[3]

In what follows, I will propose a reading of permissive law that differs from both approaches in important respects. As I will argue, in both *Perpetual Peace* and the *Doctrine of Right*, Kant takes permissive laws to indeed grant exceptions to prohibitions. However, contrary to the common reading advocated by Brandt and others, permissive laws do not permit wrongful actions, either in the sense of tolerating, or excusing, transgressions of prohibitions, or in the sense of suspending other demands

[2] Reinhard Brandt, 'Das Erlaubnisgesetz, oder: Vernunft und Geschichte in Kants Rechtslehre", in Reinhard Brandt (ed.), *Rechtsphilosophie der Aufklärung*, Berlin: De Gruyter, 1982, 233–85, see in particular 244–6, 256. In a similar vein, Oliver Eberl and Peter Niesen propose that permissive laws suspend certain legal or moral requirements, but only temporarily, thereby tolerating transgressions of the laws of pure practical reason on the grounds that this facilitates the introduction of new norms, such as institutions of international law ('Kommentar', in Immanuel Kant, *Zum ewigen Frieden*, ed. by Oliver Eberl and Peter Niesen, Berlin: Suhrkamp, 2011, 202–3). Christoph Horn, pursuing the overall aim of showing that Kant regards legal or political normativity as specifically distinct from moral normativity, submits that the permissive law allows an agent 'to violate the general law of the inviolability of external freedom', albeit on the grounds that the agent has 'the idea of right on his side' (Horn, *Nichtideale Normativität: Ein neuer Blick auf Kants politische Philosophie*, Berlin: Suhrkamp, 2014, 215; my translation).

[3] See Joachim Hruschka, 'The Permissive Law of Practical Reason in Kant's *Metaphysics of Morals*', *Law and Philosophy* 23 (2004), 45–72, and 'Das Erlaubnisgesetz der praktischen Vernunft und der ursprüngliche Erwerb von Stücken des Erdbodens', in *Kant und der Rechtsstaat und andere Essays zu Kants Rechtslehre und Ethik*, Freiburg: Karl Alber, 48–88. This interpretation is also defended by B. Sharon Byrd, 'Intelligible Possession of Objects of Choice', in Lara Denis (ed.), *Kant's* Metaphysics of Morals*: A Critical Guide*, Cambridge: Cambridge University Press, 2010, 93–110, see 96–99, and 'The Elusive Story of Kant's Permissive Laws', in Lara Denis and Oliver Sensen (eds.), *Kant's Lectures on Ethics. A Critical Guide*, Cambridge: Cambridge University Press, 2015, 156–69, at 164–6. See also their co-authored *Kant's* Doctrine of Right*: A Commentary*. Cambridge: Cambridge University Press, 2010, ch. 4. Hruschka's interpretation has been adopted, for instance, by Arthur Ripstein, *Force and Freedom*, Cambridge, MA: Harvard University Press, 2009, 103–4 n. 19, and Rainer Friedrich, *Eigentum und Staatsbegründung in Kants* Metaphysik der Sitten, Berlin: De Gruyter, 2004, 113–18.

of right or morality. As I will show, permissive laws proceed from antecedent prohibitions and specify conditions under which an action is permissible that would *otherwise* be wrongful, namely if these conditions are not fulfilled; this makes the permitted acts genuinely, albeit conditionally, allowed, not merely tolerated. This implies that the actions that fall under permissive laws are not, as Hruschka thinks, indifferent actions as such: while it is true that permissive laws grant certain legal powers to agents, I will argue that the actions in question are not indifferent, but would indeed be forbidden if they were not subject to permissive laws and the conditions they set.

I will carve out this notion of permissive law from Kant's discussion of permissive law in *Perpetual Peace*, for it is there that Kant clarifies his understanding of this type of norm. By relating Kant's remarks to the notion of *lex permissiva* found in the relevant textbooks by Achenwall and Baumgarten, I will show that Kant takes permissive law to be a special kind of prohibitive law: specifically a law that, against the background of a general prohibition, licenses certain acts under specific conditions (Section 8.2). I will then argue that we find the same basic understanding of permissive law in the *Vigilantius* lecture notes, despite the statement there that permissive law allows 'might to hold for right' (Section 8.3).

In the second half of the chapter, I will turn to the *Metaphysics of Morals*. I will first argue, against Hruschka, that the understanding of permissive law that Kant articulates in the Introduction of the *Metaphysics of Morals* does not in fact depart from that found in *Perpetual Peace* (Section 8.4). I will then turn to the *Doctrine of Right* and attend to the different instances of permissive law in Private Right. I will highlight how each instance of permissive law has to be understood as granting a permission subject to certain conditions against the backdrop of a general prohibition: it is only through the indication of certain specific conditions that the relevant acts must fulfil that these acts are permitted and the juridical institutions or relations in question can be established by them (Section 8.5).

8.2 'A Kind of Prohibitive Law': The Concept of Permissive Law in *Towards Perpetual Peace*

In his published writings,[4] Kant uses the term 'permissive law' for the first time in *Towards Perpetual Peace*, and it is there that he elaborates on his

[4] There is evidence in Kant's handwritten notes that he mentioned the concept of the permissive law in his ethics lectures (Refl 7031, 19:231; Refl 7256, 19:295). In the student notes of the moral philosophy lectures from the 1770s we find the simple statement that '*Leges* [. . .] *permissivae*' are

understanding of it. Kant introduces the notion in a remark following the presentation of the preliminary articles for establishing peace. All six preliminary articles, Kant says, are '*laws of prohibition*', but while some of them 'put[] a stop' to certain state practices '*at once*', with respect to other provisions there is the possibility of '*postpon[ing]* putting these laws into effect' (8:347).[5] The provisions in question 'contain permissions', 'taking into consideration the circumstances in which they are to be *applied*' (8:347). In a footnote to the passage, Kant explains the extent to which one can speak of permissive laws with respect to such provisions. There he clarifies his understanding of this type of norm by distinguishing it from what he considers to be two false understandings of permissive law, thus establishing the defining marks of his notion of permissive law.

8.2.1 Permissions and Prohibitions

The first understanding of permissive law that Kant rejects is the idea that permissive laws are required for indifferent acts to be possible. This, according to Kant, would be absurd. Since laws contain 'a ground of objective practical necessity' of actions, whereas permissions contain a reason 'of the practical contingency of certain actions', a permissive *law* would present a contradiction: for a permissive law would express the 'necessity to an action such that one cannot be necessitated to do it' (8:348 fn.). In other words, a permissive law regarding an action φ would, on the one hand, *qua law*, state the practical necessity to φ, but on the other hand it would at the same time, *qua permission*, imply the absence of this necessity. Thus, permissive laws are not required for actions that are morally indifferent.[6]

As Kant goes on to argue, it only makes sense to speak of permissive laws insofar as necessitation and permission refer to different actions, but not if 'the object of the law has the same meaning in both kinds of relation' (8:348 fn.). As a case in point, both in the main text and in the footnote, Kant refers to the second preliminary article, which prohibits the acquisition of one state by another 'through inheritance, exchange, purchase or

such laws 'whereby actions are permitted', and that one 'could also think of *jus permissi*' (V-Mo/Collins 27:274). I will turn to the later *Vigilantius* lecture notes in Section 8.3.

5 The articles to be implemented immediately are articles nos. 1, 5, and 6; delayed implementation is possible for articles nos. 2, 3, and 4 (8:347).

6 In an addendum to the second edition of the *Religion within the Boundaries of Mere Reason*, published one year before *Perpetual Peace*, Kant states that 'neither *command*, nor *prohibition*, nor yet *permission* (*authorization* according to law), intervenes or is necessary' with respect to 'a morally indifferent action' (RGV 6:23 fn.).

donation' (8:344). Since such acquisitions lack 'the necessary legal title', the preliminary article implies the duty that the states that have acquired other states in these ways restore the freedom of those states (8:347; translation modified). Now, while the article directly prohibits any acquisition of states by others in the future, the reversal of past acquisitions, Kant argues, can be adapted to the circumstances of each specific case. Thus, a past acquisition may still be regarded as valid for a certain transitional period until the restoration can be realized: 'the prohibition here concerns only the *way of acquiring*, which from now on shall not hold, but not the *status of possession*' (8:347). To the extent that prohibition and permission refer to different objects, it is possible, Kant submits, to speak here of a permissive *law* (8:348 fn.).

It is important to note that the prohibition is the primary component to which the permission refers, as Kant's formulations show: 'the prohibition presupposed', 'the exemption from this prohibition, i.e., the permission' (8:348 fn.).[7] On the one hand, the prohibition is a precondition of the permission, in that the conduct regulated by the law is generally prohibited and permitted in certain circumstances only. On the other hand, the prohibition sets limits to the permission by tying the permitted action to specific conditions. Thus, the restitution of state autonomy may be delayed if 'implementing the law prematurely [will] counteract its very purpose' (8:347), but the permission does not extend so far that the restitution could be postponed forever, 'to a nonexistent date', so that the delay would amount to not restoring the other state's freedom (8:347). We can therefore say that the permission is limited by the underlying prohibition, or by the grounds of that prohibition.

These observations also apply to the permissive laws that Kant hints at in the appendix of *Perpetual Peace*. There Kant argues that shortcomings in the constitution of a state do not have to be eliminated in one fell swoop but can be remedied step by step through gradual reforms: there are 'permissive laws of reason that allow a situation of public right afflicted with injustice to continue' until the conditions are such that the

[7] Accordingly, Wolfgang Kersting believes that permissive laws are 'necessarily derivative in nature'. In his view, they 'can only appear in the form of exceptional rules that restrict the scope of existing laws of prohibition and thus allow certain previously prohibited acts under the conditions formulated in them' (Wolfgang Kersting, *Wohlgeordnete Freiheit: Immanuel Kants Rechts- und Staatsphilosophie*, Berlin: De Gruyter, 1984, 65; my translation). However, as I will show in Section 8.2.2, permissive laws do not represent separate norms that would restrict laws of prohibition distinct from them; rather, the permissive law is a particular kind of law of prohibition, so that prohibition and permission are part of the same law.

constitution may safely be changed, that is, 'until everything has either of itself become ripe for a complete overthrow or has been made almost ripe by peaceful means' (8:373 fn.).[8] The permission in question applies if 'a *premature* reform' threatens to undo the juridical condition so that a relapse into the 'anarchy' of the state of nature is to be feared (8:373 fn.). The reason for the permission to change the constitution step by step accordingly lies in the fact that '*some* rightful constitution or other, even if it is only to a small degree in conformity with right, is better than none at all' (8:373 fn.; my emphasis).

As with preliminary articles 2, 3, and 4, the permission to forgo a complete revision of a faulty constitution and postpone certain changes holds against the background of a general prohibition, in this case the inadmissibility, itself grounded in 'the ideal of public right' (8:373 fn.), of an unjust state constitution. Moreover, in this case, too, the permission is at the same time limited by the prohibition: the postponement is only allowed insofar and as long as it is necessary for change to be actually possible and it is conjoined with the 'duty' to work towards the realization of the provision, to 'make reforms in keeping with the ideal of public right' (8:373 fn.). Now, it may seem as if the permissive law in question would indeed tolerate a wrongful action, insofar as it allows 'a situation of public right *afflicted with injustice* to continue' (8:373 fn.; my emphasis). But it indeed '*allow*[*s*]' deferring certain constitutional changes (8:373 fn.; my emphasis), and it does this insofar as it is required for the injustice to be remedied. The permissive law hence declares that retaining the current constitution, as long as changing it is not possible, is genuinely allowed, based, ultimately, on the idea of Public Right.

8.2.2 Permissive Law as a Kind of Prohibitive Law

The second understanding of permissive law that Kant rejects in his elaboration in *Perpetual Peace* is the idea that permissive laws are independent norms of exception that are, as it were, attached to, or placed alongside, prohibitive laws. According to Kant, examples of this are often found in positive law ('in civil (statutory) law'): 'Then it is said that this or that is prohibited, *except* for number 1, number 2, number 3, and so forth indefinitely' (8:348 fn.). In such cases, the relationship between prohibition and permission is such that 'the prohibitive law stands all by itself and

[8] Kant probably had in mind the hasty reforms implemented in Austria by Joseph II. See Brandt, 'Erlaubnisgesetz', 249–55.

the permission is not included in that law as a limiting condition (as it should be) but is thrown in among exceptions to it' (8:348 fn.). Kant's criticism of this approach is that the exemptions from the prohibition are added to the law 'only contingently, not in accordance with a principle but by groping among cases that come up' (8:348 fn.).

In contrast to this approach, Kant holds that if one wishes to identify '*permissive laws* [. . .] of pure reason' (8:347 fn.) a properly systematic approach is required in which 'the conditions [are] introduced *into the formula of the prohibitive law*' (8:348 fn.; Kant's emphasis). If this is done, that is, if the conditions under which a certain action shall be permitted are specified in the formula of the prohibition, the prohibitive law ('it') becomes '*at the same time* a permissive law' (8:348; my emphasis). By including the conditions under which the prohibition shall not hold into the law itself, the law assumes a dual character: in relation to the generally required omission of a certain course of action, the law is a law of prohibition, but in relation to those conditions under which that course of action is allowed it is a permissive law. Thus, Kant characterizes permissive law as a form of prohibitive law that specifies conditions for exemptions from its prohibition, thereby establishing a particular permission.

Permissive law is thus a kind of prohibitive law. This is reflected by Kant's distinction, in his remark at the end of the section on the preliminary articles, between prohibitive laws 'of the *strict* kind (*leges strictae*), holding without regard for differing circumstances', on the one hand, and 'laws that, taking into consideration the circumstances in which they are to be *applied*, *subjectively* widen [one's] authorization (*leges latae*) and contain permissions', on the other hand (8:347).[9] In a similar vein, in the *Vigilantius* lecture notes, Kant distinguishes between prohibitive laws that hold universally ('*universales*'), that is, which are 'valid under all circumstances, so that an exception is therefore impossible, and a permissive law not to be thought of here at all', and merely general prohibitions ('*generales*'), 'where the prohibition holds good in the great majority of cases (in

[9] I think Aaron Szymkowiak overshoots the mark when he argues that Kant would claim that 'there are prohibitive laws that become intelligible only when attended by certain permissions' and that 'the permissions must constitute laws in themselves in order to preserve the lawful status of the commands or prohibitions they are intended to supplement or complete' (Aaron Szymkowiak, 'Kant's Permissive Law: Critical Rights, Sceptical Politics', *British Journal for the History of Philosophy* 17 (2009), 567–600, at 570). As we have seen, it is the prohibitive component that makes permissive laws proper laws, not the other way around. Hence, I believe the correct picture is simply that there are certain prohibitive laws that include certain exceptions, and a permissive law is simply such a limited prohibitive law considered with respect to the exceptions, that is, permissions, it includes.

general)' and where therefore 'exceptions are conceivable' (27:514). As the texts clearly show, Kant in both cases regards permissive law as a kind of prohibitive law.

In considering permissive law as a kind of prohibitive law, Kant follows his textbook authors Alexander Gottlieb Baumgarten and Gottfried Achenwall.[10] Both regard the *lex permissiva* as a special (Baumgarten: 'peculiaris') kind of prohibitive law ('species legis prohibitivae'). Both argue that a permissive law is a law of prohibition that on the one hand establishes an obligation (in the form of a prohibition) and on the other hand grants an authorization. Thus, Baumgarten explains that 'a PERMISSIVE LAW (permission strictly considered) is a law declaring that a certain action that has indeed not been prescribed is indeed nevertheless not to be impeded'. The permissive law is therefore 'a particular species of prohibitive law' (*est peculiaris species legis prohibitivae*). It is a law 'in favour of someone who perhaps will carry out certain things' in that it 'obligates others to omit an impedition that otherwise could have been opposed to such a free determination'.[11]

Achenwall similarly elaborates:

> If a juridical law determines that a certain action, although it is not prescribed, must not be hindered either, it is a law and a kind of prohibitive law [*species legis prohibitivae*] [. . .]. But as it has a different effect with regard to him to whom it attributes the ability to do something licitly and with regard to him onto whom it imposes the obligation not to hinder the other man, with respect to the former it is a PERMITTING (permissive) law, with regard to the latter a COMMANDING one. In the former respect the law is called permitting, because by force of such law the legislator grants the ability to execute a certain action as permitted.[12]

Kant's view, however, differs from that of his textbook authors with regard to what is permitted and what is prohibited by the law. For Achenwall and Baumgarten, permission and prohibition refer to the actions of different agents addressed by the law. The law that permits an agent A to φ is a permissive law for this agent. Insofar as the law at the same time prohibits other agents from interfering with A's doing φ, it is a law of prohibition for

[10] Kant used Baumgarten's ethics textbooks for his lectures on moral philosophy from 1759 onwards, and Achenwall's textbooks for his lectures on natural law from 1767 onwards.

[11] Alexander G. Baumgarten, *Elements of First Practical Philosophy: A Critical Translation with Kant's Reflections on Moral Philosophy*, ed. and trans. by Courtney D. Fugate and John Hymers, London: Bloomsbury, 2020, § 68.

[12] Gottfried Achenwall, *Prolegomena to Natural Law* (1763), ed. by Pauline Kleingeld, trans. by Corinna Vermeulen, Groningen: University of Groningen Press, 2020, § 90.

those other agents. This is very clearly brought out by Achenwall's explanation of permissive law, quoted above: the law 'has a different effect' for the different agents. As Achenwall puts it succinctly in his *Ius Naturae*: '[S]uch a law is called "permitting" with regard to the person to whom it concedes the ability to do something licitly, but "commanding" with regard to the person whom it obligates not to hinder someone else.'[13]

On Kant's view, in contrast, permission and prohibition are directed *at the same agent*. For Kant, what differs are the forbidden and permitted *actions*, namely the respective 'object[s] of the law' (8:348 fn.), and they differ on the basis of the conditions or circumstances in which an agent subject to the law finds herself. Thus, while agent *A* is generally prohibited from φ-ing, *A* is permitted to φ under certain circumstances as specified by the law. Thus, it is forbidden for states to acquire another state, while they are allowed to retain their prior acquisitions until restitution of wrongful acquisition can successfully commence.

Now, Kant's notion of permissive law, like that of Achenwall and Baumgarten, also implies that other agents are prohibited from preventing the addressee of a permissive law from exercising his authority. Within the scope of the conditions specified by the permissive law, *A's* doing φ is permitted, that is, it is not subject to any prohibition. Hence, insofar as *A's* doing φ conforms with law, other agents may not interfere with it. Thus, other nations may not force state *S* to restore freedom immediately to those states it had illegitimately acquired in the past. Indeed, owing to the permissive law, *S* may rightfully resist any such attempts at interfering with conducting its own affairs. This aspect, however, is not the essence of permissive laws for Kant. In fact, the account of permissive law found in Achenwall and Baumgarten cannot suffice in Kant's eyes. On their account, the normativity of the permissive law (its being a practical law) does pertain only to the agents who are prohibited from interfering with the permitted action.[14] But unless the permitted action is also prescribed, it does not make sense, as we have seen in the previous section, to speak of

[13] Achenwall, *Natural Law* (1763), ed. by Pauline Kleingeld, trans. by Corinna Vermeulen, London: Bloomsbury, 2020, part I, § 48.

[14] Achenwall uses the term 'lex iubens' to describe any law that imposes an obligation on an agent ('obligationem imponit': *Ius Naturae*, Göttingen 1763, part I, § 48). Depending on whether the omission or the commission of an act is prescribed, it can be a law of prohibition ('LEX [...] PROHIBITIVA (vetans, negans)') or a prescriptive law ('LEX [...] PRAECEPTIVA (praecipiens, aiens[])') (*Prolegomena*, § 19). For Achenwall, then, the character of the permissive law to be a particular kind of law is due to the fact that a binding force correlating to the permission is created on the side of the other agent(s). Kant himself articulates such an understanding of permissive law in a note in the preliminary drafts for the *Metaphysics of Morals* (cf. 23:384).

laws for permitted acts. On Kant's account, in contrast, the permissive law is a proper law *for the addressee of the permission* insofar as she is at the same time the addressee of the antecedent prohibition.

Given Kant's understanding of permissive law as a kind of prohibitive law, it is clear that permissive laws do not authorize doing something that is still forbidden: as Kant says, a generally prohibitive law is turned into a permissive law by inserting 'into the formula of the prohibitive law' the conditions under which the action regulated by the law is to be permitted (8:348 fn.; emphasis removed). Since prohibition and permission are for Kant part of the same law, the permission has genuinely to allow the action in question, rather than merely tolerate it as a transgression of the prohibition: for it would be contradictory for a law to establish a prohibition and at the same time allow a contravention to it. Moreover, like all practical laws, the permissive laws with which Kant is concerned are principles of (pure practical) reason (8:347 fn.; 8:373 fn.), and reason cannot issue a prohibition while at the same time allowing its transgression. Indeed, Kant emphasizes that the authorizations granted by permissive laws do 'not' allow the agents 'to make exceptions to the rule of right' (*nicht als Ausnahmen von der Rechtsregel*; 8:347). Far from taking permissive laws as suspending the validity of the prescripts of reason, Kant thus understands permissive law as conditionally allowing, or licensing, a course of action that is otherwise forbidden, namely if the conditions contained in the law do not obtain. In this sense, a permissive law merely limits the scope of an antecedent prohibition.

8.3 Permissive Law in *Metaphysics of Morals Vigilantius*

I now want to turn briefly to the discussion of permissive law in the *Vigilantius* lecture notes from 1793/4 which can be easily misread as implying that permissive laws would sanction forbidden actions. Against the backdrop of our discussion of permissive law in *Perpetual Peace* one can see, however, that Kant already entertains the same notion of permissive law in the lecture.

The discussion of permissive law in *Vigilantius* revolves around the question whether there are permissive laws in natural law just as they exist in positive law. Kant submits that 'if there are *leges permissivae*, they have to be accompanied with a prohibition' (27:514). This, however, is only possible if the prohibition in question is not a universal prohibition that is 'valid under all circumstances' but merely a general prohibition that holds for most but not all cases (27:514). It is with respect to these general prohibitive laws that 'there are permissive laws as exceptions' (27:514).

The prohibition that Kant takes as case in point is the principle that 'might must not replace right' (27:514). He submits that with respect to this prohibition a permissive law exists if 'the conditions exist, under which we may assume that might replaces right' (27:515). These conditions exist, as Kant goes on to argue, in the state of nature, before a legal condition is established. According to Kant, the only way for a state, and hence for a legal order, to come into existence is the use of force. There is therefore, he argues, a permissive law that allows might to precede right in this case (27:515–16).

Now, since the use of unilateral force (that is, of the use of might) is morally forbidden one could assume that the permissive law here functions to tolerate an immoral action or that it suspends that prohibition. However, as Kant's elaboration makes clear, the permissive law grants the use of force only if it is used for establishing right. And this is morally justified because the state of nature, due to its lack of legal institutions and the ensuing ubiquity of unilateral exercise of choice, is a condition that we are morally required to overcome:

> this is a state of affairs in conflict with the universal imperative of morality, and we thus have to assume that nature allows us, in this fashion, to bring man's free choice into agreement with general freedom, by means of universal law; and so here there is a natural law in effect, to permit the force employed. (27:515)

The use of unilateral force, while generally prohibited, is not prohibited when it is used in the state of nature in order to establish legal institutions; indeed, it is actually obligatory insofar as it is the only way to leave the state of nature.[15] Thus, as in *Perpetual Peace*, the permissive law in question only exists, first, with respect to an antecedent prohibition and, secondly, it limits the permission to the condition that the action in question is necessary to accommodate the demand of morality.

8.4 The Concept of Permissive Law in the Introduction of the *Metaphysics of Morals*

In the preceding two sections I have established that, contrary to the common view, Kant in *Perpetual Peace*, as well as in the *Vigilantius* lecture

[15] Cf. Byrd, 'Elusive Story', 161–2.

notes, does not regard permissive law as a norm for tolerating wrongful conduct. Rather, he situates permissive laws within the overall class of prohibitive laws. The specific difference of permissive law as a kind of prohibitive law is that it specifies conditions under which the prohibition in question does not hold, thereby establishing a permission to act in a certain way. In the remainder of the chapter I will attend to Kant's understanding and use of permissive law in the *Metaphysics of Morals*, specifically in Private Right in the *Doctrine of Right.*[16]

While most interpreters assume that Kant did not change his understanding of permissive law between the publication of *Perpetual Peace* and the *Doctrine of Right*, Joachim Hruschka has argued that in the *Doctrine of Right* we find a notion of permissive law different from that in *Perpetual Peace.* This revised type of permissive law, according to Hruschka, does not formulate an exemption from a prohibition, but is an authorizing, power-conferring norm by which practical reason enables the establishment of the institutions of private right.[17] In this function, Hruschka argues, the permissive law does not refer to acts that are as such prohibited, but rather relates to acts that are fundamentally morally indifferent, that is, simply permitted.[18] While I agree with Hruschka that the permissive laws coming into play in the *Doctrine of Right* concern the establishment of legal institutions and thus can be regarded as power-conferring norms, I submit that Hruschka is mistaken in assuming that Kant in his later work takes permissive law to relate to indifferent actions only and that it does not presuppose an antecedent prohibition.

Hruschka primarily justifies his interpretation with reference to a passage in the Introduction of the *Metaphysics of Morals* in which Kant briefly brings up the question of the existence and function of permissive laws. At the beginning of the passage Kant distinguishes two meanings of the term 'permitted', a general and a more narrow sense. In the general sense, any act is permitted ('*licitum*') 'which is not contrary to obligation' (6:222), that is, any act that is 'morally possible' (6:221). With regard to permitted acts, the agent possesses an authorization ('*facultas moralis*'), so that with respect to this act his 'freedom [. . .] is not limited by any

[16] Because I am here only concerned with Kant's legal philosophy, I will not attend to the two passages in the *Doctrine of Virtue* where Kant employs the concept of permissive law (6:426, 453). (Regarding the first passage, see Martin Brecher, 'Ehelicher Geschlechtsgebrauch und Fortpflanzungszweck in §7 der Tugendlehre', in Violetta Waibel et al. (eds.), *Natur und Freiheit: Akten des XII. Internationalen Kant-Kongresses*, Berlin: De Gruyter, 2018, 1761–8.)

[17] Hruschka, 'Permissive Law', 47; 'Erlaubnisgesetz', 55.

[18] Hruschka, 'Permissive Law', 50–3; 'Erlaubnisgesetz', 59–60.

opposing imperative' (6:222). All morally possible acts are permitted acts in this sense, including those acts that are actually obligatory, namely 'morally necessary' (6:221), for no other imperative stands in the way of the performance of acts to which we are obliged. In a narrower sense, Kant labels as 'merely permitted' those acts that are 'neither commanded nor prohibited': merely permitted actions are not subject to practical necessity in any way; in relation to them there is 'no law limiting one's freedom (one's authorization) [. . .] and so too no duty' (6:223; emphasis removed). An action that is merely permitted is 'morally indifferent (*indifferens, adiaphoron, res merae facultatis*)' (6:223). While the freedom of the agent is restricted in the case of an obligatory action insofar as she may not refrain from the action, in the case of a merely permitted action the agent is free to decide whether or not to perform it.

So far, Kant's exposition of these terms leaves open whether there actually are any merely permitted actions at all and, if so, whether these would require the existence of permissive laws:

> The question can be raised whether there are such actions and, if there are, whether there must be permissive laws (*lex permissiva*), in addition to laws that command and prohibit (*lex praeceptiva, lex mandati* and *lex prohibitiva, lex vetiti*), in order to account for someone's being free to do or not to do something as he pleases. (6:223)

While Kant leaves open at this point the question whether there are morally indifferent actions or not, he points out that permissive laws will not concern this class of actions:

> If so, the authorization would not in any case [*nicht allemal*] have to do with an indifferent action (*adiaphoron*); for, considering the action in terms of moral laws, no special law would be required for it. (6:223; translation modified)

Hruschka argues that in the passage just cited Kant would state that permissive law would apply to some merely allowed actions and that some merely allowed actions would accordingly require a permissive law (namely the actions by which agents can acquire rights to external objects). However, I think it is clear from the above quotations that this is not the case. If there are actions for which a permissive law is required ('If so') these actions will not be indifferent acts: for with regard to such an action, there is no practical necessity whatsoever anyway, which is why 'no special law would be required for it'. Thus, just as in *Perpetual Peace*, Kant here holds that permissive laws are not concerned with acts that are as such indifferent.

In his interpretation of the passage above, Hruschka reads the qualification 'nicht allemal' in the sense of 'not always',[19] to substantiate his assumption that Kant would distinguish between different types of merely permitted acts: namely, that he would only designate as *adiaphora* those actions that do not require a permissive law, whereas an act *qua 'res merae facultatis'* (6:223) would indeed require a permissive law.[20] However, Hruschka does not show why the obvious reading of 'nicht allemal' in the sense of 'not in any case' (or 'certainly not', *gewiss nicht*) should not apply here.[21] Moreover, one would expect Kant to provide some information about the cases in which a permissive law concerns a morally indifferent act and the cases in which it does not.[22] But since Kant does not make any explicit terminological distinction in the way Hruschka claims, we must assume that in the formulation 'morally indifferent (*indifferens, adiaphoron, res merae facultatis*)' Kant uses the three expressions mentioned in the brackets synonymously (6:223).[23]

8.5 The Permissive Laws in Private Right of the *Doctrine of Right*

Contrary to Hruschka's reading, Kant in the Introduction of the *Metaphysics of Morals* retains his view from *Perpetual Peace* according to which permissive laws do not refer to indifferent actions, but make certain

[19] Hruschka, 'Permissive Law', 50–1 n. 16 and 'Erlaubnisgesetz', 57. This is also the way in which Gregor, in my eyes incorrectly, translates the passage. In this way Kant uses the expression in two other places in the Introduction to the *Metaphysics of Morals*: once when he explains that the 'pleasure or displeasure in an object of desire does not always precede the desire' and accordingly 'need *not always* be regarded as the cause' of desire, 'but can also be regarded as the effect of it' (6:211; my emphasis), and when he says 'that all duties belong to ethics merely because they are duties, but their legislation [. . .] is therefore *not always* contained in ethics, but of many of them outside it' (6:219; my emphasis and translation).

[20] Hruschka, 'Permissive Law', 50–1 n. 16.

[21] See Heyse's *Handwörterbuch der deutschen Sprache*, vol. 1, Magdeburg 1833, s.v., allemal'. The Grimms' dictionary also points to this shift in meaning (*Deutsches Wörterbuch*, vol. 1, Leipzig: Hirzel, 1854, col. 218).

[22] Klein criticizes the distinction made by Hruschka along similar lines (Klein, 'Permissive Laws', 218).

[23] See also, first, *On the Common Saying*, 8:282, where Kant clearly understands the term '*res merae facultatis*' simply as a legal synonym ('as the lawyers say') to designate indifferent 'acts of freedom', and, secondly, in RL § 15, where Kant also uses the term '*res merae facultatis*' for actions that are at the discretion of the agent: thus, the way in which peoples 'wish to settle on the face of the earth' – for example, as 'a pasturing people', as 'tillers' or 'planters' – 'is a matter of mere discretion (*res merae facultatis*)' (6:266; my translation). These passages provide further evidence that Kant does not use the term *res merae facultatis* to mark a terminological distinction, as Hruschka thinks, within the class of permitted indifferent actions.

actions legally possible that are otherwise prohibited. I will now show that this also applies to the permissive laws employed by Kant in the *Doctrine of Right.*

The permissive laws in Private Right allow certain actions by which legal institutions can be established, specifically they enable the establishment of legal possession in general (RL § 2), the original acquisition of land in the state of nature (§ 16), and the acquisition of another person (§ 22). As Hruschka points out, the permissive laws in these cases confer legal powers on the agents who carry out the corresponding acts, namely the power to establish new relations of right. These actions, however, are not as such indifferent, as Hruschka maintains. Rather, outwith the scope of the permissive law these acts would indeed be contrary to right. On the other hand, while the permissive laws thereby formulate exceptions to prohibitions, they do not suspend the rule of right: the actions in question are not merely tolerated, they do not remain as such wrongful, as the common reading holds, but are genuinely allowed. Finally, the permissive laws make the actions that they allow subject to certain requirements and restrictions that have to be fulfilled for the permission to take effect.[24]

8.5.1 The Juridical Postulate of Practical Reason as a Permissive Law (§ 2)

According to Kant, the 'juridical postulate of practical reason' (6:246) that he introduces at the beginning of Private Right can be described as a permissive law (6:247).[25] The postulate states that it must be possible 'to have any external object of my choice as mine' (6:246). By means of the postulate, practical reason 'extends itself' beyond innate right and opens up the sphere of the external mine and thine (6:247). The postulate thus lays the foundation of Private Right as a whole.

By virtue of the postulate – and the concept of merely juridical possession it serves to establish (6:252) – it is possible for agents to put others under obligation with regard to external objects, namely by restricting their

[24] For an interpretation of the permissive laws in Private Right, which focuses on the aspect of provisionality of rights in the state of nature, see Section 9.3 of Alice Pinheiro Walla's contribution to this volume (Chapter 9).

[25] Note that it is the postulate that is called a permissive law and not the other way around, as Klein claims ('Permissive Law', 219) and which leads him to develop a general interpretation of permissive law that builds on Kant's theory of postulates from the second *Critique*, in my eyes mistakenly. Permissive laws are not theoretical judgments, but normative principles, namely practical laws, as we have seen in the section on *Perpetual Peace*.

freedom with regard to these objects. For this reason the postulate can be called a permissive law:

> This postulate can be called a permissive law (*lex permissiva*) of practical reason, which gives us an authorization that could not be got from mere concepts of right as such, namely to put all others under an obligation, which they would not otherwise have, to refrain from using certain objects of our choice because we have been the first to take them into our possession. Reason wills that this hold as a principle, and it does this as *practical* reason, which extends itself a priori by this postulate of reason. (6:247)

How do we have to understand this extension of practical reason by the postulate? The 'mere concepts of right as such', and the universal principle of right that follows from them (6:230), contain only the power to bind other agents with regard to one's own inner freedom. Thus, the innate right of freedom allows us to use coercion if and only if another person restricts our freedom in a way that violates the universal law of right. To be sure, this also applies to objects that are in our physical possession, insofar as someone who 'wrest[s] the apple from my hand' against my will harms me 'with regard to what is *internally* mine (freedom)' (6:248). However, the permission to use coercion based on the innate right does not extend to objects that are not in my physical possession. Rather, restricting another agent's use of an object that I do not physically possess constitutes a wrong. On the basis of the universal principle of right alone, it would be morally prohibited to make juridical claims and to use coercion against other persons with regard to external objects that are not under one's physical control. With the introduction of the postulate that prohibition is restricted: on the basis of the postulate, we are justified in preventing other agents from using certain objects which are not in our physical possession but belong to us in terms of merely juridical (non-physical, but intelligible) possession only.

The juridical postulate clearly refers to an antecedent prohibition and establishes as rightful certain actions that would otherwise be prohibited. This means that the actions in question are not indifferent as such, as Hruschka holds. On the other hand, the postulate does not permit wrongful acts: it does not allow a transgression of the universal principle of right or of others' inner right. Instead, the postulate specifies conditions under which the external use of freedom is compatible with everybody's freedom. In this sense the universal principle of right is synthetically extended by the postulate. The postulate predicates the permission to restrict other agents' freedom in relation to external objects on the condition that the objects in question be in one's merely juridical possession. Of course, legitimate merely juridical possession can only come about in the course of a legitimate process of acquisition. It is the task of the three parts of the second chapter of Private Right, 'How to acquire something external', to spell out the specific conditions under which this is possible with regard to things, services, and persons, respectively. The postulate only states that it must be possible, in principle, for agents to put each other under obligation with regard to external objects subject to the condition of merely juridical possession.

8.5.2 Possession in the State of Nature by Favour of a Permissive Law (§ 16)

Like the postulate in RL § 2, the permissive law in § 16 also refers to an antecedent prohibition and, by specifying conditions, excludes certain actions from its scope. The object of the permissive law in § 16 is the original acquisition of external things, specifically pieces of land, in the state of nature. Prior to the establishment of the juridical condition, the original acquisition of land by an agent amounts to an act of unilateral obligation of others. Considered as such, imposing obligations on others unilaterally is a violation of the universal law of right: 'the law which is to determine for each what land is mine or yours' can only originate 'from a will that is united *originally* and a priori'; such acquisition can thus only be rightful in civil society (6:267). According to Kant, however, the original acquisition in the state of nature is possible, and only possible ('needs'), by virtue of a permissive law: the agent in question has the 'favor of a law (*lex permissiva*)' on his side (6:267).

In the state of nature, the permissive law authorizes the obligation of others through the unilateral will of the first occupant of the thing in question. In virtue of the juridical postulate from § 2, mere juridical possession of things, which are one kind of external object of the faculty of choice, must be possible. Since we are not originally in possession of things, an original *acquisition* must be possible for this to have effect. Original acquisition, however, can only occur unilaterally, through first acquisition, since otherwise it would be a derivative acquisition, which would in turn presuppose the possession of the thing to be transferred. Original acquisition through a unilateral act must, hence, be possible. The permissive law grants this acquisition.

However, the permissive law in question qualifies the right of the agent who originally acquires a thing. The acquisition must take place in conformity with the idea of the general will (see 6:259–60, 6:268) and it can only happen in the state of nature and thus only until – and in conjunction with the willingness not to resist – the establishment of the juridical condition, that is, the state. As Kant emphasizes, the 'favor' granted by the permissive law 'does not extend beyond the point at which *others* (participants) consent to its establishment', namely the juridical condition (6:267). Prior to the foundation of the state, the rights of the first occupant are merely provisional; only within the juridical condition can they be peremptory (6:267, 264; cf. 256–7).

Of the different cases of permissive laws in the *Doctrine of Right*, the case in § 16 bears the most resemblance to the cases in *Perpetual Peace*. The permission here refers to a condition that pure practical reason obliges us to overcome and is thus subject to a temporal condition. And just as in *Perpetual Peace*, for example, the toleration of unlawful possessions under international law is only permitted with a view to restitution, so too, in RL § 16, the act of unilateral first occupation of a piece of land is only permissible insofar as it is a prerequisite for possession of property.[26]

8.5.3 *Legitimating the Possession of Persons: The Permissive Law in RL § 22*

The third instance where Kant makes use of a permissive law is the acquisition of other persons – 'wife' or 'husband', 'children', and 'servants' (6:280; 6:277) – in the form of a personal right in the manner of rights to things ('auf dingliche Art persönliches Recht', which Gregor translates as 'rights to persons akin to rights to things'). Such an acquisition, Kant states, is made possible by the 'favor' of a 'natural permissive law' (6:276).[27] Since the personal right in the manner of rights to things allows the agent to act towards the other person in a certain way, namely, as if the other person were a thing, one might think that the permissive law in question would

[26] Oliver Laschet also highlights this point (*Metaphysik und Erfahrung in Kants praktischer Philosophie*, Freiburg: Alber, 2011, 278).

[27] Why is this law called 'natural'? I submit that Kant merely points out that the permissive law belongs to natural law. For Kant, marital, parental, and domestic right are a priori juridical institutions that can exist in the state of nature. In this sense, they are based on a permissive law, which, as a '*natural*' law, 'can be recognized [. . .] a priori by reason' (MS, Introduction, 6:224). The explicit qualification of the permissive law as 'natural' in RL § 22 stresses that the conditions that make the domestic relationships morally legitimate (and that are grounded in our very personhood, namely, humanity in our own person) must not be subject to arbitrary state legislation, but are grounded in natural law. For a detailed discussion of the status of the 'natural' permissive law in RL § 22 see Brecher, *Vernunftrecht und Verdinglichung*, ch. 8, sect. 4.

indeed permit a violation of the general prohibition against treating another person as a thing, thus condoning certain violations of the other person's humanity. The permissive law in § 22 might thus be taken as a case in point for the common reading of permissive laws as allowing or condoning morally impermissible actions. However, as I will sketch out, this is not the case.

Kant defines the personal right in the manner of rights to things as the right 'of possession of an external object *as a thing* and use of it *as a person*' (6:276). The right thus has two components, possession and use of the other person, and it is only the possession of the other person that obtains in the manner of rights to things. Thus, Kant argues, the agent can fetch back the other person if he or she has 'gone astray' and the agent can vindicate the other person from any third party in whose possession the person might be (6:278, 282, 284; 6:361). It is because of this legal capacity that Kant, when he introduces the permissive law in question, states that the basis of such a right to another person must lie 'beyond any rights to things and any rights against persons' (6:276): it is the right of humanity, Kant argues, that provides this basis and from which the permissive law in question 'follows' (6:276).

Humanity – namely, the property of a human being to be a free rational being and thus a person (6:239) – limits the extent to which we can make use and dispose of our own person as well as that of others. The use a person makes of herself or of others must always conform with her own personhood and that of others, respectively (6:270). From the fact that the normative basis of personal rights in the manner of rights to things is the right of humanity it should be clear that the permissive law that grants the acquisition of such rights cannot be meant to permit wrongful actions. Rather, the permissive law attaches certain conditions to the possession of one's spouse, children, and household servants that indeed guarantee the conformity with the personhood of the persons involved. That is, in the form of the permissive law following from the right of humanity, while practical reason enables the legal possession of one person by another it at the same time ensures that the persons are *not* treated like things.

In the following, I will provide a brief sketch of how the permissive law in RL § 22 enables the acquisition of another person by imposing requirements both on the possession and on the associated use of the other person in terms of compatibility with their humanity. In the individual sections of The Right of Domestic Society, Kant emphasizes that practical reason clearly delineates what is permissible, that is, in conformity with the right of humanity, from what is impermissible, (i) in sexual relationships, (ii) in the parent–child relationship, and (iii) in the relationship of master and servant.

(i) Our humanity limits the extent in which we can make use of our own person, and this includes the use we make of our body. Thus, according to Kant, the right of humanity in our own person rules out all forms of sexual intercourse in which agents make themselves into a mere object of pleasure for the other, as this would amount to treating humanity as a thing (6:278). According to Kant, this problem indeed pertains to all relationships that fall short of being a monogamous and lifelong marriage, for as Kant argues, only exclusive and permanent relationships can avert the problem of sexual objectification that our sexual desire naturally gives rise to (6:277–8).[28] Because marriage alone eschews sexual objectification and thus conforms with the right of humanity it is the only 'sexual union [. . .] according to the *law*' (6:277), that is, according to 'pure reason's laws of right' (6:278). Only in establishing a marriage can persons, therefore, acquire each other as spouses in terms of the right to persons in the manner of rights to things. All non-marital sexual relationships, including polygamy and concubinage, Kant argues, cannot be legally valid because they necessarily involve sexual objectification; in the case of such relationships the spouses do therefore not acquire rights to each other, making the relationships legally 'null and void' (6:278–9). By permitting the acquisition of another person as a spouse only in marriage, the permissive law clearly confines the legal powers that it confers on agents to certain conditions. Rather than permitting acts that would run counter to humanity and the personhood of the persons involved, the permissive law indeed specifies that legally valid sexual relationships have to conform to the right of humanity; it is thus based on the normatively antecedent prohibition, established by reason, not to treat persons as things or mere means (6:270; 6:236).

(ii) We find a similar argument in Parental Right. As Kant makes clear, the right of parents to their children is limited such that the parents' power over their children may only serve to maintain, raise, and educate the children. In particular, parents may not treat their children like pieces of property that could be mutilated, destroyed, consumed, or alienated (6:280–2), and their right automatically ceases when the children reach the age of majority (6:282). As Kant argues, the parents' right, both in terms of personal right and in terms of right in the manner of rights to things, is grounded in the parents' duty towards their children: because the parents through their act of procreation have brought a new person into

[28] For a detailed account of Kant's theory of sexual objectification and his conception of marriage see Brecher, *Vernunftrecht und Verdinglichung*.

the world without her consent, they are required to care for this person until she can do so on her own (6:280–1). Indeed, not doing so would amount to treating the child as a thing, thereby violating the child's humanity. As Kant explains, it is the parents' duty that leads to the acquisition of their rights to the child, and it is this duty that in particular gives rise to parents' right to 'handle' their children, including the right to reclaim them from any third parties and, if necessary, to bring them back under their own control by force (6:281). Hence, while the permissive law establishes the right of parents to their children as a right to a person in the manner of rights to things, it on the one hand grounds this right in the children's humanity and, on the other, limits the parents' handling of their children to conformity with the children's status as persons.

(iii) Similarly, the master's power over his domestic servants is limited in that 'he can never behave as if he owned them (*dominus servi*)' (6:283). For instance, the labour of the servants, that is, their use by the master of the house, may not amount to consumption. In this respect, domestic servants have the right to judge the master's treatment of them and they may report violations of their rights, although, according to Kant, they may not leave the household on their own authority (6:283; 6:284). Furthermore, the employment relationship cannot be for life in a strong sense, but it must always be possible to terminate the contract (6:283). The acquisition of domestic servants is thus only possible insofar as the right to freedom of the servant, namely his humanity, is preserved. This distinguishes a contract for domestic services from the conditions of serfdom or slavery, which as Kant points out, are null and void (6:283). So in this case, too, the permissive law makes possible a certain type of legal relation, which it subjects to strict conditions, and it does so with reference to a normatively antecedent prohibition.

CHAPTER 9

Bridging the Juridical Gap

Ethical and Juridical Duties in the Absence of Political Institutions

Alice Pinheiro Walla

9.1 Introduction

The main question addressed in this article is how to understand duties and rights in the *transition* towards a juridical condition. Does the fact that we are 'in transition' impact or shape our duties and rights from a Kantian perspective?

According to Kant, we have a duty to bring about political institutions ('to leave the lawless state of nature and enter the civil condition with all others' (*exeundum esse e statu naturali*).[1] Although juridical in nature, this duty is necessarily pre-institutional, and thus *non-positive.* Kant's *exeundum* thus commands the transition from a lawless towards a (relatively) lawful condition.[2] The lawful condition is 'relative' because the state of nature needs to be overcome at different levels and a civil condition will be implemented in degrees.[3] Although Kant's ideal of a fully just civil condition (*respublica noumenon*) is unattainable, it does not undermine our duty constantly to strive towards it and approach the ideal.[4] Consequently, legal orders will be more or less developed depending on how close they are to embodying the Kantian principles of external freedom, equality, and independence. However, whatever civil condition happens to exist

I would like to thank Martin Brecher and Philipp-Alexander Hirsch for their detailed and insightful feedback; Daniel Häuser, Logan Ghinter and audiences at the Georg-August University of Göttingen, the University of Toronto, Guelph University, and The Hebrew University of Jerusalem for their very helpful comments on earlier versions of this chapter.

1 RGV 6:97 footnote.

2 The duty to leave the state of nature is juridical because it is based on external freedom and the inevitability of impacting each other externally. This calls for the regulation of external relations through positive public laws.

3 Even if the state of nature is overcome between individuals in a particular geographical area or group, the state of nature still persists in regard to other areas and groups. Particular legal orders still need to be regulated externally in regard to each other. The Kantian ideal requires that all external relations between persons be regulated by external right.

4 SF 7:91. See also RL 6:350.

(*respublica phenomenon*) is legitimate and binding, regardless of its imperfection in regard to the normative ideal.

I will argue that when a duty is juridical in nature and yet must be discharged in the state of nature, this has significant *ethical* and *juridical* implications. Kant discusses the juridical implications in the private law section of the Doctrine of Right: although it is possible to acquire rights in the state of nature, the legal status of these rights must remain *indeterminate* until a condition of public (positive) law has been implemented.[5] In this chapter, I will stress two ethical implications, which I believe provide additional *ethical* arguments for Kant's *exeundum*: firstly, addressing wrongs (*Unrecht*)[6] as a matter of beneficence is incompatible with the dignity of the right holders; secondly, a civil condition is needed in order to avoid overburdening morally responsible agents and thus reconcile moral agency and the human need for happiness. Further, I will also criticize the way Kant's theory of acquired rights in the state of nature has been misrepresented into a theory of 'provisionality' or 'transitionality', able to guide us through messy political developments in the manner of non-ideal theory.[7] I argue that the way Kant connects provisional rights and permissive laws has little to do with non-ideal theory, and follows entirely from Kant's apagogical argument for acquired rights in the state of nature.[8]

9.2 Duties of Right in the Absence of Juridical Institutions: Three Problems

Although certain rights and their corresponding juridical duties can be said to be of a purely positive nature (their bindingness is wholly contingent upon the legal order under which they were posited), Kant argues that certain individual rights can be acquired in the state of nature and are to be

[5] RL 6:267.

[6] I will be using the idea of a 'wrong' (*Unrecht*) exclusively in the sense of a violation of a right, that is, in a juridical sense. Kant also uses *Unrecht* in the sense of injustice in a broad sense (6:223f). I do not refer to the failure to comply with an ethical duty towards another person as a wrong, although this imprecise use of the term is often found in the Kant literature.

[7] See for instance, Christoph Horn, 'Kant's Political Philosophy as a Theory of Non-Ideal Normativity', *Kant-Studien* 107 (2016), 89–110, and Christoph Horn, *Nichtideale Normativität: Ein neuer Blick auf Kants politische Philosophie*, Berlin: Suhrkamp, 2014.

[8] See Kant's argument in Private Right § 2, RL 6:246. Apagogical arguments are types of transcendental arguments in Kant's philosophy. An apagogical argument asserts that a premise must be accepted in order to avoid a contradiction. Ultimately the contradiction would undermine a required end of reason (practical or theoretical). The assumed premise is thus necessary for preserving a required end of reason.

taken over into the civil condition.[9] Rights and corresponding duties which are not 'merely' created in the civil condition arise from private right (*Privatrecht*) in the state of nature. A defining feature of acquired rights in the state of nature is their *inconclusive* status, and I will argue that this is what Kant means by *provisional* rights. Rights in the state of nature are inconclusive by definition, since only a condition of public law can provide binding closure in the event of contestation, thereby rendering the right *conclusive*. 'Providing binding closure' presupposes the *authority* to issue a binding verdict and is not exhausted by a claim to truth or correctness about one's interpretation of rights (since disagreement about how rights should be interpreted lies at the root of bona fide rights disputes). In other words, authority to bind in Kant's framework is not grounded on an epistemic claim.[10] As we will see, it is precisely the indeterminate status of acquired rights in the state of nature that motivates the duty to leave that state.[11]

Because we can already identify rights in the state of nature, individuals will be called upon to satisfy their corresponding duties despite the absence of juridical institutions. For instance, if A and B have agreed to buy and sell with each other, A will acquire a duty of right towards B, while B acquires a right towards A.[12] Although A has a duty of right towards B (as the primary duty bearer), B is not able to claim her right in a proper manner in the absence of a court of justice; however, this leaves it unchanged that A has a duty of right against B. B's claim is *provisional* in the sense that it cannot be made determinate (*bestimmt*) unless certain external conditions obtain (namely, the existence of a legal order, rules of legal procedure, etc.). Until then, B can only hope that A will honour the terms of their agreement or attempt to enforce her right unilaterally (without authority to do so) in case A violates their agreement.[13]

9 RL 6:256, 6:312.

10 Elsewhere, I argued that, setting aside duties based solely on the positive laws of a given legal order, the difference between juridical duties in the state of nature and in the civil condition is a matter of the *modality* of these duties, which changes once under a public legal order. See Alice Pinheiro Walla, '*Honeste vive*: Dignity in Kant's *Rechtslehre*', in Adam Cureton and Jan-Willem van der Rijt (eds.), *Human Dignity and the Kingdom of Ends: Kantian Perspectives and Practical Applications*, London: Routledge, 2021, 109–31. See also Philipp-Alexander Hirsch, *Freiheit und Staatlichkeit bei Kant: Die autonomietheoretische Begründung von Recht und Staat und das Widerstandsproblem*, Berlin: De Gruyter, 2017, 210ff. and 248ff.

11 RL 6:312–13, § 44.

12 I will set aside the question of what is actually being acquired in a sales agreement according to Kant's theory of contracts (See RL 6:285). For the purposes of my argument it is sufficient to acknowledge that the voluntary agreement between two persons according to the principles of private right can give rise to rights and duties already in the state of nature.

13 Cf. RL 6:219–20. 'It can be seen from this that all duties, just because they are duties, belong to ethics; but it does not follow that the lawgiving for them is always contained in ethics: for many of

However, addressing rights claims may be 'left to individuals' in a different way. This may be because the *content* or *matter* of individual rights can *overlap* with that of duties of beneficence. In this case, respecting rights (giving someone what is their due) and helping them (in Kant's terminology: 'adopting their happiness my end'[14]) may not be clearly differentiated in the agent's perspective, especially when agents must rely solely on internal motives to comply with duties of right.[15] As external duties, duties of right allow a wider range of motives for compliance than duties of virtue. Although duties of right do not require ethical motivation,[16] duties of right are nevertheless 'indirect-ethical', that is, virtue prescribes internal motivation for the compliance with right.[17]

In such a scenario, A could come to regard her contractual duty towards B as merely 'meritorious', since no one has the authority externally to coerce her to honour her agreement. Or if A defaults and B is left in a situation of need as a consequence, C could decide to help B and enforce B's right unilaterally. In another scenario, C could decide to provide materially for B, even though C is neither the primary duty bearer of her right nor responsible for her deprivation. In the latter case, C is addressing the *need* that results from A's violation of B's right and not the wrong as such. She is neither enforcing B's right unilaterally nor addressing the right as a right. She is simply addressing the need that results from B's deprivation of her right and I will assume she is acting from an ethical motivation, that is, out of respect for the moral law which commands one to take the permissible ends of others as one's own end.

From the above, it is possible to identify three distinct problems in the state of nature:

1. Individuals lack the *authority* to issue binding interpretations of what they take to be legitimate right claims and to coerce these rights (*unilaterality problem*);
2. Individuals may fail to uphold the *dignity* of others when they conflate the strict duties corresponding to their rights with meritorious ethical duties (*dignity concerns*);

them it is outside ethics. Thus ethics commands that I still fulfil a contract I have entered into, even though the other party could not coerce me to do so; but it takes the law (*pacta sunt servanda*) and the duty corresponding to it from the doctrine of right, as already given there.' The duty in question is thus still a duty of right, despite its lack of enforceability and the possibility of addressing it from an ethical perspective.

[14] TL 6:386.

[15] By internal motives I mean motives that are not also externally given (e.g. threats and sanctions). However, internal motives could be based on the agent's inclinations (her desires and impulses), and not only on the recognition of her duty.

[16] RL 6:219 and 231. [17] RL 6:220.

3. Individuals may be badly positioned to discharge such duties, such that what seems right to do in the eyes of the agent may end up being *too demanding* for individuals (*demandingness problem*).

9.2.1 Unilaterality Problem

Even though persons can identify rights in the state of nature through reason (objectively), these judgements have private character and cannot authoritatively bind others externally.[18] Distinctive of Kant's legal theory is the idea that one's correct but *private* judgement about rights does not warrant the authority to decide and coerce others in matters of right. One may indeed do so (without authority), due to the normative *vacuum* of the state of nature, that is, the fact that there is no public enforcement of rights. However, in contrast to John Locke,[19] the unilaterality problem arises for Kant because even though one may have 'right on one's side', the authority to impose one's judgements about rights on others externally requires omnilaterality.[20] Omnilaterality is the condition of reciprocity in external relations. Therefore, the unilaterality problem in the state of nature concerns the *moral possibility* of binding others, which is also directly connected with the moral possibility of externally coercing them.[21] Although Kant derives the concept of rightful coercion analytically from the concept of a hindrance of freedom (which coercion then logically negates), the *authority* to coerce is not analytically derived from the concept of a 'negation of a negation' of external freedom.[22] Instead, the authority to coerce is derived synthetically from the united will of all under

[18] This means that they may choose to recognize these claims voluntarily (perhaps because they think they are justified), but cannot be externally coerced to do so (with normative authority, as opposed to mere violence).

[19] Locke in contrast argued that individuals have a natural right to execute the law of nature. John Locke, *Second Treatise of Government* (1689), ed. by Richard Howard Cox, Wheeling, IL: Harlan Davidson, 1982, ch. II, 8.

[20] Kant recognizes that one can have the 'prerogative of right' in regard to certain actions in the state of nature, namely when a deed is compatible with a future condition of public law or helps bring it about (RL 6:257). This however may still require a special 'power' to bind others by a permissive law of practical reason. Examples are the permission to coerce other individuals (albeit not nations!) to enter a civil condition (RL 6:264, 312; TP 8:349) and provisional acquisition in the state of nature (RL 6:257, 312). More on this last point in my discussion of provisional rights and permissive laws.

[21] See also Hirsch's contribution in this volume (Chapter 5), and Hirsch, *Freiheit und Staatlichkeit bei Kant*.

[22] While the concept of coercion is derived analytically from negation of a rights violation, it does not entitle one to *unilateral* coercion (RL 6:256).

public law (instituted, not original).[23] The unilaterality problem thus arises because the normative condition for the enforcement of rights is not given in the state of nature and needs to be brought about in a condition of public law that has yet to be established.

9.2.2 *Dignity Concerns*

In certain passages, Kant expresses concerns about addressing the consequences of violations of rights as a matter of meritorious duty or virtue. Since it is possible to discharge duties of right from ethical motivation, the problem is not that relying on ethical motivational while discharging duties of right is problematic (since it is clearly *permissible* from a legal perspective and *required* from an ethical perspective). The difficulty arises from addressing the rights of others as if they were *only* matters of virtue, since this would be incompatible with the dignity of the right holders. There is something humiliating about someone's right claim being made into the object of another's beneficence, even though the line between moral concern for another's wellbeing and respecting the dignity of persons may not always be clear. Depending on the goodness of others to have one's right respected is problematic because beneficence is not something one can demand from others as a matter of right; one also becomes *indebted* to the benefactor since beneficence is freely bestowed.[24]

Even under a civil condition agents may tend to treat right claims as a matter of beneficence. Further, it is more convenient to regard oneself as doing something meritorious for others rather than giving others what is owed to them. Duties of right are strict, while duties of virtue are wide. Assuming a duty of virtue would allow the agent more flexibility for compliance and the possibility to do less than the duty of right would prescribe, not to mention the idea that one would be acquiring merit as a consequence of one's conduct (as opposed to doing one's strict duty). Although the possibility of genuine ignorance must be granted, *self-deceit* can also motivate such a *vitium subreptionis*. A vice of subreption is a mistake in cognition; in this case, in the recognition of the appropriate moral category (the type of duty in question). Self-deceit is a psychological mechanism allowing an agent to rationalize away her own awareness of

[23] TP 8:292. The exception is coercing another individual or individuals to enter a civil condition with oneself or to leave one's vicinity (TP 8:349 note).

[24] Beneficence is freely bestowed in the sense of non-coercively bestowed; from a Kantian perspective beneficence is still obligatory and never supererogatory, although it allows latitude for choice.

possibly objectionable conduct and thus to stop scrutinizing her motivations. Since complete honesty with oneself would require recognizing oneself as morally unworthy, which is painful, self-deceit allows agents to believe that they are being moral when they are not, which feels better than acknowledging blame and taking full responsibility for one's conduct.[25]

Rights preserve an important sphere of external freedom that (in principle) allows right holders to pursue ends, including providing for themselves, to a certain extent independently of constraints imposed by the arbitrary choice (*Willkür*) of others; having their rights violated means that they may be in a position where they will need the beneficence of others to satisfy their needs. Kant identifies two ethical dangers in this scenario: the humiliation of the helped and the self-glorification of the helper.

1. *Humiliation of the helped*: Beneficence *binds* the beneficiary towards the benefactor. Kant acknowledges that being indebted towards one's benefactor can be humiliating to a certain extent, and may cause resentment towards the benefactor as a result of one's hurt pride.[26] While the duty of gratitude is a means to counteract the tendency of beneficiaries towards resentment, benefactors are required to be beneficent in ways that do not cause the beneficiary to feel humiliated, since this would be incompatible with adopting the happiness of others as one's end. For instance, Kant acknowledges that it is better to practise beneficence in secret or anonymously than to let one's identity be known.[27]
2. *Self-glorification of the helper*: The benefactor, who may be in a position to do beneficence with no considerable cost to herself, may revel (*schwelgen*) in moral feelings at the thought of her beneficent action. Whatever the source of the need, if the benefactor is well situated to help another at no significant cost to herself, Kant suggests that she should not regard her action as meritorious, but in the manner of strict duty instead.[28] A further reason for Kant's claim that one should treat beneficence subjectively as a strict duty, this time specifically under a civil condition, is that systemic injustice through the shortcomings of

[25] GMS 4:405. The moral law 'strikes down self-conceit' and humiliates it. This is why it is painful to recognize one's moral shortcomings. See KpV 5:73. For work on Kant and self-deception, see Laura Papish, *Kant on Evil, Self-Deception, and Moral Reform*, New York: Oxford Academic, 2018; Martin Sticker, 'When the Reflective Watch-Dog Barks: Conscience and Self-Deception in Kant', *The Journal of Value Inquiry* 51 (2017), 85–104; and Maria Eugênia Zanchet, 'Towards a Holistic View of Self-Deception in Kant's Moral Psychology', *Con-Textos Kantianos* 16 (2022), 194–219.

[26] TL 6:458. [27] TL 6:453. [28] TL 6:453.

existing governments may be at the root of the poverty individuals are addressing through beneficence. Since wealthier individuals may be indirectly benefiting from the injustice of their governments and society, their merit is questionable.[29]

9.2.3 Demandingness Concerns

Rights preserve the individual sphere of external freedom that allows persons to set and pursue their own ends by providing them with *immunity* from the arbitrary interference of others.[30] Therefore, thwarting this sphere of freedom can bring about material dependence on the means of others. Although as finite beings we are by nature vulnerable and mutually dependent on each other, rights violations can be a cause of human dependence on the charity of others.

If an agent takes seriously Kant's admonitions about avoiding humiliation to others and treating wide duties as if they were strict ones (given the possibility of systemic injustice), she may find herself in a situation that is extremely morally demanding. Since the acute needs of others would trigger a duty of beneficence (to which morally conscientious agents are more responsive than other, less morally attuned agents), morally conscientious agents would find themselves in a situation in which they would bring it upon themselves to compensate for these needs. Since we can assume that morally conscientious agents constitute a minority of all agents who are actually under the duty, depending on the degree of deprivation, the help required to bring about a satisfactory level of support would require such agents to weigh beneficence against the promotion of their own ends and happiness. A paradox arises from this scenario. A morally good agent is actually *worthy* of happiness.[31] However, being a morally good agent, especially under *acutely* demanding scenarios, would mean that precisely these agents may need to sacrifice their own happiness to address need. Therefore, the best moral agents may be less likely to enjoy the happiness they morally deserve.

Elsewhere I argued that moral overdemandingness is not intrinsic to Kant's moral theory, but contingent upon external circumstances.[32]

[29] TL 6:454.

[30] Immunity is here understood as a legal *title* to protection from interference. It does not entail *actual* protection in the lack of public legal orders.

[31] KpV 5:130; TP 8:278.

[32] Alice Pinheiro Walla, 'Kant's Moral Theory and Demandingness', *Ethical Theory and Moral Practice* 18 (2015), 731–43. See also Alice Pinheiro Walla, 'Kant and the Wisdom of Oedipus', *Jahrbuch*

Injustice and lawlessness do not only bring about need but also directly contribute to moral demandingness. This means that protecting moral agents provides an additional ethical argument for Kant's *exeundum*, which I take to imply not a mere 'one off' move out of a state of nature. As stressed earlier, the state of nature is a matter of *degree*: although a group may have left the absolute state of nature by entering a legal order, they are still in a *relative* state of nature in regard to other polities, towards whom their external relations remain unregulated. Further, their internal public institutions will be still very far from the rational ideal of a Kantian *res publica*, according to which the principles of external freedom and equality before the law are the basis of legislation. There is thus a duty continually to improve this legal order in order to bring it closer to the rational ideal. The *exeundum* is thus an ongoing obligation to transition towards a more *inclusive* condition of public law, both domestically and internationally. It is inclusive because arbitrary discrimination and interference must be gradually abolished and the scope of those included in the juridification of external relations is enlarged, compatible with hierarchies of legal orders, at different levels.[33]

The argument presented above lends support to the idea that Kant's legal-political thought has a *transitional* character. It enables us to address real-world politics and institutions with the guidance of pure principles derived from *Vernunftrecht*, or Right of Reason. There is something very appealing about this picture. It allows us to dismiss the cliché of Kant's theory as empty formalism; we find instead a versatile theory that can guide us through the messiness and complexity of real political practice. It is thus not surprising that Kant's theory was recently rediscovered and celebrated as a promising theory of *transitionality*.[34]

While I do not dismiss the potential of Kant's legal theory, which proponents of a Kantian theory of transitionality are very correct to stress, in Section 9.3 I will address what I take to be a misunderstanding of Kant's theory in the recent literature: the conflation of 'transitionality' with what Kant scholars have referred to as 'provisionality'. While there is a sense in

Praktische Philosophie in globaler Perspektive/Yearbook Practical Philosophy in a Global Perspective 3 (2019), 126–44.

[33] I take hierarchies of legal orders to be required if we are to avoid a world state. Further, the ethical argument I have sketched is an imperfect duty of individuals, which must be subordinated to perfect ones, therefore, no 'conflict of duties' follow from this argument. As stressed earlier, the fact that an existing civil condition does not correspond to the perfect ideal of justice of the *respublica noumenon* does not undermine its legitimacy as *respublica phenomenon*.

[34] See Claudio Corradetti, 'Kant's Legacy and the Idea of a Transitional *Jus Cosmopoliticum*', *Ratio Juris* 29 (2016), 105–21.

which provisional rights are rights under transitional circumstances (i.e. in the development towards a condition of public law), I argue that talking about 'provisionality' in general, or applying this notion to duties, misses the point. Kant restricts the attribute 'provisional' to acquired rights, and for a good reason: it is the indeterminate status of acquired rights in the state of nature that compels us to leave that state.[35] Once we understand why acquired rights in the state of nature are deemed 'provisional', it becomes clear that it does not make sense to talk about provisional *duties* or 'provisionality' in general. While there is indeed a connection between 'transitionality' and 'provisionality', this relation pertains exclusively to provisional *rights*.

9.3 The Meaning of 'Provisional'

Kant's conceptions of provisional rights and of permissive laws have received growing attention in recent Kantian philosophy and Kant scholarship. Although Kant himself reserves the attribute 'provisional' (*provisorisch*) to rights, Kantians have extended the attribute 'provisional' also to duties. It has also become common to refer to 'provisionality' in general.[36]

In her article 'Kantian Provisional Duties', Heather Roff argued that in the state of nature we can identify duties that are 'provisional', that is, 'conditional' upon the agent's ability to act. In the state of nature, duties of justice are thus 'conditional duties'. According to Roff,

> 'conditional' or 'provisional' duties are conditioned by structural requirements, i.e. they have *enabling* conditions. As long as people are enabled, then they are under a strict necessitation to act. But if some people are disabled or disempowered, then there is (or at least might be) no duty for those agents. If it is determined that an agent has a duty, then that duty still stands as a necessitation to act. Thus *provisional here means limited by some special nullifying hindrance of a temporary nature*, e.g. the hindrances of a

[35] 'Determined' means *morally necessary*, namely conclusively binding. Unilaterally acquired rights to external things are 'indeterminate' in the sense of 'morally contingent', that is, insufficient to impose an external obligation. See RL 6:256–7 (§9) and RL 6:267. Since innate right is *original* and a *liberty* ('no duty not to'), and by definition not a unilaterally acquired right to something *external*, its content does not need to be 'determined' by an omnilaterally binding authority; the distinction provisional/peremptory does not apply to innate right. See Pinheiro Walla, '*Honeste vive*: Dignity in Kant's *Rechtslehre*' in Adam Cureton and Jan-Willem van der Rijt (eds.), Human Dignity and the Kingdom of Ends: Kantian Perspectives and Practical Applications, London: Routledge.

[36] See for instance J. P. Messina, 'Kant's Provisionality Thesis', *Kantian Review* 24 (2019), 439–63; Rafeeq Hasan, 'The Provisionality of Property Rights in Kant's *Doctrine of Right*', *Canadian Journal of Philosophy*, 48 (2018), 850–76; Christopher Yeomans, 'Kant and the Provisionality of Property', in Ansgar Lyssy and Christopher Yeomans (eds.), *Kant on Morality, Humanity, and Legality: Practical Dimensions of Normativity*, Cham: Palgrave Macmillan, 2021, 253–78.

> state of nature, civil war, civil breakdown during a natural disaster, or anything *which makes some incapable of fulfilling duties of justice*. In the absence of an authoritative neutral judge and the rule of law backed by a coercive force, duties of justice are provisional. Some examples might be helpful here. Looking solely at Kant's works, four provisional duties are easily identifiable: initial acquisition of property, initial institution of civil society, autocrats governing in accordance with republican principles, and sovereigns delaying preliminary articles 2, 3 and 4 of *Perpetual Peace*.[37]

The idea that certain duties have 'enabling conditions', that is, that they may only apply to agents who are *materially* able to discharge them, is barely something that applies only to duties of justice in the state of nature. Latitude in general signalizes that practical reason is taking into account the limitations of finite rational agents for discharging a duty. All imperfect duties, insofar as they are *wide duties*, allow agents some latitude in deciding how to discharge the obligation, permitting them to circumvent material limitations (temporary or otherwise) or to reconcile the duty in question with other indirect duties that also require the agent's time and resources. In the *Groundwork*, Kant refers once to strict duty as allowing 'no exceptions to the principle of duty', indirectly suggesting that wide duties would allow such 'exceptions'.[38] However, the idea of a duty allowing an 'exception' is misleading (and Kant himself acknowledges this later on, appearing to contradict himself).[39] It is not the case that a duty 'ceases' to apply to the agent if she is incapacitated; it is only a determinate act token or course of action which is ruled out as an option for the agent if she is incapable to act in a specific way. The view that the duty 'ceases to apply' is due to a confusion between the principle of duty (the ground of obligation) and particular actions that would discharge the obligation.[40] From a Kantian perspective, the obligation lies in the *principle* of duty, and not in the token actions we consider required by the principle. Actions are *applications* of maxims of duties to the particular circumstances of a concretely situated agent. They result from our judgement or interpretation of what we are required to do in a specific scenario, or from what is generally considered to discharge or comply with a certain obligation.

[37] Heather Roff, 'Kantian Provisional Duties', *Jahrbuch für Recht und Ethik* 18 (2010), 533–62, at 547, emphasis in original.

[38] In GMS 4:421n, Kant states: 'I here understand by a perfect duty the one that allows of no exception to the advantage of inclination.' I adopted the translation by Timmermann in Immanuel Kant, *Groundwork to the Metaphysics of Morals: A German–English Edition*, Cambridge: Cambridge University Press, 2011. See also RL 6:232–3.

[39] GMS 4:424. See also TL 6:390.

[40] See RL 6:224 and Hirsch, *Freiheit und Staatlichkeit bei Kant*, 373ff.

Paradigmatically, imperfect duties are derived from second-order moral ends that all agents are required to adopt.[41] If a specific act-token that would fall under the description of the duty must be *contingently* discarded as an option for discharging the duty, this does not extinguish the duty itself, but only a possible way of complying with the duty. The agent can discharge the duty in other ways or at a later time, although she may feel sorry or even guilty that she cannot act when *prompted* to. This is especially the case when the need of specific persons must go unattended, since agents who are genuinely committed to a moral end will *particularize* moral requirements: concrete external circumstances may trigger a specific duty (say of beneficence or justice). Responding to these external circumstances is thus considered in the agent's judgement as her *moral task* (what she is required to do under the circumstances). Not being able to comply with one's moral tasks of the moment will be perceived by conscientious moral agents (i.e. agents who genuinely *care*) as a moral failure and a reason for regret, although this may not be *objectively* the case.

The comparison with wide duties of virtue seems to beg the question, since Roff is talking about duties of *justice* in the state of nature as being 'conditional duties'. These are not duties involving latitude; paradigmatically they are strict and in principle externally coercible. However, there are cases in which a duty is *objectively* strict and yet must be treated *subjectively* as wide. Kant's ethical and legal-political works are strewn with examples of objectively strict duties that are treated subjectively as wide ones.[42] Consider the examples mentioned by Roff, namely, preliminary articles 2, 3, and 4 of *Towards Perpetual Peace*. In Kant's own words, these are laws that:

> taking into consideration the circumstances in which they are to be *applied, subjectively* widen his authorization (*leges latae*) and contain permissions, not to make exceptions to the rule of right, but to postpone putting these laws into effect, without however losing sight of the end; he may not *postpone* to a nonexistent date (*ad calendas graecas*, as Augustus used to promise) [. . .] For the prohibition here concerns *only the way of acquiring*, which from now on shall not hold, but not the *status of possession*.[43]

Under the wide laws (*leges latae*) mentioned above, we see not an 'exception' to the principle of right, but the preservation of an acquisition title

[41] See TL 6:390–5.

[42] For examples of such ethical duties see for instance the duty to cultivate morality in oneself (TL 6:392–3) and Kant's discussion of one's perfection as a moral end (TL 6:446).

[43] ZeF 8:347, my emphasis.

together with the commitment to refrain from a specific *mode of acquisition* in the future. The title of acquisition is not deemed invalid, although its mode of acquisition is now considered prohibited. The wide law thus allows states of affairs to be brought gradually in line with the rule of right, as opposed to being retroactively corrected.[44] This case in which a strict duty (to abstain from certain modes of acquisition) is treated subjectively as wide is what I will call a matter of *moral prudence* (when being too strict or too hasty in its implementation would result in undermining the moral end altogether). True, moral prudence enables a transition towards a more just legal order by allowing gradual change. But does it mean that we are dealing with a 'provisional' duty?

Roff argues that provisional *duties* are strict duties turned wide, thus enabling postponement. Roff's interpretation is a clear response to the demandingness problem I sketched before. Because compliance with juridical duties can be extremely burdensome on individuals in the state of nature, those duties must allow for leniency. This point, she states, is not merely that 'ought implies can', but that there is something 'distinctive about provisional duties that deserves attention'.[45]

However, identifying wide principles of duty (*leges latae*) with 'provisionality' ultimately obscures the reason why we should leave the state of nature in the Kantian framework. The rationale behind the duty to 'bridge the juridical gap' becomes unintelligible, if not circular. While latitude may be understood as a policy of 'moral prudence' by allowing us to protect the moral ends reason commands us to realize and avoid being overly demanding on individuals, the attribute 'provisional' refers to the conditions required for the possibility of obligation. At stake in the case of provisional *rights* is precisely *their capacity to bind*, that is, the moral faculty of the right holder to impose a duty on others. As I will explain, duties corresponding to acquired rights in the state of nature are possible due to permissive laws of practical reason. In contrast to the acquired rights to which they correspond, corresponding duties need not be deemed 'provisional'.

The interpretation I defend in this chapter is that provisional rights are rights whose status is still indeterminate; provisional rights are thus still

[44] Does Kant's view not allow for a theory of reparation for past wrongs? It certainly does. However, it may be the case that rectifying past wrongs retroactively may be 'too messy', since, for instance, ongoing possession or occupation of territory creates a rightful title over time. The way forward is thus to implement the new principle forbidding previously accepted modes of acquisition (say, through marriage, as usual among royal houses in Europe, or through colonial rule) while accepting as valid past acquisition.

[45] Roff, 'Kantian Provisional Duties', 548.

vulnerable to *contestation* by competing rights claims. Peremptory rights, in contrast, have a *conclusive* status. All other competing rights claims are thus ruled out. Provisional (*provisorisch*) alludes to the *modality* of a right. Provisional rights are rights in *expectation* of a future civil condition, under which they can become peremptory or conclusive, that is, morally *necessary*.[46] It is thus imprecise to think about provisional rights as being 'temporary' as opposed to 'permanent', although these meanings may seem very close to the idea of a modality of rights.

9.3.1 Acquired Rights and Permissive Laws of Practical Reason

Before developing my argument in more detail, I will point out a related problematic interpretation, this time focusing on the notion of *permissive laws*.[47] Permissive laws are directly connected to provisional rights. It is thus not surprising that the way 'provisionality' has been constructed in the secondary literature has direct implications for the interpretation of permissive laws, namely as principles that *temporarily permit the morally impermissible*.

Lea Ypi, in her influential article 'A Permissive Theory of Territorial Rights', offers the following interpretation of permissive laws:

> A permissive law, according to Kant, is 'necessitation to an act such that one cannot be necessitated to do it' (8:348; 321 fn). This apparently obscure definition is meant to introduce a third kind of norm (in addition to commands and prohibitions) required to exceptionally justify acts that we would ordinarily consider incompatible with principles of right. The Kantian idea that an action is incompatible with principles of right if it cannot coexist with everyone's freedom in accordance with universal law (6:231; 387) has already been discussed by other authors [. . .]. What bears emphasis is the relationship of this definition to permissive principles, i.e. their employment to assess normatively relevant circumstances in which a course of action incompatible with the idea of equal freedom is pursued.[48]

According to Ypi, permissive principles justify states of affairs incompatible with the idea of right 'only provisionally and conditionally'. They are thus

[46] §9 and §15 of Private Right (RL 6:256–7 and 6:264–6 respectively) deal with the distinction provisional/peremptory. 'Possession in anticipation of and preparation for the civil condition, which can be based only on a law of common will, possession which therefore accords with the possibility of such a condition, is provisionally rightful possession, whereas possession found in an actual civil condition would be conclusive possession.'

[47] For the concept of a permissive law, see also Brecher in this volume (Chapter 8).

[48] Lea Ypi, 'A Permissive Theory of Territorial Rights', *European Journal of Philosophy* 22 (2014), 288–312, my emphasis.

provisional in the sense that they temporarily permit an unrightful state of affairs 'as long as principles of right are not in place'. Therefore,

> it might be possible that, at T1, an action is incompatible with principles of right but justified because it is the only way through which those principles could be realized. This does not mean that the same permission is also required at T2, where other avenues might be available. Hence, permissive principles are principles of transition: they apply to past actions but not necessarily to future ones.[49]

This reading presupposes the idea that an unrightful state of affairs must precede the implementation of a condition of public justice. Violence is nothing other than coercion without law, the difference being that under the circumstances specific coercive acts may actually be conducive to the institution of a civil condition. As necessary means to a morally required end, violence and thus injustice must be tolerated, but only 'conditionally', that is, as long as required to further the moral end. The problem with this view is the idea that something incompatible with right is permitted for the sake of right itself, a view that may sound strikingly consequentialist to Kant's stunned readers. As Bernd Ludwig observed, although Kant did express this view earlier[50] (and we also see it expressively formulated in 1795 in *Towards Perpetual Peace*),[51] Kant seems to have abandoned the 'experimental' idea that violence must necessarily precede Right before the creation of a civil state.[52] How should we thus understand the idea of a permissive law in the absence of a condition of public law? Ludwig suggests that the use of coercion must be *already rightful* from the very beginning, but does not elaborate the claim further.[53]

In Section 3.2, I will develop the idea that permissive laws enable certain legal positions in the state of nature. It is not that something unrightful must be accepted as a necessary bridge towards a rightful condition, but that rightfulness must be established *ex-ante* as a *precondition* to a future civil condition. The reasons for this are not empirical considerations about implementing ends in transitional scenarios but a *rational requirement* to adopt certain normative assumptions. Therefore, while the idea of permissive laws as principles of transitionality indeed applies to *Perpetual Peace*,[54]

49 Ypi, 'A Permissive Theory of Territorial Rights', 290.
50 V-MS/Vigilantius, 27:515.
51 ZeF 8:371
52 Bernd Ludwig, *Kants Rechtslehre*, Hamburg: Meiner, 1988/2005, 157, fn. 123.
53 Ibid.
54 Here is a perfect example of Kant's position in *Perpetual Peace*: 'These are permissive laws of reason that allow a situation of public right afflicted with injustice to continue until everything has either of itself become ripe for a complete overthrow or has been made almost ripe by peaceful means; for some rightful constitution or other, even if it is only to a small degree in conformity with right, is

it cannot be conflated with the concept of provisional rights. As already pointed out by Joachim Hruschka, we are dealing with two distinct meanings of permissive laws in *Towards Perpetual Peace* and the *Doctrine of Right*.[55]

9.4 Permissive Laws as Power-Conferring Norms

Joachim Hruschka argued that in order to understand permissive laws in the Doctrine of Right one must distinguish between two meanings of permitted actions: actions that are 'allowed' (*erlaubt*) and actions that are 'merely allowed' (*bloß erlaubt*).[56] The actions and states of affairs that are the subject matter of permissive laws are 'merely allowed': they are neither prohibited nor commanded. One is at liberty to perform or not perform them. For instance, all things equal, I am at liberty to touch the tip of my nose with my finger. I am neither obligated to nor prohibited from touching the tip of my nose. What is distinctive of permissive laws in general is therefore not that they turn the prohibited into permitted, but that they turn the *morally indifferent* into a *morally relevant* action or state of affairs.

Drawing upon Achenwall, Hruschka's insight is that permissive laws transform mere liberties (i.e. actions that are morally indifferent) into *moral faculties*, that is, into morally relevant actions with the power to bind others, giving rise to a proper *individual right*. The permissive law in the Doctrine of Right should be thus understood as a *power-conferring norm*.[57] Its role is to create obligations from deeds or states of affairs that

better than none at all, which latter fate (anarchy) a premature reform would meet with. Thus political wisdom, in the condition in which things are at present, will make reforms in keeping with the ideal of public right its duty; but it will use revolutions, where nature of itself has brought them about, not to gloss over an even greater oppression, but as a call of nature to bring about by fundamental reforms a lawful constitution based on principles of freedom, the only kind that endures.' ZeF 8:373 note.

55 Joachim Hruschka. 'The Permissive Law of Practical Reason in Kant's "Metaphysics of Morals"', *Law and Philosophy* 23 (2004), 45–72, and Joachim Hruschka. 'Das Erlaubnisgesetz der praktischen Vernunft und der ursprüngliche Erwerb von Stücken des Erdbodens', in *Kant und der Rechtsstaat und andere Essays zu Kants Rechtslehre und Ethik*, Freiburg im Breisgauand Munich: Karl Alber, 2015, 48–88. See also Reinhard Brandt. 'Das Erlaubnisgesetz, oder: Vernunft und Geschichte in Kants Rechtslehre', in Reinhard Brandt (ed.), *Rechtsphilosophie der Aufklärung*, Berlin: De Gruyter, 1982, 233–85.

56 'An action is allowed (*licitum*) which is not contrary to obligation. [. . .] An action that is neither required nor prohibited is merely allowed.' Introduction to the Metaphysics of Morals, RL 6:222 and 223. I follow Hruschka in using 'allowed' as the translation of 'erlaubt', as opposed to 'permitted' as used in Immanuel Kant, *Practical Philosophy*, ed. and trans. by Mary Gregor, Cambridge: Cambridge University Press, 1996.

57 Hruschka. 'The Permissive Law of Practical Reason in Kant's "Metaphysics of Morals"', 47.

otherwise would not give rise to rights. Note that this takes place outside a condition of public law (i.e. in the state of nature).

> This postulate can be called a permissive law (*lex permissiva*) of practical reason, which gives us an authorization that could not be got from mere concepts of right as such, namely to put all others under an obligation, *which they would not otherwise have*, to refrain from using certain objects of our choice because we have been the first to take them into our possession. Reason wills that this hold as a principle, and it does this as practical reason, which extends itself a priori by this postulate of reason.[58]

Kant claims that 'reason wills that this holds as a principle'. What does it mean to say that 'reason wills' *x*? Provisional rights are acquired rights in the state of nature. As acquired rights, they rely on the notion of a permissive law of reason for their bindingness. In contrast to Achenwall, who believed that self-preservation provided the moral basis for certain moral faculties,[59] Kant thought that only an act of choice (*Willkür*) that also had *universal* character (i.e. not contingent, not unilateral) could be the basis of a moral capacity to coerce others externally. Since these conditions are only fulfilled in a condition of public right, and yet acquisition must take place *before* the implementation of a condition of public right, the permissive law is called upon to create a moral faculty in the state of nature. The permissive law turns a mere liberty ('no-duty') into a moral faculty, which creates rights and corresponding obligations. Provisional rights are thus *ex ante* rights.

The way Kant connects permissive laws and provisional rights follows from his apagogical argument for acquired rights in the state of nature.[60] An apagogical argument is an indirect proof of a proposition (from the Greek *apagein,* 'to lead away'). Something must be assumed to be true given another proposition, whose truth cannot be denied.[61]

> For an object of my choice is something that I have the physical power to use. If it were nevertheless absolutely *not within my rightful power* [*sollte es nun doch rechtlich schlechterdings nicht in meiner Macht stehen*] to make use of it, that is, *if the use of it could not coexist with the freedom of everyone in accordance with a universal law (would be wrong)*, then freedom would be

58 RL 6:247, my emphasis.

59 Gottfried Achenwall and Johann Stephan Pütter, *Anfangsgründe des Naturrechts (Elementa Iuris Naturae)* (1750), ed. and trans. by Jan Schröder. Frankfurt am Main: Insel, 1995, § 182, p. 63.

60 RL 6:246.

61 Eugen Bucher, 'Der von den Juristen verkannte apagogische Beweis – dazu auch Kant und Kelsen', in Andreas Heldrich et. al. (eds.), *Festschrift für Claus-Wilhelm Canaris zum 70. Geburtstag*, Munich: C. H. Beck, 2007, 991–1016.

> depriving itself of the use of its choice with regard to an object of choice, by putting usable objects beyond any possibility of being used; in other words, *it would annihilate them in a practical respect and make them into res nullius*, even though in the use of things choice was formally consistent with everyone's outer freedom in accordance with universal laws. – But since pure practical reason lays down only formal laws as the basis for using choice and thus abstracts from its matter, that is, from other properties of the object provided only that it is an object of choice, it can contain no absolute prohibition against using such an object, since this would be a contradiction of outer freedom with itself.[62]

It is possible to think of each person making use of objects of choice (whatever these are) as mutually compatible with the freedom of everyone else. But how can we be sure that it is *rightful* to make use of objects of choice? For the sake of the argument, we could try to imagine what would be the implications of deeming the use of objects of choice *impossible* from the perspective of right. We do not need to assume that using these objects is *prohibited* by reason; our assumption is instead that objects of choice are beyond the scope of the principles of right. They cannot belong to anyone because the juridical concept of possession (as something that belongs to another as a matter of title), cannot apply to any external objects. In this case, we would need to assume that all objects of choice are *res nullius*, that is, things that cannot possibly be or become the Mine or Thine of any person. A *res nullius* is not merely a *res vacua* (a 'vacant' object which contingently happens to have no possessor); it is something that *in principle* cannot belong to anyone, that is, *out of reach* from the perspective of rights. However, if we take into account the very concept of practical reason, we realize that the fundamental end of practical reason itself must be *Willkür* or choice. Choice is about setting and pursuing ends for ourselves. It follows that if we assume, at the same time, that objects of choice (the very matter of choice) are outside the scope of Right, this would amount to denying choice as the fundamental purpose of practical reason. It would imply a contradiction.

Apagogical arguments are often identified with *reductio* arguments (*reductio ad absurdum*). However, this comparison is not very helpful for understanding how apagogical arguments can function as indirect proofs in Kant's theory. Kant makes wide use of apagogic argumentation in the *Groundwork*, more precisely, in the way duties are derived from the categorical imperative. For instance, the prohibition against suicide arises from the insight that universalizing a maxim of taking one's life whenever

[62] RL 6:246.

one is distressed would be incompatible with 'the end of nature'; similarly, a false promise, when universalized, would contradict the very end of communication and speech. The opposite maxim of veracity must be thus adopted as a duty. Similarly, we must admit the possibility of acquired rights in the state of nature (i.e. provisional rights) because assuming the contrary would lead to a contradiction of practical reason with itself: freedom would be depriving itself of its own rationale, that is, its exercise of choice in regard to external objects (the objects of *one's choice*). Therefore, it must be possible to make use of external objects (they must be included within the scope of rights) and a permissive law must be posited to confer persons a power to bind others that they could not otherwise have (i.e. unilaterally).[63]

Which kind of contradiction does Kant identify in his argument for the possibility of possessing objects of choice? Comparing the above *Doctrine of Right* passage with the *Groundwork*, it is not a contradiction in thought or in conception, but a contradiction in *the will.*[64] We cannot *will* that such a state of affairs (external objects as *res nullius*) be the case. Why not? The assumption is a *substantive* one: it presupposes a *conception* of the nature of practical rationality in its external orientation. Reason 'wants' objects of choice to become the objects of choice of *someone.* Given the end of practical reason, it is therefore fundamental to assume that we can incorporate our use of objects under the scope of external freedom and thus of rights.

If so, why are rights to objects of choice 'provisional' in the state of nature? Why can't reason also fully settle their status as the *conclusive* rights of someone in the state of nature? This is because even though it is possible to have objects of choice, *acquiring* specific objects in such a way as to *enable* the exercise of choice also entails an entitlement against arbitrary interference from others; my immunity from interference requires an ability to impose a corresponding liability on all others not in possession of my object not to interfere with my exercise of choice. I must thus be able to *bind* all others to respect my possession. The right is provisional because I can only bind under universal conditions (omnilaterality), and these conditions are not given in the state of nature.

A possible objection to the interpretation of permissive laws as power-conferring norms in the *Doctrine of Right* would be the idea of *natural*

63 RL 6:247.

64 The distinction was introduced by Onora O'Neill in her 'Consistency in Action', in Nelson T. Potter and Mark Timmons (eds.), *Morality and Universality: Essays on Ethical Universalizability*, Dordrecht: Reidel, 1985, 159–86.

permissive laws. These appear in his discussion of personal rights akin to rights to things.[65] I have argued that the role of permissive laws in the case of provisional rights is creating a moral faculty, not turning the morally impermissible into the morally permissible. At least in the case of sexual/marital relations, Kant did seem to think that the permissive law would be turning something prohibited, namely, enjoying another person as an object, into something permissible, that is, an exclusive and reciprocal personal relationship in which the partners mutually acquire each other (Kant's conception of marriage). Kant postulates that sexual relations between persons of the opposite sex are permitted by a 'natural' permissive law.[66] One may wonder why the permissive law is deemed 'natural' in this and in the other two types of personal rights. For the sake of brevity, I will focus on marital rights.

As Kant explains, in the state of nature 'there can be societies compatible with rights (e.g. conjugal, paternal, domestic societies in general, as well as many others); but no law "you ought to enter this condition" holds a priori for these societies'.[67] There is thus *no duty* to enter such personal relations. And yet, there is something about our human nature that makes these personal relations both *unavoidable* and *morally problematic*. They have to do with facts about the human species (sexual desire, procreation, the need to form a household). While biological facts *per se* do not give rise to rights, we see the rational need to bring personal relations that are shaped by these fundamental biological facts under the scope of Right. The permissive law is 'natural' in this case because it involves empirical aspects of human life that would not automatically involve rights; however, these relations must nevertheless be brought into the sphere of right for their very moral possibility.[68] And this seems to contradict my previous interpretation of permissive laws.

Unlike external objects of choice, there would be no contradiction of practical reason with itself in depriving oneself of sexual relations with

[65] RL 6:276–84.

[66] Several Kant scholars have criticized Kant's exclusion of same-sex relationships from permissible sexual relations. For a criticism of Kant's position given his own theoretical commitments, see Martin Brecher, 'Animal Desire and Rational Nature: Kant's Argument for Marriage and the Problem of "Unnatural" Sex', in Pärttyli Rinne and Martin Brecher (eds.), *Kant on Sex, Love, and Friendship*, Berlin: De Gruyter, 2023, 35–61 and Martin Sticker, 'The Case against Different-Sex Marriage in Kant', *Kantian Review* 25 (2020), 441–64. For a revised Kantian account of sexual relationships see Helga Varden, 'A Kantian Conception of Rightful Sexual Relations: Sex, (Gay) Marriage and Prostitution', *Social Philosophy Today* 22 (2006), 199–218, and Helga Varden, *Sex, Love, and Gender: A Kantian Theory*, Oxford: Oxford University Press, 2020.

[67] RL 6:306.

[68] For an alternative interpretation of 'natural' permissive laws, see Martin Brecher, *Vernunftrecht und Verdinglichung: Eine Rekonstruktion von Kants Eherecht*, Berlin: De Gruyter, 2025.

another person. In fact, Kant is puzzled about the idea of enjoying another person sexually; he suggests that sex is the most objectionable way in which one could instrumentalize another rational being. However, Kant is ambivalent about why one should nevertheless allow heterosexual sexual relations between consenting adults. While he argues that reproduction of the species requires sexual relations (and this is his argument for rejecting same-sex sexual relations and bestiality) he nevertheless does not restrict heterosexual sexual relations to reproduction; surprisingly, a possible motivation he acknowledges for engaging in sexual relations is not the intent to procreate but the enjoyment of each other's sexual organs for the sake of pleasure.[69]

> The end of begetting and bringing up children may be an end of nature, for which it implanted the inclinations of the sexes for each other; but it is not requisite for human beings who marry to make this their end in order for their union to be compatible with rights, for otherwise marriage would be dissolved when procreation ceases.
>
> Even if it is supposed that their end is the pleasure of using each other's sexual attributes, the marriage contract is not up to their discretion but is a contract that is necessary by the law of humanity, that is, if a man and a woman want to enjoy each other's sexual attributes they must necessarily marry, and this is necessary in accordance with pure reason's laws of right.[70]

For Kant, sexual relations must be regulated by Right not because they promote external freedom, but because only exclusive rights to each other can ensure the reciprocity required for sexual relations to qualify as compatible with the right of humanity in our persons. The argument seems to be the following: since engaging in sexual relations amounts to enjoying a person similarly to a *thing* and threatens to reduce them to their sexual organs, *mutually acquiring* each other (possessing each other as a *whole* person) to the exclusion of others from the same relation, is necessary for restoring the spouses' status as *complete* persons within their sexual relationship with each other. Does the natural permissive law turn a morally 'abhorrent' state of affairs into a morally acceptable relationship in the case of marriage?

Again, the permissive law plays a power-conferring function, this time within a personal relationship. It is the permissive law that creates the moral faculty that enables the spouses to possess each other in the first place. Note that the claim goes beyond the mere consent of the involved

[69] RL 6:277. [70] RL 6:277–8.

parties to be in such a relationship. Sexual relations *per se* do not give rise to any claims to exclusive possession of one's partner; only a permissive law can do that. There is something a spouse can claim against the other spouse even if she is no longer invested in or committed to the relationship.

The difference between a natural permissive law and the permissive laws I discussed before is that a natural permissive law does not need to give rise to *provisional* rights; the duties and rights arising from marriage do not *commit us* to entering a civil condition for their bindingness as does possession of external objects in the state of nature. This is because we are dealing with claims to *persons*; no possession of external things is involved.[71] Despite Kant's claim that one can fetch a partner who ran away[72] similarly to the way one would recover a lost thing, 'possession' in that case is a metaphor for the *privilege* spouses have over each other and in regard to everyone else. Although marriage benefits from the existence of a civil condition, the obligations marriage impose on other people (their lack of privilege in regard to one's spouse) does not require omnilaterality conditions to be in place in the way possession of external objects does.

9.5 Conclusion

Kant's apagogical argument is driven by the rational requirement to avoid a contradiction of reason with its own fundamental assumptions. *Rechtswidrig* (what is 'against Right') is thus defined as what would be self-contradictory, given fundamental, *Kantian* assumptions about the nature of practical reason and external freedom. The postulate thus *extends* practical reason by creating a moral faculty to bind.[73] Provisional rights are rights in expectation of a future civil condition.

According to the transitionality reading sketched before, Kant's concern in formulating his legal-political theory is to account for the implementation of principles of justice under non-ideal conditions: the imperfection or complete absence of political institutions, the messiness of politics, the frailty of human nature, the need to overcome past practices that are incompatible with right and to progress gradually towards a condition that is closer to rational ideals. My criticism is aimed at accounts that identify or conflate 'transitionality' with 'provisionality'. I have argued that Kant's

[71] In the case of external objects, one must assume a common possession of all things in order to derive the idea of a division (acquisition) of the earth's resources. No such presupposition is required in the case of personal rights, which are merely 'akin to rights to external objects', but actually involve persons.

[72] RL 6:278. [73] RL 6:247.

account of provisional rights is based on the avoidance of contradiction; the argument is thus purely formal ('rational' in Kant's sense of the term). This does not mean that his theory does not have the advantages highlighted by the proponents of the transitionality reading. But in the spirit of *Theory and Practice* and of transcendental idealism, the view I defended in this article is that Kant's theory can be applied to the real world primarily because it is rational, not because it is sensitive to 'non-ideal' conditions. *Prima facie*, the requirements of reason stand in a strong contrast to the complexity and messiness of reality. In order to be feasible and realistic, it seems intuitive to expect normative theories to be able to be sensitive to the particularities of a world in transition, and to allow for flexibility and a certain degree of compromise in the implementation of its goals. This is certainly true of some aspects of Kant's political thought, namely, the *leges latae* (the imperfect, wide principles) discussed in *Towards Perpetual Peace*. In their case, a permissive law is a principle of moral prudence, allowing the postponement of reforms to a later, more opportune moment. In regard to provisional rights, however, Kant's message is instead that reason itself must interpret the world as a normative landscape, structured into a coherent system by rational principles. Where coherence is not given within the system, it must be *brought about as a matter of duty*. In this case, it is our task to change the world to conform to the requirements of reason, and not the other way around. My recommendation is thus to keep what can be rightly identified as Kant's theory of transitionality apart from his theory of provisional rights, and not to confuse the two.

PART IV

External Freedom and Kantian Legal Philosophy

CHAPTER 10

The Kantian Legal Relation as Radical Non-Positivism

George Pavlakos

10.1 Introduction

Contemporary legal non-positivism still remains hostage to the idea that state law is the main paradigm of law. As such it shares with its rival, positivism, some deeper assumptions about the grounds of legal obligations mainly by subscribing to an account of legal rights and duties that rests on the existence of established legal practices and institutions.

The chapter suggests that Kant's relational account of legal obligation enables us to push the boundaries of non-positivism beyond any established legal practices. Accordingly, over and above any other substantive contribution that Kant's Doctrine of Right may make to debates on law and morality, it effects a deeper and more radical change at the level of theory: it prioritizes legal relations over law-practices in the explanation of legal obligations. Kantian non-positivism, as I claim in this chapter, supports a relations-first account of legal obligation. To defend the plausibility of this claim, I undertake to develop some of its key building blocks,

Ancestors of this chapter were presented as papers at the Aristotle University of Thessaloniki; the conference 'Law and Morality in Kant' at the University of Göttingen; the Legal Theory Workshop at UCLA; the University of Bologna; the Psychopedis Seminar in Political Theory in Athens; the University of Glasgow; the Vienna Lectures on Legal Philosophy; a conference on Kant and Marx at the Erasmus University of Rotterdam; the University of Frankfurt; the Yeoh Tiong Lay Centre at King's College London; the Surrey Centre for Law and Philosophy; the Toronto Faculty of Law Colloquium and the Irish Jurisprudence Society. I am indebted to the respective audiences for valuable feedback, and for detailed and written comments to Tom Bailey, Sam Chilovi, Connor Crummey, Katrin Flikschuh, Mark Greenberg, Carsten Heidemann, Katharine Jenkins, A J Julius, Daniel Murata, Hilary Nye, Hamish Stewart, Federico Szczaranski, Andreas Takis, and Nicholas Vrousalis. Luke Davies acted as my brilliant commentator at the Göttingen conference, rescuing me from many a mistake. Ultimately, the chapter owes its existence to Martin Brecher, Philipp Hirsch, and Bernd Ludwig, the organizers of the Göttingen conference, who invited my contribution and patiently discussed my interpretation of Kant's legal philosophy. Some of the ideas in Sections 10.2.1, 10.2.2, and 10.3.2 were first aired in considerably less detail in Toni Marzal and George Pavlakos, 'A Relations-First Approach of Choice of Law', in Roxana Banu, Michael Green, and Ralf Michaels (eds.), *Philosophical Foundations of Private International Law*, Oxford: Oxford University Press, 2024, 346–68.

even though I cannot do full justice to the complexity of the issues involved within the limited space I have here.

In Section 10.2, I discuss the positivist commitments of contemporary non-positivism[1] and demonstrate that a key consequence is the mischaracterization of the existence conditions of legal relations. Legal positivism understands legal relations as obtaining when some institutional rule imposes an obligation on two or more parties. Accordingly, its explanation of legal relations subsists on the standard positivist explanation of legal obligations, as obtaining exclusively in virtue of their social sources. As it turns out, non-positivists fail to challenge the positivist picture by assigning to legal relations a more prominent role in the explanation of legal obligations. And yet, as the evidence from both the phenomenology of legal practice and legal scholarship suggests, it is imperative to seek an independent explanation of legal relations which, in turn, would facilitate an account of the grounds and scope of legal obligations, in a radical non-positivist manner.

Section 10.3 uses a Kantian account of juridical relations to suggest a route for reversing the explanatory priority of institutional rules over legal relations in the account of legal obligations. To explore the possibility of a relations-first or radical non-positivism, I propose an avant-garde reading of Kant's Universal Principle of Right (UPR) as a pre-institutional moral principle that grounds omnilateral demands of rightful action. Meanwhile, I seek to remove two key obstacles which threaten to undermine the proposed reading: the first emerges from a more standard reading of Kantian right, according to which juridical relations rely on some prior notion of individual freedom or autonomy; to counter it, I follow the lead of Katrin Flikschuh, who in recent work has launched a powerful challenge to this quasi-Lockean reading. Second, in response to the objection that the relational reading of Kantian right actually necessitates positivism, instead of combating it, I offer the preliminaries of an argument about how UPR can generate standards which are expressions of an omnilateral will, without requiring the presence of the state or its institutions.

Ultimately, the chapter points to the significance of legal relations for legal theory: when accounting for legal relations is made an independent explanatory task, then the current boundaries between positivism and non-positivism need to be redrawn, to accommodate the possibility of radical

[1] I shall limit the scope of the discussion to authors working in analytical legal theory broadly construed, owing to the centrality of this tradition in recent debates between positivism and non-positivism.

non-positivism. A Kantian, relations-first, account of legal rights seems to me to offer currently the best way forward for delivering this important task.

10.2 Legal Relations: An Explanatory Challenge for Legal Theory

Much in the phenomenology of legal reasoning suggests that it is of independent value to take an interest in relations between parties to a legal dispute when looking to determine what the law requires in terms of rights and obligations: take for instance cases in private international law which involve transnational dealings between private actors and which, when brought before a judge, require the court to determine the applicable law.[2] Judges in this field operate under a requirement not to assume that the applicable law is the law of their own jurisdiction (*lex fori*) but to first locate the legal relation which would eventually licence an inference to the applicable law, often residing in the legal order of another jurisdiction. Or take any of the classic cases where courts develop legal principles in the interstices of established[3] rights and duties to determine the legal consequences of an interaction between parties. Thus, in *Donoghue v. Stephenson* – for many the case introducing the modern law of negligence in the common law jurisdictions – the relation between Ms Donoghue and the tortious manufacturer of poisonous ginger beer became the primary focus of the judicial inquiry, in the absence of any legal rights and duties rested in earlier institutional action.[4] More dramatically, when we move to the global context, international lawyers often depart from established understandings of international responsibility, whereby only states count as subjects of attribution, and instead investigate the relations among a variety of non-state actors to determine the relevant legal obligations.

This explanatory importance of relations resonates diachronically in the legal literature: Friedrich Carl von Savigny, writing in the nineteenth century, initiates a radical shift from state legal rules to pre-institutional relations between parties to a dispute, as determining factors of the choice of law methodology.[5] In a more contemporary key, Arthur Ripstein

[2] Marzal and Pavlakos, 'A Relations-First Approach'.

[3] In the present context I understand as established those legal obligations that have been created by institutional action (legislation or adjudication).

[4] *Donoghue v. Stevenson* [1932] A.C. 562 (26 May 1932).

[5] Friedrich Carl von Savigny, *System des heutigen römischen Rechts*, 2nd reprint of the 1840 edition, Aalen: Scientia Verlag, 1981; Friedrich Carl von Savigny, *A Treatise on the Conflict of Laws*, trans. by William Guthrie, Edinburgh: T&T Clark Law Publishers, 1880.

suggests that legal 'right(s) to security of person and property must be analysed in terms of your *already* standing in a certain type of relation to other people'.[6] Such reflections can be understood as recommending that one resist an outright reduction of relations that generate legal obligations to standards which rest on prior action taken by legal institutions.[7] Meanwhile, they suggest the possibility of legal relations which escape a ready-made characterization that traces them back neatly to a state-based legal order.

But if such relations can play some role in the explanation of legal rights and duties, we are in need of an account that does not pre-empt their dependence on practices of state officials or, for short, *law-practices*.[8] On a fairly neutral characterization, which does not commit itself to the dependence of legal relations on law-practices, *that a relation between two or more parties is legal implies that their interaction is subject to one or more legal obligations*.[9] This formulation makes no assumption about which of either the relation or the obligation enjoys explanatory priority over the other, remaining thus open to at least two readings. On the first one, 'legal relation' is just another name for the range of persons that fall within the scope of antecedently established legal requirements; call this reading *scope-oriented*. In this version, legal relations subsist entirely on pre-existing law-practices and the obligations those engender. A more demanding reading would have 'legal relation' playing the role of a criterion for the obtaining of legal obligations, which is independent of law-practices; call this the *ground-oriented* reading. On this reading, the fact that legal relations may serve as self-standing grounds posits a noteworthy demand on the explanation of legal obligations: namely, the requirement that law-practices be merely a *contingent* ground of the relevant legal obligations.[10]

[6] Arthur Ripstein, *Private Wrongs*, Cambridge, MA: Harvard University Press, 2018, 81.

[7] Throughout the chapter, I will count as relevant institutional action any actions taken by state officials and proceed on the understanding that legal institutions and their practices are state-based; see also n. 8.

[8] I adopt here standard use, whereby the term 'law-practices' refers to collections of ordinary empirical facts about the sayings, doings, and mental states of members of constitutional assemblies, legislatures, courts, administrative agencies, and the like (Mark Greenberg, 'Hartian Positivism and Normative Facts: How Facts Make Law II', in Scott Hershovitz (ed.), *Exploring Law's Empire: The Jurisprudence of Ronald Dworkin*, Oxford: Oxford University Press, 2006, 265–90; Samuele Chilovi and George Pavlakos, 'Law-Determination as Grounding', *Legal Theory* 25 (2019), 53–76).

[9] For convenience, I will use 'legal obligation' also to denote powers, rights, permissions, and so on.

[10] Accordingly, the 'ground-oriented' reading does not entirely exclude law-practices: it remains possible that law-practices are among the grounds of legal obligations, in which case the relevant legal relation will fall entirely within the scope of the relevant institutional obligations. Importantly, however, it submits that legal obligations may obtain even in the absence of law-practices. I am grateful to Marcus Willaschek for pressing me to formulate better this point.

To preserve neutrality in a manner that accommodates our earlier intuitions about legal phenomenology, we should opt for the demanding, ground-oriented reading. For, the scope-oriented reading appears to operate under a key disadvantage: it forecloses the obtaining of legal relations independently of law-practices because it regards them as mere accessories of one or other institutional obligation that is the result of actions taken by the officials of some legal system. Accordingly, the scope-oriented reading leaves no space for relations to play any role in the explanation of legal obligations, suggesting instead that any explanation of the latter necessarily rests on facts of law-practices. In contrast, the demanding reading allows that those legal relations may become independent, self-standing grounds of legal obligations, taking over from law-practices which are demoted to merely possible grounds. It is only on the ground-oriented reading that we can avoid begging the question against the neutrality of legal relations, in violation of the role those play in legal phenomenology. I will proceed to suggest that the main theoretical accounts of legal obligation in contemporary legal philosophy assume a scope-oriented understanding of legal relations and end up violating the *neutrality constraint*, by begging the question in favour of law-practices *qua explanantia* of legal obligations.

Notwithstanding their explanatory potential, legal relations have not been subjected to extensive discussion by any of the dominant stands of contemporary legal theory, of either positivist or non-positivist orientation. An early suspicion that the reason might relate to a breach of the neutrality constraint will be confirmed on closer inspection of the standard accounts from each camp. Following on from this diagnosis, I will argue that respect for the neutrality constraint supports a radical version of non-positivism, which regards relations as prominent explanantia of legal obligations. Kant's relational account of legal rights will be employed in Section 10.3 to flesh out such a version of a relations-first account of legal obligations.

10.2.1 Positivism is Question-Begging

Positivist explanations violate neutrality in a more or less predictable manner: a positivist account of legal obligations cannot afford involving anything other than law-practices in their explanation, on pain of contradicting its own commitment to an understanding of legal phenomena exclusively in terms of their social sources. If positivism left space for legal relations to operate as self-standing grounds of legal obligations, it would be inviting the suspicion that the determinants of law might include elements other than law-practices. Instead, legal relations must be strictly understood as descriptions of the scope of rules which are grounded exclusively in law-practices. Here is Scott Shapiro confirming this picture in his book *Legality*:

> [T]he normativity of law is 'institutional' in nature, which is to say that the legal relations may obtain between people independently of the particular intentions of those people. *This institutionality is made possible by the structure of master legal plans.* Master plans [. . .] contain authorizations [. . .] (that) will typically set out formal procedures which allow people to exercise power even without the intention to do so.[11]

Accordingly, and setting aside finer nuances of Shapiro's terminology, legal relations obtain when the law assigns rights, obligations, and powers on the basis of institutional rules whose existence or validity can be accounted for by exclusive reference to law-practices. In other words, from a positivist perspective, there is no room for legal relations to play an independent role as grounds of legal obligations. Instead, any account of the grounds of legal obligations would need to revert to the typically positivist explanation, as exemplified by the long-standing tradition introduced by H. L. A. Hart.[12] This familiar story submits that legal obligations are determined, at the most fundamental level, exclusively by social facts, even though a legal system might incorporate other normative (e.g. moral) considerations, on the condition that the standards of incorporation are laid down in a rule of recognition whose existence can be traced back to sources that are exclusively social.[13] In this landscape, the only role left for legal relations is that of describing the scope of whatever, on the positivist story, may count as a legal obligation.

Along these lines positivism embraces the scope-oriented understanding of legal relations and demotes them to descriptions of scope of rule-based obligations, which are ultimately grounded exclusively in law-practices. In ruling out any deeper explanatory role for legal relations, the positivist strategy is begging the question of the explanation of legal obligations in favour of law-practices and, ultimately, positivism. Conversely, to steer away from that fallacy, positivism would need to allow for explanations of relations that do not involve law-practices.

[11] Scott Shapiro, *Legality*, Cambridge, MA: Harvard University Press, 2011, 16 (my emphasis).

[12] H. L. A. Hart, *The Concept of Law*, 2nd ed., Oxford: Clarendon Press, 1994.

[13] Kenneth E. Himma, 'Inclusive Legal Positivism', in Jules L. Coleman and Scott Shapiro (eds.), *Oxford Handbook of Jurisprudence and Philosophy of Law*, Oxford: Oxford University Press, 2004, 125–65.

10.2.2 *How Non-Positivism Inherits Circularity*

To a significant degree, contemporary non-positivism stands out from its predecessors by its effort to pinpoint the question-begging character of positivism.[14] Contrary to earlier critics of positivism, contemporary non-positivists 'do not focus on the classical problem posed by a clash between positive law and natural, as epitomised in the Antigone story, to argue that the former is ultimately subject to an additional test of validity contained in higher morality'.[15]

Instead, they appeal to an explanatory gap between social sources and legal obligations to demonstrate the question-begging character of positivism.[16] The charge they level at positivism is that it cannot bridge the gap between social sources and legal obligations, in order to explain how the latter obtain. The thrust of these strategies is an argument *that law-practices cannot determine their own relevance to the content of legal obligations unless further elements are added.* As the argument goes, there are multiple (epistemically) possible mappings from the social facts of law-practices to the content of legal obligations, the result being that what we know about the facts of the practice cannot settle which of the alternative candidate mappings from a set of social facts to possible meanings is actual.[17] This indeterminacy is then used as a *reductio* of the positivist notion of validity. Conversely, to counter the threat of indeterminacy the proposed solution is to supplement substantive moral principles which can determine the relevance of social facts and, thus, block the possible deviant mappings.[18]

However, despite early appearances, the non-positivist strategy fails to set itself altogether free from the predicament of circularity, in the form of a commitment to law-practices at the most fundamental level of

[14] Greenberg warns that relying on explanations that exclude pre-institutional evaluative facts would be question-begging. See Mark Greenberg, 'How Facts Make Law', *Legal Theory* 10 (2004), 157–98, at 159.

[15] Marzal and Pavlakos, 'A Relations-First Approach', 349.

[16] Greenberg, 'How Facts Make Law; 'Hartian Positivism and Normative Facts'; 'On Practices and the Law', *Legal Theory* 12 (2006), 113–36; Nicos Stavropoulos, 'Legal Interpretivism', in Edward N. Zalta (ed.), *The Stanford Encyclopedia of Philosophy* (2021), www.plato.stanford.edu/archives/spr2021/entries/law-interpretivist/ (accessed 1 June 2024); Samuele Chilovi and George Pavlakos, 'The Explanatory Demands of Grounding in Law', *Pacific Philosophical Quarterly* 103 (2022), 900–33. And for cortical discussion, see Hasan Dindjer, 'The New Legal Anti-Positivism', *Legal Theory* 26 (2020), 181–213.

[17] Chilovi and Pavlakos, 'Law-Determination as Grounding'.

[18] Greenberg, 'How Facts Make Law'; 'On Practices and the Law'; Chilovi and Pavlakos, 'Explanatory Demands'.

law-determination.[19] I will argue that the reason for that failure is closely tied to non-positivism's reluctance to conceive of legal relations independently of law-practices and assign to them an autonomous role in the explanation of legal obligations (what I earlier called the ground-oriented reading of legal relations). As I will turn to demonstrate next, the dominant strand of non-positivism departs only marginally from the positivist understanding of legal obligation, by continuing to regard law-practices as necessary, albeit partial, grounds of all legal obligation.[20] In effect, these non-positivists end up sharing the basic positivist premise which binds legal requirements to law practices, and merely supplement it with an additional premise requiring moral facts as additional grounds. While the adding of a moral component evades partially the charge of circularity in the explanation of obligations, it does not with respect to relations. For, in confirming the role of law-practices as necessary grounds of legal obligations such accounts also uphold the limited role of legal relations, which continue to appear as the shadows of institutional rules, incapable of materializing outside law-practices. Ultimately, as it turns out, the non-positivist idea of legal relations violates the neutrality constraint as much as its positivist counterpart.

To illustrate the point, think of the broadly Dworkinian strategy[21] of involving principles of political morality to 'close' the gap of indeterminacy that arises when social sources are considered as the exclusive determinants of legal obligations. Although involvement of moral considerations might be suitable for tackling indeterminacy, it does not cure circularity entirely. This is because, in any of the known renderings of the interpretivist strategy, the relevance of any pre-institutional moral considerations, appeal to which is rendered necessary for law-determination, is itself conditioned by the law-practices of some legal system. For, to specify in any given case whether and in what manner political morality is involved in law-

[19] For a related argument that contemporary non-positivism shares positivism's view about the role of law-practices in law-determination, see Larry Alexander, 'In Defense of the Standard Picture: The Basic Challenge', *Ratio Juris* 34 (2021), 187–206.

[20] Another way to put it is to say that while positivism takes law-practices to be necessary and sufficient grounds for the obtaining of all legal obligation contemporary non-positivist rivals regard them as always necessary but never sufficient grounds of legal any obligation.

[21] Although Dworkin and his epigones represent what is arguably the dominant strand of contemporary non-positivism, other influential accounts share the same predicament: Robert Alexy's influential account considers the 'claim to correctness', which is raised by legal propositions, to be at the centre of an argument for linking law and morality. The claim to correctness is relevantly raised by propositions which count already as legal, based on existing law-practices. See Robert Alexy, *A Theory of Legal Argumentation*, Oxford: Clarendon Press, 1989; *The Argument from Injustice*, Oxford: Clarendon Press, 2002.

determination, we need first to refer to the actions taken by legal institutions, including other relevant aspects of the law-practices of a legal system. Be it in terms of a demand for justification that those actions raise, or in terms of their normative footprint on the overall moral profile, these actions together with further aspects of law-practices *determine* the relevance and extent of the inclusion of moral facts in law-determination.

But this strategy is glaringly weak to escape circularity, if what is needed – when facts of law-practices are absent or cannot steer the explanation of legal obligations – are grounds whose existence does not rely directly on any law-practices.[22] For no sooner has our appeal to a moral principle of duty of care, which governs the relation between Ms Donoghue and the tortious manufacturer of ginger-beer, been framed by the law-practices of the system – say, the actions taken by the judges – than the relation between the parties fails to operate as an independent explanation.[23] It is precisely because this strategy leaves no room for legal relations to operate as independent grounds for legal obligations that contemporary non-positivism ends up conceding the primacy of positivist ontology. By this I mean an account of legal obligations that is, at the most fundamental level, determined by law-practices or a collection of social facts that count as legal in virtue of a master rule of recognition.[24]

10.2.3 Legal Practice as Basic Structure of Governance

Although non-positivists disagree with positivists about the full range of facts contained in the grounding base of legal obligations, they seem to agree that law-practices form a necessary part of that base. How is this convergence of the two camps to be explained? Simplifying a lot, both camps think of law-practices as forming a basic structure of public governance (for short, *basic structure*), which we usually identify with the

[22] For examples, see earlier this chapter (Section 10.2).

[23] The explanatory demands of grounding in law do not favour standard non-positivism over positivism (Chilovi and Pavlakos, 'Explanatory Demands'). Things might turn out differently when the target of the explanation is refocused on legal relations and a more radical form of non-positivism is taken on board. In Section 10.3, I present the contours of a Kantian version of radical non-positivism, without however addressing in detail questions of law-determination and grounding.

[24] Non-positivists discuss and reject this picture by saying that the key difference between positivists and them is at the most fundamental level of legal determinants – there the non-positivist, but not the positivist, would include moral facts. But if, as I claim, the reason for the inclusion of non-positivist moral facts is the existence of law-practices (because they trigger moral principles, or because they are determining the relevant moral footprint) then the primacy of the positivist ontology remains intact!

existence of law and political association. While the positivist account focuses on the description of the basic structure, what excites the non-positivist imagination is its normative impact on the reasons for action of those governed by it. Meanwhile, both approaches agree that the scope of all relations characterized in terms of legal rights and duties must be confined within the site of a basic structure of law-practices.[25]

As it turns out, the disagreement of the two camps is not about the site or the grounds of the basic structure; it is only about *how* (the site of) the basic structure contributes to the content of legal obligations. According to the non-positivist account, any determination of legal requirements that cites exclusively collections of facts in the basic structure would be incomplete. For, *in virtue of* imposing centrally terms of interaction on everyone living under it, the basic structure triggers the morality that regulates the governance of political association.[26] Although not stated in so many words, an implied premise of the non-positivist line of argument seems to be that individuals are endowed with pre-institutional autonomy or freedom, which triggers a demand of justification, when impacted by the centrally imposed acts of governance of the basic structure. Notably, any such instance of interference with individual autonomy requires that one make additional reference to the justificatory grounds for the interference, in order to work out the obligations imposed by the basic structure. Such grounds consist in so-called principles of political morality (such as justice, fairness, due care, democracy, and so on) and are typically evoked to justify collectively distributed interferences with individual autonomy. Consequently, the *way in* which the basic structure of public governance contributes to the production of legal obligations is through its moral impact, that is, the way in which actions taken within its remit affect or modify the all-things-considered reasons that pertain to individuals.[27]

Notice, however, the modesty of the non-positivist argument: it draws attention to the relevance of political morality but does not challenge the site of its application. True enough, for any determination of legal rights and duties a contribution from political morality is necessary, but no legal

[25] This follows from the scope-oriented reading of legal relations, according to which these are merely descriptions of the scope of the legal obligations generated by law-practices. On this reading, the scope of legal relations is merely a reflection of the scope of legal obligations.

[26] Ronald Dworkin, *Law's Empire*, London: Fontana Press, 1986, esp. 192–5, 197–8, 208–15; Dworkin, *Justice for Hedgehogs*, Cambridge, MA: Harvard University Press, 2011, ch. 14; and for critical discussion, see George Pavlakos, 'Revamping Associative Obligations', in Salman Khurshid, Lokendra Malik, and Veronica Rodriguez-Blanco (eds.), *Dignity in the Legal and Political Philosophy of Ronald Dworkin*, Oxford: Oxford University Press, 2018, 337–60.

[27] Mark Greenberg, 'The Moral Impact Theory of Law', *Yale Law Journal* 123 (2014), 1288–1342.

relation can obtain outside the site of the basic structure, precisely because political morality cannot make any contribution to the determination of legal obligations outside that structure. The basic structure delineates the scope of legal relations because it marks the boundaries of the relevance of political morality. Outside the site of the structure, questions about whether some relation is legal or not do not even get off the ground.

Adding moral facts to law's determinants amounts only to a modest modification of the positivist picture, making as a result contemporary non-positivist positions vulnerable to the same predicament of circularity that is endemic to positivist reasoning. Instead, to overcome these problems, a radical non-positivist strategy must overcome the straitjacket of positivist ontology, or the view that legal relations are limited by the site of the basic structure of law-practices.[28] To do so, it must reverse the order of the inquiry by posing the question about the grounds of legal relations *directly*, and only after answering that question to proceed and specify their site. At the same time, a relations-first strategy would need to preserve the valuable intuition that not any moral facts, but only those that pertain to public forms of governance are relevant grounds for legal obligation.

But in the absence of a basic structure of public governance, how can relations trigger facts of political morality and together with them ground the kind of rights and duties that govern legal relations? I will argue in the next section that Kant's Doctrine of Right provides us with a valuable insight:[29] his Universal Principle of Right (UPR) may serve as the moral footprint of public governance, independently of the ontology of the specific structure that may exemplify it. As such it serves the role of a 'compass' for identifying as legal any relations which can trigger it. Accordingly, it takes the place of a formal ontology of governance and explains the idea of political association and public governance by imposing a threshold demand on interactions between agents: 'any interaction that triggers UPR counts as an instance of public governance, which is accountable to principles of political morality'. The Kantian strategy, in refocusing the explanation from legal facts to rightful relations, gives explanatory priority to the grounds over the site of legal relations and thereby enables a radical form of non-positivism to take hold, which steers

[28] There is a question whether what needs to be bypassed is ontology altogether, or the particular kind of ontology proposed by positivism. Thanks to Katharine Jenkins for bringing this issue to my attention.

[29] Although most of the proposed account can be attributed to Kant, the value of the argument is independent of its exegetical accuracy. For that reason, it is more apposite to talk of a Kantian argument.

clear of the question-begging positivist ontology of legal relations. To that extent the Kantian legal relation paves the way to a *relations-first* and *radical* non-positivism.

10.3 Kantian Legal Relations

Legal relations become explanatorily less load bearing if their own explanation relies on an institutional basic structure, or so I have argued. Meanwhile the reason why contemporary non-positivists are wedded to the idea of a basic structure is that reference to a system of *public* or *omnilateral* justification serves as remedy to the coercive effects of pre-political autonomy. Exploring the possibility of a radical non-positivism, I will suggest that Kant's Doctrine of Right can be understood as supporting a relations-first account of law, which does not rely on further intermediaries, originating in state-bound institutions.[30] Although I do not aim at exegetical accuracy, I will assume throughout that my view reflects sufficiently Kant's key concern to explain the demands of right as constitutive of the type of moral freedom that ought to characterize interactions among agents (external freedom or freedom as independence).

The proposed *relational reading* of Kant will eventually be contrasted with a more standard one, which takes the demands of Kantian right to be the downstream effect of pre-institutional autonomy and freedom, much like the moderate forms of non-positivism discussed in the previous section. In conclusion, I will point to some of the strengths of the radical non-positivist version.

10.3.1 The Relational Reading

Kant's account of legal right centres on his Universal Principle of Right [UPR], which aims to explain legal obligations through the notion of rightful action conceived of in relational terms:

[30] A potential objection to the proposed approach is that it violates common understanding of Kant's methodology: often Kant moves from common experience to the necessary conditions for that experience. But attributing radical non-positivism to Kant would require setting aside actual legal institutions and practices. A sceptical reply to this criticism proceeds to draw a distinction between the actual contribution that Kant made to the philosophy of law and his own understanding of that contribution. A more constructive reply, and one I aspire to in this project, would aim to show that radical non-positivism is supported by the phenomenology of legal reasoning which does not disregard actual law-practices altogether, but reassigns them to the role of non-necessary grounds of legal obligation. I am indebted to Tom Bailey and Luke Davies for raising this point and to Luke Davies for suggesting the contours of the sceptical reply.

> Any action is right if it can coexist with everyone's freedom in accordance with a universal law, or if on its maxim the freedom of choice of each can coexist with everyone's freedom in accordance with a universal law.[31]

This makes UPR a direct account of legal relations which moves beyond both positivist accounts and those among the non-positivist accounts which rely for the explanation of legal rights and duties on the priority of a basic structure. With respect to positivism, UPR reverses the order of explanation between law-practices and legal relations, by opening the possibility of an explanation of legal obligations that dispenses with appeals to formally ordained legal sources *qua* necessary grounds. Meanwhile, against those non-positivist accounts that remain wedded to an institutional basic structure of governance, the Kantian UPR offers a way out of the priority of individual autonomy over omnilateral authorization, which otherwise would require a reference to law-practices and the state. I turn next to discuss each of these contributions. Taken together they encourage a full-blown turn to a relations-first account of law.

10.3.1.1 Against Positivism: UPR as Pre-institutional and Moral

UPR supports the explanatory priority of legal relations over a legal basic structure because it understands them as moral relations, which are not tied down to any specific institutional arrangement. On a widespread understanding, UPR is a pre-institutional moral principle that specifies standards of interaction among a plurality of persons.[32] Acting on these standards enables each to act consistently with the freedom of others in the sense of remaining independent from the way others exercise their choice. To that extent, the morality of independence takes centre stage in Kant's account of law as the condition for any act to count as 'rightful'.

Ultimately, this reading supports an understanding of law as forming that domain of morality which is dedicated to external freedom,

[31] Kant, RL 6:230.

[32] See, Arthur Ripstein, *Force and Freedom: Kant's Legal and Political Philosophy*, Cambridge, MA: Harvard University Press, 2009; Katrin Flikschuh, 'Human Rights in Kantian Mode: A Sketch', in Rowan Cruft, S. Matthew Liao, and Massimo Renzo (eds.), *Philosophical Foundations of Human Rights*, Oxford: Oxford University Press, 2015, 662–70; Barbara Herman, 'Juridical Personality and the Moral Role of Juridical Obligation', in Tamar Shapiro, Kyla Ebels-Duggan, and Sharon Street (eds.), *Normativity and Agency: Themes from the Philosophy of Christine Korsgaard*, Oxford: Oxford University Press, 2022, 240–63. However, it cannot be emphasized enough that this view is far from mainstream. There is a large body of influential literature that disputes the moral character of UPR. See, instead of others, the influential paper by Marcus Willaschek 'Which Imperatives for Right? On the Non-prescriptive Character of Juridical Laws in Kant's Metaphysics of Morals', in Mark Timmons (ed.), *Kant's Metaphysics of Morals: Interpretative Essays*, Oxford: Oxford University Press, 2002, 65–88.

understood as independence from the choice of others. Rather than assuming law's dependence on state institutions and regarding its relationship with morality only as derivative, the constitutive role law plays for freedom should be regarded as the strongest proof of its moral quality. Explaining the constitutive contribution of law for freedom facilitates an understanding of law's moral nature: freedom materializes through the law precisely in the sense that rightful conduct consists of synergetic patterns whose components are act-tokens of individual agents, each of whom is comporting themselves in accordance with the recommendation of UPR for freedom-consistent action. Individual act-tokens can only contribute to a rightful pattern of action if they are 'carved out' in ways that help them to latch on to each other, with an eye to forming composite rightful patterns of action. But notice that for this to happen, each individual act-token must already have in view the shape of the final rightful product, which is described by the Kantian UPR and the principles that instantiate it.[33]

Notably, this picture is not one where the freedom of choice of each is *ex post* subjected to rightful constraints of an institutional pedigree. Rather, it is the demand of freedom consistency that renders free the choice of any interacting party. As such, freedom of choice of each is not some *monadic state* but obtains in virtue of a *relation*: namely, coexistence with everyone's freedom under standards of freedom consistent action. Accordingly, free action is constitutively law-governed, that is, governed by the standards that instantiate the demands of UPR, or in Katrin Flikschuh's words: 'UPR is constitutive of external freedom; it is not an external constraint upon external freedom.'[34]

Ultimately, the picture painted by UPR can explain legal relations as obtaining when two or more individuals stand under the demand of engaging in structured tokens of action requiring their mutual contribution. Accordingly, legal relations can be employed in direct explanations of legal facts (facts about legal obligations),[35] without any residual need to refer to preordained legal institutions.

10.3.1.2 Radicalness: UPR as Source of Omnilateral Demands

Meanwhile the relational reading of UPR, in exemplifying freedom as independence, can purge the lingering commitment to positivist grounds, which brands many contemporary non-positivist accounts. Recall that a

[33] By principles I mean what UPR denotes as 'universal laws'. In developing this picture, I am relying heavily on A. J. Julius, "Independent People", in Sari Kisilevsky and Martin J. Stone (eds.), *Freedom and Force: Essays on Kant's Legal Philosophy*, Oxford: Hart Publishing, 2017), 91–110.

[34] Katrin Flikschuh, *What Is Orientation in Global Thinking?*, Cambridge: Cambridge University Press, 2017, 84.

[35] I am following here the definition of 'legal fact' proposed by Greenberg, 'How Facts Make Law'.

key reason for resorting to law practices and a preordained structure of governance was a concern about unilateral exercises of coercion in the name of a pre-institutional right to individual autonomy. Thus, in contrast to positivists who prioritize institutionalized legal sources over relations for the explanation of the content of the law, the non-positivist appeal to institutions has a different source: the basic structure of governance becomes now necessary because pre-institutional legal rights are, in the absence of a scheme of public authorization, bound to generate illegitimate coercion.

This concern with state institutions often assumes different guises: for Dworkin and other broadly interpretivist accounts of law, appeal to law-practices as grounds serves the purpose of triggering principles of political morality, which may legitimize the coercion exercised by the state on behalf of individual claims of autonomy. A less demanding view, and one that is of consequence for a Kantian account of legal relations, departs from a thinner requirement of legitimacy. In contrast to interpretivist non-positivism this view does not require any thick political morality to legitimize coercive exercises of individual autonomy, but merely appeals to the public structure of state coercion as a source of omnilateral authorization of enforceable claims of individual autonomy. I will coin the expression 'quasi-Lockean reading' for this interpretation of the Doctrine of Right and postpone its discussion until the next section, where I will also touch upon the idea of omnilaterality in more detail.

Meanwhile, on the relational reading, UPR demands that subjects undertake 'structured' actions which are composed by mutual contributions of the interacting parties. In that respect UPR offers a direct moral backing or justification for the recommended course of action, leaving no residual need for reference to an institutional basic structure. Let us revert to our example of Ms Donoghue, the unlucky consumer of poisoned ginger-ale, and ask how UPR would structure her relations with the careless manufacturer. Under its authority the manufacturer, Mr Stevenson, should be making ginger-beer consistently with the freedom of Ms Donoghue; namely, in such a manner that his act-tokens and those of Ms Donoghue compose a joint pattern of action, which enables Mr Stevenson and Ms Donoghue to interact in a mutually independent manner; which is to say, in a manner whereby the actions of each becomes a 'step' or a 'landing' for the actions of the other to lean on; or in more poetic terms, for performing together a dance 'in the steps of independence'. Here, the much celebrated 'duty of care', which was found to determine the relevant obligations in this landmark case of negligence, is but one among the principles that describe the structure of the pattern of independence which each of the parties must anticipate in performing their acts. In the celebrated words of Lord Atkin:

> I content myself with pointing out that in English law there must be, and is, some general conception of relations giving rise to a duty of care, of which the particular cases found in the books are but instances. [...] The rule that you are to love your neighbour becomes in law, you must not injure your neighbour; [...] You must take reasonable care to avoid acts or omissions which you can reasonably foresee would be likely to injure your neighbour. Who, then, in law is my neighbour? [...] this sufficiently states the truth if proximity be not confined to mere physical proximity, but be used [...] to extend to such close and direct relations that the act complained of directly affects a person whom the person alleged to be bound to take care would know would be directly affected by his careless act.[36]

On this occasion, any reference to law-practices, as enablers of an invitation for moral justification, is redundant. The legal relation between Donoghue and Stevenson comes first and is itself the source (or ground) of the relevant legal obligations.

The crux of radicalness in the proposed reading consists in the fact that UPR does not require the state and its institutions to ground its moral contribution to legal demands.[37] With respect to interpretivist non-positivists, Kantian right serves directly as ground of the moral content of the law, leaving no space for a basic structure to play a role in the justification. Equally, when confronted with the quasi-Lockean reading, the relational reading of Kantian right rejects individual autonomy as an antecedent moral demand, relinquishing the burden of justification that accompanies it. Significantly, as I am going to suggest in the closing section, omnilaterality is already involved in the demands of independence, with no need to appeal to some source external to UPR to retrieve it.

10.3.2 The Quasi-Lockean Reading

The defended reading of Kantian right clashes with a standard interpretation, which for expository reasons I shall label 'quasi-Lockean'. On this standard reading, independence is grounded in a pre-institutional principle

[36] *Donoghue v. Stevenson*, 1932.

[37] Tom Bailey has objected that my argument establishes at most that UPR grounds one pre-institutional legal obligation: the Kantian duty to enter the civil condition. All other legal obligations must lie downstream of that one and be grounded in the institutions of the civil condition (or law-practices, in the terminology of this chapter), because they presuppose the existence of an omnilateral will, which in Kant cannot be conceived of independently of the civil condition. In Section 10.3.3, I discuss the requirements of a pre-institutional conception of omnilaterality, which would counter the above objection at least in part. I am indebted to Bailey for raising this important point.

of individual autonomy, which partly overlaps with Kant's idea of innate right (IR):

> *Freedom* (independence from being constrained by another's choice) [. . .] insofar as it can coexist with the freedom of every other in accordance with a universal law, is the only original right belonging to every man by virtue of his humanity.[38]

This reading affirms the priority of individual autonomy qua IR and seeks to understand UPR's relational account of right as derivative. However, in its more sophisticated version, the quasi-Lockean reading introduces an interpersonal dimension to Kantian independence by suggesting that, although grounded in an absolute innate right, it cannot materialize independently of the public institutions of a political community.

To understand why, one must appreciate that pre-institutional autonomy is merely *provisional.* In contrast, for a full enjoyment of independence persons must acquire *conclusive* property titles in the material means of their actions. This requirement, eloquently defended by Arthur Ripstein in recent years, relies on an understanding of action whereby securing the means is conceptually prior to setting the ends of the action. To that extent, setting the ends of one's action independently of the choice of others would require having secured the relevant means: 'I can choose to Φ only if I can set about doing Φ, which requires that I have a right in the means that enable me to Φ.'[39] Accordingly, the negation of independence is a state of affairs in which others are equally entitled, in virtue of their innate right, to use the same means when they come to physical possession of them. Importantly, independence breaks down because any act based on the provisional entitlements of each is rendered an instance of unilateral coercion towards others.

This understanding of action, and the idea of independence that informs it, considers conclusive property titles as enabling the independence of an actor *because* they alone can ground legitimate exclusion of others from the means of her action. The condition of legitimacy requires in turn a system of public law which finalizes provisional entitlements and enforces them in an omnilateral manner, namely, in the name of all those who belong to the same political community. To that extent, pre-institutional individual autonomy (innate right) plays the role of a

[38] Kant, RL 6:230.

[39] Ripstein, *Force and Freedom*, 14; 40. This leads to a fundamental distinction between actions and their contexts; and between choosing and wishing: I can only choose something only if I consider it to be within my power to pursue. Otherwise, I am only wishing it.

background structuring ground of legal relations, which however can only be fully constituted by the public institutions of state-based law.[40] Thus, we read in Ripstein: 'People are entitled to independence simply because they are persons capable of setting their own purposes.'[41] And elsewhere, 'the consistent exercise of the right to freedom by a plurality of persons cannot be conceived apart from a public legal order'.[42] Taken together, these statements amount to the standard liberal understanding of independence and freedom, according to which law is a legitimate external constraint on a pre-existing, unconstrained notion of individual autonomy.[43]

10.3.3 The Rejection of the Quasi-Lockean Reading

Appealing as it might appear at first sight, the standard reading struggles to withstand closer scrutiny, as recent work has suggested. For, it seems to subsist on a mischaracterization of the relation between the two central principles of Kant's account of legal rights, namely, the UPR (universal principle of right) and IR (innate right). In contrast to the relational reading defended earlier, the standard reading suggests that individual autonomy operates as an antecedent ground of independence which does not rely on the juridical relations between parties. Accordingly, a key strategy for resisting this move requires the inversion of the explanatory

40 The *locus classicus* is Arthur Ripstein's *Force and Freedom*, which has set the agenda of the debate on Kant's philosophy of right. Although Ripstein proposes to understand Kantian right in a relational manner, his focus on innate right ultimately renders his account a version of the quasi-Lockean reading. Sorin Baiasu regards this reading as a viable strategy for defending the independence of Kantian right from ethics (Baiasu, Chapter 4, this volume). See for related criticism of the philosophical premises of the quasi-Lockean reading, Flikschuh, *What Is Orientation*, 69–99; 'Innate Right and Acquired Right in Arthur Ripstein's *Force and Freedom*', *Jurisprudence* 1 (2010), 295–304; 'Justice without Virtue', in Lara Denis (ed.), *Kant's Metaphysics of Morals: A Critical Guide*, Cambridge: Cambridge University Press, 2010, 51–70; Julius, 'Independent People'; George Pavlakos, 'Coercion and the Grounds of Legal Obligation: Arthur Ripstein's *Force and Freedom*', *Jurisprudence* 1 (2010), 305–16. And for responses to Flikschuh and Pavlakos see Arthur Ripstein, 'Reply to Flikschuh and Pavlakos', *Jurisprudence* 1 (2010), 317–24.

41 Ripstein, *Force and Freedom*, 17.

42 *Force and Freedom*, 9. Pauline Kleingeld (Chapter 13, this volume) understands Kantian external freedom as consisting of two interdependent dimensions: a negative one, which rests with IR as the most fundamental right, and a positive dimension as a requirement for the realization of the demands of IR, which consists in collective self-legislation. It is debatable whether this conception differs from Ripstein's reading.

43 See Paul Guyer, *Kant on Freedom, Law and Happiness*, Cambridge: Cambridge University Press, 2000; Louis-Philippe Hodgson, 'Kant on the Right to Freedom: A Defense', *Ethics* 120 (2010), 791–819; Otfried Höffe, *Kategorische Rechtsprinzipien*, Frankfurt am Main: Suhrkamp, 1990; Wolfgang Kersting, *Wohlgeordnete Freiheit*, 2nd ed., Frankfurt am Main: Suhrkamp, 1993; Bernd Ludwig, 'Kants Verabschiedung der Vertragstheorie', *Jahrbuch für Recht und Ethik/Annual Review of Law and Ethics* 82 (1993), 221–54.

priority between the two principles, as I read Katrin Flikschuh to suggest in recent work.[44]

On her proposal, UPR subjects the interacting parties to standards that secure the consistency of the action of each with the independence of everyone else. Meanwhile, innate right does not constitute an additional ground of UPR or the relation it specifies, but merely announces or summarizes the moral status enjoyed by anyone who is subject to the requirements of UPR, namely, the status of an agent as independent of the choice of others, because everyone is under an obligation of acting on principles that secure consistency with each other's independence. Providing ample textual evidence, Flikschuh argues convincingly that UPR specifies the central moral relation in Kant's account of legal rights, while innate right captures the moral status that pertains to anyone who stands in that moral relation.[45] Accordingly, the general concept of right pertains to a 'formal, external, strictly reciprocal moral relation':

> [T]he concept of right, insofar as it is related to an obligation corresponding to it, has to do, *first*, only with the external and indeed practical relation of one person to another [. . .] But *second*, it does not signify the relation of one's choice to the mere wish of the other, but only in relation to the other's *choice*. *Third*, in this reciprocal relation of choice no account at all is taken of the *matter* of choice [. . .] All that is in question is the *form* in the relation of choice on the part of both.[46]

Flikschuh's reconstruction consolidates a reading of Kantian right that moves away from the quasi-Lockean picture and closer to the relational reading that was defended earlier: on the standard view independent persons are understood as 'each [having] an equal right to exercise [their] power of choice consistently with everyone else having an equal such right'.[47] Conversely, her reading highlights the *constitutive role* of UPR for independent action: 'each has a right to being treated by all others as someone who is capable of right action',[48] in a manner that supports the relations-first reading of Kantian right.

Another notable account that underscores the constitutive priority of UPR over IR has been recently advanced by Rafeeq Hasan and Martin Stone.[49]

44 Flikschuh, *What Is Orientation*.
45 Flikschuh, 'Human Rights in Kantian Mode'; *What Is Orientation*, 82–7.
46 Kant, RL 6:230; text edited and quoted by Flikschuh, 'Human Rights in Kantian Mode', 662.
47 Flikschuh, *What Is Orientation*, 85. 48 Flikschuh, *What Is Orientation*, 85.
49 Martin J. Stone and Rafeeq Hasan, 'What Is Provisional Right?', *Philosophical Review* 131 (2022), 51–98. Their account is much more nuanced than my summary suggests, which however should suffice for present purposes.

On this proposal, what distinguishes juridical right within Kant's division of morality is its provisionality. Importantly, this property grounds a *conceptual link* between pre-relational entitlements (including innate right) and their fully realized instantiations (as specified by UPR), because a complete explanation of anything that is provisional must involve as ground the conditions of its possibility: 'provisional right expresses the intrinsic connection between rightful relations and political association by marking the defective character of rights where a state is absent'.[50] Ultimately, on their account, UPR 'grounds and unifies the domain of juridical principles by exhibiting them as stages of its own explication'.[51] Here, as with Flikschuh earlier, the *provisionality account* vindicates a relational reading of Kantian right, which takes the ultimate ground of independence to be the relation in UPR rather than some self-standing notion of individual autonomy (which in the authors' account can only be thought of as provisional).

Both these accounts cast serious doubt on the quasi-Lockean reading of Kantian right.[52] Importantly, they identify and remove the misconceived priority of IR over UPR in the explanation of Kantian freedom as independence, which was responsible for demoting legal relations to tools for 'realizing' antecedent claims of individual autonomy. In contrast, when the order of explanatory priority between UPR and IR is restored, a compelling new understanding emerges of the relation between rights and legal relations: rights are then grounded in the relation specified by UPR, the legal relation. In this context innate right functions merely as a

50 Stone and Hasan, 'What Is Provisional Right?', 53.

51 'What Is Provisional Right?', 93. The authors supplement the 'centripetal' role of UPR, of unifying the juridical domain by grounding itself in its instantiations, with a claim about the necessary role of institutions in the juridical domain: because UPR is a purely formal principle, it affords nothing that can play the role of a unifying end; accordingly, accessing the requirements of right can only be a matter of its specification via additional principles and determinate judgements applying those principles, both of which need to be procured by legal intuitions and officials occupying roles in them ('What Is Provisional Right?', 92). This further claim is clearly not necessitated by the *provisionality* thesis, as I will argue in Section 10.3, even though it might be valid as an exegetical point about Kant.

52 In recent work Barbara Herman develops a holistic reading of Kant's practical philosophy, according to which the Doctrine of Right complements his earlier moral philosophy. Her view, rich and subtle in its detail, resists an easy classification under either of the camps suggested here. In a nutshell, she takes duties of right to 'flesh out' moral agency by providing standards for action which enhance our moral powers as autonomous persons. To that extent, her view seems to side with quasi-Lockean readings that affirm the primacy of Innate Right. Meanwhile, on a par with relational strategies that subsist on institutionalization, Herman argues that the obligation to act as law requires is instantiated only if everyone is equally constrained – and not just obligated – to conform. See Barbara Herman, 'Juridical Personality and the Moral Role of Juridical Obligation', in Tamar Shapiro, Kyla Ebels-Duggan, and Sharon Street (eds.), *Normativity and Agency: Themes from the Philosophy of Christine Korsgaard*, Oxford: Oxford University Press, 2022, 240–63.

signpost for the moral status of each of the interacting persons, *once they are parties to legal relations.*

10.3.4 The Publicity of Legal Relations

Despite the progress made by recent defenders of relational strategies of Kantian right, there remains a key difference from the version put forward in this chapter, whose identification will help us consolidate the possibility of a *relations-first* or *radical* non-positivism. Both the account of Flikschuh and the *provisionalist* one read Kant's universal principle of right [UPR] as necessitating the existence of a basic structure of legal institutions [basic structure].[53] In doing so they hold juridical relations to be constitutively dependent on the law-practices of the basic structure.[54]

This belief is equally shared by the quasi-Lockean reading of Kant but also other moderate versions of non-positivism, as previously indicated. In these accounts the basic structure is a means for evoking a collective 'we'-agent, on whose name pre-political individual claims can become binding on others.[55] While the significance of omnilateral justification and the institutions that procure it is obvious for modest non-positivists, it is less clear why a relational account (including those of Flikschuh and the provisionalists) should commit to them. I turn next to two reasons why a relational reading of Kantian right does not necessitate the presence of a basic structure in its explanation of legal relations.

To begin with, any retreat to the basic structure would struggle to account for legal relations as an independent explanatory tool in line with the phenomenology of legal practice.[56] In particular, making reference to the basic structure, qua necessary ground of legal obligations, would revive the problem of circularity that we encountered in positivist accounts of law. Meanwhile, if the requirements of juridical relations are ultimately

[53] For the definition of basic structure, see Section 10.2.3.

[54] For a similar approach, see Herman, 'Juridical Personality'.

[55] Flikschuh also appeals to a version of the basic structure argument to ground the idea of an omnilateral will as the source of legal obligations (see, 'Justice without Virtue', 63–9). In her case, however, the concern is not to legitimize legal restrictions on antecedent, pre-political individual rights, but to demonstrate that omnilateral willing is fundamental in the explanation of legal rights and, therefore, not reliant on any antecedent notions of individual willing or autonomy. Specifically, she argues that the omnilateral will is constituted by the subordination relation that obtains between a commander and their subject(s), making facts of authority the basic determinants of legal rights. Below I propose a constitutive account of omnilateral will that avoids grounding legal rights exclusively in authoritative institutions while, at the same time, it steers clear of the fallacies committed by the non-relational readings of Kant.

[56] See Section 10.2.

grounded in institutional sources, then a fresh need to appeal to pre-institutional considerations would arise, in order to counter the indeterminacy of institutional sources.[57]

The second reason is deeper and demonstrates why the relational reading of Kantian right is uniquely suited to vindicate the possibility of radical positivism. It points at the redundancy of state law in the context of the relational reading: why turn to law-practices to establish the interpersonal or public dimension of juridical demands if we have *already* established that the pre-institutional grounds of legal relations are public? Recall our earlier discussion of freedom as independence. Freedom as independence is premised on a particular kind of *interdependence* from others: one obtaining when each of the interacting parties is acting with a view to the freedom of everyone else. If that is the kind of demand that is grounded by the UPR, then why appeal to an additional source of publicity?

To put it differently, the question of publicity arises about the range of those who can partake in relations of independence. It asks: 'who can be included in the scope of collectives whose members act on demands that help each to act consistently with the freedom of others?' It was demonstrated earlier that a typical route for answering this question looks to identify a 'collective' agent in whose name the said demands can become binding for all those involved. But there is no symmetric demand to resort to an institutional public structure once we have adopted the relational interpretation of legal rights. For, the UPR bestows on juridical demands a public dimension in virtue of recommending them 'in the name of' all those who are parties to the relation.[58] It does so because the demands of

[57] See Section 10.2.1. Although there is no space for detailed discussion, this seems to me to be the upshot of Flikschuh, *What Is Orientation*. After having disentangled UPR from innate right, she reverts somewhat puzzlingly to public institutions. But this is too quick; UPR, as she has argued, is a moral principle that explains what counts as rightful action among a plurality of persons and should not be collapsed into the conditions of an institutional legal order. The two issues should be kept analytically distinct, even though UPR can be employed to support the Kantian duty to enter the civil condition. Ultimately, her suggestion invites two criticisms: apart from reviving the thread of circularity, it is also redundant, as I explain next.

[58] Notably, in his theory of citizenship, Kant does not include every subject of the state in the citizenry. Instead, he takes citizenship to require *Selbständigkeit* (civil self-sufficiency) as the specific aspect of independence that comprises not only the rights and powers of persons but also the conditions for their exercise. The importance of this move cannot be overrated: in suggesting that independence operates as an autonomous normative threshold for citizenship, Kant questions the role of the state as the primary source of public standards for independent interaction. My reading of the relation between citizenship and *Selbständigkeit* follows the illuminating discussion in Nicholas Vrousalis, 'Interdependent Independence: Civil Self-Sufficiency and Productive Community in Kant's Theory of Citizenship', *Kantian Review* 27 (2022), 443–60.

independence stipulated by UPR define those requirements as the features of a pattern of interaction whose subject is the joint agent made up by everyone who is under the general, abstract obligation to interact with others in a freedom-consistent manner.[59]

But perhaps one might object that a more precise understanding of the omnilateral scope of UPR is needed, for the reason that by removing altogether institutions as necessary grounds of legal relations, we also remove the possibility of accounting for the scope of legal relations through the idea of an omnilateral we-subject. For, that possibility would ultimately require a scaffolding enabling the interpersonal relevance of a domain of interactions. Here the issue is not one of (omnilateral) *justification*, but the simpler and more basic one about the *boundaries and relevance* of the legal domain.

To this we must reply by looking closer at how 'omnilaterality', qua joint authorship of standards of rightful action, is *already* incorporated in the normative meaning of UPR. Key in this context is to realize that publicity is part of the practical necessity of UPR: the Kantian principle, in virtue of constituting independence, involves a notion of universalization which is specific to independence. When UPR enjoins 'according to a universal law' the stated universality is not the universality of autonomy (as affirmed by the categorial imperative) but the universality of independence, which, I would like to suggest, involves omnilaterality.[60] This is a robust claim whose full demonstration would have to wait for a future occasion. Within the confines of this short chapter, I can only limit myself to a sketchy demonstration. To reflect on the separateness of the universalization that pertains to independence, just think that many of the maxims that would pass the test of universalization under the categorical imperative may fail under the test of independence.[61] In other words, the

[59] A. J. Julius, 'Reconstruction', unpublished MS, version 7 December 2013, www.ajjulius.net/reconstruction.pdf, chs. 7, 9, and 11 (accessed 9 July 2025).

[60] Owing to lack of space, I cannot here elaborate on the complex relation between universality (in autonomy) and omnilaterality (in independence). By way of quick comment, I am inclined to understand them as interdependent parts in a unified conception of practical thinking, whereby independence plays the role of a *condition* on autonomy, much in the way the 'reasonable' can be thought of as a constrain of the 'rational' in Rawls's account of the original position. Here I draw on recent proposals on the problem of practical unity in Rawls's account of justice as fairness (Micha Gläser, 'The Reasonable and the Rational in General and in Particular', unpublished MS). Marcus Willaschek's distinction between the ethical and legal domain relies implicitly on a distinction between two kinds of universalization, which reflects mine between universalization and omnilaterality (Willaschek, Chapter 1, this volume).

[61] Willaschek provides several very helpful examples to disprove the coextensiveness of ethical and legal universalisation (Willaschek, Chapter 1, this volume).

set of valid moral maxims of autonomy is not coextensive with the set of maxims of independence. That much might already be familiar and not terribly surprising. My further suggestion is that the universal test of independence *is that of omnilaterality*: only omnilateral maxims can pass it. Here is an example:[62] I am standing in a room with others and there is only one chair. Striving toward autonomy, I act on the maxim: 'occupy chair'. I think this is perfectly consistent with the demands of autonomous agency. But it would, arguably, fail on the demands of independence, precisely because it fails to ground a rightful course of action (i.e. if abided by, it would violate independent interaction among those present in the room). In its stead, a different maxim is in the offing that would enable each one of us in the same room to engage in patterns of action consistent with the freedom of everyone else; perhaps something like 'occupy chair, unless occupied'; or even better, 'occupy chair, consistently with the freedom of others'.

I suggest that omnilaterality is this version of universalization that considers (explicitly) the freedom of others, and as a result cares for maxims that require from a plurality of persons to act as an interdependent or omnilateral subject.[63] If this is not an outlandish suggestion, then omnilaterality and freedom as independence turn out to be co-original. And the Universal Principle of Right, as a pre-institutional moral standard, comes out as constitutive of both.

Where does this leave us? In contrast to the liberal reading, legal rights are not antecedent entitlements that need to be mutually reconciled within an institutional matrix that is acceptable to all. Legal rights, on the relational reading, are grounded from the outset on the interpersonal

62 Both the example and the argument of this paragraph are inspired by Julius, 'Independent People'.

63 A potential concern arising with respect to the idea of pre-institutional omnilaterality submits that it would violate the requirement of formality of Kantian right, because individuals must (a) either assume unilateral authority to interpret the demands of UPR or (b) defer such authority to others; however, the objection continues, neither of these options would be consistent with Kantian independence. In reply, I note that the above worry presupposes that outside the state everyone is endowed with some form of pre-institutional autonomy, whose unilateral exercise threatens their independence. In contrast, the picture I am developing here aims to show that precepts of right remain formal, but their formality is omnilateral: in acting on these laws none of the agents is deferring to the other's ends; instead, they are all willing together principles that afford to each right exercising actions, consistent with the freedom of others. In consequence, these principles commit interacting parties to deliberative practices of interpretation and application which do not require the presence of state institutions or law-practices. I am especially grateful to Luke Davis who pressed me to discuss this issue.

normative demands of the legal relation.[64] Although a more detailed analysis of these demands escapes the confines of this chapter, they will typically include a principle of fair distribution and a collective duty of care, alongside the class of responsibilities that apply reciprocally to each party to avoid engaging in wrongdoing and other *pro tanto* unjustifiable acts that one person might commit against another on a particular occasion.[65] Taken together these standards formulate the central qualitative features of patterns of action through which each of the parties to the legal relation acts consistently with the principled actions of the others.[66] Acting on such patterns safeguards the *distinctness between persons*[67] among pluralities of interacting agents, each of whom is typically in the pursuit of separate systems of ends.

10.4 Conclusion

I began by raising some concerns about the possibility of an explanation of legal relations in the contemporary landscape of legal theoretical positions. I am now a little more reassured that this might not be a doomed project, given the potential of Kantian right to hold out the possibility of radical non-positivism.

64 Figuratively speaking, while the liberal reading sees rights as part of a Natural Private Law, the relational reading I propose defends something akin to a Natural Public Law (Julius, 'Independent People'; George Pavlakos, 'Redrawing the Legal Relation', in Jorge L. Fabra-Zamora (ed.), *Jurisprudence in a Globalised World*, Cheltenham: Edward Elgar, 2020, 173–94; 'Agent-Relativity without Control: Grounding Negligence on Normative Relations', in Veronica Rodriguez-Blanco and George Pavlakos (eds.), *Negligence, Agency and Responsibility*, Cambridge: Cambridge University Press, 2021, 118–35).

65 For an account of the morality of social practices, see Aaron James, 'Distributive Justice without Sovereign Rule: The Case of Trade', *Social Theory and Practice* 31 (2005), 533–59. Essentially, James develops principles of interpersonal morality which regulate interactions of a plurality of persons, when those interactions constitute a social practice, in virtue of passing a threshold test.

66 See Julius, 'Reconstruction', 107. Notice that on the proposal I am defending, the requirements of legal relations are structural principles which aim also to safeguard conditions for the exercise of persons' normative powers, in addition to enforcing individual entitlements against others. Compare the inclusive reading of civil independence developed in Nicholas Vrousalis, 'Interdependent Independence'.

67 John Rawls, *A Theory of Justice*, Cambridge, MA: Harvard University Press, 1971, §5.

CHAPTER 11

What Is External Freedom?

Japa Pallikkathayil

The foundational claim of Kant's political philosophy is that we each have an innate right to external freedom: '*Freedom* (independence from being constrained by another's choice), insofar as it can coexist with the freedom of every other person in accordance with a universal law, is the only original right belonging to every man by virtue of his humanity.'[1] I take external freedom to involve already a normative component: one is free insofar as one has effective rights against others. The innate right to freedom is thus essentially a right to have a secure place in a system of universal rights. My aim in this chapter is to defend this normative understanding of external freedom as the basis of a compelling argument justifying the state. This will not be primarily an interpretative project and my argument will explicitly differ from Kant's own at points. But I aim to display the virtues of some of the insights that I take to be at the heart of his political philosophy.

In what follows, I begin by considering Arthur Ripstein's prominent reconstruction and development of Kant's argument for the state.[2] Ripstein employs a normative conception of external freedom very similar to the one that I propose. I then survey powerful objections that Kyla Ebels-Duggan presses against Ripstein's view.[3] I take these objections to tell decisively against Ripstein's argument for the state, whatever the merits of that argument as a reconstruction of Kant's own. While Ebels-Duggan takes the problems with Ripstein's argument to provide support for relying on a descriptive rather than a normative conception of external freedom, I think these problems turn on other features of his argument. After showing that the descriptive conception of external freedom preferred by

[1] Kant, RL 6:237.

[2] Arthur Ripstein, *Force and Freedom: Kant's Legal and Political Philosophy*, Cambridge, MA: Harvard University Press, 2009.

[3] Kyla Ebels-Duggan, 'Critical Notice', *Canadian Journal of Philosophy* 41(2011), 549–74.

Ebels-Duggan faces problems of its own, I give an argument for the state that is inspired by but distinct from Kant's argument. My argument employs a normative conception of external freedom and yet avoids Ebels-Duggan's objections.

11.1 Ripstein's Normative Conception of External Freedom

In this section, I describe Ripstein's reconstruction and development of Kant's argument for the state and highlight the ways in which that argument incorporates a normative conception of external freedom. In the course of this discussion, I introduce Ebels-Duggan's objections to Ripstein's view.

Ripstein claims that '[y]ou are independent if you are the one who decides what ends you will use your means to pursue, as opposed to having someone else decide for you.'[4] This is a normative conception of external freedom in that its content depends on a determination of what constitutes one's means. And the distinction between what is mine and what is yours is itself a normative matter. There are some subtle differences between this characterization of external freedom and the one I gave above in terms of having effective rights against others. I will return to these differences in Section 11.3. But for now, let us proceed with Ripstein's characterization in mind.

Ripstein takes Kant's argument for the state to proceed as follows. One innately possesses one's own body – it is one's basic means. This innate right to one's own body gives one a derivative right to whatever one physically possesses. But if I put down the apple I have just picked, my innate right to my own body does not prohibit you from taking it. We move beyond the rights secured by mere empirical possession with Kant's Postulate of Practical Reason with Regard to Right, which holds that it must be possible to have objects external to oneself as property. Ripstein's defence of the Postulate relies on his normative conception of external freedom. As he puts it:

> No other person is wronged by another's having an object subject to his or her choice. The freedom of others would only be compromised if one person's having a proprietary or contractual right deprived some other person of something he or she already had. From the standpoint of each person's right of humanity in his or her own person, the acquired rights of others are just parts of the context within which they choose.[5]

[4] Ripstein, *Force and Freedom*, 33. [5] Ripstein, *Force and Freedom*, 63–4.

In other words, given that freedom consists in choosing what to do with what is yours, others having rights over objects to which you do not have a right does not deprive you of freedom.

Ebels-Duggan argues that relying on a normative conception of freedom causes trouble for Ripstein's defence of the Postulate.[6] It may be true that having rights to external objects does not deprive anyone of anything that is theirs. But a system of rights in which nothing external is owned also does not deprive anyone of anything that is theirs. A conception of freedom as control over one's own means lacks the resources to adjudicate between different specifications of one's means.

Ripstein claims that

> any restrictions on the possibility of a person having objects as her own would restrict one person's purposiveness for the sake of something other than freedom, and so interfere with each person's right to be *sui juris*, her own master. That is, they would limit freedom on the basis of something other than its own conditions.[7]

But recall that on the normative conception of freedom, freedom is limited only if others take control of one's means. Since precisely what is at issue in the Postulate is what can potentially be part of one's means, talk of freedom being limited is out of place. The normative conception of freedom does not support the claim that a system of rights in which external objects of choice may not be owned has any less freedom than a system of rights in which they may be owned.

I take this to be a deep problem with Ripstein's defence of the Postulate. Perhaps the Postulate can yet be rescued. I am sceptical though, and my own argument for the state will not rely on the Postulate. For now, however, let us set aside these concerns and consider the next step in Ripstein's reconstruction of Kant's argument for the state. While the Postulate tells us that it must be possible to have external objects as one's own, it does not tell us how to acquire rights to such objects. And it turns out that in the state of nature we are unable to acquire property in external objects for three reasons, which Ripstein glosses as follows. First, individuals cannot unilaterally choose to put others under obligation by acquiring property. Second, property rights in the state of nature would be indeterminate, and no individual could unilaterally resolve this indeterminacy. Third, one is not required to respect others' property rights in the absence of assurance that they will do likewise, assurance that no individual can

[6] Ebels-Duggan, 'Critical Notice', 569–70. [7] Ripstein, *Force and Freedom*, 64.

unilaterally provide. Since we cannot unilaterally solve these problems, their resolution requires an omnilateral will. And this is precisely what the establishment of the state makes possible.[8]

Ripstein also goes beyond reconstructing Kant's view by providing a novel argument for why the state must establish and regulate public roads. This argument begins by considering what would happen if all the land around you was privately owned. In that case, '[p]rivate ownership of land does not simply foreclose some particular purpose that you might happen to have, but also forecloses the entire formal class of purposes involving voluntary interactions with others'.[9] But as Ebels-Duggan correctly points out, being boxed in by one's own neighbours would not prevent all voluntary interactions with others – one could still enter into voluntary agreements with one's immediate neighbours.[10] Why then think that there is something problematic about having the possibility of voluntary interactions with one's mediate neighbours depend on the permission of one's immediate neighbours to cross their land?

It seems that any answer to this question that is consistent with the normative conception of external freedom has to identify a way in which such a scheme would deprive one of something that was already among one's means. In the circumstance we are imagining you are not being deprived of any external object of choice to which you already have a right. That leaves innate right as the only potential ground for objection. And sometimes Ripstein seems to gesture in this direction, suggesting that being blocked in by one's neighbours 'is in conflict with each person's right to associate with others as those others see fit, which [. . .] is simply an aspect of "a human being's quality of being *his own master*" [. . .] A neighbor who is entitled to decide who you can associate with would be your master.'[11]

Kant takes each human being's status as his own master to be an aspect of innate right. As an interpretative matter, Ripstein may well be right to hold that the freedom to associate with others on mutually agreeable terms is part of this aspect of innate right. As Ripstein puts it, 'Part of your entitlement to set and pursue your own purposes is the entitlement to choose those with whom you will make arrangements, subject only to their entitlement to decline to enter into arrangements with you.'[12] But we are not imagining a situation analogous to a parent who forbids her child from

[8] Ripstein, *Force and Freedom*, 183.
[9] Ripstein, *Force and Freedom*, 247.
[10] Ebels-Duggan, 'Critical Notice', 566.
[11] Ripstein, *Force and Freedom*, 247–8.
[12] Ripstein, *Force and Freedom*, 210.

associating with what she takes to be a bad crowd – that really is a case in which one person restricts with whom another may associate. In contrast, the neighbours who block you in exercise no authority over your choice of with whom to associate. They simply decline to provide you with the means needed to make your overtures audible or visible to those with whom you wish to associate. As Ebels-Duggan points out, this seems very like the situation in which you need milk to make pancakes, but I have purchased the last carton.[13] And that is Ripstein's paradigmatic example of a case in which I do not deprive you of anything to which you have a right. Thus, the normative conception of external freedom makes it difficult to see how the neighbours who block you in infringe your freedom – you are still free to control the means that are yours.

Ebels-Duggan takes this be a symptom of a larger problem with reliance on a normative conception of freedom.[14] Since the Kantian argument takes the state to be needed to give determinate content to what is mine and yours, and thus to what our respective freedom consists in, 'it looks like no matter how the state assigns acquired rights, it will count as securing the freedom of all, so long as it enforces those very rights'.[15] I take this to be a serious challenge for relying on a normative conception of freedom in the Kantian argument for the state. How can a concern for freedom constrain the legitimate activities of the state if the state itself is what makes freedom determinate? In Section 11.3, I will try to answer this question. But at this point one might instead be tempted to jettison the normative conception of freedom. In the next section, I argue that the most obvious alternative to the normative conception of freedom faces serious problems. This is why I take the best hope for something in the spirit of the Kantian argument for the state still to lie in the normative conception of freedom.

11.2 The Descriptive Conception of Freedom

Ebels-Duggan proposes a descriptive conception of external freedom according to which a person is externally free 'just in case she can move her body around in space to pursue her ends unfettered by others'.[16] This conception is descriptive in that it does not take the content of freedom to depend on the application of any other normative concepts. I take it there may be other descriptive conceptions of freedom. But the one to which

[13] Ebels-Duggan, 'Critical Notice', 567.

[14] Ebels-Duggan, 'Critical Notice', 563.

[15] Ebels-Duggan, 'Critical Notice', 563.

[16] Ebels-Duggan, 'Critical Notice', 563.

Ebels-Duggan gestures is one on which Kantians often implicitly or explicitly rely.[17] I therefore take this descriptive conception of freedom to be worth singling out for attention.

Ebels-Duggan argues that this descriptive conception of freedom can better defend the Postulate. Let us briefly take a look at that argument. With regard to the Postulate, Ebels-Duggan notes that many of our ends require using more objects than we can physically possess at one time and using those objects for longer than we hold them. If I may snatch whatever you put down, my choices will frustrate your pursuit of your ends. For this reason, she takes it that a system of rights without private ownership of external objects of choice severely limits external freedom. She acknowledges that private ownership also restricts people's freedom in certain ways – now I may not snatch an object you have put down if you own it. But she argues 'this restriction is much less serious than the restriction that I would face if I couldn't establish property rights. In the former case, I may be coerced not to interfere with what you own. But in the latter case, all of my ends could be severely curtailed.'[18]

The problem with this argument is that whether property rights enhance or limit our freedom to pursue our ends unfettered by others depends on what our ends happen to be. If I want to live the life of nomadic hunter-gatherer, I may be able to pursue more of my ends without interference if no one including me has property rights. To determine whether property rights enhance or limit freedom understood as the absence of interference we need to settle which ends we are trying to secure against interference. But doing that requires going beyond the idea of freedom.

This is a familiar problem for the conception of freedom as the absence of interference, or as it is often called, negative liberty. H. L. A. Hart suggests a similar objection to Rawls's original formulation of his first principle of justice, which holds that 'each person is to have a right to the most extensive basic liberty compatible with a similar liberty for others'.[19] Hart asks what it is to limit liberty for the sake of liberty and takes up

[17] For example: '[T]he freedom that is to be preserved and promoted by right action, whether it is motivated by virtue or not, is in all cases freedom not only of choice but also of action in the world, the freedom of human beings to move their own bodies and to exercise them upon other objects in nature in accord with their own choices to the extent compatible with a like freedom for all other human beings' (Paul Guyer, *Kant on Freedom, Law, and Happiness*, Cambridge: Cambridge University Press, 2012, 237).

[18] Kyla Ebels-Duggan, 'Moral Community: Escaping the Ethical State of Nature', *Philosophers' Imprint* 9 (2009), 1–19, at 3.

[19] John Rawls, *A Theory of Justice*, Cambridge, MA: Harvard University Press, 1971, 60.

Rawls's example of 'the introduction of rules of order in a debate, which restrict the liberty to speak when we please'.[20] As Hart observes, 'what such rules of debate help to secure is not a greater or more extensive liberty, but a liberty to do something which is more valuable for any rational person than the activities forbidden by the rules, or, as Rawls himself says, something more "profitable."'[21] What I have suggested about attempting to use the conception of freedom as non-interference to justify the Postulate comes to the same thing. That defence of the Postulate requires us to specify some ends relative to which schemes of freedom as non-interference may be judged.

Rawls went on to modify his first principle in response to Hart's objection. Instead of focusing on the extent of liberty, he moved to focusing on a scheme of liberty 'fully adequate' for the development and full and informed exercise of the capacity for a sense of justice and the capacity for a conception of the good.[22] In terms of Rawls's project, singling out these capacities is well motivated. He presupposes that society is 'a cooperative venture for mutual advantage' and seeks to identify principles that would fairly distribute the benefits and burdens of such cooperation.[23] The idea of fair cooperation for mutual advantage requires that individuals have both a sense of justice and a conception of the good. Thus, ensuring that people can adequately realize their capacities for a sense of justice and a conception of the good is required for Rawls's principles of justice to have application. But the Kantian project seeks to answer a prior question, namely, why are we required to cooperate with anyone at all? From the point of view of that prior question, there is no particular reason to assume that people must be able to develop the aforementioned capacities.

Of course, concern for agency is a recognizably Kantian concern. And we may well have duties of virtue that orient us towards ensuring that others are able to develop their agential capacities adequately. But that does not yet indicate why we may be *compelled* to ensure that others are able to develop their agency. And, indeed, there are many duties of virtue that Kantians deny may be coercively enforced. For this reason, assessing the extent of freedom in terms of any particular end, even one required by

[20] H. L. A. Hart, 'Rawls on Liberty and Its Priority', *The University of Chicago Law Review* 40 (1973), 534–55, at 543.

[21] Hart, 'Rawls on Liberty and Its Priority', 543.

[22] John Rawls, *Political Liberalism: Expanded Edition*, New York: Columbia University Press, 2005, 331–2.

[23] Rawls, *A Theory of Justice*, 4.

virtue, fails to engage with the main question of the Doctrine of Right. Since the extent of freedom as non-interference cannot be assessed without reference to some privileged end or another, I take this to be a decisive reason to set this conception of freedom aside here.

11.3 The Normative Conception of Freedom Revisited

In Section 11.1, I noted three problems facing Ripstein's use of a normative conception of external freedom: (1) the Postulate seems undermotivated; (2) the aim of securing external freedom seems to provide no constraints on the state; (3) Ripstein's argument for public roads is unsuccessful. In this section, I consider how a normative conception of freedom might be employed in ways that overcome these three problems. Before doing so, I will briefly comment on the differences between Ripstein's conception of freedom and my own. As I noted at the outset, these differences are subtle. And I do not think that the differences matter much for what follows. It is Ripstein's particular use of the normative conception of freedom rather than the conception itself that is problematic. But since I will often frame the discussion that follows using my preferred articulation, it may be helpful to draw out the differences between these views.

Recall that Ripstein claims that '[y]ou are independent if you are the one who decides what ends you will use your means to pursue, as opposed to having someone else decide for you'.[24] The gloss strikes me as misleading. No one can decide what ends you will use your means to pursue. Choosing ends is something one can do only for oneself. What matters is instead simply that others leave our means available for our use. I suspect this is actually closer to what Ripstein himself has in mind even though references to setting ends is sprinkled throughout his text. With this correction in view, we might then gloss external freedom as having effective control over one's means.

My preferred conception of external freedom, however, makes no explicit reference to one's means. Instead, I take external freedom to consist in having effective rights against others. But in my view having effective control over one's means and having effective rights against others comes to the same thing. What it is for something to be among my means rather than among yours is for me to have rights against you with respect to it. I prefer to gloss external freedom as consisting in effective rights

[24] Ripstein, *Force and Freedom*, 33.

against others because doing so makes salient a question about what rights against others I must have, a question I take Ripstein to fail to appreciate fully because he considers the idea of having control over one's means to have more determinate content than it does.[25] Be that as it may, I treat these ways of talking about the subject matter of external freedom as interchangeable in the discussion that follows.

11.3.1 The Argument for the State without the Postulate

With this in mind, we can turn to the first of the three problems that Ripstein's use of the normative conception of freedom faces. Recall that the normative conception of freedom does not support the claim that a system of rights in which external objects of choice may not be owned has any less freedom than a system of rights in which they may be owned. Neither system denies anyone anything that is theirs. Since, in Kant's view, securing the possibility of property rights provides the reason for establishing the state, this is a serious problem for that argument. I believe, however, that the basic structure of Kant's argument for the state can be successfully repurposed by focusing on bodily rights rather than property rights. I have developed this argument at length elsewhere.[26] Here I briefly rehearse this argument, which has two steps. Kant seems to assume implicitly that one has a right to one's body. The first step in my argument involves motivating this claim. Next, I show that bodily rights are subject to problems that largely parallel the problems faced by property rights in the state of nature. They can thus be used to justify establishing the state without relying on the Postulate.

Let us consider each of these steps in turn. Recall that the basic problem faced by the normative conception of freedom is that a conception of freedom as having effective rights does not tell us what rights people have (or, alternatively, identify the means over which they should have effective control). In one way, the right to one's body is no exception – it would be a mistake to say that we would be less free without rights to our bodies. In another way, however, the right to one's body occupies a special place in a scheme of rights. We must attribute bodily rights to people in order for the idea of external freedom to have application. You cannot have effective control over anything if you do not have effective control over yourself.

[25] Japa Pallikkathayil, 'Persons and Bodies', in Sari Kisilevsky and Martin Stone (eds.), *Freedom and Force: Essays on Kant's Legal Philosophy*, Oxford: Hart Publishing, 2017, 35–54, at 38.

[26] Pallikkathayil, 'Persons and Bodies'.

And since we are embodied beings that requires effective control over your body.

Notice that this is not just the claim that your body is your most basic means, though that is true. The important point is rather that in order for you to show up in my practical reasoning as the kind of being to whom things can belong, you must belong to yourself. If you are simply among my potential means, anything that is 'yours' is really mine. In order to not simply be among my potential means, you must have rights against my use.

I take the foregoing to establish that we must have bodily rights if we are to have any rights at all. But this does not yet settle what bodily rights we must have. There are differing views about how indeterminate bodily rights are in the state of nature. Ripstein often seems to take them to be all but settled. But there are some aspects of bodily rights that are undoubtedly indeterminate in the state of nature. One of Ripstein's own examples suggests this:

> If I shout loud enough to startle you when you stand on the edge of a cliff, but do not touch you, do I wrong you? This seems to be a question about our respective rights, which is not resolved by some factual consideration about the number of molecules that my shout displaced toward you.[27]

Does shouting in this context constitute a violation of one's bodily rights? How loud is too loud? What circumstances are too dangerous for shouting? Reason alone does not settle precise answers to these questions. This suggests that bodily rights are at least in some respects indeterminate. Moreover, for the purposes of the argument that follows, it would be fine if bodily rights were completely indeterminate in the state of nature. For this reason, I am largely going to set aside the question of how indeterminate bodily rights are, though I will return briefly to this issue in Section 11.3.2 after the argument for the state has been laid out.

I take indeterminacy to be the basic problem in the state of nature. This contrasts with Ripstein's position, which begins with the problem of unilateralism.[28] Ripstein takes it that the basic problem with property rights in the state of nature is that we cannot unilaterally impose duties on others and hence cannot unilaterally claim property rights. I, however, argue that the reason we cannot unilaterally impose duties on others in the state of nature is that the indeterminacy in the rights correlative to those

[27] Ripstein, *Force and Freedom*, 176–7.

[28] For a discussion of the problem with this position, see Pallikkathayil, 'Persons and Bodies', 45–6.

duties is not something we are unilaterally entitled to settle. Why not? A unilateral right to settle indeterminacy would be in tension with the innate right to freedom's requirement that rights be *universal.* I take this requirement to imply that we must all have the same rights prior to any exercise of those rights. This is the truth in Kant's claim that the innate right to freedom involves a conception of innate equality, that is, 'independence from being bound by others to more than one can in turn bind them'.[29] For this reason, the right to settle the indeterminacy of bodily rights is not one any individual can claim for him- or herself alone.[30] This means that this right is one that we must all share. And that is something we can only do via a decision-making procedure that unites us.

Bodily rights also give rise to problems of adjudication and assurance. Consider first the problem of adjudication. Even if we settle principles determining the content of bodily rights, no one can have a unilateral right to settle disputes over the application of those principles. Likewise, unilateral assurance that others will respect our bodily rights falls short of the kind of security that innate right demands that we have.[31] With this brief characterization of how bodily rights give rise to problems that parallel the problems Kant attributes to property rights in the state of nature in view, we can construct an argument for the state that takes bodily rights rather than property rights as its starting point:

(1) The innate right to freedom requires bodily rights.

(2) Bodily rights are subject to indeterminacy, adjudication, and assurance problems in the state of nature.

(3) These problems can be resolved in a way that is consistent with the innate right to freedom only in a properly constituted state.

(4) Therefore, the innate right to freedom requires the establishment of a properly constituted state.

We have already seen that premise (1) requires care in its interpretation. The innate right to freedom requires bodily rights not because we would

[29] Kant, RL 6:237–8.

[30] Although 'settlement by me' is certainly not a universalizable principle, one might think that 'settlement by the first to do so' is. We could each have a right to settle the indeterminacy problem conditional on being the first to do so. But precisely because bodily rights involve no original act of acquisition, it is unclear what sense we could make of being first in this context. We each are already enacting our own interpretation of our bodily rights simply by conducting ourselves in a world that we share with others.

[31] Proper specification of the assurance problem is controversial. I treat this matter at length in Pallikkathayil, 'Persons and Bodies'.

be less free without bodily rights but because the idea of freedom would lack application without those rights. And although the indeterminacy problem referenced in premise (2) may be interpreted in more or less expansive ways, any interpretation will suffice for the argument. Finally, the foregoing discussion has brought us most of the way to premise (3). Each of the three problems finds its solution in a branch of the government – the indeterminacy problem in the legislative branch, the adjudication problem in the judicial branch, and the assurance problem in the executive branch. Of course, a full defence of premise (3) would require a much closer examination of each of these three branches of government and the way in which they solve the corresponding problem from the state of nature. Although I cannot undertake that full defence here, I draw out some important features of the legislative branch in the next section. For now, however, this should suffice to show how the normative conception of freedom can support an argument for the state. There are three key moves in this argument. First, this argument bypasses the problematic Postulate and focuses instead on bodily rights. Second, the argument treats bodily rights as a precondition for freedom rather than as increasing freedom. And, finally, the argument treats the problems faced by bodily rights in the state of nature as stemming from the innate right to freedom's demand that rights be universal. Thus, the heavy lifting in the argument is done not by the mere concept of freedom but rather by the innate right to freedom in accordance with a universal law.

11.3.2 Constraints on the State

Recall that the second problem faced by Ripstein's use of the normative conception of freedom is that it is unclear how that conception places any constraints on the state. As Ebels-Duggan puts it, 'the notion of freedom receives determinate content only from the very institutions for which it is supposed to provide a normative standard'.[32] One initial reply involves clarifying that the notion of freedom alone is not supposed to provide a normative standard for the state. Rather, as we have just seen, the standard is provided by the *innate right* to freedom and the demand for universalizability which that includes. The general question, however, remains. If freedom just consists in having effective rights, how can a right to freedom in that sense constrain the organization of the state or the laws that it enacts? I am going to begin by considering the organization of the state and that will lead us naturally to a discussion of particular laws.

[32] Ebels-Duggan, 'Critical Notice', 563.

Ripstein claims: 'All that is required for the legislative will to be omnilateral is for the distinction between public and private purposes to apply to it in the right way . . . the only public purpose that is relevant is the public purpose of creating and sustaining a rightful condition.'[33] He then compares the relationship between public officials and citizens to the relationship between trustees and those with whose affairs they have been entrusted. He indicates that a trustee must act to ensure the ongoing purposiveness of the one for whom arrangements are being made and a trustee is precluded from making those arrangements for his own private purposes. Moreover, '[e]ven the power to ensure the ongoing purposiveness of another person can only be exercised on terms to which that person could consent'.[34] Since people cannot consent to slavery or to forfeiting the innate right to freedom, certain institutions that may superficially resemble states do not qualify as embodying an omnilateral will. Ripstein treats Nazi Germany as an apt example of an entity that fails to embody an omnilateral will in this way.[35]

Ruling out Nazi Germany is not nothing, but it is still less than one might hope for. In particular, nothing in this line of argument requires anything like democratic governance. Readers of Kant will not find this surprising. Kant's discussions of democracy are a bit muddled and sometimes express a somewhat negative attitude towards that organizational form.[36] What is important for both Kant and Ripstein is that the people be represented by the legislative branch of government. But that is consistent with playing no actual role in decision-making.

We should pause here, however, to question why we should accept Ripstein's characterization of an omnilateral will solely in terms of the purposes it pursues. Ripstein suggests that:

> if a group of officials make, apply and enforce law in a given region of the Earth's surface, in so doing they thereby unite the inhabitants of that region into a people. By becoming an agent for the people, the state creates that people as a moral subject to whom its acts can be imputed.[37]

But to begin simply making laws is to claim for oneself a right that all others cannot have. In contrast, if I begin to act as if we all share legislative authority, I claim for myself only the same right that I also attribute to

[33] Ripstein, *Force and Freedom*, 192. [34] Ripstein, *Force and Freedom*, 192.

[35] Ripstein, *Force and Freedom*, 341.

[36] For a helpful discussion of Kant's writings on democracy and a distinct argument that Kant's view ultimately requires it, see Christoph Hanisch, 'Kant on Democracy', *Kant-Studien* 107 (2016), 64–88.

[37] Ripstein, *Force and Freedom*, 195.

you. In this way, democratic decision-making procedures alone reflect the kind of formal equality that universalizability demands.

For this reason, I take it that in a legitimate state the ultimate legislative authority must be literally held by the people collectively. This is not merely an idea of reason. Nevertheless, on this view the distinction between public and private purposes remains significant. The people have a collective right to settle the indeterminacy problem. To undertake any other task like, say, maximizing welfare or supporting the development of virtue, would take the legislative body outside its mandate. Thus, just as Ripstein claims, state officials must act for the public purpose of establishing a rightful condition. My claim has simply been that a legitimate state is one in which all citizens hold the office of legislator.

To be clear, the requirement that ultimate legislative authority be held by citizens collectively is still compatible with very different forms of governance. The people might legislate directly or via chosen representatives, who might be numerous or even just a single individual. Although such elected officials would have rights that not all have, these rights would be bestowed on them through the exercise of rights held by everyone and thus in a way that respects the innate equality that is an aspect of the innate right to freedom.

But even if most actual legislating is done by representatives, the fact that the ultimate legislative authority is held by citizens has far-reaching implications for the constitution of a legitimate state. Whatever indeterminacy there is in the state of nature must be settled in a way that enables citizens to satisfy the duties of their offices as legislators. Although a full discussion of what this entails is far beyond the scope of this chapter, I will briefly gesture towards two broad sets of constitutional provisions that are suggested by this requirement. First, the familiar liberties of speech, conscience, and association may each be thought to play an indispensable role in enabling citizens to fulfil their duties as legislators. Without these liberties, citizens would be unable to think for themselves and together in the ways required by their offices. Second, consider the resources needed for decision-making. Human bodies need food, water, and shelter to do anything at all, including legislating. Any settlement of the indeterminacy problem that left citizens without access to these resources would be inconsistent with enabling them to do their jobs as legislators and hence inconsistent with the only organizational form permitted by the innate right to freedom.[38]

[38] For an insightful discussion of this point, see Suzanne M. Love, *The Material Conditions of Freedom*, PhD Dissertation, University of Pittsburgh, 2018. I am indebted to Suzie for many helpful discussions of these issues.

This brief list of constraints on a legitimate constitution is not meant to be exhaustive. I mean here only to highlight how the innate right to freedom's requirement that citizens hold the ultimate legislative authority may yield such constraints even if the content of freedom is otherwise indeterminate in the state of nature. With this picture in view, we may turn to how these constitutional constraints shape the task of legislators. Legislators are tasked with settling on a specific scheme of rights. The constitutional constraints I have just discussed mean that not just any assignment of rights will do to resolve the indeterminacy problem in a way that is consistent with the innate right to freedom. Legislators must therefore engage in two somewhat different activities when they pass laws: checking potential laws for consistency with the constitutional constraints and choosing among the potential laws that survive this initial scrutiny. For example, the constitutional imperative that citizens qua legislators must have access to food, water, and shelter does not by itself distinguish among subsidizing those who are impoverished, providing a universal basic income, having the state stand as an employer of last resort, or some other organizational scheme directed at the same end. Of course, there may ultimately be public considerations that weigh in favour of one of these rather than another. It may be, for example, that some schemes of rights minimize the chance of misapplication or corruption of the law. Or it may be that some schemes of rights are more conducive to a state's stability over time. These, then, are the challenging issues that legislators are called on to evaluate or to elect representatives to evaluate in their place.

In this section, I have argued (1) that the innate right to freedom requires democratic governance, (2) that that entails certain constitutional requirements, and (3) that those constitutional requirements in turn constrain the laws legislators enact. Before closing this section, it may be helpful to contrast my argumentative strategy on a particular matter of law with Kant's own. He attributes to the state a right to tax citizens to provide sustenance for those who are unable to provide for themselves on the basis of the state's end of maintaining itself perpetually. It is, however, not clear from Kant's text why sustaining those who are impoverished is necessary for the state to maintain itself.[39] Ripstein argues that the state must provide for those who are impoverished in order to prevent them from falling into a condition of dependence that is inconsistent with the idea of sharing in a united will: 'a social world in which one person has the rightful

[39] For a helpful discussion of Kant's argument for poverty relief, see Sarah Williams Holtman, 'Kantian Justice and Poverty Relief', *Kant-Studien* 95 (2004), 86–106.

power of life and death over another is inconsistent with those persons sharing a united will, even if the situation came about through a series of private transactions in which neither did the other wrong'.[40] As I indicated above, if there were no constraints on how I interacted with your body, you would be merely a means to me, and I agree that this precludes the possibility of uniting our wills. But the situation Ripstein is envisioning is not one in which individuals lack bodily rights altogether. Those who are rich still may not assault those who are poor. Since freedom just consists in having effective control over one's means and you may be secure in the very limited means you have, for all that has been said this still seems to be a condition in which we are both free.[41] It is therefore unclear what precludes conceiving of our wills as united in a state that allows me to have so much and you to have so little.

The problem here is, as it was before, treating the idea of a united will as a mere idea of reason. In contrast, since I hold that citizens must literally share legislative authority, my view has the resources to explain a very different way in which the requirement that citizens have access to the resources needed to meet their basic needs follows from the state's end of maintaining itself perpetually.[42] I doubt that this is what Kant had in mind himself. My argument also potentially goes further than requiring the kind of poverty relief Kant envisioned as the resources needed to enable citizens to satisfy their duties as legislators may outstrip those needed for sustenance. It may be, for example, that this same style of argument can be used to ground a requirement that citizens have access to the kind of education needed to satisfy these duties. In this way, although my argument begins with Kantian commitments, it has the potential to justify more far-reaching required state action than Kant himself envisioned.

11.3.3 Public Roads

This brings us directly to the final problem facing Ripstein's use of the normative conception of freedom. His attempt to argue that the state is required to establish public roads is unsuccessful. The normative conception of external freedom makes it difficult to see how the neighbours who block you in infringe your freedom. You are still free to control the means

[40] Ripstein, *Force and Freedom*, 278. [41] Ebels-Duggan, 'Critical Notice', 568.

[42] For an argument in broadly the same spirit as my own, see Ariel Zylberman, "Bread as Freedom: Kant on the State's Duties to the Poor', in Dai Heide and Evan Tiffany (eds.), *The Idea of Freedom: New Essays on the Kantian Idea of Freedom*, Oxford: Oxford University Press, 2023, 245–64.

that are yours and to associate with anyone you choose. Your neighbours simply decline to provide you with the means needed to contact those with whom you wish to associate.

My argument suggests a different basis for a state's duty to provide public roads. Citizens qua legislators must be able to discuss matters of state together in order to satisfy the duties of their office. For example, they must be able to discuss whether various schemes of rights are consistent with ensuring that citizens have access to the resources needed to sustain themselves in a condition that enables them to satisfy the duties of their office. They must be able to disseminate information about the implementation and effects of existing laws. They must be able to exchange information about the conduct of elected representatives. And so on. Democratic governance requires open avenues of communication. And notice that what this requires in practice may depend on the particular society in question. In addition to public roads, the state may need to fund a postal service or public internet connections.

Moreover, citizens have to be able to reach the resources they need to sustain themselves adequately. They do not actually have effective access to food if they cannot get to the grocery store. Likewise, access to education requires effective access to schools and the like. Here again, there are potentially many ways of settling rights that might be compatible with the innate right to freedom. But given certain ways of setting up access to the resources that citizens need, the state may be required to go beyond merely providing public roads and to provide public transportation as well.

This discussion has necessarily been rather schematic. Full consideration of any of the potential state programmes discussed in this section would require detailed consideration of the scheme of rights in which the programme is supposed to be embedded. The demands on the state to provide public services may differ considerably against the backdrop of different economic systems. Here I simply want to draw out the way in which the demand that citizens be equipped to carry out their legislative duties puts pressure on the systems of rights states may enact consistently with the innate right to freedom. This pressure potentially provides the argumentative basis not just for public roads but for much else besides.

11.4 Conclusion

I have argued that conceiving of freedom as consisting in having effective rights against others sets up a powerful argument for the state and one that constrains both the organization of legitimate states as well as the legislation those states enact. Although this argument was not Kant's, it relies on his idea of an innate right to freedom and draws on his diagnosis of the problems inherent in the state of nature. I thus hope to have shown how a normative conception of freedom can be used productively by those attracted to some of the core elements of Kant's political philosophy.

PART V

Law and Morality in Kant's Political Theory

CHAPTER 12

Two Conceptions of Freedom in Kant's Political Philosophy

The Moral Foundations of Kantian Politics

J. P. Messina

12.1 Introduction

If scholars of Kant's political philosophy agree on anything (and it is not clear that they do), it is (1) that Kant political philosophy is a doctrine of 'external freedom'.[1] If they agree on two further things, they are (2) that external freedom is a univocal notion in Kant's political philosophy, and (3) that, though there may be connections between moral and political freedom, Kant emphasizes the latter's externality to signal clearly that autonomy (often associated with internal freedom[2]) is not the freedom

This chapter benefitted tremendously from the discussion at the conference that shares the title of this volume. It was also much improved by detailed comments from the volume's editors, Martin Brecher and Phillip Hirsch. I am grateful for their guidance.

[1] For example, Jennifer Uleman writes that 'External freedom (*äussere Freiheit*) is the central concept in Kant's 1797 *Rechtslehre* [. . .] Our only innate right is to it (MS 6:237). The Universal Principle of Right governs it (MS 6:231). Positive ("juridical") law is justified just insofar as it protects it (MS 6:214)' (Jennifer K. Uleman, 'External Freedom in Kant's "Rechtslehre": Political, Metaphysical', *Philosophy and Phenomenological Research* 68 (2004), 578–601, at 578). The earliest passage (214) refers to Kant's discussion of juridical law, which does state that these laws refer only to freedom in the external use of choice. But he does not say that juridical law *only* protects external freedom in *this* sense. And it is not obvious that it does. For juridical law might 'refer' to external freedom by governing it and constraining it, just as well as by protecting it. The next passage (231) refers to Kant's formulation of the universal principle of right (UPR), where Kant does indeed say that the UPR governs external actions, for these are the only ones that affect others. Finally, the last passage (237) does indeed refer to our one innate right, but Kant manifestly does not say that this right is to external freedom only. See also: Arthur Ripstein, *Force and Freedom: Kant's Legal and Political Philosophy*, Cambridge, MA: Harvard University Press, 2009; Allen W. Wood, *The Free Development of Each: Studies on Freedom, Right, and Ethics in Classical German Philosophy*, Oxford: Oxford University Press, 2014; L.-P. Hodgson, Kant on the Right to Freedom: A Defense', *Ethics, 120* (2010), 791–819; L.-P. Hodgson, 'Kant on Property Rights and the State', *Kantian Review* 15 (2010), 57–87; Kyla Ebels-Duggan, 'Kant's Political Philosophy: Kant's Political Philosophy', *Philosophy Compass* 7 (2012), 896–909; Reidar Maliks, *Kant's Politics in Context*, Oxford: Oxford University Press, 2014; and Ariel Zylberman, 'The Public Form of Law: Kant on the Second-Personal Constitution of Freedom.' *Kantian Review* 21 (2016), 101–26.

[2] *Nota bene*: it is a mistake to conflate inner freedom with autonomy as many do. For accounts that closely identify internal freedom with autonomy, see Katrin Flikschuh, *Kant and Modern Political Philosophy*, Cambridge: Cambridge University Press, 2000, 85–91; and Maliks, *Kant's Politics in Context*, 66–71. For a corrective, see: P.-A. Hirsch, *Freiheit und Staatlichkeit bei Kant: Die*

concept central to his political thought.[3] Despite agreeing that Kant's treatment of external freedom is unambiguous and that it is sharply distinct from autonomy, it is a striking fact that commentators disagree (sometimes without noticing) about what exactly external freedom is.

On the classic view, especially popular in German accounts of Kant's political philosophy, external freedom consists in free choice *simpliciter*, without regard for its determining grounds.[4] Newer, especially anglophone, work emphasizes the republican idea that you are (externally) free just in case you are your own master. For some Kantian republicans, you are your own master, in turn, provided you are free to use your means for your (external) purposes without anyone else's say-so.[5] Others understand republican self-mastery in terms of 'capacity to make choices independently of constraint by the choices of others'.[6] Though intended to be compatible with these republican ideas, some characterize external freedom instead as the ability to move about in space.[7] On these pictures, the *Rechtslehre* is designed to discover those institutions (e.g. property schemes) that maximize such an ability. Still others take it that Kant's

autonomietheoretische Begründung von Recht und Staat und das Widerstandsproblem, Berlin: De Gruyter, 2017, 73 n. 24.

[3] Compare McKean, who writes that 'external freedom [...] is the chief concern of his political philosophy' while 'internal freedom is central to his moral and theoretical philosophy' (B. L. McKean, 'Kant, Coercion, and the Legitimation of Inequality', *Critical Review of International Social and Political Philosophy*, 4 (2019), 1–23); see also Ripstein, *Force and Freedom*, 14–18). On (3), it's important to note that some think the two notions of freedom are necessarily connected. See Hirsch, *Freiheit und Staatlichkeit bei Kant*, 139ff. As will become clear below, I am broadly sympathetic with this line.

[4] E.g. Bernd Ludwig, *Kants Rechtslehre: Mit einer Untersuchung zur Drucklegung Kantischer Schriften von Werner Stark*, Hamburg: Meiner, 1988; Otfried Höffe, 'Kant's Principle of Justice as Categorical Imperative of Law', in Yirmiyahu Yovel (ed.), *Kant's Practical Philosophy Reconsidered: Papers Presented at the Seventh Jerusalem Philosophical Encounter*, Dordrecht: Springer, 1989, 149–67, at 163–4); Burkhard Kühnemund, *Eigentum und Freiheit: Ein kritischer Abgleich von Kants Rechtslehre mit den Prinzipien seiner Moralphilosophie*, Kassel: Kassel University Press, 2008, 25–6; Philipp-Alexander Hirsch, *Kants Einleitung in die Rechtslehre von 1784: Immanuel Kants Rechtsbegriff in der Moralvorlesung 'Mrongovius II' und der Naturrechtsvorlesung 'Feyerabend' von 1784 sowie in der 'Metaphysik der Sitten' von 1797*, Göttingen: Universitätsverlag Göttingen, 2012, 28–37.

[5] Ripstein, *Force and Freedom*, 8–9; 18–24; 33. [6] Wood, *The Free Development of Each*, 73–4

[7] Ebels-Duggan, 'Kant's Political Philosophy', 901; Sharon B. Byrd, and Joachim Hruschka, 'The Natural Law Duty to Recognize Private Property Ownership: Kant's Theory of Property in His *Doctrine of Right*', *The University of Toronto Law Journal*, *56* (2006), 217–82, at 275; Rafeeq Hasan, 'The Provisionality of Property Rights in Kant's *Doctrine of Right*', *Canadian Journal of Philosophy* 48 (2018), 850–76; Helga Varden may accept a similar view. See Helga Varden, 'Kant's Non-Voluntarist Conception of Political Obligations: Why Justice Is Impossible in the State of Nature', *Kantian Review* 13 (2008), 1–45, at 4–5, although note also that her account shares several affinities with the one I develop in detail below.

'clearest statement'[8] of external freedom marks it out as a second-personal 'title' not to be dependent on the will of any other – a title fully realized only insofar as each person's will is dependent upon positive law.[9] So understood, external freedom specifies an 'irreducibly relational norm, linking the right of one agent to the duty of another' – which means that there is no purely individual capacity for external freedom that can be cashed out in terms of deploying means, setting ends, or moving through space.[10]

Though related (and often self-consciously so), it is implausible that these views come to the same thing. Rather, we should see in these formulations subtle disagreement about the meaning of 'external freedom' in Kant's politics. Interpretative disagreement like this is common enough in philosophy and can have many sources (misreadings, misunderstandings, missed context, logical error, different emphasis, different aims, and so on). But I submit that disagreements concerning external freedom have their source in the Kantian texts themselves. Against what the standard view suggests, Kant's *Rechtslehre* treats at least two distinct notions of freedom, each of which has a clear claim to the title 'external freedom'. This fact has not always been clearly recognized in the scholarly literature (though scholars are usually at least inchoately aware that there are distinct notions and tacitly switch between them in their analyses).

The purpose of this chapter is to do what others have not: carefully and explicitly mark external freedom's distinct meanings (Section 12.2). While this exercise may seem pedantic at times, stressing this distinction will put pressure on the claim, (3), that autonomy fades from relevance when Kant's attention turns to politics. Whereas others have wondered why a philosopher concerned with autonomy would make such a big deal out of external freedom, I argue that this question rests on a false premise. If autonomy is the property of our will according to which we are subject only to those normative constraints that we ourselves legislate, political principles treat what seems on its face like an affront to autonomy: normative constraints grounded in *another's* power of choice (Section 12.3). Kant's political philosophy aims to show that, under certain conditions, such alien constraints are grounded in a principle of authority that we legislate ourselves, and so are, in the end, consistent with autonomy. Or so I argue below, closing my argument by considering a pair of objections (Section 12.4) and ending the chapter with a brief concluding section (Section 12.5).

[8] Zylberman, 'Public Form of Law', 104. [9] Ibid. 107–8. [10] Ibid.

12.2 Kantian Freedom

Before beginning, it is useful to rehearse some details about how Kant thinks about freedom across his corpus. As may by now be familiar, Kant accepts a generic negative notion of freedom, understood as independence (*Unabhängigkeit*), alongside a generic positive notion of freedom, understood as capacity (*Vermögen*). The negative *theoretical* notion of freedom is independence from determination by prior causes (KrV A446/474; A447/B475), whereas the positive theoretical notion of freedom is the capacity to initiate a series of causes (KrV A445/B473, A448/B476).[11] The negative *practical* notion of freedom is the independence of the human power of choice from determination by prior sensible impulse (e.g. inclination) (KrV A802/B830, GMS 4:446), whereas the positive practical notion of freedom is the capacity of reason to determine practically the power of choice to action (KpV 5:33).

When it comes to external freedom, then, we should expect Kant to offer a negative characterization (independence), followed by a positive characterization (capacity). These expectations are in part supported by the way Kant describes our innate right to freedom: the (negative) independence (*Unabhängigkeit*) of each from the constraining choice of every other, so far as it is compatible with everyone's freedom under universal law (MS 6:237). But unlike in the theoretical and practical cases, Kant offers no corresponding positive characterization.[12] Moreover, the kind of freedom described in our innate right is not the only claimant for the title external freedom.

Indeed, Kant makes clear early and often that the *Rechtslehre* concerns only 'freedom in the external use of choice' (*Freiheit in dem 'äußeren Gebrauche der Willkür'*), rather than freedom in the internal use of choice (MS 6:220). Relatedly, principles of right govern only 'the external and indeed practical relation of one person to another, insofar as their actions, as facts, can have (direct or indirect) influence on each other' (MS 6:230).

[11] For an account of how Kant's precise understanding of the positive conception of freedom developed between the publication of the *Critique of Pure Reason* and the *Metaphysics of Morals*, see Bernd Ludwig, 'Positive und negative Freiheit bei Kant? Wie begriffliche Konfusion auf philosophi(ehistori)sche Abwege führt', *Jahrbuch für Recht und Ethik* 21 (2013), 271–305.

[12] This has not stopped scholars from developing often insightful accounts of positive political freedom. Proposals include: legislative willing (Sharon Byrd and Joachim Hruschka, *Kant's* Doctrine of Right*: A Commentary*, Cambridge: Cambridge University Press, 2010; desire-based willing (Flikschuh, *Kant and Modern Political Philosophy*); and action under public political principles (Zylberman, 'Public Form of Law'). See also Pauline Kleingeld's essay in this volume (Chapter 13).

As Kant tells us, 'anyone can be free' in the sense relevant to Right 'as long as I do not impair his freedom by my *external action*' (MS 6:231). These remarks direct us to look for one notion of external freedom as a *capacity* – one that allows us to interfere with others through outer *actions* – and a second notion of external freedom as *norm*, proscribing certain uses of that capacity.[13] I submit that freedom in the external use of choice offers Kant's account of the first notion; the right to freedom as independence, the second.[14] Let us treat each in turn.

12.2.1 External Freedom as Capacity

To understand what Kant means by freedom in the *external use of choice*, it is natural to begin with Kant's notion of choice (*Willkür*), abstracting from its various use cases. In Kant's metaphysics of action, choice is an aspect of the capacity of desire. Specifically, choice is the capacity for doing as one pleases, insofar as one is conscious 'of the capacity to bring about [one's desired] object by one's action' (MS 6:213). So understood, choice plays a crucial role in Kant's broader action theory, which distinguishes between determining grounds of choice and objects of choice. Understanding these related notions, I argue, yields an attractive distinction between internal and external *uses* of choice.

12.2.1.1 Determining Grounds of Choice

In the *Groundwork* Kant argues that, in addition to being subject to rational norms, human beings are sensible creatures with inclinations. By the time he writes the *Metaphysics of Morals*, Kant distinguishes clearly between two grounds capable of determining choice: rational incentives (which proceed from the will (*Wille*) as practical reason), and pathological incentives (which proceed from sensibility).[15] Incentives of both kinds partially explain why we prefer to do this, rather than that, when we choose. For instance: I determine my power of choice by means of rational incentives when, for example, I determine that I will not steal because

[13] As Kant puts the point, 'the part of the general doctrine of duties that brings inner, rather than outer, freedom under laws is a doctrine of virtue'; that which brings outer freedom under laws (of freedom) is a *Rechtslehre* (MS 6:380).

[14] To be clear: I am not saying that freedom in the external use of choice provides the positive notion of freedom corresponding to the kind of independence in Innate Right all by itself. That is too quick. It is, however, an important part of that story (see in particular the last paragraph of this chapter).

[15] Compare Lewis W. Beck, *A Commentary on Kant's* Critique of Practical Reason, Chicago: University of Chicago Press, 1996.

I recognize that it is wrong to do so (categorical imperative) or that I will keep to my exercise regime because prudence demands it (hypothetical imperative). By contrast, I determine it by means of pathological incentives, for example, when omit to steal because I see a camera hovering over the goods I covet or when I impulsively sneak a dram during an allegedly dry January.

The distinction between types of determining grounds explains why Kant treats choice, but not the will, as characteristically free. While the human will (*Wille*) necessarily furnishes rational laws of freedom as grounds capable of determining choice, we can determine our power of choice with respect to these laws or incentives drawn from sensibility. These determining grounds relate to freedom in the following way. Choice is *negatively* free because it is not inescapably determined by sensible impulses. We achieve positive freedom of choice when we determine ourselves to act on the basis of the dictates of our rational wills (MS 6:226). Because it has access to rational determining grounds, our power of choice is necessarily negatively free. Our *Willkür* is not inescapably determined by sensible impulse. Yet we only contingently determine our powers of choice itself on these rational grounds. Determining ourselves to act according to rational principles against the pull of sensibility is a demanding business. Negative freedom is constitutive of human agency; positive freedom, in the sense of determining our powers by rational determining grounds, is an achievement.

Some suppose that the distinction between 'inner' and 'outer' uses of choice is just the difference between *Wille* (inner) and *Willkür* (outer).[16] But this cannot be. Kant speaks of the 'äußeren oder inneren Gebrauche der Willkür' (MS 6:214), not 'äußeren Gebrauche der Willkür' and 'inneren Gebrauche des Willens'.[17] It is, I think, more promising to locate the difference Kant actually marks in his treatment of objects, rather than determining grounds, of choice, as I now argue.

12.2.1.2 Objects of Choice

Whereas a determining ground of choice is that incentive by which we determine choice (e.g. fear of punishment or respect for the moral law), an

[16] Maliks, *Kant's Politics in Context*, 66.

[17] There is, of course, a central sense in which the obligations issuing from *Wille* (rational will) are inner, whereas those issuing from another agent's *Willkür* (arbitrary power of choice) are outer (see V-Mo/Collins 27:255). But it is important to be precise here, and, in fact, in his treatment of freedom in Kant's politics, Maliks tacitly appeals to the contrast I've developed here (see e.g. *Kant's Politics in Context*, 66, 71).

object of choice is that at which choice aims. More simply, the object of one's choosing is that which one aims to affect, shape, or bring about through choice.[18]

Now, Kant explicitly observes that our power of choice can aim at external objects. Among the explicitly classified external objects, Kant counts corporeal objects (including land, corporeal things, and others' bodies; others' services through contract; and certain status relations with respect to others).[19] I want to suggest that to use choice externally just is to direct it to external objects. If this is right and the difference between internal and external uses of choice is supposed to be grounded in the different kinds of objects (inner and outer) that choice can take up, then we must search for some class of internal objects.[20]

This is harder work, for Kant does not provide a taxonomy of internal objects (as he does with external objects). Still, he does offer some clues in the way he describes internal or 'inner' actions (the result of exercises of choice in its internal use). For example, he claims that to set an end is '*an internal act of the mind*' (MS 6:329, emphasis added). Moreover, he suggests that the contrast class to external actions (presumably internal actions) involves adopting maxims and principles. For instance, if I make the Universal Principle of Right (UPR) 'the principle of my action', this is an internal rather than an external act (and a matter for internal rather than external lawgiving). In addition, Kant characterizes the modulation of our attitudes as consisting in internal acts. After all, when I wish 'to infringe upon your freedom', or am 'indifferent to it', these are internal, rather than

[18] In *The Critique of Practical Reason*, Kant tells us that every action has a matter (KpV 5:34), and that this consists in a desired object (KpV 5:21).

[19] These three external objects of choice divide the three sections of Private Right: property right, contract right, and status right (MS 6:247).

[20] One suggestion, drawing on Kant's intellectual environment and the draft materials for various essays, is to treat outer freedom as that which results in observable actions that occur in space and time, whereas inner freedom results in unobservable actions that occur in time only (see e.g. V-MS/Vigilantius 27:572–3). This is how I understood the distinction in previous work (J. P. Messina, 'Kant, Smith and the Place of Virtue in Political and Economic Organization', In Elizabeth Robinson and Chris W. Surprenant (eds.), *Kant and the Scottish Enlightenment*, New York: Routledge, 2017, 267–85). But Kant does not characterize things this way in the *Rechtslehre*. Moreover, inner actions understood as those that occur only in time can still concern outer objects (as when I intend to exclude you from my plot of land and give rise to an act of lawgiving through first appropriation). When so (and when accompanied by the right kinds of actions in space), they (sometimes) implicate *Recht*. Still, most of what I say in the main text is compatible with this interpretative alternative: the lion's share of external actions occurs observably in space and time (because most of how we engage with external objects of choice does), and no internal actions do. Thanks to Philipp Hirsch for pressing me on this point.

external, matters (see again MS 6:231).[21] Finally, whereas the *Rechtslehre* 'dealt only with the *formal* condition of outer freedom [...] ethics goes beyond this and provides a *matter* (an object of free choice), an **end** of pure reason that it presents as an end which is also objectively necessary' (MS 6:380). In simpler terms, whereas right leaves our internal ends up to us, ethics prescribes an end 'it is a duty to have' (ibid.). We comply with this duty by exercising inner freedom, taking as our object of choice the relevant end.[22]

These passages suggest the following picture. Since (1) objects of choice are those things we aim to affect or bring about by means of the exercise of choice, and (2) we set ends, adjust attitudes, and adopt maxims (MS 6:225) by exercising internal freedom, it is reasonable to infer that (3) objects of an agent's internal choice are (perhaps among other things) ends, maxims, attitudes, and other mental items.[23] This picture is further supported by Kant's definition of an end: 'an object of the choice (of a rational being)', albeit one to which we can only constrain ourselves (MS 6:381).

Given that choice can be used to realize, alter (or otherwise affect) internal or external objects, we can understand freedom in the internal use of choice to involve directing choice inwardly, towards internal objects.[24] Freedom in the external use of choice, by contrast, is freedom of choice so far as it ranges over external things. Thus, by setting my mental faculties into motion, I can act to bring it about (1) that I have a certain end or goal, (2) that this goal plays a certain systematic role in organizing my further actions, (3) that I struggle against my inclinations to take a certain attitude towards the obstacles I face, (4) that I wish it were easier to satisfy, and so on, just as I can bring it about that (5) I paint a canvas by setting my body in motion. (1)–(4) are internal acts, whereas (5) is an external act (though partly constituted by antecedent internal acts).[25] If so, Kant's claim that 'anyone can be free as long as I do not impair his

[21] Inner freedom's role in moderating our passions and affects is made clear in the *Doctrine of Virtue*, around 6:407.

[22] For further support, see MS 6:408.

[23] This reading is supported by Achenwall's (§ 77) definition of inner liberty as liberty of the mind. See Gottfried Achenwall, *Natural Law*, ed. by Pauline Kleingeld, trans. by Corinna Vermeulen, with an introduction by Paul Guyer, London: Bloomsbury, 2020.

[24] Notice on this picture that freedom in the internal use of choice will be governed by laws of virtue, just as freedom in the external use of choice will be governed by laws of right. When we succeed in governing inner freedom (freedom in the internal use of choice) by laws of virtue, the result will be, in a distinct sense, inner freedom. When we succeed in governing freedom in the external use of choice by laws of right, the result will be, in a distinct sense, external freedom. More on this below.

[25] This implies that any single thing that we are inclined, in natural language, to call an action, is likely to be analysed in terms of multiple actions, some internal and some external. I do not myself find this implication counterintuitive, but others have reported otherwise.

freedom by my *external action*' makes perfect sense (MS 6:231). What you do with inner objects of choice has no direct impact on me. You can take whatever ends and adopt whatever maxims and take whatever attitudes towards me you want without infringing on my freedom. By contrast, what you do with outer objects of choice can compromise my bodily integrity (as when you hit me with a bat) and reduce the number of things at my rightful disposal (as when you originally claim the bat as your own).[26]

In sum, the first contender for the title of external freedom in Kant's *Rechtslehre* is nothing other than our free power of choice, directed externally. It is this notion that explains those views according to which external freedom refers to an ability to move about in space or to pursue one's purposes by the use of one's external means.[27] So far as principles of right are silent with respect to an agent's ends, this also explains neatly those accounts that take external freedom to amount to the freedom to take up any end you choose: principles of right leave this genuinely up to us. For the same reason, external freedom as freedom in the external use of choice explains Kant's remarks to the effect that 'Right generally has as its object only what is external in actions': what is internal in actions is not subject to outer constraint because it does not itself constrain outwardly (MS 6:232). If freedom in the external use of choice were the only candidate for the title external freedom, the classical account, according to which external freedom is free choice, *simpliciter*, would need only a minor amendment. Yet, as I have suggested, there is another contender for this title, to which we should now turn.

12.2.2 *External Freedom as Independence*

Kant holds that freedom, understood as 'independence from being necessitated by another's choice [. . .] insofar as it can coexist with the freedom of every other in accordance with a universal law is the only original right belonging to man' (MS 6:237).[28] Like freedom in the external use of

[26] Because this is so, the ordinary notions of positive and negative freedom of choice apply here. Our freedom in the use of external choice (like internal choice) is constitutively negatively free, insofar as it is not necessarily determined by sensible impulse, even when we succumb to temptation. Like internal choice, it is positively free when I set it into motion because the moral law requires it (e.g. when I pick up a book in order to perfect my talents, though I'd prefer to watch TV; or when I return the excess change I was given to avoid ripping you off, though I'd prefer the extra money).

[27] See for reference the discussion on pp. 242–3, including notes.

[28] My translation – for discussion, see J. P. Messina, 'The Paradox of Outer Necessitation in (and after) Kant's 1784 Course on *Naturrecht*', in Margit Ruffing, Annika Schlitte, and Gianluca Sadun Bordoni (eds.), *Kants Naturrecht Feyerabend: Analysen und Perspektiven*, Berlin: De Gruyter, 169–83.

choice, commentators refer to this notion too as 'external freedom'.[29] So understood, external freedom is not (an aspect of) a capacity that we have, but instead describes a normative principle governing the relationship between persons' powers of choice. If the institutional preconditions of right are realized, the result is that we are independent (externally free) in just this sense.

We should now dig deeper and try to get clear on what exactly innate right demands. Innate right prescribes independence from others' *necessitating powers of choice.* Readers will recognize necessitation as a technical term, introduced in the context of Kant's famous treatment of moral rationality. It refers to human choice insofar as it is contingently, not infallibly, determined by rational practical laws but necessitated to them by practical reason (GMS 4:413, 4:439; MS 6:379). On the Kantian picture, moral obligation is paradigmatic of this kind of constraint.

It is thus tempting to read the notion of necessitation drawn from Kant's moral philosophy into Kant's statement of our innate right. On this reading, innate right protects against obligations imposed on us from without (so far as such independence is *compossible*, i.e. can coexist with everyone else's freedom under universal law). But this is just to be compossibly free from obligations grounded in acquired rights and positive law. After all, positive law is that act of lawgiving by which a moral agent binds 'another by mere choice' rather than through laws recognizable as obligatory by reason alone (MS 6:224). And acquired rights are those 'moral capacities for placing others under obligation' that are authored by a person's lawgiving, juridical act, rather than obtaining simply by nature independently of such an act (6:237).

The temptation is now to say that the right to independence is nothing other than the compossible freedom from others' positive lawgiving – lawgiving that obtains both when the state enacts laws and when individuals acquire rights.[30] But this is too quick. After all, necessitation admits of a broader interpretation than the above reading suggests. *Nöthigung* can

[29] See Wood, *The Free Development of Each*, 94; Hodgson, 'Kant on the Right to Freedom' and 'Kant on Property'; Ebels-Duggan, 'Kant's Political Philosophy', 897; Maliks, *Kant's Politics in Context*, 1; and Zylberman, 'The Public Form of Law', 104, in which innate right is called Kant's 'clearest statement' of external freedom.

[30] This element of Kant's thought makes good sense of the concern Ripstein's interpretation registers about unilateral attempts to 'change the normative situation of another' (*Force and Freedom*, 24; 123). But what it is to change another's normative situation is left vague. Moreover, such changes to another's normative situation do not obviously impede a person's ability to be her own master, and so it is not obvious what is problematic about them. On my account, things are clearer, as I hope emerges below.

simply indicate *constraint* without any relation to obligation or law.[31] Moreover, this rendering makes sense of the emphasis Kant places on coercion (*Zwang*) throughout the *Rechtslehre* – the two words after all can be used interchangeably. Yet, there are three good reasons to prefer the narrow reading suggested above.

First, the main virtue of the broad reading, namely that it accounts well for Kant's focus on coercion, is not completely lost to the narrower reading. To see this, recall that, on my preferred interpretation, the necessitation that we are guaranteed against is that which results from others' lawgiving wills. Notice further that, on Kant's account, lawgiving necessarily involves two components: (i) giving a law, and (ii) providing an incentive (see e.g. MS 6:218–19). The relevant incentive in the case of outer lawgiving is explicitly cashed out in terms of coercion's ability to provide incentives of hope (and, especially, fear).

Admittedly, this means that our innate right does not pick out *all* coercion as potentially concerning – only that which is part of issuing law. By the same token, however, it is only if Kant's remarks about coercion clearly and unequivocally imply that we are to be compossibly free from coercion in a perfectly general way that appeal to the broader notion is necessary. But in suggesting this, the broader reading presents a puzzle about the systematic place of coercion in Kant's broader thought. To read Kant as concerned with necessitation in the broad sense is to read him as introducing a new kind of concern with the *Rechtslehre*, one that is absent in his earlier moral thought. Notice: there is no analogous question if we read necessitation more narrowly, such that it essentially involves lawgiving. For (as I explain below) Kant is famously sceptical that we have reason to acknowledge alien constraints on our free choosing (GMS 4:432 compare V-MS/Vigilantius 27:500 and MS 6:379–80).

Third, if Kant is focused on bare coercion (without connotations of law and obligation), it is hard to make sense of the structure of private right and various claims that Kant makes in it. For instance, he explicitly claims that 'lawgiving is involved in the expression, "this object is *mine*," *since by it an obligation is laid upon all others* (weil allen andern dadurch eine Verbindlichkeit auferlegt wird), *which they would not otherwise have*, to refrain from using the object' (MS 6:253, emphasis added). But if coercion in the wider sense is what is normatively relevant as far as right is concerned, then the focus on new obligations is out of place. What matters

[31] 'Der Pflichtbegriff ist an sich schon der Begriff von einer Nöthigung (Zwang) der freien Willkür durchs Gesetz' (MS 6:379).

in the case of property claims is that they are frequently enforced through violence. In line with this, the analysis should proceed explicitly with reference to the way that property rights involve coercion. But it does not so proceed.

For these reasons, I suggest that we reject interpretations which rely on the broader notion of necessitation. So far as we do, Kant's statement of our innate right invites a question: How far can we remain free of external positive lawgiving, consistent with everyone's like freedom under universal law? Put differently: how far must we admit a capacity on the part of others to give practical laws that necessitate our own powers of choice?[32]

Such questions would have been salient to Kant. After all, Achenwall (author of Kant's textbook on natural law) simply defines freedom in terms of an independence from so-called overlordship. 'A person enjoys full liberty', he writes, 'if he is independent of another's overlordship in all his actions [...] Hence someone is *free* (autonomous) in as far as he is not subjected (heteronomous)' (§ 83). Moreover, overlordship specifically involves having a right over someone's otherwise rightful actions along with a capacity to *oblige* her (§§ 74–7). And yet liberty is not an all-or-nothing affair – a person's liberty might be partial, in which case they are only free in some of their actions from the overlordship of others.[33] In Achenwall's language, the question that Kant's innate right asks is: how far is our freedom from others' overlordship compatible with everyone's like freedom?

Now, importantly, when it is understood this way, external freedom as independence has nothing to do with others constraining us by moving about in space – except insofar as what we do in space places others under new normative constraints. It says nothing directly about choosing means to various ends or manipulating which purposes we pursue with our means – except insofar as our doing so has the effect of necessitating others. It has nothing obvious at all to do, in other words, with freedom in the external use of choice *at all*. And yet, *right* clearly has to do with the latter. What's the connection?

The fact that it is only by exercising external choice that we can compromise others' freedom as independence ('anyone can be free', recall, 'as long as I do not impair his freedom by my *external action*') suggests an answer. Right is concerned with freedom in the external use of choice in the specific sense that this is what principles of right *constrain*. You may not use your external freedom to necessitate me unless doing so is required by universal law. In turn, if I have a right, by the lights of universal law, to

[32] Compare Messina, 'The Paradox', from which the next several paragraphs draw.
[33] See again Achenwall, *Natural Law*.

constrain you against some action (e.g. interference with my property), then you cannot use your external freedom in the ways specified. Right is *not*, as is commonly suggested, concerned with freedom in the external use of choice because this is the kind of freedom that it matters to protect (*pace* Uleman). Right *will*, of course, protect freedom in the external use of choice. It will do so simply by virtue of the fact that, when persons' freedom in the external use of choice is limited as right requires, each will remain free to perform those external actions still within her rightful power. But this is not because freedom in the external use of choice is intrinsically valuable or anything like that. It is because we have a very narrow mandate for binding others through our mere choice. Such others are, after all, *laws to themselves.*[34] Our authorization to bind them is properly limited to those instances when submitting to our binding is a necessary condition of everyone's independence.

12.3 Autonomy and Kant's Politics

So far, I have urged that we should distinguish between freedom in the external use of choice (external freedom as capacity) and the kind of freedom to which we have an innate right (external freedom as independence). I have also argued for a particular reading of the latter that, I think, implies that Kant does not change the topic with respect to freedom when his attention turns to politics. In this section, I want to substantiate that claim. I will show that the principle encoded in our one innate right picks up directly where Kant's moral philosophy left off: with the idea of an autonomous human will, independent of alien lawgiving.

Towards this end, it is helpful to recall a few familiar details from Kant's ethics of autonomy and how it differs from the systems that came before it. In his moral philosophy, Kant seeks to arrive at the philosophical foundations of the common-sense view that morality is binding in a special way. Whereas several constraints that we face are *hypothetical*, that is, derive their grip on us from something that we desire or a goal that we've set, morality has a *categorical* character that makes its demands unconditional with respect to our desires and goals (GMS 4:414–16). If I want to live a healthy life, the requirements to eat well, exercise regularly, and get sufficient sleep are good ways of realizing my desire. Give up the desire, though, and I may live in a sleepless haze of gluttony and sloth. As Kant sees it, morality is not like this. That I must refrain from murdering you does not depend upon whether omitting to slay you has any particular

[34] For a complementary but distinct account, see Hirsch's contribution to this volume (Chapter 5).

benefit to me or advances some goal of mine. I must refrain from slaying you whatever else I want.

On Kant's reckoning, past moral systems searched for a ground of morality's special bindingness (they too wished to account for this aspect of common sense). But their efforts were in vain for having built systems according to which our wills were necessitated (*genöthigt*) to moral action by something alien to them – either principles of purposiveness like perfection or principles of sensibility like happiness (GMS 4:434; GMS 4:442). Give up the goal of making myself perfect (or change or abandon my conception of happiness), and there with it goes the practical imperative by which I took myself to be bound. To overcome this defect in past systems, Kant rejects the supposition that generates it: that the will must be bound by something else to moral action.

Rejecting this assumption leaves Kant with a picture according to which we are necessitated by our own internal lawgiving capacity (practical reason), which is necessarily rational, and represents our proper self.[35] In his lectures on ethics nearly ten years later (1793), Kant allegedly formulated a principle – call it the Autonomy Principle – which makes clear that, to bear the weight of the above features of morality, our capacity for practical reason must be independent—not just from objects of inclination and feeling – but also from determination by others' wills.

> All autonomy of reason must therefore be independent, (a) of all empirical principles, such as the principle of personal happiness, which may be called the physiological principle; (b) of the aesthetic principle, or that of moral feeling; and (c) of any alien will [*von allem fremden Willen*] (the theological principle) [. . .] it cannot be assumed that the principle of the choice to be determined lies in an object of purposiveness, sensibility or alien will, without perpetrating a heteronomy; it is supposed, after all, to be independent of any object of choice. (V-MS/Vigilantius 27:500)

Dependence upon sensible objects of choice is not the only threat to autonomy; dependence upon alien wills constitutes heteronomy, too (compare Refl. 3872 (17:319-20) and Refl. 4549 (17:590)). If practical reason (*Wille*) recognizes constraints in others' contingent power of choice, the question raised so poignantly in the *Groundwork* re-arises: why must we recognize unconditional obligations that are grounded in others' wills?

But this isn't quite right either: Kant's position in the moral philosophy suggests that the question is *confused*. Because Kant accepts the strong view

[35] Compare V-NR/Feyerabend 27:1322–5.

that constraints grounded in alien sources are not categorically binding, he appears to reject outright the possibility of genuine political authority. For on the above picture, genuine obligation is always *self-obligation*, that is, obligation by means of laws generated by our rational will, laws that are universal, necessary, and unconditional.[36] By contrast, obligation by others' power of choice appears to be arbitrary, contingent, and dependent upon the constrained agent's desire to avoid any sanctions the other might threaten. Thus, Kant's moral theory can seem to entail a kind of philosophical anarchism.[37]

And yet, political obligations appear to be no less a feature of ordinary moral cognition than the unshakeable sense that morality binds unconditionally. We recognize in our ordinary lives, in other words, several demands that are at least *prima facie* laid down by others' arbitrary and contingent acts of choice. Our political duties are grounded in large part by acquisitive acts and legislative choices that long preceded our birth. The demands these acts make upon us extend to nearly every aspect of our lives. That Kant's notion of autonomy appears *prima facie* inconsistent with *any* obligation that has its source in the particular will of another is bad news for a metaphysics of morals that seeks to rationalize commonsense practical cognition.

As he is typically read, Kant's goal in the *Rechtslehre* is to show that *external freedom* is inconsistent with anarchy.[38] Indeed, securing external freedom winds up demanding that we acknowledge an absolute duty to obey the political authorities over us in whatever does not conflict with 'inner morality' (MS 6:371). This means, as Ripstein puts it, that Kant's approach to political questions leaves no room for any 'general objection to authority as such'.[39] The fact that his moral principles (with their embrace of autonomy) seem so naturally to lead to the rejection of political authority while his political principles are almost designed to embrace it

[36] 'What I cognize immediately as a law for me I cognize with respect, which signifies merely consciousness of the *subordination* of my will to a law without the mediation of other influences on my sense. Immediate determination of the will by means of the law and consciousness of this is called *respect*, so that this is regarded as the *effect* of the law on the subject [. . .] Respect is properly the representation of a worth that infringes upon my self-love [. . .] The *object* of respect is therefore simply the *law*, and indeed the law that we impose on *ourselves* and yet as necessary in itself' (GMS 4:402n).

[37] Robert Paul Wolff saw well the tension between notions of moral autonomy and political obligation. See Robert P. Wolff, *In Defense of Anarchism*, Berkeley: University of California Press, 1970), 18.

[38] Jeremy Waldron, 'Kant's Legal Positivism', *Harvard Law Review*, 109 (1996), 1535–66, at 1554.

[39] Ripstein, *Force and Freedom*, 326.

has led scholars to conclude that Kant simply changes the subject regarding freedom once he sets his sights upon the political domain.[40]

We are now positioned to understand why claims that Kant's political philosophy is radically discontinuous from his moral theory with respect to freedom are overstated. It is true that (i) Kant's political philosophy is structured around a notion of freedom distinct from his notion of autonomy and (ii) this notion of freedom furnishes Kant with a justification – in principle – for state authority. It is, moreover, true that he does not offer political principles designed to make achieving virtue as easy as possible (by removing temptations to it). Still, the relevant sense of freedom at stake here is that each be free of every other's *necessitating power of choice.* And if to have one's power of choice necessitated is to have it subjected to law (as I have suggested above), and we are to be free from such necessitation insofar as it comes from others' acts (rather than principles internal to our will) then Kant's statement of our one innate right to freedom fits *perfectly* with a moral theory that emphasizes that genuine moral obligations are self-legislated. Still, it does not move as quickly to the anarchist's conclusion as some.[41] The catch is in the last clause, which states that we are rightfully subject to others' lawgiving insofar as our independence from such *cannot* coexist with everyone's freedom under universal law. Why? Because human reason must be universal and self-consistent. It cannot confer upon some powers that it denies to others.

The picture is this. If everyone's independence from external necessitation is incompatible with everyone's freedom under universal law, and some distinct and lawful dependence on external necessitation would change that, then our own practical reason demands that we subject our external freedom as capacity to law just that far. When this is so, we must recognize the authority of others to give law by our own lights. Put differently, there might be conditions under which I am under a self-legislated duty to acknowledge another's right to bind me by mere choice. So long as the exercise of the relevant authority stays within proper limits, the alien appearance of this duty is merely apparent.

In sum, Kant's political theory approaches alien legislative activity exactly as a theory concerned with autonomy should. Such legislative activity lacks authority over us *except* insofar as it can itself be shown to

40 Flikschuh, *Kant and Modern Political Philosophy*, 83–8.

41 See again Wolff, *In Defense of Anarchism.*

be a requirement of our own self-legislative capacities. Of course, this is a tall order and the arguments to this conclusion might fail. When so, it is possible that each of us must be completely free from standing under obligations grounded in others' acts of lawgiving. Anarchism is a genuine option on the Kantian view. But perhaps the case can be made and complete freedom from alien lawgiving cannot coexist with others' freedom under universal law. When so, it follows that we are rightfully subject to some at least apparently alien lawgiving. In the end, we recognize just as much political authority as is required for our freedom to be consistent with everyone else's freedom. We are in that sense equals.

12.4 Problems: New and Old

If the above is on the right track, our innate right protects against a kind of normative interference, *not* a kind of merely physical or spatial interference. Against this, it might be urged, Kant also very clearly claims (as we have seen) that it is by means of freedom in the external use of choice that we threaten one another's freedom. This generates two related worries. First, it is implausible that all the ways in which we can wrong one another by exercising freedom in the external use of our choice involve obligation-imposition. Second, it is not clear by what mechanism exercising freedom in the external use of choice involves lawgiving. Let us take these in reverse order.

Recall that, on my analysis, freedom in the external use of choice involves directing choice outward to objects distinct from us. Paradigm cases include: typing on a laptop, bouncing a basketball, eating an apple, painting a canvas, scaping a plot of land, and so on. Not only does none of this need to be moral to count as an exercise of freedom in the external use of choice, but also none of it seems obviously to involve lawgiving acts. My painting the canvases I can get my hands on does not compromise your ability to be a law to yourself and paint the canvases you can get your hands on. In exercising my free choice out in the world, I may take an object you wanted or previously had, but this appears not to affect, one way or the other, your will's independence from alien lawgiving.

Yet, as is by now well known, Kant does not think that mere use of objects suffices to realize the kind of freedom we are rationally committed to wanting.[42] Rather, he suggests that freedom demands extended use of objects as a *postulate*. This postulate demands that we incorporate outer

[42] Wood, *The Free Development of Each*.

objects into our purposes long term and to the exclusion of others.[43] But for this ability not to rest on mere luck (e.g. happy circumstances in which we are sufficiently isolated from others as for there to be no conflicts), extended freedom in the external use of choice requires *normatively excluding* others from the objects we incorporate into our projects. If I can paint my canvas only so long as you are not around to interfere with it or destroy it, my free choice finds its use of the object frustrated. If I can't constrain you to keep to a contract that we've made after we've made it, then I can't incorporate your behaviour into my long-term plans. And if you marry me but can't stop others from marrying me even if you want to, then our relationship cannot be incorporated into your projects in a stable way. Thus, I must take myself to have the power to stop you from using what's mine, even when it is not in my physical possession.

Kant's argument for the postulate of private right is to show exactly that we can have external objects as mine or yours and that we can constrain people in these ways. So understood, the restriction of autonomy in question is not the mere exercise of outer choice, but an extended exercise of the same that invokes at the same time a moral power[44] to impose obligations on others by merely choosing externally.[45] How do we do this? By taking control of an object, giving a sign, and intending to give a law through the general will 'in idea',[46] a law which places others under new obligation to refrain from interfering with what is mine (MS 6:258–9).[47]

Now, even if this shows that we *can* restrict one another's autonomy by exercising freedom in the external use of choice, it stops short of showing

43 See Ripstein, *Force and Freedom*; Hodgson, 'Kant on Property'; and J. P. Messina, 'The Postulate of Private Right and Kant's Semi-Historical Principles of Property', *British Journal of the History of Philosophy* 29 (2021). 64–83.

44 Pat Kain asks (in conversation) if this moral power is really activated by exercising external choice. If not, then Kant will have trouble vindicating his claim that external actions are the only things that can impinge upon another's rightful freedom. The problem appears especially stark if external actions are to be those and only those that occur in space as well as time. But on my account, exercises of this moral power, though perhaps only in time, are nevertheless directed at external objects, and so qualify as external in my sense. See note 20 and the surrounding discussion above.

45 Of course, as Kant later shows, exercising this capacity generates *peremptory* obligations only in the civil condition.

46 Compare MS 6:268.

47 Compare the discussion in Ludwig, *Kant's Rechtslehre*. While this shows that external choice imposes obligations at some level, one might think that Kant's argument strangely sacrifices autonomy (by allowing others to impose obligations on us) for the mere sake of securing extended freedom in the use of *things* and that this is sufficient to re-raise the puzzle posed at the outset. What gives? Here, I think the idea is that we can reasonably accept these restrictions because, without them, our outer freedom would be not just seriously curtailed but annihilated. External objects present to our embodied rationality as usable in this way. If reason were to veto their use, practical reason would not be self-consistent.

that this is the only – or even the paradigmatic – way we interfere externally with one another's freedom. After all, if *anything* violates my innate right to freedom, the thinking goes, your murdering or assaulting me does. And yet neither murder nor assault involve placing others under new obligations. Moreover, Kant seems to accept assault as a paradigmatic violation of innate right: the reason that property rights are not needed to explain why it is wrong to snatch the apple out of my hand or force me off the land I occupy is that such acts already wrong me with respect to 'what is *internally* mine (freedom)' (MS 6:247–8). And in case that leaves room for doubt, Kant is clear early on that innate right belongs to everyone by nature and can also be regarded as the 'internally mine or yours' (MS 6:237). But, on the account developed above, the fact that these violations of freedom do not place me under any new normative constraints straightaway implies that they are not inconsistent with innate right. A major problem.[48]

In response, notice that we might pursue an indirect grounding of the freedom from assault. Failing to guarantee such freedom, the argument would go, is a requirement of innate right because failing to place others under obligation to refrain from assaulting us would be inconsistent with freedom under universal law. Consider Kant's notion of the internally mine. On this notion, what's internally mine belongs to me without requiring any special act to establish it as mine. What Kant is saying when he calls freedom as independence our innate right is, in effect, that the obligation to refrain from violating that right does not stem from any particular agent's act of *Willkür*, but from every agent's *Wille* as practical reason. And yet asserting my claim over what is internally mine *is* an act of *willkürlich* lawgiving. Only, rather than being one in which I am the author of the *law* (as in the case of positive law), it is instead one in which I am the author of the *obligation* in accordance with the law, that is, an act of lawgiving in which a natural law serves as its ground (MS 6:227). In those cases where my act of necessitation merely directs someone to comply with a natural law, the thought goes, it is easy to satisfy the compossibility condition. The absence of a norm against assault cannot coexist with everyone's freedom in accordance with a universal law, and so necessitation to this effect immediately satisfies the constraint specified in our innate right. Those bound by such lawgiving acts have no legitimate complaint.[49]

48 Thanks to Luke Davies for pressing me on this point.

49 Thanks to Philipp Hirsch for helpful discussion; see also Hirsch, *Freiheit und Staatlichkeit bei Kant*, 123ff.

This picture might seem to leave Kant unable to claim that we have only one innate right, namely to independence. For surely saying that each of us has, in addition, a right to freedom from assault (which is internally ours) suggests a second entitlement that exists merely in virtue of our humanity.[50] But it is unclear how much this should disturb us. For long before Kant decided that parsimony demanded that we accept only *one* innate right, he included the right to be secure in one's body and person in that category (see e.g. V-MS/Vigilantius 27:588–93; V-NR/Feyerabend 27:1338). So while Kant may have been experimenting with a more parsimonious account, it is clear that he thinks that innate right includes rights over one's person (and that others' innate rights constrain the way we may act towards them).[51] He is simply mistaken in thinking that innate right itself (as he formulates it) logically entails these sorts of strong rights to the integrity of the person without recourse to independent natural laws.

12.5 Conclusion

Although readers of Kant's political philosophy frequently claim that the relevant notion of freedom for understanding his thought is external freedom, unclarity remains about the precise meaning of external freedom. I have argued that this is not the fault of commentators, but of Kant's own unclear exposition. For there are two distinct notions of freedom in the *Rechtslehre*, both of which have a plausible claim to the title. By specifying each clearly, we better understand their systematic place in Kant's political philosophy. What I have called freedom in the external use of choice allows us not just to interact with the outside world but also to interfere with and constrain one another's by engaging in acts of external lawgiving. By contrast, our innate right to freedom demands that impinging on our autonomy through such lawgiving is to be tolerated only insofar as it is necessary to secure everyone's freedom under universal law.

[50] Compare Huber on a similar issue with cosmopolitan right: Jakob Huber, 'Cosmopolitanism for Earth Dwellers: Kant on the Right to be Somewhere', *Kantian Review*, 22 (2017), 1–25, at 7–16.

[51] This may become somewhat less mysterious on a particular reading of what Kant means when he says that innate right can be treated in 'the prolegomena', such that the *Rechtslehre* can focus on acquired right. There are two natural contenders. On the first, Kant means to refer to the introduction to the *Rechtslehre* as the prolegomena. On the second, however, he might mean to refer to the *Grundlegung*, which establishes the special dignity that inheres in humanity and precludes that human beings can be permissibly used as mere means to others' ends. For discussion, see: Messina, 'Kant, Smith and the Place of Virtue' and Hirsch's essay in this volume (Chapter 5).

All of this suggests an answer regarding Kant's unstated positive notion of political freedom. If negative political freedom amounts to compossible independence (*Unabhängigkeit*) from external necessitation, positive political freedom amounts to the capacity (*Vermögen*) to necessitate others externally when doing so is necessary to preserve freedom under universal law, or, what comes to the same thing: the capacity to exercise justified political authority. Unfortunately, making this case must be left for another time. What is important for now is to notice how well Kant's political philosophy coheres with his moral philosophy on the story told above.[52]

[52] This stops short of saying that Kant's politics can be derived straightforwardly from his moral theory, much less the categorical imperative. See Marcus Willaschek, 'Right and Coercion: Can Kant's Conception of Right Be Derived from His Moral Theory?' *International Journal of Philosophical Studies* 17 (2009), 49–70; and Paul Guyer, 'The Twofold Morality of *Recht*: Once More unto the Breach', *Kant-Studien* 107 (2016), 34–63.

CHAPTER 13

Independence and Kant's Positive Conception of Freedom

Pauline Kleingeld

13.1 Introduction

The resurging interest in the republican tradition of legal and political theory – thanks largely to Quentin Skinner and Philip Pettit[1] – has shed new light on Immanuel Kant's conception of freedom, revealing that it is best understood along republican lines.[2] The discussion of Kant's republicanism to date, however, has focused on what he calls the 'negative' conception of freedom. This is the conception of freedom as defined in terms of the *absence* of something, that is, as consisting in '*in*dependence', '*non*-domination', and '*not* being subject to another master'. What has received much less attention is Kant's 'positive' conception of freedom, that is, his definition of freedom in terms of the *presence* of something else, and the relation between these two conceptions has hardly been examined.[3]

I am grateful for helpful comments from Martin Brecher and Philipp-Alexander Hirsch, and from Sorin Baiasu, Vinicius Carvalho, Micha Gläser, Michael Gregory, Daniel Häuser, JP Messina, Arthur Ripstein, Janis Schaab, Mark Timmons, Fiorella Tomassini, Elisabeth Widmer, Wouter Wiersma, Garrath Williams, Lu Zhao, the audience at the 2021 online workshop on 'Independence in Kant's Political Philosophy', organized by Nicholas Vrousalis, and organizers and online audiences at Bilkent University, Lancaster University, San Raffaele University, Humboldt University, the Digital Kant Center, the online 2021 UK Kant Society Lecture, and the 2022 Central Division meeting of the APA, as well as the two commentators there, Geraldine Ng and Jeffery Kinlaw. I thank the Netherlands Organization for Scientific Research (NWO) for financial support.

1 See Quentin Skinner, 'The Idea of Negative Liberty: Philosophical and Historical Perspectives', in Richard Rorty, Quentin Skinner, and Jerome B. Schneewind (eds.), *Philosophy in History: Essays in the Historiography of Philosophy*, Cambridge: Cambridge University Press, 1984, 193–221; Quentin Skinner, *Liberty before Liberalism*, Cambridge: Cambridge University Press, 1998; and Philip Pettit, *Republicanism: A Theory of Freedom and Government*, Oxford: Oxford University Press, 1997.

2 See especially Arthur Ripstein, *Force and Freedom: Kant's Legal and Political Philosophy*, Cambridge, MA: Harvard University Press, 2009; also, Louis-Philippe Hodgson, 'Kant on the Right to Freedom: A Defense', *Ethics* 120 (2010), 791–819; Helga Varden, 'Kant's Non-Absolutist Conception of Political Legitimacy: How Public Right "Concludes" Private Right in the "Doctrine of Right"', *Kant-Studien* 101 (2010), 331–51.

3 Sharon Byrd and Joachim Hruschka as well as Ariel Zylberman also note that Kant's positive conception of freedom has not received sufficient attention, but they do not examine the relation between his positive and negative conceptions of freedom in detail. See B. Sharon Byrd and Joachim

This terminology of 'negative' and 'positive' conceptions of freedom is Kant's own (e.g. GMS 4:446; RL 6:213), and in discussions of his account of freedom of the *will* the distinction between negative and positive conceptions of freedom is well known. Negatively conceived, he describes freedom of the will as its *independence* from compulsion by the impulses of sensibility (e.g. KrV A 534/B562; GMS 4:446; RL 6:213). Positively conceived, he describes it as the will's being *subject to its own legislation* (*eigene Gesetzgebung*, GMS 4:440, 447, 450; KpV 5:33).[4]

Although it has not received much attention, we find the same distinction in Kant's *Metaphysics of Morals.* In the Doctrine of Right, external freedom conceived negatively, as independence from compulsion at the private discretion of another, is distinguished from freedom conceived positively, as being subject to one's own legislation. Positively conceived, the freedom of a citizen of a republic consists in the 'legal attribute' of 'obeying no other law than that to which he has given his consent' (RL 6:314; ZeF 8:350n.).[5] Kant here defends a notion of freedom that is akin to that articulated by Jean-Jacques Rousseau, who writes in the *Social Contract* that 'obedience to the law one has prescribed to oneself is freedom'.[6]

One reason why Kant's positive conception of freedom has not received much attention in discussions of his political philosophy is the fact that he does not flag it as such; another may be Isaiah Berlin's influential critique of the perversions of the ideal of 'positive liberty', which gave the ideal itself a rather bad reputation.[7] Kant's distinction between the negative and the positive conception of freedom does not map onto Berlin's distinction

Hruschka, *Kant's* Doctrine of Right*: A Commentary*, Cambridge: Cambridge University Press, 2010, 77, and Ariel Zylberman, 'The Public Form of Law: Kant on the Second-Personal Constitution of Freedom', *Kantian Review* 21 (2016), 101–26.

[4] On Kant's conception of freedom of the will, see Pauline Kleingeld, 'Me, Myself, and I: Kant's Republican Conception of Freedom of the Will and Freedom of the Agent', *Studi Kantiani* 33 (2020), 103–23. I leave aside Kant's later distinction between *Wille* and *Willkür*, since it is not relevant to the argument of this chapter.

[5] In the *Groundwork* and the *Critique of Practical Reason*, Kant explicitly equates the positive conception of freedom with autonomy. In *Towards Perpetual Peace* and the Doctrine of Right of the *Metaphysics of Morals*, however, he does not do so. In this chapter, I bracket the associated difficulties and focus exclusively on Kant's notion of freedom. For discussion, see Pauline Kleingeld, 'The Principle of Autonomy in Kant's Moral Theory: Its Rise and Fall', in Eric Watkins (ed.), *Kant on Persons and Agency*, Cambridge: Cambridge University Press, 2018, 61–79.

[6] Jean-Jacques Rousseau, *The Social Contract* (1762) in *'The Social Contract' and Other Later Political Writings*, ed. by Victor Gourevitch, Cambridge: Cambridge University Press, 1997, 1.8.

[7] Isiah Berlin, *Two Concepts of Liberty: An Inaugural Lecture delivered before the University of Oxford on 31 October 1958*, Oxford: Clarendon Press, 1958.

between negative and positive liberty, however.[8] Berlin uses the term 'negative liberty' for the absence of interference or coercion limiting the actions open to individuals. He uses 'positive liberty' to refer to the ability to pursue and realize one's fundamental purposes, individually or collectively. Berlin tends to see negative and positive liberty as rival political ideals. As I explain below, for Kant, by contrast, freedom negatively conceived consists not in the *mere absence* of interference or coercion but in *independence* from interference and coercion at the discretion of other individuals. Freedom positively conceived consists in being subject to one's own laws, in contrast to laws imposed by another. Furthermore, for Kant these are not two different *kinds* of freedom (let alone rival kinds) but two aspects of *one and the same condition*, namely external freedom.

In this chapter, I argue that Kant's positive conception of external freedom plays a crucial role in his theory of right because freedom in the negative sense *requires* and *is realized by* freedom in the positive sense. I also show that this applies to each of the three branches of public right – state right, international right, and cosmopolitan right. I first examine the content and status of the innate right to freedom (Section 13.2). I then show how Kant's account of the innate right to freedom as independence relates to his positive conception of freedom: mutual independence requires and is realized by joint self-legislation (Section 13.3).

13.2 The Innate Right to Freedom

13.2.1 Kant's Conception of Freedom as Independence

In the Introduction to the Doctrine of Right, Kant argues that all human beings have one and only one right simply by virtue of their humanity, independently of any juridical act. This is the right to external freedom, that is, freedom in the sphere of interaction with others. He calls this right 'original' and 'innate', to distinguish it from 'acquired' rights, and formulates it as follows:

> Freedom (independence from being compelled by the choice of another), insofar as it can coexist with the freedom of every other in accordance with a general law, is the only original right belonging to every human being by virtue of his humanity. (RL 6:237)

[8] See also Howard Williams, *Kant's Critique of Hobbes*, Cardiff: University of Wales Press, 2003, 96 n. 48.

The parenthetical negative definition of freedom as 'independence from being compelled by the choice of another' places Kant clearly in the republican tradition of thinking about freedom. In this tradition, freedom is defined neither in terms of a particular substantive entitlement (say, a right to property) nor as the mere *absence* of interference and compulsion by others. Rather, freedom is defined in terms of a particular quality of your *relation* to others. It is the condition of *not being subordinate* to others who have the unilateral power to compel you at their private discretion (that is, compelled by their choice in the sense of it being at their discretion, not in the sense of randomness or caprice). This is why, in the republican tradition, freedom is opposed to slavery, dependence, domination, despotism, and similar relations with asymmetrical power structures.

Note that on this conception of freedom, it is possible for you to be unfree even when *de facto* you can do what you want without interference or compulsion by others. This is illustrated by the fact that the unfreedom of enslaved persons is not restricted to the moments when their masters make active use of them. If the master grants them a break or temporarily refrains from giving orders, this does not mean they are free. They are still enslaved, and it remains up to the master alone to decide whether and when they are to resume their activities. Thus, if your ability to do what you want is subject to the discretion of another person who has unilateral power over you, then you are not free in the republican sense of the term. Within the republican tradition of political theory, other relationships with asymmetrical power structures similar to that between master and slave also count as forms of unfreedom – such as the relationship between a colonial power and the colony under its jurisdiction, or that between a despot and their subjects.

The republican background of Kant's conception of freedom helps to explain the sense in which individual freedom has limits. Kant writes that the innate right is a right to freedom *insofar as* it can coexist with the freedom of every other in accordance with a general law. This locution does not mean that your freedom is somehow *reduced* by the freedom of others. You have a right to *full* independence from being compelled at others' discretion. This does not include a right on your part to compel others at your discretion, however, and this is the sense in which your innate right to freedom is limited by that of others.

Immediately after introducing the innate right in the Introduction to the Doctrine of Right, Kant highlights two implications. The first is that the innate right to *freedom* is at the same time a right to *equality*. The two are 'not distinct', he claims. The innate right is a right to:

> innate *equality*, that is, independence from being bound by others to more than one can in turn bind them; hence a human being's quality of being *his own master* (*sui iuris*), as well as being a *respectable* human being (*iusti*) [. . .]. (RL 6:237–8)

Kant here explains freedom in terms of a relation of equal and reciprocal independence. Freedom does not mean that you are not subject to any constraints or obligations. Rather, it means that you are *not asymmetrically* subject to constraints or obligations that stem from the *unilateral* power of *others*.[9] If others have the power to impose obligations on you, then your freedom requires that you have equal power to impose obligations on them. Hence the right to innate equality also means that, by birth, no one has a lower social standing (rank, estate, class, caste) than any other.

The second implication that Kant highlights is that the innate right includes the right to *attempt to engage in interaction* with others, on the condition that this initiative does not deprive others of what is theirs without their consent. He describes a person's innate right as:

> the authority to do to others anything that does not in itself diminish what is theirs if they do not want to accept it – such things as merely letting them know his thoughts, telling them or promising them something [. . .]. (RL 6:238)

Thus, the innate right to freedom is not a unilateral right to get others to interact or cooperate with you; it is not a right to involve others in your private projects. You have the right to approach others, to speak to them, and to attempt to initiate interaction, as long as you do not already wrong them in doing so.

Kant's negative description of freedom as *independence* from compulsion by others, in his formulation of the innate right, does not contain a positive characterization of the proper forms of interaction among free individuals. This raises the question: *How* can they interact without violating each other's right to independence? Kant's positive account of external freedom answers this question.

To anticipate, the key to understanding Kant's positive conception of freedom is the requirement, expressed in the formulation of the innate right, that the right of each coexists with the right of all others 'in accordance with a general law'. As mentioned, the innate right of each extends no further than what is compossible with the same right on the part of all others. Securing everyone's independence from discretionary

[9] Contracts are a good example: contractual obligations should result from a free and voluntary agreement between the parties, not from coercion within an asymmetrical power relation.

compulsion by others therefore requires general principles that apply to all, and this in turn requires establishing a *state* with general coercive laws. Now if these laws were unilaterally imposed by some on others, this would be inconsistent with the others' right to independence. Hence, Kant argues, the laws of the state must be *jointly self-given by the citizens.* Thus, the realization of external freedom in the negative sense (individual independence) *requires and is realized by* freedom in the positive sense (citizens' self-legislation). Or so I will argue.

Before turning to this argument, however, I first address a worry concerning the role and status of the innate right to freedom. It has seemed to several authors that this right has only a small role to play. On the view I defend, by contrast, it is the most important and most fundamental right in Kant's Doctrine of Right and grounds the entire system of rights. This is why the scope and status of the innate right must be clarified first.

13.2.2 The Scope and Status of the Innate Right in Kant's Doctrine of Right

Kant introduces the innate right to freedom in no more than a paragraph. In the rest of the book, he offers lengthy discussions of the various types of acquired rights, such as property rights, contractual rights, status rights, and civil rights. As a result, the innate right may seem little more than a 'starter' without a further role to play in the Doctrine of Right as such. Katrin Flikschuh, for example, has argued that the innate right is merely a formal *precondition* for acquiring substantive rights, with no other scope or content than that of allowing the emergence of acquired rights. She claims that the innate right itself is 'empirically non-instantiable' and lacks any substantive content of its own.[10]

Others have argued that the innate right does have a substantive domain of its own, namely a limited right to one's own *body.* Japa Pallikkathayil, for example, has argued that Kant acknowledges a right to one's own body – albeit a limited right that does not include, say, the right to sell one's body parts – and that this is plausibly innate rather than acquired.[11]

Kant does not explicitly limit the innate right to a merely formal precondition for acquiring rights, however. As shown in the previous section, his description of the innate right – for example, his claim that

[10] Katrin Flikschuh, 'A Regime of Equal Private Freedom? Individual Rights and Public Law in Ripstein's Force and Freedom', in Sari Kisilevsky and Martin J. Stone (eds.), *Freedom and Force: Essays on Kant's Legal Philosophy*, Oxford: Hart Publishing, 2017, 55–74, here 70–1.

[11] Japa Pallikkathayil, 'Persons and Bodies', in Kisilevsky and Stone (eds.), *Freedom and Force*, 35–54.

it includes a right to approach others – indicates that he saw it as implying certain substantive entitlements. Furthermore, although it is plausible that he endorses everyone's (limited) right to their own body – say, to defend it against illegitimate attacks – and that he would regard such a right as innate, he does not restrict innate right to the right to one's body.

Others, including Arthur Ripstein, Sharon Byrd and Joachim Hruschka, Bernd Ludwig, and Philipp-Alexander Hirsch, defend a third interpretation, namely that the innate right to freedom under general law is the most *fundamental* right, the right that normatively governs the acquisition of any other rights – that is, the right that provides the norm for all acquired rights. On this interpretation, the innate right is indeed a precondition of any acquired rights, but it is not non-instantiable. Rather, it is *the* basic right that is to be fully realized by the entire system of rights.[12]

On this issue I agree with Ripstein, Byrd and Hruschka, Ludwig and Hirsch. There is strong textual evidence in support of this reading. This evidence is found not just in Kant's argument for the moral necessity of establishing a juridical condition, but also, and more importantly, in the argument that precedes the formulation of the innate right in the Introduction to the Doctrine of Right.

An overview of the steps of the latter argument reveals that it yields all the elements contained in the formulation of the innate right. Kant formulates the 'General Principle of Right' (*allgemeines Princip des Rechts*) and, on its basis, the 'General Law of Right' (*das allgemeine Rechtsgesetz*) in the form of a categorical imperative: 'Act externally in such a way that the free use of your faculty of choice (*Willkür*) can coexist with the freedom of everyone in accordance with a general law' (RL 6:231). This imperative tells you to act in such a way that your actions can coexist with the external freedom of everyone in accordance with a general law, that is, in accordance with a law that applies equally to all. Kant subsequently argues that since, as a matter of right, your external freedom is restricted in this way, others have the authority to prevent you from infringing on theirs: to the relevant extent, your freedom 'may be actively limited by others' (RL 6:231). Kant then argues that having a 'right' and having the 'authority to coerce' are equivalent (RL 6:231–2). On the basis of these steps, he concludes that right 'is grounded on the principle of the

[12] Ripstein, *Force and Freedom*, 51, 56; Byrd and Hruschka, *Kant's Doctrine of Right*, 77–93; Bernd Ludwig, *Kants Rechtslehre*, Hamburg: Meiner, 1988; Philipp-Alexander Hirsch, *Freiheit und Staatlichkeit bei Kant: Die autonomietheoretische Begründung von Recht und Staat und das Widerstandsproblem*, Berlin: De Gruyter, 2017.

possibility of external coercion that can coexist with the freedom of everyone in accordance with general laws' (RL 6:232).

Taken together, these steps imply the innate right to external freedom. If, as Kant argues, (1) everyone has the authority coercively to prevent others from infringing on their freedom, (2) this authority is equivalent to having a right to freedom, and (3) everyone's freedom must be able to coexist with the freedom of all in accordance with a general law, then it follows that everyone has a right to freedom to the extent that it can coexist with the freedom of everyone in accordance with a general law. In other words, the argument in support of the innate right to external freedom is found in the Introduction. Kant's argumentation is brief and clearly calls for further analysis, but for the purposes of this chapter the relevant point is merely to explain why he may not have seen a need to explicate and defend the innate right in the paragraph in which he formulated it: in essence, he had already done so.

According to this reconstruction, the innate right is not a merely formal precondition for rights nor a limited right to one's body. Rather, being based directly on the General Law of Right, it is the most fundamental right. It animates the entire system of right.

13.2.3 How to Acquire Rights without Dominating Others

According to Kant, acquiring and owning something external means being entitled to constrain the conduct of all others with regard to it: it means being entitled to prevent them from taking or using it. But is it possible to constrain the conduct of others in this way without compelling them at one's own discretion, that is, without violating their innate right to freedom? If so, how?

In the state of nature, Kant argues, this is indeed impossible. The problem with the state of nature is not just a matter of human nastiness. Irresolvable disagreements will arise even among friendly, upright, and reasonable people. In the *Feyerabend Lectures on Natural Law* from 1784, Kant gives the following example: if, in the state of nature, he shoots a wild animal and it runs onto someone else's land and dies there, he may believe he has the right to retrieve it, but the other person may claim that it belongs to him because it is on his land (V-NR/Feyerabend 27:1337). They each have grounds for claiming that the dead animal is theirs: Kant because he shot it, the other because he found it on his land. Whoever unilaterally imposes his will on the other, however, violates the other's innate right.

To solve this structural problem endemic to the state of nature, there needs to be a general positive law that covers such cases. Kant reportedly explained: 'I do wrong to others if I wanted to make my will into their law, hence I am obligated to subject myself to an external law that is valid for everyone' (V-NR/Feyerabend 27:1338).

In the *Metaphysics of Morals,* Kant develops this point in more detail, explaining that even 'good-natured and right-loving' people (RL 6:312) ought to leave the state of nature and enter a civil condition, that is, they ought to subject themselves to general laws, law enforcement, and impartial arbitration.[13] Having something external as mine entails obligations on the parts of others, such as the obligation not to take it or use it without my permission. Kant argues that this is possible – without violating the freedom of others – only under general laws (RL 6:255–6). In order for an owner's entitlement not to boil down to the authority to compel others unilaterally, that is, for the owner's freedom to be compatible with the freedom of others, the entitlement must itself derive from a 'general' or 'omnilateral' authorization by the united citizens, expressed in a general law (RL 6:245–57). Or, to use Ripstein's apt terminology, rightful unilateral acquisition requires omnilateral authorization.[14]

This explains why Kant writes that 'it is possible to have something external as one's own only in a rightful condition, under a public-legislative power, that is, in a civil condition' (RL 6:255). In the state of nature, there can be 'only provisional' possession (RL 6:256). This applies to each of the three kinds of objects to which one can acquire rights: (1) material objects (things I own), (2) the substance of contractual agreements (that which others have promised me), and (3) persons to whom I stand in certain status relations (which Kant revealingly describes in terms of a person's being 'my wife', 'my child', or 'my domestic servant', as part of 'my belongings', RL 6:248; for discussion see Section 13.3.2).

Kant's account raises the question, of course, where the required general laws are to come from. Clearly, the laws in the state must not stem from the unilateral imposition of some people's wills on others. This would yield a despotic state, and it would violate the innate right to freedom.

In Section 13.3 I show that Kant's considered answer is that the united citizens *themselves* should legislate and that freedom conceived positively consists in being subject to *one's own legislation.* Or, more precisely, this is

[13] See also Helga Varden, 'Kant's Non-Voluntarist Conception of Political Obligations: Why Justice Is Impossible in the State of Nature', *Kantian Review* 13 (2008), 1–45.

[14] Ripstein, *Force and Freedom*, 148–59; see also Ludwig, *Kants Rechtslehre*, 115–20.

the answer Kant gives starting with *Towards Perpetual Peace* (1795) and the *Metaphysics of Morals* (1797). According to Ripstein, by contrast, Kant holds that state officials should take up a general (omnilateral) perspective and give *to* the people laws that the people *could* give to themselves. In what follows, I shall frequently refer to Ripstein's account, since he offers the most comprehensive, detailed, and philosophically astute discussion of Kant's republicanism. Like most others who discuss the topic, however, Ripstein focuses entirely on Kant's negative conception of freedom as *independence*.[15] By comparing his interpretation to the one I propose in this chapter, I aim to clarify the important role Kant attributes to the positive conception of freedom as *joint self-legislation*.

Furthermore, I argue that this *positive* conception of external freedom structures not only Kant's account of the state but each of the three levels of public right in the Doctrine of Right. Only once a rightful condition exists at the levels of the state, international right, and cosmopolitan right can rights be definite and secure ('peremptory') (RL 6:266, 311; ZeF 8:349n.).

13.3 Freedom and Public Right

13.3.1 Independence and Self-Legislation in the republic

The question raised at the end of the previous section was how individual 'independence from compulsion by the choice of others' (the innate right to freedom) can be secured through laws without introducing new forms of unfreedom in the process, namely domination by those giving the laws.

One answer found within contemporary republican theory is that the state should ensure non-arbitrary rule, without this requiring self-legislation by the people. Philip Pettit, to mention one prominent example, has argued that democratic participation has some instrumental value but is not valuable in and of itself. Pettit distances himself from what he calls the 'populist' view that freedom consists in democratic self-rule, a view which he associates with Rousseau and Kant.[16] The better kind of republicanism, Pettit argued in his influential 1997 book *Republicanism*,

[15] According to Byrd and Hruschka, freedom conceived positively is 'dependence on public law in a juridical state' (*Kant's Doctrine of Right*, 92–3, also 87, 88). This formulation seems too broad, however, since it leaves open the question of who legislates the law.

[16] Pettit, *Republicanism*, 8, 30; as for Kant, see Pettit, 'Two Republican Traditions', in Andreas Niederberger and Philipp Schink (eds.), *Republican Democracy*, Edinburgh: Edinburgh University Press, 2013, 169–204.

'sees the people as trusting the state to ensure a dispensation of non-arbitrary rule'.[17]

On Ripstein's interpretation, this last statement in fact comes close to Kant's view. He argues that Kant sees it as the role of the state, and 'state officials', to 'make arrangements for the people'.[18] Ripstein says very little about how these officials receive their mandate, but he seems to conceive of them as being elected. At least on one occasion he refers to 'chosen representatives' of the citizens who act 'on their behalf'.[19] These officials are to give laws to the people that the people 'could' give themselves, laws that it would be 'possible' for the citizens to adopt.[20] The officials are to take up, vicariously, an omnilateral perspective and give laws that make it possible for the people to interact on terms of equal freedom.

Thus, to put it in terms of Hanna Pitkin's influential distinction between trustee and delegate models of representation,[21] Ripstein seems to conceive of these state officials as elected representatives who act as *trustees* to whom the citizens have *outsourced* the business of legislation – not as elected delegates through whom the citizens *themselves* give laws. Ripstein does not describe the citizens as legislating. He consistently describes the task of the state officials as that of giving *to* the people laws that the people *could* give themselves.

When introducing this view, Ripstein quotes a passage from 'What Is Enlightenment?' (1784), in which Kant writes: 'The touchstone of whatever can be decided upon as law *for* a people lies in the question: whether a people *could* impose such a law upon itself' (8:39, emphasis

[17] Pettit, *Republicanism*, 8. In more recent work, Pettit strengthens the role of democracy considerably. He argues that the citizens should have a suitable form of control over government, via elections and contestatory influence, but he maintains the division between the state and the people, and he does not conceive of those in power as the citizens' agents. See Philip Pettit, *On the People's Terms: A Republican Theory and Model of Democracy*, Cambridge: Cambridge University Press, 2012. For critical discussion, see Rainer Forst, 'A Kantian Republican Conception of Justice as Nondomination', in Andreas Niederberger and Philipp Schink (eds.), *Republican Democracy*, Edinburgh: Edinburgh University Press, 2013, 154–68, and Rainer Forst, 'Kantian Republicanism versus the Neo-Republican Machine: The Meaning and Practice of Political Autonomy', in Julia Christ, Kristina Lepold, Daniel Loick, and Titus Stahl (eds.), *Debating Critical Theory: Engagements with Axel Honneth*, Lanham: Rowman and Littlefield, 2020, 17–34.

[18] Ripstein, *Force and Freedom*, 194–5; see also Horn in this volume (Chapter 3).

[19] Ripstein, *Force and Freedom*, 203.

[20] Ripstein, *Force and Freedom*, 25, 26, 183, 206–13, 241, 243.

[21] Hanna Fenichel Pitkin, *The Concept of Representation*, Berkeley: University of California Press, 1967, esp. 112–43. For discussion of this distinction, see also Suzanne Dovi, 'Political Representation', in Edward N. Zalta (ed.), *The Stanford Encyclopedia of Philosophy*, Fall 2018, www.plato.stanford.edu/archives/fall2018/entries/political-representation/, section 1 (accessed 1 June 2024).

added).[22] In the *Feyerabend Lectures on Natural Law* from the same year, Kant makes similar claims (V-NR/Feyerabend 27:1382). Neither in 'What Is Enlightenment?' nor in the Feyerabend Lectures, however, is there any indication that Kant argues that legislation ought to be enacted by *elected* representatives. Thus, the role Kant attributes to the people seems significantly *weaker* than Ripstein assumes it is. Kant seems to present this 'touchstone' as a normative criterion for autocratic rulers. He presents the rulers as 'representing' the people (V-NR/Feyerabend 27:1382), but without suggesting that these rulers should be elected by the citizens.[23]

By the mid-1790s, however, Kant's position has changed significantly, and he now attributes a much *stronger* role to citizens than Ripstein claims he does. In *Towards Perpetual Peace* and the *Metaphysics of Morals*, Kant explicitly emphasizes that laws should be adopted *by the citizens.* He defends the separation of powers and argues that this requires a representative system in which different subsets of citizens are active in the different branches of government (RL 6:313–17, 341).

It is not hard to see why, philosophically speaking, it made sense for Kant to introduce the requirement of actual self-legislation.[24] If the people must obey laws that are unilaterally imposed on them by an unelected ruler, then strictly speaking this ruler is a despot, no matter how enlightened and benevolent. Whatever an enlightened despot decides, he *unilaterally* decides which law to impose on the people (even if he chooses from among laws the people *could* give themselves). In such cases, the people are subject to the compulsion of another who binds them through his choice, without their having the reciprocal power to bind him. This asymmetry is precisely what Kant, in the *Metaphysics of Morals*, describes as a violation of the innate right to freedom under general laws (see Section 13.2.1).

Accordingly, in the Doctrine of Right Kant now argues that the right to freedom requires that the united people give themselves the laws to which they are subject:

> When someone decrees something over *another* [etwas gegen einen *anderen* verfügt], it is always possible that he thereby wrongs the other, but he can never do wrong in what he decides about himself [. . .]. Therefore, only the concurring and united will of all, insofar as each decides the same thing for

[22] Quoted in Ripstein, *Force and Freedom*, 207.

[23] See also Kant's two arguments against selecting monarchs via elections (V-NR/Feyerabend 27:1388–9).

[24] I here bracket the biographical issue as to what circumstances may have prompted Kant to change his mind.

> all and all for each, and hence only the general united will of the people can be legislative. (RL 6:313–14)

He now emphasizes that 'the only qualification for being a citizen is being fit to vote' (RL 6:314) and that the laws should 'spring from [the citizens'] own legislating will' (RL 6:316; cf. SF 7:91). The ideal representative political system is what Kant calls a 'genuine' or 'pure republic', and he claims that this is 'the only constitution that accords with right' (RL 6:340). Here citizens are 'united for the purpose of legislation' (RL 6:314), and they have the right 'to manage the state itself as active members of it, to organize it or to cooperate for introducing certain laws' (RL 6:315). In a genuine republic every citizen is a 'co-legislating member' of the body politic (*mitgesetzgebendes Glied*, RL 6:345, also 6:335).

This normative ideal of joint *co-legislation* by the citizens is clearly quite different from Kant's earlier defence of the unelected enlightened ruler who was to give laws to the people that the people could give themselves. Moreover, his terminology of the citizens as 'co-legislators' and laws being given 'by the citizens, by means of their delegates' (RL 6:341; cf. ZeF 8:352–3), presents elected representatives as *delegates* who are the voice of the citizens themselves, rather than as *trustees* to whom citizens transfer the task of legislation (which is how Ripstein presents them).

Kant conceives of the co-legislating citizens as *free* in a positive sense, that is, as being subject to their own legislation. As mentioned at the beginning of this chapter, he describes the freedom of the citizen as the 'legal attribute' of 'obeying no other law than that to which he has given his consent' (RL 6:314). In *Towards Perpetual Peace*, he similarly describes 'external (rightful) freedom' as 'the authority to obey no external laws other than those to which I have been able to give my consent' (ZeF 8:350n.).[25] By calling freedom a 'legal attribute' and an 'authority', he indicates that his point is not that the freedom of citizens consists in their *following* the law.[26] The contrast case is not disobedience but despotism. The freedom of the citizens consists in their not having to obey laws given *by another* but those given *by themselves*.

We can now see that the two conceptions of freedom are intimately connected. As long as you must obey laws that are imposed on you by

[25] In the Cambridge Edition, Mary J. Gregor translates this as 'those to which I could have given my consent', but the German text says 'zu denen ich meine Beistimmung habe geben können'.

[26] Zylberman argues that, for Kant, positive freedom consists in following the law, Zylberman, 'The Public Form of Law', 102–8. This is not exactly how Kant puts it, however, and it would have the implausible implication that citizens who break the law lack external freedom.

someone else at their discretion, you are not free in the negative sense. Freedom in the negative sense – independence from compulsion by the choice of others – is possible and secure only through everyone's subjection to jointly self-given laws; that is, it requires freedom in the positive sense. Only if and when the united citizens jointly give *themselves* the laws to which they are subject are they no longer subject to the discretionary choice of *another*.

Thus, the relation between freedom in the negative sense and freedom in the positive sense is not merely additive, as if you could first have mutual independence without joint self-legislation and then add it. Rather, genuine freedom in the negative sense (independence from compulsion by the choice of another) *requires* and *is realized by* freedom in the positive sense (joint self-legislation). Kant's view is that the citizens become genuinely independent of each other by virtue of subjecting themselves to collectively self-given laws in a republican state.

In other words, for Kant the fact that the citizens of a republic are subject to coercive laws does not run counter to their freedom – on the contrary, in instituting a system in which they give themselves general laws that they must all obey, they make themselves independent of each other. They are no longer in a condition where the more powerful individuals can compel the others at their discretion: under the rule of law they are each other's equals. Here Kant agrees with Rousseau, who claims in the *Social Contract* that citizens become independent of each other as they become dependent on the (jointly self-given) laws of their state.[27] Incidentally, this thought explains the otherwise rather puzzling fact that Kant sometimes groups together 'freedom, equality, and independence' and at other times 'freedom, equality, and dependence'. In the first case, he is referring to independence from other individuals (RL 6:314). In the second case, he is referring to everyone's dependence on their own laws, for example in *Towards Perpetual Peace*, where he describes the republic in terms of the 'freedom', 'equality', and 'dependence of all upon a single common legislation (as subjects)' (ZeF 8:349–50).

Kant's argument shows that the innate right to freedom requires a genuine republic. Indeed, his description of the legal properties of citizens in a republic echoes his description of the different aspects of innate right (RL 6:237, quoted above) and articulates how this right is realized in the republic. The characteristics of the citizen are as follows:[28]

[27] Rousseau, *The Social Contract*, 2.12.

[28] The passage does not refer to the right to approach others, perhaps because interaction is the very premise of the state.

> Lawful *freedom*, obeying no other law than that to which he has given his consent; civil *equality*, not recognizing among the people any superior with regard to him, except one that he has the moral capacity legally to bind, just as the other can bind him; and third, the attribute of civil *self-sufficiency*, of owing his existence and preservation to his own rights and powers as a member of the commonwealth, not to the choice of another among the people; and hence his civil personality, not needing to be represented by another in juridical matters. (RL 6:314)

Freedom in the state is here described as subjection to public laws to which the citizen has agreed – the positive conception of freedom. *Equality* is again explained in terms of the citizens' reciprocal power to impose obligations, now further specified as *legal* obligations. *Independence* is realized in the form of *civil* independence from the discretionary choice of others, and the right to speak for oneself is specified as *civil* personality in legal affairs. Thus, by institutionalizing a legal system that determines and secures the different aspects of this right, the republic realizes the innate right to freedom.

Kant's claim that the citizen's freedom consists in the entitlement to obey only those laws 'to which he has given his consent' might make it sound as if one need not obey laws to which one has not given consent. But this is clearly not his view. In fact, he is notoriously committed to the opposite view (RL 6:320). Citizens ought to obey the law regardless of how they voted. In some texts, Kant endorses the majority principle, according to which a decision of the majority counts as a decision of all (TP 8:296; cf. VARL 23:351). Kant fails to address the position of outvoted citizens in detail, however, and a discussion of the majority principle is strikingly absent from the *Metaphysics of Morals*.[29]

Importantly, the fact that external freedom requires joint self-legislation does not imply that all positive laws passed by citizens actually realize external freedom. Although Kant does not discuss the procedural requirements for proper legislation in much detail, it is obvious that the innate right to freedom imposes normative constraints on the citizens' legislation. Positive laws must be compatible with the innate right to freedom of all. For Kant this means that laws must be truly general. They should not, say, include exceptions on behalf of special interests (see e.g. TP 8:298n.) or

[29] For a more detailed discussion of the majority principle, the original contract, and the status of the outvoted voter in Kant's theory, see Mike Gregory, 'Does the Kantian State Dominate? Freedom and Majoritarian Rule', *Ratio* 36 (2023), 124–36. For Kant's conception of the relation between citizens and their elected representatives, see Pauline Kleingeld, 'Kant's Formula of Autonomy: Continuity or Discontinuity?', *Philosophia* 51 (2023),555–69.

usurp what belongs to minorities for the sake of majority interests.[30] In other words, Kant retains the earlier criterion that it must be possible for the entire people to adopt a law (e.g. RL 6:329). But this requirement is now a *necessary* condition for rightful legislation and no longer a *sufficient* condition. Thus, the shift in Kant's stated position does not imply that he has dropped the earlier 'touchstone'. Rather, he has *added* a further normative condition for rightful legislation, namely that laws *actually* be adopted by the people.[31]

As a result, for a positive law to meet Kant's requirements it is not sufficient that the citizens' representatives happen to enact it. Kant should not be misunderstood as claiming that whatever the citizens happen to prefer is just. Any law must also satisfy the criterion (now as a necessary condition) that the entire people *could* impose it on itself. This criterion makes it possible to distinguish between just laws and those resulting from a despotic majority or powerful special interests. Another important reason why Kant preserved this criterion may well have been the fact that on his own account the set of citizens with voting rights was a small subset of the people, excluding all so-called 'passive' citizens. The 'active' citizens should give laws *for* the passive citizens that the latter *could* give themselves. To this issue I now turn.

13.3.2 Not All Humans Become Herren

Thus far, I have used Kant's terminology and discussed the innate right of 'every human being' and the freedom of 'the citizens' or 'the people'. This may give the mistaken impression that he endorses universal adult suffrage. In fact, however, he limits the full enjoyment of the *human* right to freedom to a small subset of adult males. Therefore, before I turn to relations among states, an important qualification is in order regarding

[30] Discussing the substantive implications of this criterion in detail would take me beyond the scope of this chapter. For a good argument in support of the thesis that legislation should prevent not only dependence and power inequalities among individuals but also structural power inequalities, see Rafeeq Hasan, 'Freedom and Poverty in the Kantian State', *European Journal of Philosophy* 26 (2017), 911–31. For an interesting defence of a public and collective notion of freedom, see Garrath Williams, 'Between Ethics and Right: Kantian Politics and Democratic Purposes', *European Journal of Philosophy* 20 (2012), 479–86.

[31] In the interim, that is, before a genuine republic has been established, it is the duty of autocrats to give laws in the spirit of republicanism, even if they do not literally ask their subjects for consent. Kant's ideal, however, is a constitution in which 'those who obey the law are also simultaneously, united, legislating' (SF 7:90–1, cf. 88).

Kant's claim, quoted in Section 13.2.1, that 'every human being' has the innate right to freedom.

Kant distinguishes between active and passive citizens, as did the French Constitution of 1791. He asserts that those who depend on others for their livelihood do not qualify for the right to vote and are hence passive citizens. His examples include shop assistants, day laborers, domestic servants, children, and 'all women' (RL 6:314). He argues that these groups are dependent on others, whereas store owners, artisans, and heads of households are not.

Kant recognizes that the distinction might seem problematic. He admits that it seems to be at odds with his own account of citizenship and that it is hard to draw the line. He nevertheless claims that the difference in civil status is justified as long as it is possible for passive citizens to work their way up to active status (RL 6:314–15). It is not entirely clear what the precise nature of the relevant dependency relation is or why Kant sees dependence as disqualifying someone from the right to vote.[32] Nor does he explain why he argues in favour of restricting voting rights rather than in favour of abolishing social, economic, and juridical dependency relations among private individuals as far as possible – especially since the latter argument would have been more in line with the innate right to freedom of all. I leave these issues aside here, since my focus in this chapter is on the relation between Kant's positive and negative conception of freedom, not on his political theory in general. The status of women as dependents deserves further comment, however, for reasons that will become clear.

By placing *all* women in the category of dependents (RL 6:314), Kant in effect denies them the possibility of ever working their way up to active status. And indeed, he claims elsewhere that women do not qualify for the right to vote because they lack an unspecified allegedly 'natural' prerequisite ('that it not be a child or a woman', TP 8:295). Nowhere does he criticize the inferior legal status of women as passive citizens or call for their emancipation.

This reveals clear tensions in the Doctrine of Right. Recall that Kant describes the innate right to freedom as a right that 'belongs to *every human being* by virtue of his humanity' and that it includes the right to equality and independence, including the right 'to be one's own master'

[32] For discussion see Luke Davies, 'Kant on Civil Self-Sufficiency', *Archiv für Geschichte der Philosophie* 105 (2023), 118–40; Kate Moran, 'Kant on Traveling Blacksmiths and Passive Citizenship', *Kant-Studien* 112 (2021), 105–26; Nicholas Vrousalis, 'Interdependent Independence: Civil Self-Sufficiency and Productive Community in Kant's Theory of Citizenship', *Kantian Review* 27 (2022), 443–60.

(*Herr*, meaning 'master', 'lord', 'gentleman'). Yet he also claims that *women* are naturally unfit for the right to vote, arguing that the 'natural superiority' of men in promoting the common interest of the household gives a husband the right to command over his wife as *her master*. He writes that the law is right to say to the wife: 'he shall be your master [*Herr*] (he the commanding, she the obeying part)' (RL 6:279). Furthermore, in the *Anthropology from a Pragmatic Point of View* (1798) Kant again appeals to 'nature' in explaining why women cannot represent themselves in court (7:209).

Thus, in the Doctrine of Right women lack each of the three essential characteristics of the citizen described above. They lack the lawful *freedom* to obey no other law than that to which they have given consent, since they lack active citizenship; they lack civil *equality*, since they cannot legally bind men in the way men can bind women; and they lack civil *independence*, including the power to represent themselves in court. Thus, despite his claim that *every human being* has the right to be 'his own master' (*sein eigener Herr*) by virtue of 'his humanity' (*seiner Menschheit*), Kant simultaneously denies this right to women. In light of this, I have followed Kant in his use of male pronouns. Gender-inclusive language ('he or she', 'she', or the non-binary singular 'they') would be misleading and in many cases factually incorrect.[33]

13.3.3 Freedom and the Republican Federation of States

Kant famously argues that states ought to leave the international state of nature (ZeF 8:354–7). Rather than advocating the establishment of an internally undifferentiated world state, however, he writes that '[i]nternational right shall be based on a *federalism* of free states' (ZeF 8:354).

Kant's terminology of a 'federalism of *free* states' has often been read as indicating that he advocates only a loose form of association without any coercive powers. In light of the analysis in Section 13.3.1, however, the expression as such could also refer to a federation with legislative, executive, and judicial powers. After all, he also conceives of the citizens in a republic as *free*. Thus, a republican federation with coercive powers could in principle be called a federation of *free* states – in both the negative and the positive sense of 'free' – if states were independent of each other by virtue of living under collectively self-given international laws.

[33] For further discussion, see Pauline Kleingeld, 'On Dealing with Kant's Sexism and Racism', *SGIR Review* 2 (2019), 3–22.

Given the predominant emphasis in the literature on Kant's *negative* conception of freedom as independence, it is not surprising that his emphasis on the 'freedom' of states is usually seen as evidence that he endorses only a loose league of states. In this vein, Arthur Ripstein reads Kant as rejecting an international federation of states with public laws and law enforcement. He claims that Kant defends only a voluntary league 'for deciding disputes', but one without any power to enforce its rulings.[34] To defend his reading, Ripstein argues, first, that 'no "mine or yours" structure' applies to the acquisition of state territory, since 'the state does not acquire its territory'; consequently, 'there is no need for omnilateral authorization of a unilateral acquisition' and hence no need for public international law and coercive enforcement.[35] Second, Ripstein points to Kant's claim that the federation of states should not only be entered into voluntarily but also remain 'dissoluble' (cf. RL 6:351), assuming, as many authors do, that the voluntary character of the federation implies that it lacks coercive laws.[36]

A closer look at the texts reveals, however, that Kant does argue that states have an external 'mine and yours' and should join a federation with public international laws to make rights peremptory. In the *Metaphysics of Morals,* he writes:

> [In the international state of nature] all international right and all [...] external mine and yours of states is merely *provisional*; and only in a general *union of states* [*allgemeiner Staatenverein*] (analogous to that by which a people becomes a state) can it come to have *peremptory* validity and become a true *condition of peace*. (RL 6:350, orig. emphasis)

He claims that states ought to leave the international state of nature and enter into a condition in which their conflicts are decided on the basis of international public laws (RL 6:350–1; cf. ZeF 8:358).[37]

[34] Ripstein, *Force and Freedom*, 229; Arthur Ripstein, *Kant and the Law of War*, Oxford: Oxford University Press, 2021, ch. 8; similarly, Reidar Maliks, *Kant's Politics in Context*, Oxford: Oxford University Press, 2014.

[35] Ripstein, *Force and Freedom*, 228–30.

[36] Ripstein, *Force and Freedom*, 230. He further claims that genuine republics do not pursue private purposes and that they will therefore never have grounds for war except to defend themselves or their allies, *Force and Freedom*, 228–9. It seems, however, that purposes that are public within a state can become 'private' purposes of that state at the international level, for example its purpose of maintaining certain socio-economic arrangements, when faced with challenges from other states. Moreover, the duty to leave the state of nature applies to republics for the same reason that it applies to 'good-natured and right-loving' individuals (see the beginning of Section 13.2.3).

[37] See also Martin Brecher, 'Konsequenter Kosmopolitismus', in Andree Hahmann and Stefan Klingner (eds.), *Konsequenter Denkungsart: Studien zu einer philosophischen Tugend*, Hamburg: Meiner, 2024, 62–100.

Kant's claim that the 'external mine and yours of states' requires an international legal order is not surprising given his scathing criticism of the belligerent and imperialist behaviour of the European states of his time, many of which were actively striving to enlarge their own territory at each other's expense and to appropriate additional territory overseas. Against this background of war, conquest, and colonialism, the territorial claims of states do call for just laws on the basis of which international disputes can be settled, such that all states receive what is rightfully theirs. Such international laws should not be unilaterally imposed by a subset of states – say, European colonial powers – on the rest of the world.[38] Given Kant's positive conception of freedom, public international laws should rather be the states' *jointly self-given* laws.

This does not entail that states (or groups of states) have a right to *coerce* other states *into* a federation against their will. In *Towards Perpetual Peace*, Kant argues that the only way to leave the international state of nature is for states to form a *voluntary* federation (ZeF 8:357). This argument has often been read as inconsistent. After all, he argues that *individuals* do have a right to coerce each other to leave the state of nature (ZeF 8:349n.).[39] But Kant's positive account of freedom within the republic, discussed above, clarifies why his position is not inconsistent. Given their innate right to freedom, individuals in the state of nature are entitled to coerce each other into a state with common legislation, to secure their mutual independence from each other's discretionary choice. If states had a general right to coerce other states into a world state or an international federation, however, against the will of their citizens, the citizens would once again be compelled by the discretionary choice of another – namely, foreign states. Thus, there can be no such right, and joining an international federation should be a *voluntary* decision by the citizens of a state.[40] The fact that joining should be voluntary does not mean that it does not matter whether

[38] This is a scenario that Kant envisioned before he became a forceful critic of European colonial practices about ten years later (see Pauline Kleingeld, 'Kant's Second Thoughts on Colonialism', in Katrin Flikschuh and Lea Ypi (eds.), *Kant and Colonialism: Historical and Critical Perspectives*, Oxford: Oxford University Press, 2014, 43–67). On his theory of territorial rights, see Alice Pinheiro Walla, 'Private Property and Territorial Rights: A Kantian Alternative to Contemporary Debates', in Alice Pinheiro Walla and Mehmet Ruhi Demiray (eds.), *Reason, Normativity and Law: New Essays in Kantian Philosophy*, Cardiff: University of Wales Press, 2020, 213–32.

[39] See, for example, Byrd and Hruschka, *Kant's Doctrine of Right*, 2010, 195.

[40] For further discussion of the disanalogy between the permitted ways of leaving the individual and the international state of nature, see Pauline Kleingeld, 'Approaching Perpetual Peace: Kant's Defence of a League of States and His Ideal of a World Federation', *European Journal of Philosophy* 12 (2004), 304–25.

they do: Kant argues that states have a *duty* to work towards the ideal of a union of states (RL 6:350).

Kant ends this discussion in the *Metaphysics of Morals* with the claim that the federative union of states should remain *dissoluble*, unlike the US constitution, which prohibits secession (RL 6:351). Ripstein sees this as indicating that Kant rejects the ideal of an international federation with public laws enforced by a federal executive.[41] Kant's rejection of the US model, however, does not concern the fact that it has a federal legislature and executive.[42] Rather, it concerns the fact that it is *not a real federation*, in Kant's eyes, because it is 'based on a state constitution [*Staatsverfassung*] and hence indissoluble' (RL 6:351). It starts with 'We the people' – as if it were a single people – rather than with 'We the states' or 'We the peoples', and it does not grant its member states a right to secession. Kant's claim that the federation should grant states the right to exit does not imply that he denies that it should have a federal legislature, executive, and judiciary – just as little as in the analogous case of a state and its citizens' right to emigrate. The current example of the European Union demonstrates that the member states' right to leave is compatible with their being subject to common coercive public laws while their membership lasts. In practice, it may be difficult to carry out – and carry out consistently – the demands of public international law, as Kant was well aware (ZeF 8:357) and as is attested by the difficulties surrounding international economic boycotts and peace-keeping efforts. But the fact that membership in the federation should remain voluntary does not entail that it should lack coercive public laws.

Why would Kant view it as important that states retain the right to exit? His positive conception of freedom, in particular the crucial role of the ideal state in securing the freedom of citizens under their own public laws, again suggests an explanation. Recall that the state is to secure individuals' innate right to freedom under general laws, and that the international federation is in turn to secure the freedom of member states under general international laws (thus securing the innate right of the citizens who compose these member states). If the international federation were to prevent its members from leaving, it would undermine the very thing it seeks to promote, namely their citizens' innate right to freedom. For example, if the federation has a

41 Ripstein, *Force and Freedom*, 229–30.

42 The passage often seen as evidence that Kant rejects a federation with coercive laws is his claim that states 'need not subject themselves (like human beings in the state of nature) to public laws and coercion under such laws' (ZeF 8:356). However, this passage is best read as rejecting the coercive incorporation of states into a federation with coercive laws. Moreover, as indicated in this section, Kant repeatedly emphasizes that the federation is to have common public laws.

'despotic' political structure but some of its member states are republics, and if the latter's citizens wanted to leave the federation, their right to freedom would be violated if they were prevented from doing so. On this suggested reading, Kant's reason for emphasizing that states ought to have a right to *leave* the federation, then, turns out to be akin to his reason for claiming that states must not be forced to *join* it: the individual innate right to freedom, conceived both negatively and positively.

13.3.4 Cosmopolitan Right

In addition to state right, which is to govern interactions among individuals, and international right, which is to govern interactions among states, Kant adds a third branch of public right, which is to govern interactions between states and individuals or groups who are neither their citizens nor official representatives of other states. His examples include the interaction between a state and shipwrecked foreigners stranded on its beach (VAZeF 23:173), between a state and foreign trading companies wanting to enter the country (ZeF 8:359), and between non-state peoples and a state attempting to appropriate their hunting grounds (RL 6:353). This third branch of public right is called cosmopolitan right.

Cosmopolitan right articulates the conditions under which states and foreign individuals or groups can interact without one party's violating the freedom of another. Its core is the right to hospitality, by which Kant means the right of persons and states to request peaceful interaction without being treated with hostility (ZeF 8:357–8). He discusses the circumstances under which parties have a right to refuse such requests, arguing, for example, that they do not have this right in cases where refusal would lead to the other's 'demise' or the annihilation of their freedom (ZeF 8:358). Thus, he denies that states have a right to send shipwrecked sailors back into the sea (VAZeF 23:173). Furthermore, he denies that foreigners (such as representatives of trading companies) have a right to enter another state at will. They do have the right to *request* entry (without being treated with hostility), but the state in turn has a right to refuse their request, except in cases where this would lead to their demise. Finally, states do not have the right to seize land used by non-state peoples, and any settlement in regions used by others requires their informed agreement (RL 6:353). Accordingly, Kant argues that the colonialism and imperialism of the European states of his day constitute flagrant violations of cosmopolitan right (ZeF 8:358–9; RL 6:353).

Kant's description of cosmopolitan right clearly echoes his description of the innate right to freedom conceived negatively as independence from compulsion by the choice of another. It echoes his description of the innate right as including the right to attempt to engage in interaction with others (see Section 13.2.1), while others have the right to refuse (unless this leads to the demise of the first). Moreover, by highlighting the illegitimacy of states' unilateral acquisition of territory used by others and the illegitimacy of nonconsensual entrance into states, Kant's examples also re-emphasize the normative importance of freedom and equality.

Kant provides hardly any details on how he envisions the legislation of cosmopolitan law, but the link with his positive conception of freedom is visible even in this case, albeit less clearly. He writes that it is a task of the 'peoples' (in the political sense, 'peoples as states', ZeF 8:354) to unite for the sake of giving cosmopolitan law. The peoples are to establish 'right, which can be called *cosmopolitan* right, insofar as it concerns the possible union of all peoples for the purpose of certain general laws of their possible interaction' (RL 6:353). This legislation is to yield a 'rightful connection of human beings under public laws' (RL 6:355). Thus, even in the case of cosmopolitan right we encounter Kant's positive conception of freedom: the peoples of the world are to unite for the purpose of giving themselves the laws that govern the cosmopolitan interaction between states and foreigners.

13.4 Conclusion

On Kant's republican account, freedom, negatively conceived, consists in independence from compulsion at the discretion of another. Freedom, positively conceived, consists in being subject to one's own legislation. The mutual independence of a plurality of individual agents can be achieved only through their joint subjection to collectively self-given public laws. Thus, the innate right to external freedom requires the realization of freedom in *both* senses, and this holds for each of the three domains of public right (ZeF 8:349n.; RL 6:311).

The interpretation proposed in this chapter is different from how Kant's republicanism is usually described. Most authors focus on his negative conception of freedom as independence. The argument of this chapter suggests that, in doing so, they overlook his thesis that mutual independence requires collective self-legislation. The current focus on independence, in republican readings of Kant, should be complemented with an increased emphasis on Kant's account of citizenship, co-legislation, and the appropriate mode of political representation.

CHAPTER 14

Morality, Right, and Responsibility

Paul Guyer

Throughout the volume, especially but not just in Part I, it has been debated whether Right, that is, public law enforced by the coercive juridical and penal instrumentality of the state, is part of morality for Kant, thus whether its basic principle, the Universal Principle of Right, can and must be derived, in some way or other, from the fundamental principle of morality in general. Most of the contributions to the volume have defended the dependence of the principle of Right on the principle of morality in general, while recognizing the distinction between Right and Ethics, that is, the non-coercive part of morality in general, although several, notably Marcus Willaschek, have defended the independence of Right from morality. In this chapter, which has been placed in the position of a conclusion to the volume, I will not get further into the trenches of this debate than I have previously done.[1] Instead, I will frame the debate with two general points. First, I argue that Kant recognizes only two forms of practical reason, namely pure practical reason, based on the fundamental principle of morality, and empirical practical reason, based upon the principle of prudential self-love (see especially RGV 6:35–6), so if the necessity of Right does not depend upon the latter, it must derive in some way from the former; and since Kant makes it clear that his philosophy of Right is fundamentally opposed to that of Hobbes (TP, 8:289), it is clear that he intends it to be grounded in pure practical reason and derived from its principle.[2] Whatever the details of Kant's derivation of Right from

[1] I have previously discussed this issue in 'Kant's Deductions of the Principles of Right', in Mark Timmons (ed.), *Kant's Metaphysics of Morals: Interpretative Essays*, Oxford: Oxford University Press, 2002, 23–64, reprinted in Paul Guyer, *Kant's System of Nature and Freedom*, Oxford: Clarendon Press, 2005, 198–242, and 'The Twofold Morality of *Recht*', *Kant-Studien* 107 (2016), 34–63.

[2] I thus agree with the conclusion of Philipp-Alexander Hirsch (*Freiheit und Staatlichkeit bei Kant: Die autonomietheoretische Begründung von Recht und Staat und das Widerstandsproblem*, Berlin: De Gruyter, 2017) when he writes that 'Kant's *Rechtslehre* can be sensibly interpreted only as an equally justifiable part of a unitary critical moral philosophy under the categorical imperative as supreme practical principle' (p. 69).

morality, they must be consistent with this premise. In the second part of this chapter, I turn from this foundational question to the question of the role of individual morality in the actual practice of law and politics. Here I argue that although Kant's conception of justice places moral burdens on individuals in the state of nature and on both subjects and rulers in existing states, Kant is particularly concerned to argue that the operations of the juridical and penal institutions of the state, indeed of the state as a whole, are dependent upon the free acts of individual human beings in positions of power, thus that there are no mechanisms that can guarantee the realization of justice through the state apart from the moral conduct of such individuals. All of this makes no sense unless the necessity of the institution and maintenance of the state is a moral duty, that is, the duty of both citizens and rulers to institute and maintain a system of juridical duties is itself a moral duty.

14.1 The Morality of Right

All parties to the debate acknowledge Kant's distinction between duties of Right and Ethics as respectively coercively enforceable or not, and thus that '[a]ll lawgiving can [...] be distinguished with respect to the incentives' (*Triebfedern*) for compliance with it: in the case of *ethical* duty, at least if moral worth is at stake, the moral law that makes an action a duty must also be the incentive for compliance with it; but *juridical* duty 'does not include the incentive of duty in the law and so admits an incentive other than the idea of duty itself' (MS, Introduction, section IV, 6:218–19).[3] Or, '*ethical* laws' 'require that they (the laws) themselves be the determining grounds of action' in compliance with them, while '*juridical* laws', which define the duties of Right, are, first, 'directed merely to external actions and their conformity to law' (MS, Introduction, section II, 6:214), and, second, permit of other, external incentives, that is, '*pathological* determining grounds of choice, inclinations and aversions, and among these, from aversions; for it is a lawgiving, which constrains, not an allurement, which invites' (MS, Introduction, section IV, 6:219). More precisely, ethical duties *require* an internal incentive (*Triebfeder*) or determining ground of choice (*Bestimmungsgrund der Willkür*), in part

[3] I follow Marcus Willaschek (Chapter 1) in capitalizing 'Right' as the translation of *Recht* when it refers to the whole body of coercively enforceable rights rather than to a particular right, and then correspondingly capitalizing 'Ethics' when it refers to the whole body of our non-coercively enforceable duties. Our difference is whether *Recht* is a proper part of morality in general.

because some of them, the duties of virtue properly speaking,[4] involve the adoption of an end rather than the performance of specific actions in specific circumstances, and the adoption of an end always is or at least begins with a mental act, an internal matter,[5] and in part because Ethics aims at moral worth and is thus concerned with the character of our motivation (e.g. TL, Introduction, section XVII, 6:410); juridical duties, however, *allow* the application of coercion as an external incentive or determining ground of choice because they are not concerned with moral worth. 'Ethical lawgiving (even if the duties might be external), is that which *cannot* be external; juridical lawgiving is that which *can* also be external' (MS, Introduction, section IV, 6:220, second emphasis added). But while making this contrast, Kant does not suggest that juridical duties have some ultimate ground different from that of ethical duties, or that the content of juridical duties, what it is that they require of us, is any less derived from the fundamental principle of morality than is the content of ethical duty. Rather, he says, 'The doctrine of right and the doctrine of virtue are [. . .] distinguished not so much by their different duties as by the difference in their lawgiving, which connects one incentive or the other with the law', and an 'obligation is assigned to ethics not because the duty is of a particular kind (a particular kind of action to which one is bound)' – for there are external duties in ethics as well as in right – but rather because the lawgiving in this case is an internal one and can have no external lawgiver. It is because of this that an act required by juridical legislation *can* be performed out of respect for the moral law, and it is morally worthy to do so, although there is no virtue or merit in performing the act in the face of an external incentive, namely a threatened coercive sanction (TL, Introduction, section VII, 6:390–1), while an ethical duty cannot be coercively enforced.[6] Thus Kant writes: 'It is no duty of virtue to keep

[4] Some duties that are not coercively enforceable according to Kant, such as the perfect duties to oneself to avoid suicide and self-mutilation or the duties of respect to others to avoid arrogance, defamation, and ridicule, are therefore ethical duties, and part of what it is to treat oneself and others as ends not merely as means, but they are not part of what it is to adopt the two ends that are also duties, namely self-perfection and the happiness of others, so they are not duties of virtue. See TL, Introduction, section II, 6:383.

[5] Although it could be argued that the adoption of an end begins with a mental act, the formation of an intention, but is not complete without at least the effort to perform some external action designed to realize this end, whether that action is successful or not.

[6] To be sure, outward compliance with ethical duties can be motivated by 'external' incentives such as a concern for one's reputation or even unjustified legislation of what should be ethical duties, but in such cases the agent's motivation will presumably be prudence rather than respect for the moral law, and the end adopted will not be self-perfection or the happiness of others per se, but one's own happiness, or avoidance of unhappiness.

one's promises, but a duty of right, to the performance of which one can be coerced. But it is still a virtuous action (a proof of virtue) to do it even where no coercion may be *applied*, and even though 'it is an external duty to keep a promise made in a contract [. . .] the command to do this merely because it is a duty, without regard for any other incentive, belongs to *internal* lawgiving alone' (MS, Introduction, section IV, 6:220). Juridical duties are just the subset of moral duties that may be coercively enforced, indeed on moral grounds themselves *must* be coercively enforced if the incentive of respect for the moral law is not forthcoming, but they *can* be fulfilled out of respect for the moral law if that is forthcoming; and this is possible just because juridical duties, for example the duty to fulfil contracts, are grounded in the moral law just as much as ethical duties, such as the duties of beneficence and gratitude.[7] Of course one may not have to enter into any contracts at all, but if one does, then it is a moral obligation to fulfil them, but an obligation that may be coercively enforced if the motivation of respect for the moral law is not forthcoming.[8]

One of the strongest proponents of the 'independence' thesis that juridical duties are *not* grounded on the fundamental principle of morality was Allen Wood, but in my opinion he undermined his position in his most recent discussion of the issue when he stated that:

> The universal principle of right [. . .] cannot possibly be based on or derived from the supreme principle of morality [. . .] because a categorical imperative is one that carries the incentive to its obedience with itself, rather than borrowing the incentive from elsewhere. That is what makes the moral law governing ethics a principle of inner self-government, rather than a principle of external constraint.[9]

[7] I argue that this was the standard approach to the distinction between moral duties in general and duties of right in particular, from which Kant shows no signs of departing, in 'Enforcing the Law of Nature: 'The Background to Kant's Conception of the Relation between Morality and *Recht*', in Mark Timmons and Sorin Baiasu (eds.), *Kantian Citizenship. Grounds, Standards and Global Implications*, New York: Routledge, 2025, 15–42. It might also be argued that juridical duties *must* be fulfilled out of the motive of respect for the moral law if the external incentives of a public juridical and penal system are *not* available; see Hirsch, *Freiheit und Staatlichkeit*, 119–20, and Bader in this volume (Chapter 7). However, Kant's insistence that our fundamental *moral* obligation in the state of nature is to institute the state or 'civil condition' obviates this concern.

[8] That is, it is both morally permissible to enter into contracts under certain conditions, and both morally necessary and legally enforceable to satisfy them under appropriate circumstances. 'Permissive' laws, such as laws that certain sorts of contracts (but not all, for example a contract of self-enslavement) may be entered into under certain conditions, thus do not grant exceptions to other moral or legal laws, but simply specify that certain obligations may be undertaken within the law. On the character of permissive law, see Brecher (Chapter 8).

[9] Allen W. Wood, *The Free Development of Each: Studies on Freedom, Right, and Ethics in Classical German Philosophy*, Oxford: Oxford University Press, 2014, 82–3, 93–4.

On the contrary, the fact that we *can* fulfil duties of right from respect for the moral law show that the content of these duties *are* grounded in that law, which presents itself to us in the form of the categorical imperative, and it is the moral law itself that permits and requires the use of coercion to fulfil some of its duties when respect for it will not do the job, and that indeed requires the institution of the state to make sure that this external incentive is available when needed. But I am not going to rehash the detailed objections that I have made to earlier arguments by Wood and other proponents of the 'independence' thesis such as Thomas Pogge and Marcus Willaschek here.[10] Instead, I want to make one simple point on this general issue, and then turn to what I think is the now more interesting and more timely issue of the need for individual morality – virtue – in the actual practice of justice.

My general point is that Kant recognizes only two kinds of practical rationality, namely self-love, including prudent self-love, and morality, so that if Right were not derived from the fundamental principle of morality in general, it could be founded only on self-love or prudence. But that would be Hobbes, not Kant, and Kant clearly means to dissociate himself from Hobbes at the foundational level of his doctrine of right.[11] Clear evidence for Kant's view that there are only two possible kinds of practical rationality comes from his *Religion within the Boundaries of Mere Reason*, an indispensable work for all interpretation of Kant's thought in the 1790s (and one which Allen Wood, the editor of *Religion and Rational Theology* in the Cambridge edition of Kant as well as of a current commentary on it, knows as well as anyone).[12] Here Kant states that there are only two fundamental dispositions or maxims in human beings, the moral law and self-love, and that evil consists in subordinating morality to self-love:

> The human being (even the worst) does not repudiate the moral law, whatever his maxims, in rebellious attitude [...] The law rather imposes itself upon him irresistibly, because of his moral predisposition; and if no other incentive were at work against it, he would also incorporate it into his supreme maxim as sufficient determination of his power of choice, i.e., he would be morally good. He is, however, also dependent on the incentives of his sensuous nature because of his equally innocent natural predisposition,

[10] See again my 'Kant's Deductions of the Principles of Right' and 'The Twofold Morality of *Recht*'.

[11] See also TP, section II. For commentary, see my '"Hobbes is of the opposite opinion": Kant and Hobbes on the Three Authorities in the State', *Hobbes Studies* 25 (2012), 91–119; and Howard Williams, *Kant's Critique of Hobbes*, Cardiff: University of Wales Press, 2003.

[12] Allen W. Wood, *Kant and Religion*, Oxford: Oxford University Press, 2020.

> and he incorporates them too into his maxim (according to the subjective principle of self-love).

However,

> If he took them into his maxim *as of themselves sufficient* for the determination of his power of choice, without minding the moral law (which he nonetheless has within himself), he would then become morally evil. [. . .] Hence the difference, whether the human being is good or evil, must not lie in the difference between the incentives that he incorporates into his maxims (not in the material of the maxim) but in their *subordination* (in the form of the maxim): *which of the two he makes the condition of the other*. (RGV, Part I, 6:36)

The form of evil is to subordinate morality to self-love, whatever particular form self-love takes (always favouring oneself, favouring one's own children, etc.); the form of good is to subordinate self-love to morality, whatever morality happens to require (a large sacrifice, or not).[13]

This is not to say that juridical duties founded on self-love would be evil; they would be evil only if so founded they were also allowed to override all conflicting moral obligations. But it does show that for Kant there are only two fundamental sources of motivation, self-love and morality, and that if he rejects the foundation of juridical duties in self-love, as he clearly does, then there is no alternative foundation in practical rationality for them other than morality. There is no third kind of practical rationality.

This is also clear in Kant's earlier, foundational works in moral philosophy. Going back first to the *Critique of Practical Reason*, we see that Kant commences the argument of the book with the division of 'practical principles' into 'material' and 'formal' ones. Material practical principles are those 'that presuppose an *object* (matter) of the faculty of desire as the determining ground of the will' (KpV 5:21), and Kant asserts that 'All material practical principles as such are, without exception, of one and the same kind and come under the general principle of self-love or one's own happiness' (5:22). A formal practical principle, in contrast, is one that contains 'the determining ground of the will not by [its] matter but only by [its] form', and there is only one candidate for such a principle: 'all that

[13] Kant notoriously distinguishes 'three different grades of [the] natural propensity to evil', frailty, impurity, and depravity (RGV 6:29–30). We might understand this distinction as establishing a range of frequency, from occasionally allowing oneself to subordinate morality to self-love to always doing so, but the underlying principle of allowing oneself to subordinate morality to self-love is the same in all cases.

remains of a law if one separates from it everything material, that is, every object of the will (as its determining ground), is the mere *form* of giving universal law' (5:27), in other words, the 'Fundamental Law of Pure Practical Reason', 'So act that the maxim of your will could always hold at the same time as a principle in a giving of universal law' (5:30). In other words, there are two kinds of practical principles, material and formal, the principle of self-love and the moral law, and if the foundation of the Universal Principle of Right, as a practical principle, is not to be simply a matter of enlightened, prudent self-interest, as in Hobbes, then it can only be, whatever the precise details, the moral law.

We get the same result if we consider Kant's division of imperatives in the *Groundwork for the Metaphysics of Morals*. There of course Kant first divides all imperatives into two classes, hypothetical and categorical, the first those that represent an action as "good merely as a means *to something else*", the latter those that represent an action 'as *in itself good*, hence as necessary in a will in itself conforming to reason' (GMS 4:414). Kant then divides the class of hypothetical imperatives into two practical principles, 'problematic' and 'assertoric', the first of which say only that 'an action is good for some *possible*' purpose and the second of which say that an action is good for some '*actual*' purpose. The former, which Kant also calls 'imperatives of *skill*' (4:415) and 'technical' imperatives (4:416), prescribe means to ends that someone may or may not want to adopt, such as 'If you want to cure this patient, use this medicine', but also 'if you want to kill that patient, use that poison'. The latter, which Kant also calls 'pragmatic' (4:416), are general rules of 'prudence' for 'one's own greatest well-being' or happiness, 'a purpose that can be presupposed surely and *a priori* in the case of every human being, because it belongs to his essence' (4:415–16). However, as Kant makes clear in the *Critique of the Power of Judgment*, technical imperatives are just 'corollaries of theoretical philosophy' (KdU, Introduction, section I, 5:172) – theoretical propositions like 'This chemical causes these effects' are the basis for hypothetical imperatives like 'If you want to cure this patient, use this medicine' – so there is a sense in which these are not imperatives of practical reason at all; and we might also observe that we will need such 'corollaries of theoretical philosophy' in properly moral cases as well, like 'If you are to be beneficent to these persons, this is the (or the most) effective way to do it.' So these technical imperatives, while they are not by themselves sufficient for any principle of practical reason, are necessary for the exercise of pure as well as empirical practical reason, or we need them for purposes of either prudence or morality, and once again we end up with only those as the two main kinds of practical reason. But then, Kant also argues that pragmatic imperatives are not really 'determinate principles for the sake of being happy, but only [. . .] empirical counsels', or recommendations for happiness that depend on contingent circumstances, including any particular person's desires, since the same-sounding goal of 'happiness' is in fact nothing but the global satisfaction of any particular person's desires, which of course vary from person to person, from time to time even for the same person, and so on. Happiness is not really a single thing at all, thus there cannot be a single technical imperative stating how to achieve it. So although the ultimate moral choice for any person remains that between prudence or happiness on the one hand and morality on the other, this is not really a choice between two imperatives; it is a choice between a mere counsel or rule of thumb on the one hand and the only genuine imperative, the moral, categorical imperative, on the other. And this means that any recommendation of laws or a juridical condition based on prudence will be merely that, a mere recommendation dependent on particular circumstances, and not a genuine universal principle of Right at all, something that one might honour as long as it seems prudent but that one can violate if doing that seems prudent. A genuine universal principle of right can be founded only on the fundamental principle of morality.[14]

So when Kant says, in the Preface to the *Metaphysics of Morals*, that 'For the *doctrine of right*, the first part of the doctrine of morals, there is required a system derived from reason which could be called the *metaphysics of right*' (MS 6:205), he can only mean that the doctrine of Right, as part of morality, is derived from pure practical reason, thus from the fundamental principle of morality in some form. The only alternative would be that it is derived from prudence, but that is not an alternative for Kant. To be sure, as Kant goes on to explain, the 'concept of Right' – in this just like the concept of ethical obligation that will follow – 'is a pure concept that still looks to practice (application to cases that come up in experience', so a '*metaphysical system* of Right [will] also have to take

[14] Some 'independence' theorists have taken Kant's notorious remark that 'The problem of establishing a state, no matter how hard it may sound, is *soluble* even for a nation of devils (if only they have understanding)' (ZeF, First Supplement, 8:366) as evidence for their claim that Right need not be grounded on morality. But I take this remark to mean only that while a population of purely self-interested agents can figure out, like good Hobbesians, what the laws of a state should be ('as long as they have understanding'), they would be, severally, motivated to institute and maintain a state to enforce those laws only when they thought, severally, that it would be in their own interest – and that they would all always think so could never be relied upon. See Hirsch, *Freiheit und Staatlichkeit*, 156ff., and Ludwig (Chapter 2) and Hirsch (Chapter 5) in this volume.

account, in its divisions, of the empirical varieties of such cases', or as he says later, in the Introduction, 'a metaphysics of morals', which we have just seen must include the doctrine of Right as well as the doctrine of virtue, 'cannot dispense with principles of application, and we shall often have to take as our object the particular *nature* of human beings, which is cognized only by experience, in order to *show* in it what can be inferred from universal moral principles' (MS, Introduction, section I, 6:217). More fully, the doctrine of Right must apply the universal principle of morality in light of certain empirical but basic facts about the conditions of human interaction, such as that human beings need to have access to land and its products on the finite surface of a terraqueous globe populated by other human beings with similar needs, while the doctrine of virtue must apply the universal principle of morality in light of certain basic but still only empirically known facts about human natures, such as that humans need to perfect their physical, intellectual, and other mental capacities, for these are hardly developed at birth, and can rarely survive and flourish solely on their own resources and thus can need aid from others and must be prepared to extend aid to others. But the present point is just that in both cases these derivations of the juridical and ethical duties of human beings begin with the *same* 'universal moral principles' or more precisely principle.

Having said this, I will not delve into the details of the derivation of the Universal Principle of Right from the fundamental principle of morality beyond saying that Kant's category of the innate right to freedom, on which the further categories of private right and public right depend – private right because our innate right to freedom of action means that we all have an equal right to acquire land, goods, and services from others on mutually agreeable terms, and public right as the mechanism for making both the innate right to freedom and the acquired rights that we can acquire through the exercise of the former under appropriate conditions (as specified by permissive laws) determinate and secure[15] – can most readily be seen as derived from the formulation of the categorical imperative as the demand always to treat the humanity in every person, oneself and everyone else, as an end and never merely as a means (GMS 4:428, 429). Kant states that '*Freedom* (independence from being constrained by another's choice),

[15] See Arthur Ripstein, *Force and Freedom: Kant's Legal and Political Philosophy*, Cambridge, MA: Harvard University Press, 2009, especially 145–81, and Guyer, 'Kant's System of Duties', in *Kant's System of Nature and Freedom: Kant's System of Nature and Freedom*, Oxford: Clarendon Press, 2005, 242–74, especially 258, and Guyer, *Kant*, 2nd ed., London: Routledge, 2014, 303–51, especially 315.

insofar as it can coexist with the freedom of every other in accordance with a universal law, is the only original right belonging to every person [*Menschen*] by virtue of his humanity' (RL 6:237), and this innate right is just the correlative of our fundamental moral obligation to treat every instance of humanity, which is itself the capacity of human beings to set their own ends (TL, Introduction, 6:387, 392), as an end and never merely as a means.[16]

So much for the general framework within which Kant argues for the dependence of Right upon morality. What I now want to emphasize is, first, that in Kant's view the moral foundation of the principle of Right places every human being under the obligation, in conditions in which contact with other cannot be avoided, to enter into and maintain a civil condition or state with those others, and even gives anyone the moral right to *compel* others to enter into and maintain a state with them – certainly nothing that could be derived from the foundation of Right upon mere prudence – and, second, that in Kant's view, those in positions of authority and power in a state, who have no one *else* to *coerce* them into instituting, maintaining, and when need be improving the condition of justice, *must* be, because they *can only* be, motivated by their own respect for the *moral* law to rule justly. Or in other words, although *subjects* in an extant state can be seen as having a juridical duty, enforceable by external, aversive incentives, that is, coercion in the form of the threat and when necessary the application of sanctions, to act justly, *rulers* may be seen as having what is essentially a moral duty, enforceable only by their own respect for the moral law and in that sense an ethical duty, to rule justly.

Human beings in a state of nature who cannot avoid contact with each other, and who thereby cannot avoid threatening each other with an abridgement of their freedom, have a moral duty to enter into the civil condition, or a state. But human beings rarely if ever actually exist in a state of nature, so this duty translates into a moral duty to maintain the existence of the state in which they find themselves (along with the right to move to another), which in turn entails a duty not to return their state to a

[16] My position is thus close to that of Hirsch in *Freiheit und Staatlichkeit*, e.g. pp. 70ff. and 227ff., and to those developed in this volume by, for example, Ludwig (Chapter 2) and Kleingeld (Chapter 13). Willaschek in this volume (Chapter 1) objects to my foundation of all Right on the innate right to freedom and on the respect due to humanity as an end in itself that it entails that there would be juridical rights and obligations in the state of nature, which is a contradiction. My response is that the 'right of humanity' does exist in the state of nature: that is precisely what obligates us to exit the state of nature in order to make both innate and acquired right determinate and secure. More on this in Section 14.2.

condition of anarchy – Kant's famous denial of a right to rebellion. Rulers have a moral obligation to maintain the civil condition, but since historically rulers tend not to be duly elected officials but people who by some historical chain of events find themselves in positions of power, that translates into a duty to transform their less just states into more just ones. Both citizens and rulers may be considered to have juridical duties within extant states, but the duties to institute and maintain just states, in other words to institute and maintain a legitimate system of coercive enforcement, cannot themselves be juridical duties, on pain of infinite regress. They are moral duties that must be motivated, at some point, simply by respect for the moral law. They are not *duties of virtue* to realize either of the two ends that are also duties, self-perfection and promotion of the happiness of others – Kant's forceful rejection of paternalistic government makes that clear for the case of rulers (TP 8:290–1). But they are *ethical duties* that require motivation by respect for the moral law.

Let us now look at the steps of this argument in a little more detail.

14.2 Crooked Timber and Moral Politicians

Kant is famous for the metaphor that trees growing 'in freedom, and separated from one another, [. . .] put forth their branches as they like, [and] grow stunted, crooked, and awry', while 'trees in a forest, precisely because each of them seeks to take air and sun from the other, are constrained to look for them above themselves, and thereby achieve a beautiful straight growth' (IaG, Fifth Proposition, 8:22):[17] that is, humans whose internal incentives would not suffice for them to act justly can nevertheless be coerced into acting justly by a properly constituted and administered state. Thus they can act justly without being motivated morally, that is, by respect for the moral law. True enough, perhaps, allowing for that degree of criminality, let us hope relatively low, that persists even in the best-run state. True enough, also, only within a properly constituted and maintained state. But when such a state does not exist, its existence is morally demanded and can even be compelled, and it cannot be compelled, that is, forced on others, out of mere prudence, by people motivated merely by prudence, but must be brought into being by the internally – morally – motivated action of some body of agents. This is why a nation of devils can solve the problem of a just state intellectually, but cannot actually will one into existence (see again ZeF

[17] Kant uses the metaphor again at RGV, Part III, Division One, section IV, 6:100.

8:366). But also, once such states have been brought into existence, even with the properly constituted division of powers among lawmakers, executives, and magistrates demanded by Kant's conception of republican government (RL, §45, 6:313), there will be nobody who can coerce *them* in into correctly carrying out their obligations and maintaining the state in a condition of justice. Politicians must be, in Kant's term, moral politicians.

14.2.1 The Moral Duties of Citizens

First, then, the obligation of human beings who cannot avoid interaction with one another to enter into and maintain just states is a moral obligation.[18] This is the import of the 'postulate of public right' that is placed at the transition from Private Right to Public Right. The transition begins with the statement that 'A rightful condition is that relation of human beings among one another that contains the condition under which alone everyone is able to *enjoy* his rights, and the formal condition under which this is possible in accordance with the idea of a will giving laws for everyone is called public justice' (RL, §41, 6:305–6). This is a restatement of the Universal Principle of Right including an allusion to the rights that by this point in Kant's exposition have been established, namely the innate right to freedom of every individual and the rights to acquisition of property rights, contract rights, and rights to persons akin to rights of things that are the consequences of the innate right to freedom. Everyone's innate right to freedom, as we saw, is the correlative of everyone's obligation to respect the humanity in everyone, and so is clearly grounded in morality not prudence; thus when Kant goes on to describe the formal condition under which the rightful condition as 'accordance with the idea of a will giving laws for everyone', this too must derive from the categorical imperative, in this case from the first formulation of the categorical imperative which states that requirement of universal validity (GMS, section I, 4:402, section II, 4:421; KpV 'Fundamental Law of Pure Practical Reason', 5:30). Kant then states that the 'condition of public Right' 'contains no further or other duties of human beings among themselves than can be conceived in' private Right, rather 'the matter of private Right is the same in both' and 'The laws of the condition of public

[18] I have previously discussed the duties of citizens in the Kantian state in 'Civic Responsibility and the Kantian Social Contract', in Herta Nagl-Docekal and Rudolf Langthaler (eds.), *Recht – Geschichte – Religion: Die Bedeutung Kants für die Gegenwart*, Berlin: Akademie Verlag, 2004, 27–48.

Right [. . .] have to do only with the rightful form of [. . .] association (constitution), in view of which these laws must necessarily be conceived as public' (6:306); that is, public Right is the enforcement of conceptually prior rights of 'association' by the instruments of a state.[19] That is misleading in one, minor way: since the division of powers in a genuine condition of public right, that is, a properly constituted republic, creates certain rights of officeholders against one another and rights of subjects against their rulers as well as obligations to them, the 'laws of the condition of public right' have to include those rights and obligations. Further, the rights of 'association' that the state is instituted to secure must include innate as well as acquired Right. If the state exists to enforce rights that are conceptually antecedent to public Right, then it has to enforce innate as well as acquired rights, or to make innate as well as acquired rights determinate and secure[20] – for example, what precisely will count as working for another without violating one's right to be one's own master, or what will count as permissible free speech, needs to be legally defined and enforced just as much as property lines need to be. But the main point here is that if innate Right is grounded in the fundamental principle of morality and the possibility of acquired, private Right is grounded in innate right and is therefore also derived from the fundamental principle of morality, although with one extra step, then, as Kant next makes clear, the necessity of public Right is also morally grounded, and it is a moral obligation as well as permission to bring it about. This is what Kant makes clear with the 'postulate of public Right': 'when you cannot avoid living side by side with all others, you ought to leave the state of nature and proceed with them into a rightful condition' (RL, §42, 6:307). This is not a juridical 'ought' entailed by the laws of an extant state, but a moral 'ought', obligatory for those who find themselves in a state of nature with other people – and for any in an extant state who might want to undermine or destroy that state. It is not a matter of prudence. Kant states that the 'ground of this postulate can be developed analytically from the concept of *right* in external relations, in contrast with *violence*', but this does not mean that this postulate is independent of the fundamental principle of morality, because the concept of Right itself has been grounded on the fundamental principle of morality, beginning with innate Right.

[19] Kant resolves the tension between Hobbes, who held that there are no rights in the state of nature, and Locke, who held that there are and that the state is instituted to protect them, by means of his distinction between 'provisional' and 'conclusive' claims to rights. I will explain this shortly.

[20] See note 9.

Only a moral foundation can explain how individuals in the state of nature are under an *obligation* to institute a state and have the *right* to compel others who would resist the institution of a state to join them. Kant states that 'No one is bound to refrain from encroaching on what another possesses if the other gives him no assurance that he will observe the same restraint toward him' (RL 6:307). This may sound like a matter of mere prudence, or a natural right grounded in self-preservation, as in Hobbes or Achenwall.[21] But Kant continues in moral terms. First he states that 'No one is bound to refrain from encroaching on what another possesses if the other gives him no equal assurance that he will observe the same restraint toward him', and further 'it is not necessary to wait for actual hostility; one is authorized to use coercion against someone who already, by his nature, threatens him with coercion'. This might still sound like mere prudence, and it may be from the point of view of prudence that Kant further states that 'Given the intention to be and to remain in this state of externally lawless freedom, men do *one another* no wrong at all when they feud among themselves' (6:307). But he then takes the moral point of view when he adds that 'in general they do wrong in the highest degree* by willing to be and to remain in a condition that is not rightful' (6:307–8), and adds the note at the asterisk that this is a distinction between what is 'materially wrong' and what is 'formally wrong'.[22] The latter is, of course, an indication of *moral* wrong, so what Kant means is that while refusing to enter into the juridical condition and thereby exposing oneself to the preventative measures of others may be imprudent or not, depending upon the circumstances, refusing to enter into a state is always morally wrong, therefore all who cannot avoid contact with others altogether have a duty to enter into the judicial condition. This could not be so if entering into this condition were merely a matter of prudence.

Kant raises the question how one person can rightfully acquire property when rightful acquisition requires that the division and acquisition of land or other assets concerned could be the subject of an 'omnilateral will', that is, the possible agreement to the division among all who could lay any

[21] See Thomas Hobbes, *De Cive: The English Version*, ed. by Howard Warrender, Oxford: Clarendon Press, 1983, ch. I, paragraphs VII–IX, p. 47, and *Leviathan*, ed. by Noel Malcolm, Oxford: Clarendon Press, 2012, English text, vol. 2, ch. XIV, p. 214: 'A Covenant not to defend my selfe from force, by force, is always voyd.' Or Gottfried Achenwall, *Natural Law*, ed. by Pauline Kleingeld, trans. by Corinna Vermeulen, with an introduction by Paul Guyer, New York and London: Bloomsbury, 2020, Part I, §37: 'Because I am naturally obliged to preserve my body and life, I have the natural right, as a moral ability, to remove obstacles to my preservation' (p. 14). See also Hirsch, *Freiheit und Staatlichkeit*, 214ff.

[22] On this distinction, see Hirsch in this volume (Chapter 5).

claim to the property, when the rightful condition does not yet exist. His answer to this is his distinction between 'provisional' (*provisorisch*) and 'conclusive' (*peremptorisch*) acquisition or possession (following Achenwall's concept of 'conditional' obligation).[23] His idea is that the acquisition of property is not in fact determinate, secure, and rightful in the absence of an omnilateral will and its expression in a juridical condition, but that antecedent to the realization of that condition individuals can rightfully acquire property if they do so with the *intention* of establishing a juridical condition and in a way that is compatible with the emergence of such a condition and can lead to it: 'something external can be *originally* acquired only in conformity with the idea of a civil condition, that is, with a view to it and to its being brought about, but prior to its realization [. . .] Hence *original* acquisition can be only *provisional*. – *Conclusive* acquisition takes place only in the civil condition' (RL, §15, 6:264). In a state of nature, prudence requires that you take as much but only as much as you reasonably think you can get away with, given whatever forces you possess. Only morality requires that your acquisitions even in a state of nature be subject to the constraint of the *idea* of the possibility of an omnilateral will, and that you indeed attempt to bring about the actual juridical or civil condition that will make your possession conclusive. Only morality can justify the 'principle of private right, in accordance with which each is justified in using that coercion which is necessary if people are to leave the state of nature and enter into the civil condition, which can alone make any acquisition conclusive' (6:264). Prudence would allow and indeed require you to take as much property as you can and defend it with whatever means you can; only morality requires you to take only as much property as is compatible with an omnilateral will and then allows or even requires you to compel others to enter into a juridical condition in which the possessions of all are conclusive. (Of course Kant does not think that an omnilateral will must be established by the actual consent of everyone affected to every particular property claim; it is established by a system of laws concerning property to which everyone could freely consent.)

Thus Kant argues that individuals in a state of nature have a moral obligation to exit that state and enter into a civil condition and have a moral right and even an obligation to compel others to join them in that condition. He also argues that once in a civil condition, that is, once they are subjects of a state, individuals have a moral obligation to maintain the

[23] Achenwall, *Natural Law*, Part I, §109, p. 39.

existence of that state and avoid relapse into a state of nature. This is evident in Kant's denial of the possibility of a right to rebellion against an existing government.[24] Kant has several specific arguments against a right to rebellion. One is that a rebellion in the hope of greater *happiness* than under a current regime would be unjustified because the business of government is not to promote happiness (TP, section II, 8:298); the hope for greater happiness is no more a justification for rebellion than it is for paternalistic government. But this argument seems irrelevant to the case in which people would rebel against the *injustice* of an existing government. More plausible is Kant's constitutional argument that a right of rebellion against the designated supreme authority in a state would be incoherent because then the supreme authority would not be the supreme authority after all, but neither would be the people, so there would be no supreme authority, and therefore really no state at all (TP, section II, 8:299–300; RL, General Remark A, 6:319–20). But Kant's main idea is simply that rebellion exchanges a juridical condition, however imperfect, for a condition of lawlessness or anarchy – a return to the state of nature – and that if it is wrong to *remain* in the state of nature, then it is also wrong to *return* to the state of nature – morally wrong, that is, just as it is morally wrong to refuse to leave the state of nature in the first place. Even if a better state might emerge from a rebellion, a happier or even a more just state, the *process* of rebellion necessarily includes a phase of anarchy when the old state has been destroyed and the new one not yet created: 'the previously existing constitution has been torn up by the people, while their organization into a new commonwealth has not yet taken place. It is here that the condition of anarchy arises with all the horrors that are at least possible by means of it'. Thus Kant holds that the people do 'wrong in the highest degree by seeking their rights in this way; for this way of doing it (adopting it as a maxim) would make every rightful constitution insecure and introduce a condition of complete lawlessness (*status naturalis*), in which all rights cease, at least to have effect' (TP, section II, 8:301–2 and note). Again, Kant's use of the phrase 'wrong in the highest degree' indicates that this is not a matter of prudence, but of morality. So individuals have an obligation to enter into the civil condition, and once in it to remain in it.

[24] There is of course an extensive literature on this subject. For a few items, see Ripstein, *Force and Freedom*, 325–52; B. Sharon Byrd and Joachim Hruschka, *Kant's* Doctrine of Right: *A Commentary*, Cambridge: Cambridge University Press, 2010, 181–4; Reidar Maliks, *Kant's Politics in Context*, Oxford: Oxford University Press, 2014, 112–43l; Wood, *Free Development*, 79–9; and Hirsch, *Freiheit und Staatlichkeit*, 337–421.

They should of course have the right to petition the authorities in an imperfect civil condition to reform and improve it (*TP*, section II, 8:30304), and perhaps they even have a moral obligation to petition for reform. But the moral obligation to reform an existing civil condition in the direction of a more ideally just one falls primarily on the shoulders of those who are in a position of power in such a state. Individuals in a state of nature and subjects in an existing state have the moral obligation to enter into and maintain such a state. But authorities – politicians – have the obligation to reform it, or as Kant puts it, to be moral politicians.

14.2.2 The Moral Obligations of Rulers

The granddaddy passage on this subject is the Sixth Proposition of Kant's 1784 'Idea for a Universal History with a Cosmopolitan Aim'.[25] After having argued in the Fifth Proposition that the solution to potentially wayward *subjects* is a 'perfectly *just civil constitution*' that will if necessary subdue their 'wild freedom' with coercion and make them grow straight like trees in a forest (IAG 8:22), Kant raises a problem in the Sixth, namely that 'the *master*, who breaks [the subject's] stubborn will and necessitates him to obey a universally valid will with which everyone can be free', *must himself be found* in 'such crooked wood as the human being is made', from 'which nothing entirely straight can be fabricated', and 'who has no authority over *him* to exercise authority over him in accordance with the laws' (8:23, emphasis added). On pain of an infinite regress, at some point the chain of authority must stop with an actual human being or group of humans (a 'natural' or 'moral person' in Hobbes's terminology) who have no one to exercise coercion over *them*, and who are subject to the same temptation to misuse their freedom as is any other human being. So if a prudent regard for coercion will not restrain rulers from exploiting their own authority, what can? Only morality. Thus, although a 'perfect solution' to this problem 'is impossible [. . .] the approximation to this idea is laid upon us by nature'. Writing in his teleological voice, Kant is disposed to attribute our moral end to nature itself, but this is definitely not an appeal to prudence. On the contrary, the solution is morality on the part of

[25] I have previously discussed this passage in 'The Crooked Timber of Humankind', in Amelie Rorty and James Schmidt (eds.), *Kant's 'Idea for a Universal History with a Cosmopolitan Aim': A Critical Guide*, Cambridge: Cambridge University Press, 2009, 129–49. On the moral obligations of rulers, see also my 'Kant and the Moral Politicians', in Kyriakos N. Demetriou and Antis Loizides (eds.), *Scientific Statesmanship, Governance, and the History of Political Philosophy*, London: Routledge, 2015, 116–36, and Wood, *Free Development*, 90–118.

rulers: 'it requires correct concepts of the nature of a possible constitution, great experience practiced through many courses of life, and beyond this a good will that is prepared to accept' that constitution (8:23). We may regard each of these as a necessary condition, with their conjunction a sufficient condition for the approximation to an ideally just civil condition; the list makes it clear that a *good will*, that is, respect for the moral law, is among the necessary conditions for 'masters', authorities, or politicians to realize and maintain justice. Since there is no one to force them into acting as morality requires, only their own respect for morality can make them do so – and if it is only their good will, or respect for the moral law, that can lead them to improve the civil condition, then their doing so must itself be a requirement of morality, not a mere matter of prudence for themselves or anyone else.

A decade later, Kant reiterates the moral burden on rulers to improve the justice of their states in an Appendix to his pamphlet *Towards Perpetual Peace*.[26] This work is written in the form of a proposed treaty to bring about perpetual peace among states accompanied by recommendations to their rulers in the Appendix. Perpetual peace is a moral requirement for human beings, as Kant says in the *Metaphysics of Morals* 'the entire final end of the doctrine of right within the limits of mere right" (RL, Conclusion, 6:355), which is to say pure practical reason. The treaty itself is divided between 'preliminary' and 'definitive' articles, the former stating conditions that must be observed during the current and usual condition of warfare among states to make eventual peace even possible and the latter those conditions that will make it actual. It might be noted that this structure mirrors the distinction between provisional and conclusive acquisition of property in Kant's theory of the latter. Chief among the definitive articles is that each state must become a republic, for Kant holds the (empirical) view that republics responsive to the genuine interests of their citizens will be loath to make war upon one another (ZeF, 8:350). In the Appendix, Kant then holds that the transition of present states to genuine republics is the responsibility of 'moral politicians', who 'take the principles of political prudence in such a way that they can coexist with morals', in other words who subordinate self-interest and prudence to morality, just as demanded by Kant's *Religion* two years before *Towards Perpetual Peace*, rather than 'political moralists', who frame their 'morals to suit the statesman's interest'. Kant then writes:

[26] Again, there is a vast literature on this work. For my own interpretation, see 'The Possibility of Perpetual Peace', in Luigi Caranti (ed.), *Kant's Perpetual Peace: New Interpretative Essays*, Rome: LUISS University Press, 2006, 161–81.

> A moral politician will make it his principle that, once defects that could not have been prevented are found within a state or in the relations of states, it is a duty, especially for heads of state, to be concerned about how they can be improved as soon as possible and brought into conformity with natural right, which stands before us as a model in the idea of reason, even at the cost of sacrifices to their self-seeking. [. . .] it can be required of the one in power that he at least take to heart the maxim that such an alteration is necessary, in order to keep constantly approaching the end (of the best constitution in accordance with laws of right). A state can already *govern* itself in a republican way even though, by its present constitution, it possesses a despotic *ruling power* [*Herrschermacht*] [. . .] (ZeF, Appendix, 8:372)

Kant's language is moral throughout: the goal of republican government is a requirement of natural right, itself an idea of reason; the burden of transforming a state from a despotism into a republic falls on the head or heads of state; and it requires them to be moral politicians 'who take to heart the maxim that such an alteration is necessary', not mere political moralists who might or might not undertake such a transformation, depending on what they think is in their self-interest – giving a little to their subjects if they think that will allow them to keep their crown (as Louis XVI wrongly thought), or toughing it out if they think that will let them keep their crown (as Charles I wrongly thought). Of course the burden of the transformation of existing states must fall on their rulers rather than on their subjects, since the subjects have been deprived of the right to do that by the means of rebellion; but in the absence of the possibility of coercion either by their subjects or by anyone over them, Kant uses his most moralistic language to stress that nothing but their own moral will, or the determination of their will by the moral law, can force rulers to undertake this transition even when they might not see it as in their personal interest: they must 'take to heart the maxim that such an alteration is necessary', that is, morally necessary.

What does this mean in practice? The essay on that subject, which was clearly present in Kant's mind as he wrote the Appendix to *Towards Perpetual Peace*[27] – the Appendix begins with the statement that 'Morals is of itself practical in the objective sense, as the sum of laws commanding unconditionally, in accordance with which we *ought* to act, and it is patently absurd, having granted this concept of duty its authority, to want to say that one nevertheless *cannot* do it. [. . .] (hence no conflict of practice with theory)' (ZeF, Appendix, 8:370) – makes it clear that rulers must

[27] See also Wood, *Free Development*, 91–2.

fulfil their duty by extending to their subjects the right to criticize the government and petition for reform. The *Metaphysics of Morals* then makes it clear that rulers also have the moral obligation to *act* upon such criticisms and petitions and actually reform their governments. First, there is Kant's explication of the right to criticize and petition – which implies the obligation of governors to extend this right – in 'Theory and Practice':

> A nonrecalcitrant subject must be able to assume that his ruler does not *want* to do him any wrong. Accordingly, since every human being still has his inalienable rights [...] a citizen must have, with the approval of the ruler himself, the authorization to make known publicly his opinions about what it is in the ruler's arrangements that seems to him to be a wrong against the commonwealth. [...] Thus *freedom of the pen* – kept within the limits of esteem and law for the constitution within which one lives by the subjects' liberal way of thinking [...] – is the sole palladium of the people's rights. For to want to deny them this freedom is not only tantamount to taking from them any claim to a right with a respect to the supreme commander (according to Hobbes), but is also to withhold from the latter – whose will gives order to the subjects as citizens only by representing the general will of the people – all knowledge of matters that he himself would change if he knew about them and to put him in contradiction within himself. (TP 8:304)

This is a rich passage. It is one of the places where Kant makes clear his distance from Hobbes, who not only holds that transferring one's power to a ruler is an act of prudence but also holds that this grant of power must be absolute, exempting only the right to self-defence against the ruler which is simply a natural disposition that the subject cannot give up. (At the same time, Kant aligns himself instead with Rousseau by stating that the ruler properly gives orders to the people only as a representative of the general will).[28] Rather, Kant holds that the right to make their opinions known is a right that the people retain against a ruler, and, as a right, it implies that the ruler has an obligation to recognize this right. Although of course the people themselves must exercise their right 'within the limits of esteem (*Hochachtung*) and love for the constitution', that is, within the limits of their *own* juridical obligations, and the limits of morality more generally, of which their juridical obligations are part – Kant's term *Hochachtung*, a variation of his basic term *Achtung* for the virtuous attitude to the moral law, links the political obligations of the people to morality. Finally, Kant's phrase that the ruler will be *in contradiction* with himself suggests that his obligation to grant the people the right to bring to his attention defects in

[28] See Hirsch, *Freiheit und Stattlichkeit*, 17–21.

his constitution or administration also suggests that this is a moral obligation, for Kant's basic idea is that immorality is a self-contradiction of pure practical reason, a state in which one denies one's own and others' purely rational will even as one must admit it.[29]

As I said, in the *Metaphysics of Morals* Kant then makes clear that rulers have the obligation to respond to the proper calls for reform by their subjects. After rejecting the right to rebellion in that work, Kant then states that 'A change in a (defective) constitution, which may certainly be necessary at times, can therefore be carried out only through *reform* by the sovereign itself, but not by the people, and therefore not by *revolution*; and when such a change takes place this reform can affect only the *executive authority*, not the legislative' (RL, General Remark A, 6:321–2). If the people cannot reform their government by rebellion, it must be reformed by the government itself; and if, as *Towards Perpetual Peace* has made clear, it is a moral obligation to reform the government, in the direction of a genuinely republican regime, then it is not just the right but also the obligation of the government to undertake this reform. Kant assigns this right and obligation to the executive rather than the legislative authority because while the legislature can write laws, it is the executive who puts them into effect; and in particular, if there is going to be any coercion involved – as there inevitably will be, because in any reform there are going to be some who will see their own interests as being harmed and will be disposed to resist the change – then it must be the executive which exercises that coercion, because the division of powers in a Kantian republic reserves the coercive enforcement of law to the executive (RL, §49, 6:316–17).[30] But Kant also emphasizes that the people, in the person of their duly representative legislature or parliament, have the "negative" right of refusal 'to accede to every demand the government puts forth as necessary for administering the state' (where here 'government' must mean the executive) (RL, General Remark A, 6:322), and here one could add that even though only the executive can enforce the laws necessary for an improvement in justice, it must be the prerogative of the legislature to write those laws. Without worrying about the details, perhaps we can

[29] For further development of this approach, see Paul Guyer, *Kant on the Rationality of Morality*, Cambridge: Cambridge University Press, 2019.

[30] On Kant's approach to the division of powers in republican government, see Ripstein, *Force and Freedom*, 173–6; Byrd and Hruschka, *Commentary*, 143–67; and Guyer, 'Achenwall, Kant, and the Division of Governmental Powers', in Margit Ruffing, Annika Schlitte, and Gianluca Sadun Bordoni (eds.), *Kants Naturrecht Feyerabend: Analysen und Perspektiven*, Berlin: De Gruyter, 2020, 201–28.

simply conclude that for the purposes of approximating the ideal of justice in the civil condition, the people have the right to criticize the state, in the form of all three of its authorities (legislature, executive, and judiciary; see RL, §45, 6:313), the state must recognize that right, and the state must act to address those criticisms and resolve them. These are rights of the citizens that may be considered juridical rights, grounded in moral obligations, while the obligations of the rulers, since no one can coerce them, can only be ethical obligations, again grounded in their moral obligations.

Kant grounds the demands of Right on the fundamental principle of morality, not prudence; and only such a foundation of Right makes sense of his account of the moral obligations of citizens to enter into and maintain a state and rulers to administer the state in the way that he demands that they must. By way of conclusion, this passage from *The Conflict of the Faculties*, Kant's own concluding work,[31] sums up his position very nicely:

> The idea of a constitution in harmony with the natural right of human beings, one namely in which citizens obedient to the law, besides being united, ought also to be legislative, lies at the basis of all political forms [. . .] Consequently it is a duty to enter into such a system of government, but it is provisionally the duty of the monarchs, if they rule *as autocrats*, to govern in a *republican* (not democratic) way, that is, to treat people according to principles that are commensurate with the spirit of laws of freedom (as a nation with mature understanding would prescribe them for itself), although they would not be literally canvassed for their consent. (SF 7:90–1)

To be sure, Kant's claim that even in the absence of an ideal system of government an actual government should rule in a republican but not democratic way, and in anticipation and in the direction of an actual republican but not democratic will, sounds jarring to a contemporary ear – but what Kant meant by a 'democratic' government is straightforward rule by a majority on all possible issues, with none of the constitutional guard rails provided by the division of powers and a bill of rights to be found in a genuine republic, whereas what *we* mean by a 'democratic' government is precisely what he meant by a 'republic', that is, a government with a representative legislature expressing the sovereignty of the people but with the guard rails of a division of governmental powers and a guarantee of the components of the innate Right to freedom.[32]

[31] Except perhaps for the textbook on anthropology that he edited out of older notes and the textbooks on pedagogy and physical geography that Rink edited from the same sort of materials.

[32] See Guyer, 'Achenwall, Kant, and the Division of Governmental Powers' and 'Is Sovereignty Divided Still Sovereignty? Kant and *The Federalist*', *University of Pittsburgh Law Review* 83 (2021), 365–96.

Bibliography

Throughout this volume, all translations of Kant's works, unless otherwise specified, are drawn from the *Cambridge Edition of the Works of Immanuel Kant* published by Cambridge University Press. References to Kant's texts follow the Akademie edition. Contributors who have used different translations or editions have provided full bibliographical information at first mention.

Works by Kant

Critique of Practical Reason (1788), ed. by Mary J. Gregor and Andrews Reath, Cambridge: Cambridge University Press, 1997.

Critique of Pure Reason (1781/87), ed. and trans. by Paul Guyer and Allen Wood, Cambridge: Cambridge University Press, 1998.

Groundwork of the Metaphysics of Morals (1785), trans. by Mary J. Gregor, Cambridge: Cambridge University Press, 1998.

Groundwork of the Metaphysics of Morals: A German–English Edition, ed. and trans. by Jens Timmermann, Cambridge: Cambridge University Press, 2011.

Kants gesammelte Schriften, ed. by the Königlich Preußische Akademie der Wissenschaft, subsequently Deutsche, now Berlin-Brandenburg Akademie der Wissenschaften, Berlin: Georg Reimer, subsequently Walter de Gruyter, 1900–.

Lectures and Drafts on Political Philosophy, ed. by Fred Rauscher, Cambridge: Cambridge University Press, 2017.

Lectures on Ethics, ed. by Peter Heath and J. B. Schneewind, trans. by Peter Heath, Cambridge: Cambridge University Press, 1997.

The Metaphysics of Morals (1797), ed. and trans. by Mary J. Gregor, Cambridge: Cambridge University Press., 1996.

Practical Philosophy, ed. and trans. by Mary J. Gregor, Cambridge: Cambridge University Press, 1996.

Religion and Rational Theology, ed. and trans. by Allen W. Wood and George Di Giovanni, Cambridge: Cambridge University Press, 1996.

Vorlesung zur Moralphilosophie, ed. by Werner Stark, Berlin: De Gruyter, 2004.

Works by Other Authors and Secondary Literature

Achenwall, Gottfried, and Johann S. Pütter, *Anfangsgründe des Naturrechts (Elementa Iuris Naturae)* (1750), ed. and trans. by Jan Schröder, Frankfurt am Main: Insel, 1995.

Achenwall, Gottfried, *Natural Law* (1763), ed. by Pauline Kleingeld, trans. by Corinna Vermeulen, with an introduction by Paul Guyer, London: Bloomsbury, 2020.

Observationes iuris naturalis, Specimen II, De obligatione et imputatione, Göttingen: Bossiegel, 1754.

Prolegomena iuris naturalis, 2nd ed., Göttingen: Bossiegel, 1763.

Prolegomena to Natural Law (1763), ed. by Pauline Kleingeld, trans. by Corinna Vermeulen, Groningen: University of Groningen Press, 2020.

Alexander, Larry, 'In Defense of the Standard Picture: The Basic Challenge', *Ratio Juris* 34 (2021), 187–206.

Alexy, Robert, *The Argument from Injustice*, Oxford: Clarendon Press, 2002.

A Theory of Legal Argumentation, Oxford: Clarendon Press, 1989.

Annen, Martin, *Das Problem der Wahrhaftigkeit in der Philosophie der deutschen Aufklärung: Ein Beitrag zur Ethik und zum Naturrecht des 18. Jahrhunderts.* Würzburg: Königshausen & Neumann, 1997.

Augustinus, Aurelius, *De sermone domini in monte libri II*, ed. by Almut Mutzenbecher, Turnhout: Brepols 1967.

Bacin, Stefano, '"Only one obligation": Kant on the Distinction and the Normative Continuity of Right and Ethics', *Studi Kantiani* 29 (2016), 77–90.

Bader, Ralf M., 'Kant and the Categories of Freedom', *British Journal for the History of Philosophy* 17 (2009), 799–820.

'Kant on Freedom and Practical Irrationality', in Dai Heide and Evan Tiffany (eds.), *The Idea of Freedom: New Essays on the Kantian Theory of Freedom*, Oxford: Oxford University Press, 2023, 198–216.

Baiasu, Sorin, 'Ethical and Politico-Juridical Norms in the *Tugendlehre*', *Studi Kantiani* 29 (2016), 59–76.

'Right's Complex Relation to Ethics in Kant: The Limits of Independentism', *Kant-Studien* 107 (2016), 2–33.

Baum, Manfred, 'Freiheit und Verbindlichkeit in Kants Moralphilosophie', *Jahrbuch für Recht und Ethik* 13 (2005), 31–43.

Baumgarten, Alexander Gottlieb, *Baumgarten's Elements of First Practical Philosophy: A Critical Translation with Kant's Reflections on Moral Philosophy*, ed. and trans. by Courtney D. Fugate and John Hymers, London: Bloomsbury, 2020.

Initia philosophiae practicae primae, Halle: Hemmerde, 1760.

Beck, Lewis W., *A Commentary on Kant's Critique of Practical Reason*, Chicago: University of Chicago Press, 1996.

Berlin, Isaiah, *Two Concepts of Liberty: An Inaugural Lecture delivered before the University of Oxford on 31 October 1958*, Oxford: Clarendon Press, 1958.

Brandt, Reinhard, 'Das Erlaubnisgesetz, oder: Vernunft und Geschichte in Kants Rechtslehre', in: Reinhard Brandt (ed.), *Rechtsphilosophie der Aufklärung*, Berlin: De Gruyter, 1982, 233–85.

Brecher, Martin, 'Animal Desire and Rational Nature: Kant's Argument for Marriage and the Problem of "Unnatural" Sex', in Pärttyli Rinne and Martin Brecher (eds.), *Kant on Sex, Love, and Friendship*. Berlin: De Gruyter, 2023, 35–61.

'Ehelicher Geschlechtsgebrauch und Fortpflanzungszweck in §7 der Tugendlehre', in Violetta L. Waibel et al. (eds.), *Natur und Freiheit: Akten des XII. Internationalen Kant-Kongresses*, Berlin: De Gruyter, 2018, 1761–8.

'Konsequenter Kosmopolitismus', in Andree Hahmann and Stefan Klingner (eds.), *Konsequente Denkungsart: Studien zu einer philosophischen Tugend*, Hamburg: Meiner, 2024, 62–100.

Vernunftrecht und Verdinglichung: Eine Rekonstruktion von Kants Eherecht, Berlin: De Gruyter, 2025.

Bucher, Eugen, 'Der von den Juristen verkannte apagogische Beweis – dazu auch Kant und Kelsen', in Andreas Heldrich et al. (eds.), *Festschrift für Claus-Wilhelm Canaris zum 70. Geburtstag*, Munich: C. H. Beck, 2007, 991–1016.

Byrd, B. Sharon, 'The Elusive Story of Kant's Permissive Laws', in Lara Denis and Oliver Sensen (eds.), *Kant's Lectures on Ethics: A Critical Guide*, Cambridge: Cambridge University Press, 2015, 156–69.

'Intelligible Possession of Objects of Choice', in Lara Denis (ed.), *Kant's Metaphysics of Morals: A Critical Guide*, Cambridge: Cambridge University Press, 2010, 93–110.

'Kant's Theory of Punishment: Deterrence in Its Threat, Retribution in Its Execution', *Law and Philosophy* 8 (1989), 151–200.

Byrd, B. Sharon, and Hruschka, Joachim, *Kant's Doctrine of Right: A Commentary*, Cambridge: Cambridge University Press, 2010.

'The Natural Law Duty to Recognize Private Property Ownership: Kant's Theory of Property in His *Doctrine of Right*', *The University of Toronto Law Journal* 56 (2016), 217–82.

Campos, Andre S., 'Kant on Acting from Juridical Duty', *International Journal of Philosophical Studies* 27 (2019), 498–514.

Chilovi, Samuele, and Pavlakos, George, 'The Explanatory Demands of Grounding in Law', *Pacific Philosophical Quarterly* 103 (2022), 900–33.

'Law-Determination as Grounding', *Legal Theory* 25 (2019), 53–76.

Corradetti, Claudio, 'Kant's Legacy and the Idea of a Transitional *Jus Cosmpoliticum*', *Ratio Juris* 29 (2016), 105–21.

Davies, Luke, 'Kant on Civil Self-Sufficiency', *Archiv für Geschichte der Philosophie* 105 (2023), 118–40.

'Whence "Honeste Vive"?', *European Journal of Philosophy* 29 (2021), 323–38.

Demiray, Mehmet Ruhi, 'The Intrinsic Normativity of Law in Light of Kant's *Doctrine of Right*', *Contextos Kantianos* 3 (2016), 161–87.

'Natural Law Theory, Legal Positivism and the Normativity of Law', *The European Legacy* 20 (2015), 807–826.

Dindjer, Hasan, 'The New Legal Anti-Positivism', *Legal Theory* 26 (2020), 181–213.

Dovi, Suzanne, 'Political Representation', in Edward N. Zalta (ed.), *The Stanford Encyclopedia of Philosophy*, Fall 2018 ed., https://plato.stanford.edu/archives/fall2018/entries/political-representation/ (accessed 1 June 2024).

Dworkin, Ronald, *Justice for Hedgehogs*, Cambridge, MA: Harvard University Press, 2011.

Law's Empire, London: Fontana Press, 1986.

Ebels-Duggan, Kyla, 'Critical Notice', *Canadian Journal of Philosophy* 41 (2011), 549–74.

'Kant's Political Philosophy: Kant's Political Philosophy', *Philosophy Compass* 7 (2012), 896–909.

'Moral Community: Escaping the Ethical State of Nature', *Philosophers' Imprint* 9 (2009), 1–19.

Eberl, Oliver, and Niesen, Peter, 'Kommentar', in Immanuel Kant, *Zum ewigen Frieden*, ed. by Oliver Eberl and Peter Niesen, Berlin: Suhrkamp, 2011, 89–416.

Ebbinghaus, Julius, 'Kant und das 20. Jahrhundert', in *Gesammelte Schriften*, vol. 3: *Interpretation und Kritik: Schriften zur theoretischen Philosophie und zur Philosophiegeschichte 1924–1972*, ed. by Georg Geismann and Hariolf Oberer, Bonn: Bouvier, 1990, 151–74.

'Kants Rechtslehre und die Rechtsphilosophie des Neukantianismus', in Gerold Prauss (ed.), *Kant: Zur Deutung seiner Theorie von Erkennen und Handeln*, Cologne: Kiepenheuer & Witsch, 1973, 322–36.

'Die Strafen für Tötung eines Menschen und Prinzipien einer Rechtsphilosophie der Freiheit', in *Gesammelte Schriften*, vol. 2: *Philosophie der Freiheit: Praktische Philosophie 1955–1972*, ed. by Georg Geismann and Hariolf Oberer, Bonn: Bouvier, 1988, 283–380.

Feinberg, Joel, 'Action and Responsibility', in Max Black (ed.), *Philosophy in America*, London: Cornell University Press, 1965, 134–60.

Fernández, Graciela, 'Utopia and Perpetual Peace', in Valerio Rohden, R. R. Terra, G. A. de Almeida, and Margit Ruffing (eds.), *Recht und Frieden in der Philosophie Kants: Akten des X. Internationalen Kant-Congresses*, Berlin: De Gruyter, 2008, 311–21.

Fichte, Johann Gottlieb, *Grundlage des Naturrechts nach Prinzipien der Wissenschaftslehre*, Jena: Christian Ernst Gabler, 1796.

Flikschuh, Katrin, 'Elusive Unity: The General Will in Hobbes and Kant', *Hobbes Studies*, 25 (2012), 21–42.

'Human Rights in Kantian Mode: A Sketch', in Rowan Cruft, S. Matthew Liao, and Massimo Renzo (eds.), *Philosophical Foundations of Human Rights*, Oxford: Oxford University Press, 2015, 662–70.

'Innate Right and Acquired Right in Arthur Ripstein's *Force and Freedom*', *Jurisprudence* 1 (2010), 295–304.

'Justice without Virtue', in Lara Denis (ed.), *Kant's Metaphysics of Morals: A Critical Guide*, Cambridge: Cambridge University Press, 2010, 51–70.

Kant and Modern Political Philosophy, Cambridge: Cambridge University Press, 2000.

'A Regime of Equal Private Freedom? Individual Rights and Public Law in Ripstein's Force and Freedom', in Sari Kisilevsky and Martin J. Stone (eds.), *Freedom and Force: Essays on Kant's Legal Philosophy*, Oxford: Hart Publishing, 2017, 55–74.

What Is Orientation in Global Thinking?, Cambridge: Cambridge University Press, 2017.

Formosa, Paul, '"All Politics Must Bend Its Knee Before Right": Kant on the Relation of Morals to Politics', *Social Theory and Practice* 34 (2008), 157–81.

Forst, Rainer, 'A Kantian Republican Conception of Justice as Nondomination', in Andreas Niederberger, Philipp Schink (eds.), *Republican Democracy*, Edinburgh: Edinburgh University Press, 2013, 154–68.

'Kantian Republicanism versus the Neo-Republican Machine: The Meaning and Practice of Political Autonomy', in Julia Christ, Kristina Lepold, Daniel Loick, and Titus Stahl (eds.), *Debating Critical Theory: Engagements with Axel Honneth*, Lanham: Rowman and Littlefield, 2020, 17–34.

Friedrich, Rainer, *Eigentum und Staatsbegründung in Kants Metaphysik der Sitten*, Berlin: De Gruyter, 2004.

Geismann, Georg, 'Recht und Moral in der Philosophie Kants', *Jahrbuch für Recht und Ethik* 14 (2006), 3–124.

Gläser, Micha, 'The Reasonable and the Rational in General and in Particular', unpublished MS.

Greenberg, Mark, 'Hartian Positivism and Normative Facts: How Facts Make Law II', in Scott Hershovitz (ed.), *Exploring Law's Empire: The Jurisprudence of Ronald Dworkin*, Oxford: Oxford University Press, 2006, 265–90.

'How Facts Make Law', *Legal Theory* 10 (2004), 157–98.

'The Moral Impact Theory of Law', *Yale Law Journal* 123 (2014), 1288–1342.

'On Practices and the Law', *Legal Theory* 12 (2006), 113–136.

Gregor, Mary J., *The Laws of Freedom: A Study of Kant's Method of Applying the Categorical Imperative in the 'Metaphysik der Sitten'*, Oxford: Basil Blackwell, 1963.

Gregory, Mike, 'Does the Kantian State Dominate? Freedom and Majoritarian Rule', *Ratio* 36 (2023), 124–36.

Grimm, Jacob, and Grimm, Wilhelm (founding eds.), *Deutsches Wörterbuch*, 14 vols., Leipzig: Hirzel, 1854–1961.

Grotius, Hugo, *De jure belli ac pacis libri tres*, Paris: Nicolaus Buon 1625.

Guyer, Paul, 'Achenwall, Kant, and the Division of Governmental Powers', in Margit Ruffing, Annika Schlitte, and Gianluca Sadun Bodoni (eds.), *Kants Naturrecht Feyerabend: Analysen und Perspektiven*, Berlin: De Gruyter, 2020, 201–28.

'Enforcing the Law of Nature: The Background to Kant's Conception of the Relation between Morality and *Recht*', in Mark Timmons and Sorin Baiasu (eds.), *Kantian Citizenship: Grounds, Standards and Global Implications*, New York: Routledge, 2025, 15–42.

'Civic Responsibility and the Kantian Social Contract', in Herta Nagl-Docekal and Rudolf Langthaler (eds.), *Recht – Geschichte – Religion: Die Bedeutung Kants für die Gegenwart*, Berlin: Akademie Verlag, 2004, 27–48.

'The Crooked Timber of Humankind', in Amelie Rorty and James Schmidt (eds.), *Kant's 'Idea for a Universal History with a Cosmopolitan Aim': A Critical Guide*, Cambridge: Cambridge University Press, 2009, 129–49.

'"Hobbes is of the opposite opinion": Kant and Hobbes on the Three Authorities in the State', *Hobbes Studies* 25 (2012), 91–119.

'Is Sovereignty Divided Still Sovereignty? Kant and *The Federalist*', *University of Pittsburgh Law Review* 83 (2021), 365–96.

Kant. 2nd ed. London: Routledge, 2014.

'Kant and the Moral Politicians', in Kyriakos N. Demetriou and Antis Loizides (eds.), *Scientific Statesmanship, Governance, and the History of Political Philosophy*, London: Routledge, 2015, 116–36.

Kant on Freedom, Law, and Happiness, Cambridge: Cambridge University Press, 2000.

Kant on the Rationality of Morality, Cambridge: Cambridge University Press, 2019.

'Kant's Deductions of the Principles of Right', in Mark Timmons (ed.), *Kant's Metaphysics of Morals: Interpretative Essays*, Oxford: Oxford University Press, 2002, 23–64; reprinted in Paul Guyer, *Kant's System of Nature and Freedom*, Oxford: Clarendon Press, 2005, 198–242.

'Kant's System of Duties', in *Kant's System of Nature and Freedom*, Oxford: Clarendon Press, 2005, 242–74.

Kant's System of Nature and Freedom, Oxford: Clarendon Press, 2005.

'The Possibility of Perpetual Peace', in Luigi Caranti (ed.), *Kant's Perpetual Peace: New Interpretative Essays*, Rome: LUISS University Press, 2006, 161–81.

'The Twofold Morality of *Recht*: Once More unto the Breach', *Kant-Studien* 107 (2016), 34–63.

Habermas, Jürgen, *Between Facts and Norms: Contributions to a Discourse Theory of Law and Democracy*, Cambridge, MA: MIT Press, 1996.

Haensel, Werner, *Kants Lehre vom Widerstandsrecht: Ein Beitrag zur Systematik der Kantischen Rechtsphilosophie*, Berlin: Heise, 1926.

Hanisch, Christoph, 'Kant on Democracy', *Kant-Studien* 107 (2016), 64–88.

Hart, H. L. A., *The Concept of Law*, 2nd ed., Oxford: Clarendon Press, 1994.

'Rawls on Liberty and Its Priority', *The University of Chicago Law Review* 40 (1973), 534–55.

Hartman, Robert J., 'Kant Does Not Deny Resultant Moral Luck', *Midwest Studies in Philosophy* 43 (2019), 136–50.

Hasan, Rafeeq, 'Freedom and Poverty in the Kantian State', *European Journal of Philosophy* 26 (2018), 911–31.

'The Provisionality of Property Rights in Kant's *Doctrine of Right*', *Canadian Journal of Philosophy* 48 (2018), 850–76.

Hegel, G. W. F., *Grundlinien der Philosophie des Rechts*, Berlin: Nicolai, 1821.

Henson, Richard G., 'What Kant Might Have Said: Moral Worth and the Overdetermination of Dutiful Action', *The Philosophical Review* 88 (1979), 39–54.

Herb, Karlfriedrich, and Ludwig, Bernd, 'Kants kritisches Staatsrecht', *Jahrbuch für Recht und Ethik/Annual Review of Law and Ethics* 2 (1994), 431–78.

Herman, Barbara, 'Juridical Personality and the Moral Role of Juridical Obligation', in Tamar Shapiro, Kyla Ebels-Duggan, and Sharon Street (eds.), *Normativity and Agency: Themes from the Philosophy of Christine Korsgaard*, Oxford: Oxford University Press, 2022, 240–63.

Heyd, David, 'Moral and Legal Luck: Kant's Reconciliation with Practical Contingency', *Jahrbuch für Recht und Ethik* 5 (1997), 27–42.

Heyse, Johann Christian August, and Heyse, Karl Wilhelm Ludwig, *Handwörterbuch der deutschen Sprache*, 3 vols., Magdeburg: Wilhelm Heinrichshofen, 1833–49.

Himma, Kenneth E., 'Inclusive Legal Positivism', in Jules L. Colemann and Scott Shapiro (eds.), *Oxford Handbook of Jurisprudence and Philosophy of Law*, Oxford: Oxford University Press, 2004, 125–65.

Hirsch, Philipp-Alexander, *Freiheit und Staatlichkeit bei Kant: Die autonomietheoretische Begründung von Recht und Staat und das Widerstandsproblem*, Berlin: De Gruyter, 2017.

'Kant über Recht, Autonomie und Selbstzweckhaftigkeit: Naturrecht Feyerabend als Geburtsstunde Kants kritischer Rechtsbegründung?', in Dieter Hüning, Stefan Klingner, and Gianluca Sadun Bordoni (eds.), *Auf dem Weg zur kritischen Rechtslehre?*, Leiden: Brill, 2021, 197–228.

Kants Einleitung in die Rechtslehre von 1784: Immanuel Kants Rechtsbegriff in der Moralvorlesung 'Mrongovius II' und der Naturrechtsvorlesung 'Feyerabend' von 1784 sowie in der 'Metaphysik der Sitten' von 1797, Göttingen: Universitätsverlag Göttingen, 2012.

'Von Rechtspflichten zu vollkommenen Tugendpflichten? Kants ungelöstes Problem der Pflichtensystematik', in Beatrix Himmelmann and Camilla Serck-Hanssen (eds.), *The Court of Reason*, Berlin: De Gruyter, 2021, 1457–66.

Hobbes, Thomas, *De Cive: The English Version* (1642), ed. by Howard Warrender, Oxford: Clarendon Press, 1983.

Leviathan (1688), ed. by Noel Malcolm, Oxford: Clarendon Press, 2012.

Hodgson, Louis-Philippe, 'Kant on Property Rights and the State', *Kantian Review* 15 (2010), 57–87.

'Kant on the Right to Freedom: A Defense', *Ethics* 120 (2010), 791–819.

Holtman, Sarah Williams, 'Kantian Justice and Poverty Relief', *Kant-Studien* 95 (2004), 86–106.

Höffe, Otfried, 'Kant's Principle of Justice as Categorical Imperative of Law', in Yirmiyahu Yovel (ed.), *Kant's Practical Philosophy Reconsidered: Papers Presented at the Seventh Jerusalem Philosophical Encounter*, Dordrecht: Springer, 1989, 149–67.

'Der kategorische Rechtsimperativ: Einleitung in die Rechtslehre', in Otfried Höffe (ed.), *Immanuel Kant: Metaphysische Anfangsgründe der Rechtslehre*, Berlin: Akademie-Verlag, 2010, 41–62.

Kategorische Rechtsprinzipien, Frankfurt am Main: Suhrkamp, 1990.

Horn, Christoph, 'Kant's Political Philosophy as a Theory of Non-Ideal Normativity', *Kant-Studien* 107 (2016), 89–110.

Nichtideale Normativität: Ein neuer Blick auf Kants politische Philosophie, Berlin: Suhrkamp, 2014.

'Rousseau und Kant über Gemeinwille und Gesellschaftsvertrag', in Paul Geyer, Volker Ladenthin, and Anke Redecker (eds.), *Rousseau über Rousseau. Beiträge zum 300. Geburtstag*, Würzburg: Ergon, 2016, 31–46.

Hruschka, Joachim, 'Das Erlaubnisgesetz der praktischen Vernunft und der ursprüngliche Erwerb von Stücken des Erdbodens', in *Kant und der Rechtsstaat und andere Essays zu Kants Rechtslehre und Ethik*, Freiburg: Karl Alber, 2015, 48–88.

Kant und der Rechtsstaat und andere Essays zu Kants Rechtslehre und Ethik, Freiburg: Karl Alber, 2015.

'The Permissive Law of Practical Reason in Kant's *Metaphysics of Morals*', *Law and Philosophy* 23 (2004), 45–72.

Huber, Jakob, 'Cosmopolitanism for Earth Dwellers: Kant on the Right to Be Somewhere.' *Kantian Review* 22 (2017), 1–25.

Hufeland, Gottlieb, *Versuch über den Grundsatz des Naturrechts*, Leipzig: Göschen, 1785.

James, Aaron, 'Distributive Justice without Sovereign Rule: The Case of Trade', *Social Theory and Practice* 31 (2005), 533–59.

Julius, A. J., 'Independent People', in Sari Kisilevsky and Martin J. Stone (eds.), *Freedom and Force: Essays on Kant's Legal Philosophy*, Oxford: Hart Publishing, 2017, 91–110.

'Reconstruction', book MS, version 7, December 2013, www.ajjulius.net/reconstruction.pdf (accessed 9 July 2025).

Kahn, Samuel, 'Kant's Philosophy of Moral Luck', *Sophia* 60 (2021), 365–87.

Kalscheuer, Fiete, *Autonomie als Grund und Grenze des Rechts: Zum Verhältnis zwischen dem kategorischen Imperativ und dem allgemeinen Rechtsgesetz Kants*, Berlin: De Gruyter, 2014.

Kersting, Wolfgang, *Wohlgeordnete Freiheit: Immanuel Kants Rechts- und Staatsphilosophie*, Berlin: De Gruyter, 1984.

Wohlgeordnete Freiheit: Immanuel Kants Rechts- und Staatsphilosophie, 2nd ed., Frankfurt am Main: Suhrkamp, 1993.

Klein, Joel T., 'Permissive Laws and Teleology in Kant's Juridical and Political Philosophy', *Kantian Review* 27 (2022), 215–36.

Kleingeld, Pauline, 'Approaching Perpetual Peace: Kant's Defence of a League of States and His Ideal of a World Federation', *European Journal of Philosophy* 12 (2004), 304–25.

'On Dealing with Kant's Sexism and Racism', *SGIR Review* 2 (2019), 3–22.

'Kant's Formula of Autonomy: Continuity or Discontinuity?', *Philosophia* 51 (2023), 555–69.

'Kant's Second Thoughts on Colonialism', in Katrin Flikschuh and Lea Ypi (eds.), *Kant and Colonialism: Historical and Critical Perspectives*, Oxford: Oxford University Press, 2014, 43–67.

'Kant's Theory of Peace', in Paul Guyer (ed.), *The Cambridge Companion to Kant and Modern Philosophy*, Cambridge: Cambridge University Press, 2006, 477–504.

'Me, Myself, and I: Kant's Republican Conception of Freedom of the Will and Freedom of the Agent', *Studi Kantiani* 33 (2020), 103–23.

'The Principle of Autonomy in Kant's Moral Theory: Its Rise and Fall', in Eric Watkins (ed.), *Kant on Persons and Agency*, Cambridge: Cambridge University Press, 2018, 61–79.

Korsgaard, Christine M., *Creating the Kingdom of Ends*. Cambridge: Cambridge University Press, 1996.

'The Right to Lie: Kant on Dealing with Evil', *Philosophy and Public Affairs* 15 (1986), 325–49.

The Sources of Normativity, Cambridge: Cambridge University Press, 1996.

Kühnemund, Burkhard, *Eigentum und Freiheit: Ein kritischer Abgleich von Kants Rechtslehre mit den Prinzipien seiner Moralphilosophie*, Kassel: Kassel University Press, 2008.

Kulenkampff, Jens, 'Über die Rolle des ursprünglichen Vertrages in *Über den Gemeinspruch: Das mag in der Theorie richtig sein, taugt aber nicht für die Praxis*', *Jahrbuch für Recht und Ethik* 16 (2008), 165–81.

Larenz, Karl, 'Sittlichkeit und Recht: Untersuchungen zur Geschichte des deutschen Rechtsdenkens und zur Sittenlehre', in Karl Larenz (ed.), *Reich und Recht in der deutschen Philosophie*. Stuttgart: W. Kohlhammer, 1943, 169–402.

Laschet, Oliver, *Metaphysik und Erfahrung in Kants praktischer Philosophie*, Freiburg: Alber, 2011.

Locke, John, *Second Treatise of Government* (1689), ed. by Richard Howard Cox, Wheeling, IL: Harlan Davidson, 1982.

Love, Suzanne M., *The Material Conditions of Freedom*, PhD Dissertation, Pittsburgh: University of Pittsburgh, 2018.

Ludwig, Bernd, *Aufklärung über die Sittlichkeit: Zu Kants Grundlegung einer Metaphysik der Sitten*, Frankfurt am Main: Klostermann, 2020.

'Die Einteilungen der "Metaphysik der Sitten" im Allgemeinen und die der "Tugendlehre" im Besonderen', in Andreas Trampota, Oliver Sensen, and Jens Timmermann (eds.), *Kant's 'Tugendlehre': A Comprehensive Commentary*, Berlin: De Gruyter, 2013, 59–84.

Kants Rechtslehre: Mit einer Untersuchung zur Drucklegung Kantischer Schriften von Werner Stark, Hamburg: Meiner, 1988.

'Kants Verabschiedung der Vertragstheorie', *Jahrbuch für Recht und Ethik/Annual Review of Law and Ethics* 82 (1993), 221–54.

'"Positive und negative Freiheit" bei Kant? Wie begriffliche Konfusion auf philosophi(ehistori)sche Abwege führt', *Jahrbuch für Recht und Ethik* 21 (2013), 271–305.

'Sympathy for the Devil(s)? Personality and Legal Coercion in Kant's Doctrine of Law', *Jurisprudence* 6 (2015), 25–44.

'Von der coactio hypothetica zum kategorischen Imperativ: Was Kants Autonomie-Lehre Achenwalls Naturrecht von 1755 verdankt', *Rechtsphilosophie – Zeitschrift für Grundlagen des Rechts* 6 (2020), 352–67.

'Whence Public Right? The Role of Theoretical and Practical Reason in Kant's Doctrine of Right', in Mark Timmons (ed.), *Kant's Metaphysics of Morals: Interpretative Essays*, Oxford: Oxford University Press, 2002, 159–84.

Maliks, Reidar, *Kant's Politics in Context*, Oxford: Oxford University Press, 2014.

Marzal, Toni and Pavlakos, George, 'A Relations-First Approach of Choice of Law', in Roxana Banu, Michael S. Green, and Ralf Michaels (eds.), *Philosophical Foundations of Private International Law*, Oxford: Oxford University Press, 2024, 346–68.

Mayr, Erasmus, 'Unwitting Omissions, Mistakes and Responsibility', in George Pavlakos and Veronica Rodriguez-Blanco (eds.), *Agency, Negligence and Responsibility*, Cambridge: Cambridge University Press, 2021, 37–56.

McKean, Benjamin L., 'Kant, Coercion, and the Legitimation of Inequality', *Critical Review of International Social and Political Philosophy* (2019), 1–23.

Messina, J. P., 'Kant, Smith and the Place of Virtue in Political and Economic Organization', in Elizabeth Robinson and Chris W. Surprenant (eds.), *Kant and the Scottish Enlightenment*, New York: Routledge, 267–85.

'Kant's Provisionality Thesis', *Kantian Review* 24 (2019), 439–63.

'The Paradox of Outer Necessitation in (and after) Kant's 1784 Course on *Naturrecht*', in Margit Ruffing, Annika Schlitte, and Gianluca Sadun Bordoni (eds.), *Kants Naturrecht Feyerabend: Analysen und Perspektiven*, Berlin: De Gruyter, 2020, 169–83.

'The Postulate of Private Right and Kant's Semi-Historical Principles of Property', *British Journal of the History of Philosophy* 29 (2021), 64–83.

Moran, Kate, 'Kant on Traveling Blacksmiths and Passive Citizenship', *Kant-Studien* 112 (2021), 105–26.

Nagel, Thomas, 'Moral Luck', *Proceedings of the Aristotelian Society*, supplementary volume 50 (1976), 137–52.

Newhouse, Marie, 'Two Types of Legal Wrongdoing', *Legal Theory* 22 (2016), 59–75.

O'Neill, Onora, 'Consistency in Action', in Nelson T. Potter and Mark Timmons (eds.), *Morality and Universality: Essays on Ethical Universalizability*, Dordrecht: Reidel, 1985, 159–86.

'Enactable and Enforceable: Kant's Criteria for Right and Virtue', *Kant-Studien* 107 (2016), 111–24.

Pallikkathayil, Japa, 'Persons and Bodies', in Sari Kisilevsky and Martin Stone (eds.), *Freedom and Force: Essays on Kant's Legal Philosophy*, Oxford: Hart Publishing, 2017, 35–54.

Palmquist, Stephen R., 'How Political is the Kantian Church?', *Diametros* 17 (2020), 95–113.

Papish, Laura, *Kant on Evil, Self-Deception, and Moral Reform*, New York: Oxford University Press, 2018.

Pavlakos, George, 'Agent-Relativity without Control: Grounding Negligence on Normative Relations', in Veronica Rodriguez-Blanco and George Pavlakos (eds.), *Negligence, Agency and Responsibility*, Cambridge: Cambridge University Press, 2021, 118–35.

'Coercion and the Grounds of Legal Obligation: Arthur Ripstein's *Force and Freedom*', *Jurisprudence* 1 (2010), 305–16.

'Redrawing the Legal Relation', in Jorge L. Fabra-Zamora (ed.), *Jurisprudence in a Globalised World*, Cheltenham: Edward Elgar, 2020, 173–194.

'The Relation between Moral and Legal Obligation: An Alternative Kantian Reading', in George Pavlakos and Veronica Rodriguez-Blanco (eds.), *Reasons and Intentions in Law and Practical Agency*, Cambridge: Cambridge University Press, 2015, 228–43.

'Revamping Associative Obligations', in Salman Khurshid, Lokendra Malik, and Veronica Rodriguez-Blanco (eds.), *Dignity in the Legal and Political Philosophy of Ronald Dworkin*, Oxford: Oxford University Press, 2018, 337–360.

Pettit, Philip, *On the People's Terms: A Republican Theory and Model of Democracy*, Cambridge: Cambridge University Press, 2012.

Republicanism: A Theory of Freedom and Government, Oxford: Oxford University Press, 1997.

'Two Republican Traditions', in Andreas Niederberger and Philipp Schink (eds.), *Republican Democracy*, Edinburgh: Edinburgh University Press, 2013, 169–204.

Pinheiro Walla, Alice, '*Honeste vive*: Dignity in Kant's *Rechtslehre*', in Adam Cureton and Jan-Willem van der Rijt (eds.), *Human Dignity and the Kingdom of Ends: Kantian Perspectives and Practical Applications*, London: Routledge, 2021, 109–131.

'Kant and the Wisdom of Oedipus', *Jahrbuch Praktische Philosophie in globaler Perspektive/Yearbook Practical Philosophy in a Global Perspective* 3 (2019), 126–44.

'Kant's Moral Theory and Demandingness', *Ethical Theory and Moral Practice* 18 (2015), 731–743.

'Private Property and Territorial Rights: A Kantian Alternative to Contemporary Debates', in Alice Pinheiro Walla and Mehmet Ruhi Demiray (eds.), *Reason, Normativity and Law: New Essays in Kantian Philosophy*, Cardiff: University of Wales Press, 2020, 213–32.

Pitkin, Hanna Fenichel, *The Concept of Representation*, Berkeley: University of California Press, 1967.

Pogge, Thomas, 'Is Kant's *Rechtslehre* a "Comprehensive Liberalism"?', in Mark Timmons (ed.), *Kant's Metaphysics of Morals: Interpretative Essays*, Oxford: Oxford University Press, 2002, 133–58.

Preda, Adina, 'Are There Any Conflicts of Rights?', *Ethical Theory and Moral Practice* 18 (2015), 677–90.

Rawls, John, 'Justice as Fairness: Political not Metaphysical', *Philosophy and Public Affairs* 14 (1985), 223–51.

Political Liberalism, New York: Columbia University Press, 1993.
Political Liberalism: Expanded Edition, New York: Columbia University Press, 2005.
A Theory of Justice, Cambridge, MA: Harvard University Press, 1971.
Raz, Joseph, 'Responsibility and the Negligence Standard', *Oxford Journal of Legal Studies* 30 (2010), 1–18.
Reath, Andrews, 'Agency and the Imputation of Consequences in Kant's Ethics', in Andrews Reath (ed.), *Agency and Autonomy in Kant's Moral Theory: Selected Essays*, Oxford: Oxford University Press, 2006, 250–69.
Rehberg, August Wilhelm, 'Über das Verhältniß der Theorie zur Praxis', *Berlinische Monatsschrift* 23 (1794), 114–43.
Riley, Patrick, 'Rousseau's General Will', in Patrick Riley (ed.), *The Cambridge Companion to Rousseau*, Cambridge: Cambridge University Press, 2001, 124–53.
'Kant on the General Will', in James Farr and David L. Williams (eds.), *The General Will: The Evolution of a Concept*, New York: Cambridge University Press, 2015, 333–49.
Ripstein, Arthur, 'Authority and Coercion', *Philosophy and Public Affairs* 32 (2004), 2–35.
Force and Freedom: Kant's Legal and Political Philosophy. Cambridge, MA: Harvard University Press, 2009.
Kant and the Law of War, Oxford: Oxford University Press, 2021.
'Means and Ends', *Jurisprudence* 6 (2015), 1–23.
Private Wrongs, Cambridge, MA: Harvard University Press, 2018.
'Reply to Flikschuh and Pavlakos', *Jurisprudence* 1 (2010), 317–24.
Roff, Heather, 'Kantian Provisional Duties', *Jahrbuch für Recht und Ethik* 18 (2010), 533–62.
Rostbøll, Christian, 'Kant and the Critique of the Ethics-First Approach to Politics', *Critical Review of International Social and Political Philosophy* 22 (2019), 55–70.
Rousseau, Jean-Jacques, *'The Social Contract' and Other Later Political Writings*, ed. by Victor Gourevitch, Cambridge: Cambridge University Press, 1997.
Savigny, Friedrich C. von, *Private International Law: A Treatise on the Conflict of Laws* (1869), trans. by William Guthrie, London: T&T Clark Law Publishers, 1880.
System des heutigen römischen Rechts, Berlin: Veit, 1840; reprint Aalen: Scientia Verlag, 1981.
Schiller, Friedrich, *Sämtliche Werke*, vol. 1, Munich: Carl Hanser Verlag, 1962.
Seel, Gerhard, 'How Does Kant Justify the Universal Objective Validity of the Law of Right?', *International Journal of Philosophical Studies* 17 (2009), 71–94.
Sensen, Oliver, 'Tugendlehre als Lehre von Zwecken (Einleitung zur Tugendlehre, I–VI)', in Otfried Höffe (ed.), *Immanuel Kant: Metaphysische Anfangsgründe der Tugendlehre*, Berlin: De Gruyter, 2019, 29–43.
Shapiro, Scott J., *Legality*, Cambridge, MA: Harvard University Press, 2011.
Skinner, Quentin, 'The Idea of Negative Liberty: Philosophical and Historical Perspectives', in Richard Rorty, Quentin Skinner, and Jerome B.

Schneewind (eds.), *Philosophy in History: Essays in the Historiography of Philosophy*, Cambridge: Cambridge University Press, 1984, 193–221.

Liberty before Liberalism, Cambridge: Cambridge University Press, 1998.

Stavropoulos, Nicos, 'Legal Interpretivism', in Edward N. Zalta (ed.), *The Stanford Encyclopedia of Philosophy* (2021), https://plato.stanford.edu/archives/spr2021/entries/law-interpretivist/ (accessed 1 June 2024).

Sticker, Martin, 'The Case against Different-Sex Marriage in Kant', *Kantian Review* 25 (2020), 441–64.

'When the Reflective Watch-Dog Barks: Conscience and Self-Deception in Kant', *The Journal of Value Inquiry* 51 (2017), 85–104.

Stone, Martin J. and Hasan, Rafeeq, 'What Is Provisional Right?', *Philosophical Review* 131 (2022), 51–98.

Szymkowiak, Aaron. 'Kant's Permissive Law: Critical Rights, Sceptical Politics', *British Journal for the History of Philosophy* 17 (2009), 567–600.

Tierney, Brian, 'Kant on Property: The Problem of Permissive Law', *Journal of the History of Ideas* 62 (2001), 301–12.

'Permissive Natural Law and Property: Gratian to Kant', *Journal of the History of Ideas* 62 (2001), 381–99.

Timmermann, Jens, 'Acting from Duty: Inclination, Reason and Moral Worth', in Jens Timmermann (ed.), *Kant's 'Groundwork of the Metaphysics of Morals': A Critical Guide*, Cambridge: Cambridge University Press, 2009, 45–62.

Kant's Will at the Crossroads: An Essay on the Failings of Practical Rationality, Oxford: Oxford University Press, 2022.

'*Quod dubitas, ne feceris*: Kant on using Conscience as a guide', *Studi Kantiani* 29 (2016), 163–7.

Tomassini, Fiorella, 'Right, Morals, and the Categorical Imperative', *Kant-Studien* 114 (2023), 513–38.

Uleman, Jennifer K., 'External Freedom in Kant's "Rechtslehre": Political, Metaphysical', *Philosophy and Phenomenological Research* 68 (2004), 578–601.

Varden, Helga, 'A Kantian Conception of Rightful Sexual Relations: Sex, (Gay) Marriage and Prostitution', *Social Philosophy Today* 22 (2006), 199–218.

'Kant's Non-Absolutist Conception of Political Legitimacy: How Public Right "Concludes" Private Right in the "Doctrine of Right"', *Kant-Studien* 101 (2010), 331–51.

'Kant's Non-Voluntarist Conception of Political Obligations: Why Justice Is Impossible in the State of Nature', *Kantian Review* 13 (2008), 1–45.

Sex, Love, and Gender: A Kantian Theory, Oxford: Oxford University Press, 2020.

Vrousalis, Nicholas, 'Interdependent Independence: Civil Self-Sufficiency and Productive Community in Kant's Theory of Citizenship', *Kantian Review* 27 (2022), 443–60.

Waldron, Jeremy, 'Kant's Legal Positivism', *Harvard Law Review* 109 (1996), 1535–66.

Walschots, Michael, 'Kant and the Duty to Act from Duty', *History of Philosophy Quarterly* 39 (2022), 59–75.

Willaschek, Marcus, 'How Can Freedom Be a Law to Itself? The Concept of Autonomy in the "Introduction" to the Naturrecht Feyerabend Lecture Notes (1784)', in Stefano Bacin and Oliver Sensen (eds.), *The Emergence of Autonomy in Kant's Moral Philosophy*, Cambridge: Cambridge University Press, 2020, 141–157.

'The Non-Derivability of Kantian Right from the Categorical Imperative: A Response to Nance', *International Journal of Philosophical Studies* 20 (2012), 557–64.

'Recht ohne Ethik? Kant über die Gründe, das Recht nicht zu brechen', in Volker Gerhardt (ed.), *Kant im Streit der Fakultäten*, Berlin: De Gruyter, 2005, 188–204.

'Right and Coercion: Can Kant's Conception of Right Be Derived from His Moral Theory?' *International Journal of Philosophical Studies* 17 (2009), 49–70.

'The Structure of Normative Space: Kant's System of Rational Principles', in Beatrix Himmelmann and Camilla Serck-Hanssen (eds.), *The Court of Reason: Proceedings of the 13th International Kant Congress*, Berlin: De Gruyter, 2021, 245–66.

'Which Imperatives for Right? On the Non-prescriptive Character of Juridical Laws in Kant's Metaphysics of Morals', in Mark Timmons (ed.), *Kant's Metaphysics of Morals: Interpretative Essays*, Oxford: Oxford University Press, 2002, 65–88.

'Why the *Doctrine of Right* Does Not Belong in the *Metaphysics of Morals*: On Some Basic Distinctions in Kant's Moral Philosophy', *Jahrbuch für Recht und Ethik/Annual Review of Law and Ethics* 5 (1997), 205–227.

Williams, Bernard, 'Moral Luck', *Proceedings of the Aristotelian Society*, supplementary volume 50 (1976), 115–35.

Williams, Garrath, 'Between Ethics and Right: Kantian Politics and Democratic Purposes', *European Journal of Philosophy* 20 (2012), 479–86.

Williams, Howard, *Kant's Critique of Hobbes*, Cardiff: University of Wales Press, 2003.

Wolff, Christian, *Vernünftige Gedancken von der Menschen Thun und Lassen*, 4th ed., Frankfurt am Main and Leipzig: Johann Benjamin Andreä & Heinrich Hort, 1733.

Wolff, Robert P., *In Defense of Anarchism*. Berkeley: University of California Press, 1970.

Wood, Allen W., 'The Final Form of Kant's Practical Philosophy', *The Southern Journal of Philosophy* 36 (1998), 1–20.

'The Final Form of Kant's Practical Philosophy', in Mark Timmons (ed.), *Kant's Metaphysics of Morals: Interpretative Essays*, Oxford: Oxford University Press 2002, 1–21.

The Free Development of Each: Studies on Freedom, Right, and Ethics in Classical German Philosophy, Oxford: Oxford University Press, 2014.

Kant and Religion, Oxford: Oxford University Press, 2020.

Kantian Ethics, Cambridge: Cambridge University Press, 2008.

Kant's Ethical Thought, Cambridge: Cambridge University Press, 1999.

Yeomans, Christopher, 'Kant and the Provisionality of Property', in Ansgar Lyssy and Christopher Yeomans (eds.), *Kant on Morality, Humanity, and Legality: Practical Dimensions of Normativity*, Cham: Palgrave Macmillan, 2021, 253–78.

Ypi, Lea, 'A Permissive Theory of Territorial Rights', *European Journal of Philosophy* 22 (2014), 288–312.

Zanchet, Maria Eugênia, 'Towards a Holistic View of Self-Deception in Kant's Moral Psychology', *Con-Textos Kantianos* 16 (2022), 194–219.

Zöller, Günter, '"[O]hne Hofnung und Furcht": Kants Naturrecht Feyerabend über den Grund der Verbindlichkeit zu einer Handlung', in Bernd Dörflinger et al. (eds.), *Kant's Lectures*, Berlin: De Gruyter, 2015, 197–210.

Zylberman, Ariel, 'Bread as Freedom: Kant on the State's Duties to the Poor', in Dai Heide and Evan Tiffany (eds.), *The Idea of Freedom. New Essays on the Kantian Idea of Freedom*, Oxford: Oxford University Press, 2023, 245–64.

'The Public Form of Law: Kant on the Second-Personal Constitution of Freedom', *Kantian Review* 21 (2016), 101–26.

Subject Index

Index of Persons

Printed by Integrated Books International,
United States of America